Isaac Williams

Thoughts on the Study of the Holy Gospels

Isaac Williams

Thoughts on the Study of the Holy Gospels

ISBN/EAN: 9783337280437

Printed in Europe, USA, Canada, Australia, Japan

Cover: Foto ©Lupo / pixelio.de

More available books at **www.hansebooks.com**

Devotional Commentary on the Gospel Narrative

(VOLUME I)

THOUGHTS ON THE STUDY OF THE HOLY GOSPELS

RIVINGTONS

London	...	...	...	...	...	...	...	*Waterloo Place*
Oxford	...	...	...	...	...	...	...	*High Street*
Cambridge	...	...	...	...	...	...	...	*Trinity Street*

THOUGHTS ON THE STUDY
OF THE HOLY GOSPELS

BY THE

Rev. ISAAC WILLIAMS, B.D.

LATE FELLOW OF TRINITY COLLEGE, OXFORD

NEW EDITION

RIVINGTONS

London, Oxford, and Cambridge

1870

" O God of my fathers, and Lord of mercy, who hast made all things with Thy word, ...

" Give me wisdom, that sitteth by Thy throne; and reject me not from among thy children:

" For though a man be never so perfect among the children of men, yet if Thy wisdom be not with him, he shall be nothing regarded: . . . .

" O send her out of Thy holy heavens, and from the throne of Thy glory, that being present she may labour with me, that I may know what is pleasing unto Thee.

" For she knoweth and understandeth all things, and she shall lead me soberly in my doings, and preserve me in her power.

" So shall my works be acceptable. . . .

" For the thoughts of mortal men are miserable, and our devices are but uncertain.

" For the corruptible body presseth down the soul, and the earthly tabernacle weigheth down the mind, that museth upon many things.

" And hardly do we guess aright at things that are upon earth, and with labour do we find the things that are before us; but the things that are in heaven who hath searched out ?

" And Thy counsel who hath known, except Thou give wisdom, and send Thy Holy Spirit from above ?"

THE WISDOM OF SOLOMON.

PREFACE

THE greatest of all evils, which hath ever overtaken the sons of men, was that which befell
that faithless Apostle, who was admitted to walk
with Jesus Christ, and to see His miracles, and to
hear His word, and to witness His holiness; and yet
knew Him not! and that because he had one cherished
sin in his heart. So that, seeing, he saw not, and
hearing, he could not understand. Danger not unlike
this is incurred by every one to whom is given the
high privilege to study the holy Gospels.

We are indeed now brought into the Christian
Kingdom, which is no less than a restoration to the
Paradise of God, and the Gospels therein are no
other than that stream which flows from beneath
the Throne of God;—being parted into four heads,
and on whose banks is that Tree whose leaves are
for the healing of the nations,—which is no other
than the Cross of Christ, budding forth, like Aaron's
rod, into new life. But in this kingdom, and with

A 2

us, remains also the Old Adam of human reason, and evil concupiscence, our mother Eve; and that serpent also finds access there, telling us that we shall not surely die. So that great is our cause of fear, lest we fall from this high inheritance, and forget the Presence of God, as it were, walking among the trees that are therein, in this evening of the world that precedes the final Judgment.

In approaching the Gospels we draw near to that City of God, of which "glorious things are spoken;" but lowly is the entrance to it, and we must make ourselves small by mortification, and by humiliation bow ourselves to the ground, in order to enter by that lowly portal. There is a "knowledge" that "puffeth up," and that too even in the study of Divine things; and this is a knowledge which will profit us not towards the attainment of that wisdom which is revealed only unto babes. Thus much then is certain, that if we "count ourselves to have apprehended," and are confident in our researches, and vain of our inquiries, we are in fact afar off; for the nearer all men approach unto the knowledge of Christ, the more are they humbled. One way only is there to understand the blessed Gospels, and that is to humble ourselves under the mighty hand of God, and to knock at the door by prayer. And hence it is that this undertaking, as it is the most sweet and delightful, so is it the most awful and

serious of all studies. Bright and beautiful are
these flowers of paradise, and precious are those
jewels that lie at the bottom of these waters of
Eden; and the fruits that are therein are sweet to
the taste and pleasant to the eye; so sweet and
engaging is the study of the Gospels, and apt to
beguile and allure us by the very abundance of
every thing suited to arrest the attention of the
critic and scholar. But nothing profits but that
which humbles; and nothing can apprehend God
but humility.

The struggle, therefore, may well be great, and
great our need of circumspection, lest we take that
earthly knowledge that puffeth up, for that knowledge from above which humbleth. But blessed be
God, Who, as He has kept this knowledge in His
own especial power, so has He promised to bestow
it on every one that asketh faithfully. "If any of
you lack wisdom, let him ask of God, that giveth to
all men liberally, and upbraideth not, and it shall
be given him." But to ask is not a matter of the
lips only, but is that desire of the heart which is
expressed by the life: by a life that ever asks for
help, inasmuch as it is so conducted as ever expressing its need of help. And such a life is the most
importunate of all demands; and the words of sup-
plication that are steeped in such a desire of the
heart will not be ineffectual with God.

This study, therefore, is the more blessed, from the very difficulty and danger with which it is encompassed : for to study the Gospels is to endeavour to know God and ourselves ; and this must be done, not only by fixing our eyes on the true Light, which ever shines in the blessed Gospels, but by girding up the loins of our minds, and conforming ourselves to that Light; inasmuch as that study can be no other than a Divine life. For he that doeth the will shall know of the doctrine. And to follow Christ from the cradle at Bethlehem, when He came down to earth, to Bethany where He ascended up to Heaven : and to compare His words and His actions, and to be attendant on Him,— must be good, if it be not our own fault; yea, though it be most needful to take up the Cross daily, and to forsake all things in order to do so : yet is it exceeding blessed, and the most blessed of all things in this world; if we can but value that blessedness, so as to esteem all things else as light in comparison with it.

It is impossible to think too highly,—or, indeed, to think worthily,—of the four holy Gospels. They are spoken of by Origen as the raiment of Christ, which were white and glistening at His Transfiguration, " so as no fuller on earth could whiten them ;" so that, although they be of human texture, and the hands of men have framed them, yet are they supernaturally illuminated with the presence of Christ throughout;—wrapping around, as a garment, the Divine Person of the Son of Man. We have therein Jesus Christ speaking on earth, speaking to men like ourselves,—speaking indeed even to ourselves; for, doubtless, we were as much in the very eye of our Blessed Lord, as they were who stood around Him, when He spoke and acted, and caused His words and actions to be recorded. The circumstances under which those His words would be brought before us, were as much present to His mind, as were those of His own immediate Disciples: " Wisdom reacheth from one end to another mightily; and sweetly doth she order all things[1]." There is especially in the Gospels, as it were, an omnipresent Eye of God, a living Power residing therein;—no other than Jesus Christ, the same yesterday, and to-day, and for ever. As He is Himself especially the Word of God, so the written Scriptures are often dignified by appellations which are given even unto the Son of God Himself: as if they did also in some sense, if we may so speak, partake of His attributes; being, as it were, the very breath of His mouth; so that it is often doubtful which is most signified in the descriptions given, the written Word, or our Lord Himself. From the inanimate letter they pass to the Spirit contained

[1] Wisd. viii. 1.

therein : from the inanimate to the animate
intelligent;—nay, more than this, to that which is
Divinely living and intelligent. The Word of God
endureth for ever : " giveth light unto the eyes;" is
" sharper than a two-edged sword;" "a discerner
of the thoughts and intents of the heart." Great,
therefore, is our need of reverence when we draw
near to this place where God is ; for to approach
these Divine narratives is to approach Him Who
dwelleth therein in light incomprehensible,—a
savour of life, and also unto death. Here we approach the place where God is : the bush of fire in
which He burns; and we must take the shoes off
our feet, lay aside all carnal low conceits, remember-
ing that the ground on which we stand is holy.
This is no doubt that ladder of God on which the
true Israelite shall behold Angels ascending and
descending; and shall tremble to find that God
indeed is there. This is that bread of God that
cometh down from Heaven, to be the daily support
of our souls; here is that smitten Rock, from which,
as from a living fountain, the Holy Spirit flows; and
the pools are filled with water throughout the wilderness of the world. Here we find the Heavens
opened in very deed, as at our Lord's Baptism.
Here we find God on earth ; and Angels and Shepherds uniting together in the same song of praise.
Here we are at the gates of that Heavenly City,

where the elders cast down their crowns before the
Throne; and the Angels hide their faces, as unworthy to look upon God. This is that City which
hath "no need of the sun, neither of the moon, to
shine in it:" for it is lightened by the glory of God,
"and the Lamb is the light thereof." It hath no
need of human reason and knowledge: for by faith
we here behold the light of the Lamb; and the
feebler reflection of that light is seen in the light
of His Church below. Here we look into that sea
of glass wherein is reflected the Throne of God
itself; and in the clear and unclouded brightness of
which we may behold ourselves. Here is the threefold Witness: the works of the Father,—and the
words of the Son,—and the Holy Spirit combining
in both; while here also in the Church below, as He
inspired them that wrote, so He interprets for them
that read. And these Three also are One (O the
wonderful mystery found in all things!): for all
Three are together combined in the Gospels. What
son of man then shall stand before the threefold
Witness; unless the Spirit enter into him, and give
him power to stand, and to hear Him that speaketh[2]?
Of this, therefore, we may be sure, that so far as our
approaches to this place where God is do not partake of fear and humiliation, so far we fail of attain-

---

[2] Ezek. ii: 2.

ing that knowledge of Scripture which leadeth unto life,—yea, which itself is life.

These thoughts we must remember, and these words are the thoughts and words of the Holy Spirit, and can be understood only by him who hath the Spirit: and the Spirit dwelleth alone with the humble and the contrite; God will reveal Himself unto him who trembles at His Word. Christ appeared in His Temple, and the Scribes and the Pharisees discerned Him not; yet at the same time the children sang Hosannahs unto Him, and were the most acceptable emblems of those that should inherit His Kingdom. Christ Himself rejoices, and His Angels rejoice with Him, in this the wonderful dispensation of God; for once only is it said of the Man of Sorrows that He " rejoiced in spirit," and the cause of His rejoicing was, because God His Father had "hid these things from the wise and prudent, and revealed them unto babes." This is that holy Land of promise, of which the Lord had said by Moses, " Doubtless ye shall not come into the land . . but your little ones, them will I bring in³."

These are they of whom our Lord said, " Fear not, little flock, for it is your Father's good pleasure to give you the Kingdom." These are they whom by a figure He took up into His arms, and put His

³.Num. xiv. 31.

hands upon them, and blessed them, and said, that of such is the Heavenly Kingdom. These are the meek, to whom the inheritance of the earth is promised: for what inheritance have we upon earth but His Word in His Gospel, and in His Sacraments, —the staff to guide the steps, and the bread which strengthens man's heart; whereby He hath "filled the hungry with good things;" whereby "they that hunger and thirst" are filled,—filled doubtless with that righteousness for which they feel such longing desire? And the more they are filled, the more will they hunger and thirst: for "they that eat Me shall yet be hungry;" and the more they hunger and thirst after righteousness, the more, according to the promise, will they be filled with that fulness; till they be no longer babes, but shall come to the full stature of Christ,—shall rise up after His likeness, and shall be satisfied with it; when He shall fill them with the abundance of His house: "they shall hunger no more, and thirst no more;" when the letter shall depart, and the Spirit shall remain; when the written commandment shall be needed no more, for obedience shall be swallowed up in love that "never faileth."

BISLEY,
Feast of St. Luke the Evangelist, 1842.

CONTENTS

PART I

Characteristic Differences in the Four Gospels

PART II

Our Lord's Manifestation of Himself

PART III

The Rule of Scriptural Interpretation furnished by our Lord

PART IV

Analogies of the Gospel

PART V

Mention of Angels in the Gospels

PART VI

Places of our Lord's Abode and Ministry

PART VII

Our Lord's Mode of dealing with His Apostles

PART I

Characteristic Differences in the Four Gospels

SECTION I

NOT IRREVERENT TO NOTICE SUCH DIFFERENCES

WE insensibly notice and love the natural character and peculiarities of those we revere; and dwell in observation and memory on their characteristics of tone, gesture, and look : may we not in like manner, in the devout and humble study of the Gospels, enter without irreverence into a critical examination of their diversities and distinctive traits, and endeavour to trace out with affectionate care the indications of such character in each Evangelist! Nothing indeed is more interesting to observe than the strong individual differences that mark good men,—a diversity of moral complexion, a sort of instinctive and unconscious effluence which passes into their words and actions, and infuses into them a sort of peculiar savour of themselves. And from the notice of these we are led on to the contemplation of the great Creator Himself, Who orders all things ; Whose infinity is set forth in the variety of His manifestations, His incomprehensible wisdom in the indications of design, and His Almighty

B

power in manifold adaptations formed to meet His purposes. May we not therefore be allowed to indulge in such contemplations on the characters of the Evangelists and their writings, where the peculiarities of the inspired writers themselves are lost in the radiance of His Divine Person of Whom, and in Whom, and by Whom they speak?

These prevailing differences in the four Gospels I had myself noticed and traced out, both in the general bearing of each, and in a variety of particulars; and concluded that they were not to be attributed merely to accidental differences in the writers, nor to those fortuitous circumstances which, humanly speaking, might have been the reasons for their writing; but to some great and Divine purposes : such as might be infinitely too deep for us fully to comprehend, but into which it would not be irreverent humbly to inquire. It seemed to me that each of the four Gospels was marked with a strong diversity of character, extending more or less throughout, and that, if I may so speak, a different manifestation of our Blessed Lord Himself comes forth in each Gospel. And it has so happened that these opinions, which had been thus formed, seemed to fall in with those emblems which have been supposed to represent the four Gospels in the prophet Ezekiel and in the Revelation of St. John. So much so, that if we were to set aside all consideration of the sacred character of such symbols in Scripture, and merely to look upon them in the light of poetical figures or similes in the way of human illustration, they would serve admirably to express the preconceived notions I had formed of the differences which might be observed in the four Gospels; and would altogether be calculated to describe the highest and best conceptions we could form of them, better than any human language.

But when we come to consider the very high authority there is for supposing that these Living Creatures were prophetically intended to set forth the Gospels, it raises immeasurably this whole view of the subject, and puts all these points at once in that position of Divine dignity, in which we must ever wish to consider every part of the Holy Writings. For in the critical study of the Gospels we are too apt to forget the greatness of Divine purpose which must prevail in them throughout; and sometimes unconsciously to suspect them of imperfection, of a want of order and accuracy. Whereas it may be supposed that Revelation in these respects is like Nature and Providence: for in these we doubt not that there is the perfection of exquisite order and arrangement; but it may appear to us in many respects otherwise, because we cannot comprehend the whole design, although often forced to notice that things apparently trivial are full of Divine intent. In like manner we cannot doubt but that the Gospels are constructed with consummate arrangement to serve their ends, although we may be unable to perceive how those ends are best attained, or what they are. The one great end of the Gospels is, of course, our "instruction in righteousness," but still it seems not improbable that even in their composition they may be replete with admirable intrinsic order and arrangement, and hidden beauty of structure. For so it is in the natural world,—the plant that seems intended for the sustenance of God's creatures, is wonderful in the beauty of its formation, and forms of itself but one link and trivial part in a vast system of exquisite and harmonious correspondence. In allusion to which it seems to have been expressly said that "the Lord God made every plant of the field before it was in the earth, and every herb of the field before it grew[1]:" and the "lights in the firmament," which are "for seasons" and "to give light upon the earth," yet are discovered to be infinitely wonderful in their order and vastness and beauty. And indeed there may be some great mistake in our ever considering things Divine to be regulated only with respect to one definite end and object, as is necessarily the case in the works of men. It is remarkable with what a curious and minute particularity these Symbolical Figures are delineated, with an accuracy of detail repeated each time in the three descriptions which are given of them. And if it can be shown that there is found in the four Gospels some correspondence even to these particulars, it will teach us to speak with reverential caution with regard to the smallest incidents and expressions that occur in the Evangelical narrative, as what had been long before weighed in the balance, and measured out in Divine Wisdom. And the declaration which so often occurs, that events take place "in order that it might be fulfilled which was spoken by the Prophets," would seem to furnish us with a great principle in the Divine economy, and to intimate that the Word that has gone forth, and the Divine appointment so expressed long before, mysteriously regulates the minutest circumstances that occur; so as to induce one to suppose that every thing with respect to our Blessed Lord was but the fulfilment of the Word spoken in His prophets, by Him "Whose goings forth have been from everlasting."

The four Symbols, therefore, I have been thus led to introduce, if I may so speak with reverence, as the framework on which to delineate these peculiarities and differ-

---

[1] Gen. ii. 4, 5.

ences of character which are observable in the four Evangelists. And in order to do this, it seems necessary to make a short digression, to consider what authority can be alleged, and what reasons there are, for adopting these typical representations as descriptive of the four Gospels.

SECTION II

THE FOUR EMBLEMS IN THE PROPHET EZEKIEL AND IN THE REVELATION OF ST. JOHN

THESE four Living Creatures are described in the first and in the tenth chapters of the Prophet Ezekiel, and also in the fourth chapter of the Revelation of St. John : for they appear clearly to be the same in all these passages : and have been variously explained by modern interpreters. Mede considers them as four Churches, or rather as the Churches in the four quarters of the globe: Dr. Hammond, as four Apostles present at the first General Council at Jerusalem. They have also been said to signify four great Empires of the world. Others, as Dean Woodhouse, take them to represent some order of Angelic Beings ; others imagine them to be symbols of the Divine Nature. But there appears to be something like a general opinion among the Fathers for supposing them to be intended for the four Evangelists. St. Irenæus, Victorinus, St. Athanasius, St. Ambrose, St. Augustin, St. Jerome, Gregory the Great, and others down to our own Bp. Andrews, speak of them as having been so considered ; and adopt this mode of interpretation as their own opinion.

It is of course possible that these later suppositions alluded to may be admissible, without prejudice to this interpretation of the Ancients, but in themselves they are all at once open to great objection. With regard to the two former, it may be asked, Is there any thing in the analogy of Scripture to justify our applying the number four to Apostles or to Churches? Four worldly Empires seem unworthy of what approaches so near to the throne of God, more near even than Angels. With regard to their signifying an Order of Angels, it may be answered that there is a marked distinction in the Apocalypse between them and Angels ; nor I believe are such Cherubim ever numbered among the Angelic Orders. With regard to the last opinion, one trembles at the thought of visible symbols of the Divine Nature. But still all these may possibly be true in some sense, without prejudice to the earlier interpretation. This last opinion, for instance, however at first sight objectionable in itself, yet in some degree falls in with the ancient interpretation, as representing manifestations of God in the four Gospels. And of course the four Gospels may themselves typify and shadow forth a further development hereafter in some Angelic Creations. And the number " four,". which is the great characteristic of the symbols, may perhaps be found in other things not as independent points of coincidence, but because the things themselves may have some analogous relation to the Gospels, either by correspondence or by contrast. Four empires or powers of Evil might admit of some correspondence with four principles of good, or Evangelists. And St. Irenæus and St. Augustin both suggest that the number of the four Gospels is on account of the four quarters of the globe. And therefore, of course, there may be a corresponding Church in four quarters, for the Elect are to be gathered from the four winds. But at all events, as numbers have usually in Holy Scripture their own ap-

propriate adaptation, the number four seems particularly to
apply to Evangelists; as the four rivers of Paradise, and
the four chariots which are declared to be " the four spirits
of the Heavens, which go forth from standing before the
Lord of all the earth" in the Prophet Zechariah². And
perhaps this number is so applied as signifying universality
or completeness³; so that, as the wings of the Cherubim
filled the temple and touched its walls, so the Gospels
may be said to fill and touch the walls of the Universe.
St. Augustin and St. Jerome both speak of these living
creatures, thus explained, as "the four-horse car of the
Lord⁴," "carried on which," says St. Augustin⁵, "throughout the world He subdues the people to His easy yoke and
light burden :" taking apparently this expression of "the
car" from Ecclesiasticus, where it is said, " It was Ezekiel
who saw the glorious vision which was showed him upon
the chariot of the Cherubims." St. Athanasius alludes to
this prophetical vision as a reason why there can be but
four Gospels. St. Irenæus⁶ speaks of them, thus applied
to the Evangelists, as the four pillars upon which the
Church rests, which is spread throughout the four quarters
of the world. His words are remarkable :—" Since there
are four regions of the world in which we are, and four
Catholic Spirits, and the Church is spread throughout the
whole earth : but the pillar and confirmation of the Church,
is the Gospel and the spirit of life; it follows that it has
four pillars, breathing incorruption from every quarter, and
giving life to man. From which it is manifest that the
Word, Who is the Worker of all things, Who sitteth above
the Cherubim, and containeth all things, in being manifested

---

² Ch. vi. 5.　　³ On this number see Nativity, pp. 406. 506.
⁴ Quadriga Domini.　　　　⁵ De Conscn. Evan. lib. i. 7.
⁶ Lib. iii. 2.

to men, hath given us the Gospel, in form fourfold, but combined, or contained, by one Spirit [7]."

But in the application of each of these Living Creatures to the four Evangelists respectively, there seems to be little agreement among ancient writers. We indeed usually see them represented in one way, which seems to have descended to us through the Roman Church, according to which St. Matthew is represented as the Man, St. Mark as the Lion, St. Luke as the Calf, and St. John as the Eagle. This is the method adopted by Victorinus, St. Ambrose, St. Jerome, and Gregory. And St. Augustin expresses his full approbation in the two latter cases of St. Luke and St. John; but gives his reasons for considering that St. Matthew is the Lion and St. Mark the Man. St. Irenæus and St. Athanasius differ from both of these opinions and from each other; and yet, as may be shown hereafter, Irenæus does in one point of view appear to confirm St. Augustin. It is possible that the reason for this discrepancy in the application of them severally, may in some degree have arisen from there having been a difference in the order in which they occur; for they differ from each other in this respect in the two places in Ezekiel; and also from both of these where they are found in St. John. And this very discrepancy in these sacred writers, although it admits of an obvious explanation, may yet also contain some high significations.

But both Irenæus and Ambrose mention an opinion which perfectly coincides with the supposition that these Animals represent the Evangelists, though they take it in a higher and more Divine manner. There are some, says St. Ambrose, who suppose our Lord Himself to be re-

---

[7] τετράμορφον εὐαγγέλιον, ἑνὶ δὲ πνεύματι συνεχόμενον.

presented by these four Living Creatures, according to the different manifestations of Himself in the four Gospels, being Himself One and the Same in each, yet represented by each in a different point of view. And perhaps it is this high view which is to be considered as that of the Fathers, rather than that bearing more immediately on the inspired writers themselves. Origen applies the interpretation of these animals to certain human affections, such as anger, by which he explains the Lion, as by concupiscence the Calf. Gregory the Great, in his interpretation of the passage in Ezekiel, enters more fully into the subject, and in his various explanations appears in some measure to combine all these senses. He considers them to signify the Evangelists, adopting the order of St. Jerome and St Ambrose; but he also applies them to our Lord Himself, as differently set forth in all these manifestations of Himself in the Gospels: in which he incidentally corresponds with the beautiful interpretation of St. Irenæus and St. Ambrose. He moreover applies the representations to individual Christians also, as being members of Christ, and formed according to the image of their Lord; for it is said, "they have the likeness of a man." Each good man, he says, has within him that which is signified by the four animals, inasmuch as all goodness in God's saints consists in their resemblance to the Son of Man. "*The likeness of a man,*" i. e. the Son of Man, must be formed in us now, and also more perfectly hereafter, for "we shall see Him as He is"! This application to individuals would in some degree coincide with Origen's mode of interpreting the subject. Quesnel [*], the French writer, in the same manner, combines these significations: after saying that the victories of Christ are represented by

[*] On the Rev. ch. iv.

the Lion; the sacrifice of His death by the Ox; His divinely-human works by the Man, and the Divine mysteries by the Eagle,—he adds, that the qualities of His saints are represented by these four animals; the Lion indicating authority, the Ox patience, the Man wisdom and charity, the Eagle heavenly-mindedness. St. Gregory moreover seems to refer them to the second Advent of our Lord as well as to the first, and considers that what is now represented by the four Evangelists, will then be manifested in the perfection of God's saints who will be present to judge the world, being, as St. John says, "in the midst of the throne, and round about the throne," and perhaps as being one with Christ.

These various interpretations of Pope Gregory in no way interfere with the object we have in view, which is to show that these figures do pre-eminently signify the four Gospels; although they may incidentally be applicable to other analogous points of resemblance, and may ultimately refer to things still more Divine, which will be revealed in the Kingdom of Heaven hereafter. It is mentioned by Mede, that the first reference of these figures is to the four ensigns of the children of Israel, which attended the Tabernacle in their passage through the wilderness. The ensign of the lion, that of Judah, went first towards the east: that of Reuben, next, with the ensign of the man; afterwards, towards the sea, that of Ephraim, the calf; and lastly, the eagle of Dan. This previous retrospective signification of the symbols coincides with our supposition of their being the four Evangelists; for as those ensigns attended the Tabernacle through the wilderness, so do these their antitypes, the Presence of Christ in His Church through the wilderness of this world to the heavenly Canaan. In like manner, if we consider them as Cherubim overshadowing the mercy-seat, or as taking possession of the Jewish Temple, and the living symbols from the midst of which the glory of God appeared, it is perfectly analogous to the place the Gospels occupy in supporting the throne of God in His kingdom on earth, as represented in the Revelation. And such an interpretation of these emblems naturally turns the thoughts to an ulterior development of them, which may be in heavenly things hereafter, of which one can not presume to speak. If the former manifestations of God were between the Cherubim in the Jewish Church, and a second as it were between the Evangelists, in a manner quite defying all previous conception, in the Christian Church; there may be a third also, to which these symbols will likewise apply, in which Christ will reveal Himself hereafter, and that too in a manner quite transcending all antecedent human thought.

It may further be observed, that even beforehand, and independently of authority and proof, there appears no reason why this interpretation of these typical figures, as representing the four Evangelists, should be considered as improbable. Surely of things sensible and visible there is nothing we can conceive more important, or more worthy of Divine prophecy and figure. The Gospels are the four great manifestations of God and of Christ in His kingdom: with reference to them, we may reverently use the sacred words, "Thou that sittest between the Cherubims, show Thyself." And indeed St. Irenæus does thus apply those words of the Psalmist, saying that David thus spake, asking for Christ's coming in the Gospel; and expressly speaks of the term Cherubim as signifying the Gospels. "For the four-shaped Cherubim," he adds, "and their countenances are images of the dispensation of the Son of God." St.

Jerome also speaks of them under this term as "the four-horse car of the Lord, *the true Cherubim.*" Moreover it may be noticed, that the very signification of the term Cherubim supports the application: for Cherubim are explained by Origen as "the fulness of knowledge;" by St. Jerome as "the multitude of knowledge;" which words could apply to nothing more suitably than to the Gospels; for where is the knowledge of God more fully and abundantly disclosed, so that all other knowledge is enlightened by it? Nor indeed is there any thing unsuitable in the application of these Divine and supernatural figures to mere human agents; for, if Angels are set forth to us under the appearance of a lower nature, that is, of humanity, with superhuman powers and glory; it is agreeable to this analogy that human agents should be represented by images from a lower nature, that of animals, but gifted with powers exceeding theirs. In confirmation of this view it may be added, that the twelve Oxen, or sacrificial emblems, supporting the brazen Sea in the Temple of Solomon, looking four different ways, are supposed to signify the twelve Apostles,—upon whom the doctrine of Baptism and forgiveness of sins is founded in the Christian Church. Now it is quite in character with this supposition, to consider these four figures, proceeding in a mysterious combination four different ways, to imply the four Evangelists. While one and the same authority in the twelve Apostles is set forth by the same emblem for each; different figures in this case represent a standing diversity of character in the Gospels. It is moreover highly interesting to observe, that whereas in the earliest ages many spurious and unworthy Gospels were written, and that the writing and preservation of these four might appear to have been quite what is called accidental, yet all this was so ordered by the watchful agency and control of God, as to have been long before the subject of distinct prophecy and designation.

SECTION III

THE DESCRIPTIONS OF THESE SYMBOLICAL FIGURES

It is not to our purpose to enter into any minute investigation of these symbolical figures as described by the two sacred writers, but merely to show that there is adequate authority for our so applying them, and then to pursue the investigation in the Gospels themselves; but it seems as well to mention some few things in the description of those symbols, which may afford some clue to the mode in which they may be thus applied.

The prophet Ezekiel, in the first chapter, sees them at the very opening of his prophecies by the river Chebar: *"I looked, and, behold, a whirlwind came out of the north, a great cloud, and a fire infolding itself."* Now it is evident to all how often "the cloud" is the symbol of the Divine presence, as in the pillar of a cloud in the wilderness, the cloud that filled the Temple, and the bright cloud at the Transfiguration; and clouds attend on the comings and goings of our Lord, as at the Ascension, and in the descriptions of His final Advent. It is also obvious how often the "fire" which accompanies it is significative of the Holy Spirit. And without attempting fully to explain what the coming "out of the north" may signify, we may see thus far, that from the north, or out of the captivity, arises in the Prophets the more clear enunciation of Evangelical promises; and also how from the north or the oppression of worldly powers (which the north is, I believe, usually said to signify) arises the manifestation of Christ crucified ; and how the strength of His Church is shown under or out of persecution, out of the " whirlwind " of temporal affliction.

The prophet then proceeds, " *also out of the midst thereof came the likeness of four living creatures. And this was their appearance ; they had the likeness of a man.*" Of this " likeness of a man " Origen observes (though not applying these symbols to the Gospels), "Amongst the four faces, pre-eminent and chief is the human face." Now if we take the figures to represent our Lord Himself in each of the Gospels, it is easy to apply this expression to the Incarnation, to that subject of which generally the Evangelists speak : whatever there may be in each Gospel more particularly to characterize it, yet most prominent as seen in each is " the Son of Man."

" *And every one had four faces, and every one had four wings ;*" and afterwards, in the eighth verse, " *and they had the hands of a man under their wings on their four sides.*" Here the wings evidently represent what is Divine and soars above earth ; the " hands under the wings " are very expressive of the human agents, as writing the Gospels according to their human characters and affections, in subservience to the Divine inspiration. Or again, the Manhood and Godhead of our Lord would readily occur to us, as seen in each and in all, and expressed by these supernatural tokens.

Again, in the next verse, " *their wings were joined one to another; they turned not when they went ; they went every one straight forward :*" of which St. Jerome says, " The Gospels are mutually united and adhere together, and flying through the whole world hurry here and there ;

nor have they any termination of their flying; nor are they sometimes overcome and retire, but always proceed to things which are beyond." The description of their motion seems to imply, that they could move with equal rapidity to every quarter; not like a bodily motion, when one has to turn in order to go in another direction, but all ways at once.

Again, "*as for the likeness of their faces, they four had the face of a man, and the face of a lion, on the right side: and they four had the face of an ox on the left side; they four had also the face of an eagle.*" Now, if we take the Man for our Lord's Incarnation; and the Lion, as the regal animal, the emblem of Judah, for the sign of our Lord's eternal Kingship and Kingdom; and the Ox, or Calf, as the sacrificial animal, for the Atonement; and the Eagle, as usually supposed, for our Lord's Divinity; we should have His Incarnation, His Kingdom, His Atonement, and His Divinity, in each of the Gospels, and in all; whatever countenance may more peculiarly characterize each one severally. One face meets us more particularly, but all faces are in all;—"*they four had one likeness*[*]."

Again, "*two wings of every one were joined one to another, and two covered their bodies.*" The two "joined" wings will readily express, that they are all thus united to each other, and divinely harmonized. And that "two wings covered their bodies," at once suggests to us that their bodies—that which is human—are covered by that which is Divine; their human purposes are lost in Divine Wisdom. And this consideration must be the rule of all who would rightly interpret the Gospels. Or, again, how does "*the appearance of lamps*," to which

[*] Ch. x. 10.

they are likened, and of which it is said that "*it went up and down among the living creatures*," remind us of that awful expression of "the seven lamps that are before the throne ;" and of the frequent description of God's Word "going forth as a lamp that burneth," and being "as a lantern unto our feet" ?   And the appearance of lightning here spoken of is, we know, the symbol of our Lord's Presence.   How closely does "*the wheel in the middle of a wheel*" express the manifold senses and meanings of the Gospels, and their mysterious end and purposes, one within another, wheel within wheel ; an expression of peculiar beauty and eloquence beyond the thought of man !   And further, "*whithersoever the spirit was to go, they went, thither was their spirit to go ;*" of which Origen says, though not thus interpreting it, "The Spirit which presides to support them, is not on the right hand as the man or the lion, is not on the left hand as the calf, but exists over all the three faces together."

They had all "*hands of a man under their wings,*" for the Son of Man is in all; they have all "*the sole of their feet like the soles of a calf's foot,*" for the Atonement is in all ; they have all "*wings,*" for Divinity is in all ; and they are all, as they move, "*lifted up from the earth.*"   And again [10], "*their whole body, and their backs, and their hands, and their wings, and the wheels, were full of eyes round about.*"   It must be obvious to all, that every part whatever of the Gospel is "full of eyes round about," to search the inmost heart, and that in every quarter where they proceed, they are like the omnipresent Eye of our Lord Himself.

One passage more may be quoted, merely to afford a clue to this interpretation : "*when they went, I heard the*

[10] Ch. x. 12.

noise of their wings, like the noise of great waters, as the voice of the Almighty ;" and afterwards, *" there was a voice from the firmament that was over their heads, when they stood, and had let down their wings."* What can be more truly spoken of as "the voice of the Almighty" than the Gospels? While the noise of their wings—the effect and commotion they produce among mankind as they move—is like the sound of many waters. And what can be the voice from the firmament, when they had let down their wings, and are silent? It may be supposed to mean that when the Spirit of God speaks within us, the Scripture itself is silent, and man adores and worships: or the voice of the Almighty from Heaven, when their motion is stopped, may signify the voice of God in His Church at present;—and also the voice of Christ on the Day of Judgment, when the movement of the Gospel through the world shall have ceased, and they shall have *" let down their wings."*

In this manner might it be shown that every part of this description is capable of a striking and minute fulfilment in the Gospels. The same is the case in the tenth chapter of Ezekiel, where these Living Creatures are again described. They are, the Prophet repeats, the same figures which he saw by the river of Chebar; but here they are seen in the Temple at Jerusalem, and in a different order. And the latter circumstance is explained, by considering the figures as holding in their advance the same relative positions[1]; but by the river Chebar they are seen coming from the North; the Man therefore on the south side is seen first, the Lion on the right, the Ox on the left, and the Eagle on the north side, the last; whilst in the Temple,

---

[1] Vid. W. Lowth ad locum.

c

as the Prophet stands on the west of the Shechinah, the Ox first presents itself to view.

This very change of order may also contain spiritual significations : it may be, that it prevents our affording an exclusive pre-eminence to either of these Divine attributes or offices of Christ ; but by changing each of them, it brings them into an awful and mysterious connexion with each other.   Thus, in the first-mentioned order, in the first chapter of Ezekiel our Lord's Manhood is the first, and then His Kingdom ; His Priesthood stands between the Manhood and the Godhead.   In the Revelation His King-dom and Priesthood stand together, His Manhood and Godhead.   And again, perhaps for some mysterious reason, by the river Chebar the Manhood comes first, in the Temple the Priesthood, in the Revelation in Heaven the Kingdom.   In the tenth chapter of Ezekiel, the Cherub is substituted for the Ox, which is supposed to be another name for the same figure.   If not so, it may contain some symbolical allusion, as that the departing of the Lord (for He is there departing from the Temple) is in judgment, and not Sacrificial or Atoning.   But the Prophet says expressly that they were the same as he first saw, the faces and their appearances.

The different order in which they appear might also represent another circumstance ; for they differ as seen from a different quarter or aspect ; and may signify our Lord's manifestations of Himself to different persons, in judgment or in mercy, in human condescension or Divine power.   By the penitent the Calf is seen—" bring forth the fatted calf :" by the impenitent the Lion is beheld—"a lion out of the forest shall slay them :" by those cast down, the Man,—" one touched me like unto the Son of Man :"   by saints of God, the Eagle, — " He shall carry them on eagles' wings, and bear them unto Himself."

Or again, the different aspects in which they appear may imply that neither of the Evangelists is before the other or prior in authority : but yet their relative position with regard to each other may be divinely ordered, and their mutual affinities implied in their wings touching each other. Thus St. Luke approaches more to what is spiritual and Divine than St. Matthew does, as touching St. John. St. Mark has more of the sacrifice than St. Matthew, as approaching St. Luke ; has more of majesty than St. Luke, as approaching St. Matthew.

But with regard to the whole descriptions and the places in which they occur, we can scarcely conceive any thing more worthy of the prophetical vision, than what this interpretation suggests. And if we consider it with respect to the subjects of the other Prophets at this period, it seems not unreasonable to suppose, that when Evangelical promises were so much brought forth, this figurative Prophet should have represented in symbol the Evangelists or Gospels themselves, which were to serve as the Manifestation of Christ's Presence in the future Kingdom until the end.

There will be found the same closeness of description and accurate correspondency in the same Living Creatures, as they are spoken of in the Book of Revelation, if we interpret them as signifying the four Gospels; at all events, sufficient to indicate that there is nothing forced or overstrained in thus explaining them, whatever higher and ulterior meanings they may contain besides. It will be enough briefly to notice this description. It is in the fourth chapter. After speaking of the rainbow encircling the throne, it proceeds, " *and round about the throne were four and twenty seats : and upon the seats I saw four and twenty elders sitting, clothed in white raiment ; and they had on their heads crowns of gold.*" If these represent the four and twenty courses of the Jewish Priesthood, they may here mean the Christian Priesthood, or the Christian Church, being clothed either in the Priestly dress worn on the day of the Atonement, or in the white robes of Baptism ; and having crowns of gold on their heads, as being of the Royal Priesthood of Christ, or Kings as well as Priests, as is afterwards expressed in their Hymn. Or if " the four and twenty " are referred to the twelve Prophets and twelve Apostles, to whom our Lord promised twelve thrones in His kingdom, it would also have a meaning very consistent with the analogy of Holy Scripture ; for they in either case, when the voice of the Gospel is heard, fall down and give glory to God.

" *And in the midst of the throne,*" proceeds the account, " *and round about the throne, were four beasts full of eyes before and behind. And the first beast was like a lion, and the second beast like a calf, and the third beast had a face as a man, and the fourth beast was like a flying eagle.*" The Living Creatures are under and form part of the throne, whereas the Angels and the Elders are round about the throne and form no part of it. Now, if the Christian Church is a kingdom, and has Angels and Elders around the throne that is therein, what can we suppose to form a part of Christ's throne on earth, or to be under it, more than the Gospels? Nor need we wonder that even Angels should be less near the throne than these, and that the throne is surrounded by Angels and Elders ; for we know that Angels in heavenly places are taught by the Church, and " desire to look into " the things of Redemption, and give glory to God for it : and where can they learn more than in the words and actions of our Blessed Lord as recorded in the Gospels? We find moreover in the next chapter, that "in the midst of the throne and of the four beasts, and in the midst of the elders, stood a Lamb as it had been slain." And the song which they sing is the mysterious "new song," and "glory to the Lamb."

As moreover our Lord has said that His Word shall judge us at the last Day, and as we have His Word chiefly in the Gospels, we may well suppose that these should be in "the midst of" and "round about" His throne, both at the Day of Judgment, and now in this His kingdom. And what could more accurately describe the Gospels, both as explaining the Old Testament and as themselves also being prophetic ; or as enlightening the conscience, in repentance for what is past, and in faith for what is to come, than the eyes that look "before and behind"?

"And the four beasts had each of them six wings about him ; and they were full of eyes within: and they rest not day and night, saying, Holy, Holy, Holy, Lord God Almighty, which was, and is, and is to come. And when those beasts give glory and honour and thanks to Him that sat on the throne, Who liveth for ever and ever, the four and twenty elders fall down before Him that sat on the throne, and worship Him that liveth for ever and ever, and cast their crowns before the throne, saying, Thou art worthy, O Lord, to receive glory and honour and power: for Thou hast created all things, and for Thy pleasure they are and were created." Here the six wings may well express their Divine mode of passing through the world, being in the midst of and around the throne of Christ in His Church ; and as differing from the stationary camp of the Church in the wilderness; unlike which "they rest not day and night." The "eyes within" may well be

understood of their deep, spiritual, heart-searching meanings.   And what upon the earth can be said so fully to
give glory to the ever-blessed Trinity, as the Gospels?
As they move, the four and twenty Elders, all the
Churches of God, fall down and worship, and cast their
crowns before the throne; for that Christian righteousness, which the Gospel reveals, is founded in humiliation.

Thus are these living emblems described, as nearest of
all things to God's throne, not as mere subjects of His
dominion, but the agents of His will, and executors of His
counsels; most powerful, rapid, and subtle; not angelic,
not human, not animal; but multiform and yet uniform,
earthly yet heavenly; with powers exceeding all that is
known, and with the Holy Spirit containing them and
contained as it were by them.   Now, the four written
Gospels have been considered as in one sense a fulfilment
of the promise of the coming of the Comforter, and
assuredly we have therein the Spirit of God and the Word
of God.   Our Lord's words are, He assures us, spirit and
life.   And if we now find that the Old Testament contains
infinitely more than the Jew of old could have formed any
conception of, we may conclude that the Gospels also do
in some hidden manner contain infinitely higher and
better things than we have ever yet attained to.   The
Cherubim in the tabernacle were supposed by the Jews
to be the memorials of God's descent on Mount Sinai;
for they looked back to the past, but knew not what in
the future they portended : thus it is with the Gospels;
they are memorials of Christ's descent on earth; how
much they speak of His future descent in glory we
know not.

Enough has perhaps been said to show the mode in
which these emblems may be interpreted, as signifying the

four Gospels in this Christ's spiritual Kingdom. It would of course be impossible to prove to a demonstration that this is the interpretation of them, or to have one's imagination sufficiently under control, to be sure that one is not misled by it. But the application itself seems like one of those things that run up into the mysterious tradition of the first ages; for indeed there is no certain knowledge why or how it is applied to them, nor indeed any universal consent on the mode of doing so; only it is reported to signify them, and one attempts to apply it in this way, and another in that. The same is the case with other things in the early ages which were received with a traditionary sanction, but not explained, unless it was by the vague conjectures of those who received them; such as the habit of turning to the East in prayer, and mixing water with the wine at the Eucharist,—practices the reception of which was general, but the reasons given for their adoption, only such as occurred to individuals.

Nor is this difference of opinion amongst ancient writers so great as it may appear at first sight; for they are not only agreed in considering these symbols to signify the Gospels, but also, I believe, in this point, that the Lion signifies what is kingly; the Man, what is human; the Ox, what is sacerdotal and sacrificial; the Eagle, what is spiritual and Divine. St. Irenæus himself speaks of them in this order and to this effect. And therefore the opinion between him and St. Augustin and others, and the point left open to private judgment and discussion, would be mainly this,—in which of the Gospels, respectively, these qualities or attributes chiefly predominate.

SECTION IV

THE KINGDOM SET FORTH IN ST. MATTHEW'S GOSPEL

RESPECTING two of the emblems the concurring testimony may perhaps be supposed to be sufficiently conclusive, viz. that St. Luke's Gospel is signified by the Calf; and St. John's by the Eagle. The only doubtful point, therefore, will be with regard to St. Matthew and St. Mark, which is to be considered the Lion, and which the Man. St. Ambrose and St. Jerome consider St. Mark as the Lion, adhering to the order in which they first occur in Ezekiel, and St. Matthew as the Man. "The first face," says the latter, "that of a man, signifies Matthew, who begins to write as of a man, the 'Book of the generation of Jesus Christ, the Son of David.' The second, Mark, in which is heard the voice of the lion roaring in the desert, 'Prepare ye the way of the Lord.' The third, that of the calf, prefigures Luke the Evangelist, commencing his history from the priest Zacharias. The fourth, the Evangelist John, who, having taken the wings of an eagle, and hastening to loftier things, speaks of the Word of God." It is evident, in this place of St. Jerome, that the adaptation to the Evangelists is merely taken from the first words of each Gospel; it seems a higher and more worthy consideration to suppose with St. Augustin, that the emblems apply to some more distinguishing character which pervades the whole. And indeed St. Irenæus and St. Ambrose do so consider it. The former says, that through St. Matthew's Gospel "the meek man, and lowliness of thought, is preserved." St. Ambrose, that "the man" is

applied to St. Matthew on account of his Gospel dealing
especially with morals and manners, which are especially
human ; for St. Matthew's Gospel mentions more of precept and command than the others do. But I am not
aware that any attempt has been made to prove "the
lion" applicable to St. Mark, from any peculiar character
in his Gospel. One thing is remarkable in these discus-
sions, that the questionable point lies between those two
of the former Evangelists, who are so similar to each other,
that the Gospel of the latter is reasonably supposed to be
taken from that of the former, and adheres so closely to it,
that it would be difficult at first sight to select in it any
peculiar character of its own.

Now it may be as well to mention what first led the
writer to the consideration of these emblems. Without
any reference to these symbols, or even knowledge of
them, in considering the distinctive characters of the four
Gospels, that of St. Mark seemed to him, in a very remarkable manner throughout, to set forth our Lord's humanity
and the Son of Man, in those incidental expressions that
distinguish his Gospel : and on finding that this symbol
of "the Man" had been thus applied, it appeared a striking
confirmation of this his opinion. And yet, on referring
to St. Augustin [2], it did not appear that he had thus
arranged these symbols relative to any consideration of
St. Mark, but because he thought that St. Matthew's
Gospel was in an especial manner significative of "the
Lion ;" nor does he mention any reason for St. Mark
being "the Man," but the absence of the Priest and the
King, which the other two record. Nor does he enter
into the question as one depending on the characteristic

[2] See de Consen. Evan. and also Tract. in Johan. Evan. xxxvi.
5. 1.

tone and spirit of the Gospels, but considers it merely with regard to the particular subjects which are distinctly mentioned in the narrative.

Our object, therefore, at present, is to show that there are in the four Gospels great characteristic differences, and that these cannot be better expressed than by these four Animals, if we take them according to St. Augustin's interpretation,—the Lion for St. Matthew, and the Man for St. Mark, the Calf and the Eagle for St. Luke and St. John; which interpretation, indeed, Augustin does not mention as his own, but as that tradition which he most approved of.

Now it is evident of these Animals, that three walk on earth,—the Lion, the Man, and the Calf; and the other, the Eagle, soars above earth: and, agreeably to this, in the three first Gospels it is our Lord's human Person is mostly described, and in the last, His Divine. The Calf, being the sacerdotal animal, obviously may represent either the Priest or the Victim; and be considered to intimate the Atonement, as especially pervading St. Luke's Gospel. The Man would signify our Lord's humanity and His Incarnation, as characterizing St. Mark's Gospel; and the Lion, the emblem of Majesty —the Lion of the tribe of Judah (a title applied to our blessed Lord Himself)—would imply the sovereignty and kingdom of Christ, as more especially disclosed in St. Matthew.

But, first of all, it may be asked, what reason can there be for the Lion holding the first place? In the description in Ezekiel, "the Man" comes first, and Reuben, whose standard it was, was the first-born; but in St. John "the first beast was like a lion," and Judah had now taken the promised precedence. "The remnant

of Jacob," says the Prophet Micah [3], "shall be among
the Gentiles in the midst of many people as a lion." It
may be, that this Gospel was the first opening of the
Kingdom in which all the attributes of Christ were to be
shown; and we know what a prominent place the Kingdom of Christ holds in all prophecy : to which it may be
added, that among the ensigns of the tribes, the lion of
Judah went foremost, and when the Apocalypse was written, the Lion, the King of Judah, had already come. To
this, therefore, the first and opening of the Gospels, and to
the very first words of this Gospel, which traces Christ as
the Root of David, we may apply the words in the
Apocalypse, "I wept much, because no man was found
worthy to open and to read the book, neither to look
thereon. And one of the elders saith unto me, Weep not ;
behold, the Lion of the tribe of Judah, the Root of David,
hath prevailed to *open the book.*" St. Matthew, poor in
spirit, first discloses the Kingdom.

The commencement of St. Matthew's Gospel appears at
once to indicate the King rather than the Son of Man, for
Christ is there at once introduced as the Son of David.
This title was the highest appellation of their kings, and
for David's sake the kingdom was entailed to them. Here
it is to David and to Abraham; whereas in St. Luke it is
to Adam, that our Lord is traced. Throughout the genealogy also St. Augustin has observed that St. Matthew
adheres to the mention of kings, whereas St. Luke introduces others in the line [4]. And let us observe the circumstances of our Saviour's birth, which are recorded by St.
Matthew alone. It is revealed to the Eastern Kings, or
Wise Men, who come to wait on Him with gifts as a King,
asking for Him, and saying, "Where is He that is born

[3] Ch. v. 8.   [4] See Nativity, pp. 106. 110. 117.

King of the Jews ?" But in St. Luke it is celebrated by Shepherds, who represent Christ's little ones and His ministers, in conjunction with Angels, who say, " Unto you is born this day, in the city of David, a Saviour, which is Christ the Lord." In St. Matthew our Lord is persecuted by Herod as a King, and as a King flies into Egypt; while the Innocents, the first in His army of Martyrs, are slain, betokening the nature of His kingdom. In St. Luke, He is circumcised, which is the first shedding of the victim's blood ; and as the Priest and the Victim, He is presented in the Temple, and there attended on by the holy Simeon and devout Anna, the one a prophet and the other a prophetess, " which departed not from the temple, but served God with fastings and prayers night and day." Again, in St. Matthew's Gospel alone, our Lord on His return from Egypt retires from Judea, as the King of the Jews, to avoid Archelaus, and is taken into Galilee : but in St. Luke, the only mention of His early years is that He is at twelve years of age in the Temple, sitting among the Doctors of the Law.

Such is the commencement of the Gospels, the character, as it were, that marks the vestibule in each ; the one as that of the palace of the great King ; the other as that of the temple of our God. The nature of the Gospels is such, that it precludes our expecting to find any thing very prominent or strongly marked of this kind in the general narrative ; and yet, on a little examination, we find it is more so than we should have supposed. There appears, for instance, something throughout the Gospel of St. Matthew of a tone Majestic and Kingly, as distinguished from the rest. There is something of this character in the general narrative, which proceeds so regardless of time and place, after some Divine manner indifferent to minute particulars; all this partakes of a Majestic simplicity, a Kingly sublimity. It mentions consecutively and together things separated by intervals of days, or weeks, or months, in some mysterious mode; as coming from that Spirit to Whom all things are equally present, and "a thousand years as one day." There is, again, something great and majestic in the manner in which the Gospel throws together in groups, at one time discourses, at another miracles, and at another parables. It all partakes of a kind of greatness, notwithstanding the singular simplicity of this Evangelist. There are, indeed, in St. Matthew, indications of a very profound humility and meekness; but then it must be remembered that poverty of spirit and meekness is the very character of Christ's kingdom. There is also in St. Matthew something that is peculiarly *human*, and marks the Son of Man; but then it must be observed that our Lord is King especially as the Son of Man; and therefore a part of His kingdom and majesty are His humanity and His meekness. It is when mention is made of our Lord's humanity, whereby He is made a little lower than the Angels, that it is added, "Thou hast put all things under His feet[5]."—"What is man that Thou art mindful of him, or the son of man that Thou visitest him? Thou madest him lower than the Angels, to crown him with glory and worship." St. Ambrose, indeed, in applying "the Man" to St. Matthew, considers the precepts and moral commands which abound particularly in this Gospel, to be of a *human* character; but if we consider the authority with which these are delivered in St. Matthew they will appear more strongly, I think, as what is Kingly, and the commands of a King. Observe especially the majestic authority which appears throughout the

[5] Ps. viii. 6. 1 Cor. xv. 27.

Sermon on the Mount: through the whole of it we see
that it is the Judge Himself who is speaking; and the
King Himself who is now opening His kingdom and
laying down its laws; the very first beatitude is to declare
who shall inherit "*the kingdom.*" It is mentioned that
the multitude were amazed at "the authority" with which
He spake; and this sermon is full of indications of that
authority. We may notice such expressions as, "I say
unto you," where the King Himself comes forward to
sanction the laws of His own Lawgiver, Moses, or to set
them aside by the higher sanction and authority of His
own; and, appealing to the day when He shall visibly
establish His kingdom, "many shall come to Me in that
day, saying, Lord, Lord;" and "then will I declare unto
them, I never knew you—depart from Me." If, with this
Sermon on the Mount, we compare St. Luke's Sermon on
the Plain, we shall find this difference, that in St. Matthew there are references to Jewish customs and laws,
such as characterize the King of the Jews, but which are
omitted in St. Luke. It is as writing to Jews that St.
Matthew necessarily writes of the King; for it is of the
Jews that our Lord is King[6]; "Judah is my Lawgiver,"
"upon My hill of Sion have I set My King." And so far
as the Sermon in St. Luke differs, it is especially as being
of a compassionate character, as addressed to a mixed
multitude from both heathen and Jewish cities. We may
notice the very commencement :—"And He came down
with them, and stood in the plain,"—"and the whole
multitude sought to touch Him; for there went virtue out
of Him, and healed them all: and He lifted up His eyes
on His disciples, and said, Blessed be ye poor." The
mere circumstances of His going up to the mountain, and

[6] See Passion, p. 294.

His coming down to the plain, are supposed to contain spiritual meanings ; the one of sublimity, the other of condescension to human infirmities. And His sitting down in the Sermon on the Mount, St. Augustin speaks of as implying something of majestic authority. On the plain He stood.

We may observe, also, our Lord's discourses towards the latter part of His ministry in St. Matthew's Gospel, and the very awful majesty of His reproofs in His teaching in the Temple, as in the denunciations upon the Scribes and Pharisees, to which there is nothing precisely similar in the other Gospels. The formal manner in which the Beatitudes are brought forward in St. Matthew, at the opening of our Lord's ministry, and the Woes at its close, seem in their mode of statement to represent the King laying down the privileges and the penalties of His kingdom, like the Lawgiver on Mount Gerizim and on Mount Ebal. Add to which, that mere moral precepts and commands, which abound in this Gospel, as coming from Christ, are of themselves of a *kingly* nature, rather than of *human* character. Some of them too are so in the form and manner in which they are enunciated, as "then began He to upbraid the cities in which His mighty works were done [7]," and, "But I say unto you, That every idle word that men shall speak, they shall give account thereof [8]," and the like. There is perhaps something equally awful blended with the compassionateness of St. Luke ; but this arises rather from the lifting up of the veil from the unseen world, which is sometimes done by narrative, as in the parable of the Rich Man. What is vented in a tone of passionate complaint in St. Luke is as awful as what in St. Matthew is delivered in that of supreme authority, or

[7] Ch. xi. 20.   [8] Ch. xii. 36.

solemn admonition. Such are the two lamentations in St. Luke over the approaching destruction of Jerusalem, as compared with the accounts of that terrible visitation in St. Matthew. The first of these lamentations in St. Luke is on our Lord's entering Jerusalem on Palm Sunday ; the second, on His way to Calvary : in St. Matthew, the account is given when our Lord is sitting on the Mount of Olives. In St. Luke the picture comes before us amidst the tears of our merciful High Priest and Intercessor ; in St. Matthew it is set forth with an unmoved and calm judgment and majesty.

In addition to these points in St. Matthew,—viz. the Sermon on the Mount, the denunciations in the Temple, and the moral commands which are found in this Gospel, —may be added other lengthened discourses throughout, characteristic of this sovereignty. Such are those delivered at the last evening of our Lord's teaching, on the Mount of Olives, on the coming in of the Kingdom, in the twenty-fourth and twenty-fifth chapters ;—the return of our Lord in majesty to Judgment, and the parables concerning that Judgment. Observe the awful majesty of such words as these, " *then shall the King* say unto them on his right hand :" and again, "and *the King shall answer and say unto them:*" and " *then shall the Kingdom of* heaven be likened unto Ten Virgins :" and afterwards, " *for the Kingdom of heaven is* as a man travelling into a far country, who called his own servants." To which may be added this remarkable circumstance, that the two parables of the Marriage-Feast, one of which occurs in each of these Gospels, though in some respects so similar, yet have this difference, that in St. Matthew it is a King, making a marriage for his Son, and acting as a King throughout, sending forth his armies and putting in bonds the unworthy guest ;

but in St. Luke it is only "a certain man," and there is no allusion throughout to Kingly authority.

It may indeed be noticed as remarkable, how frequently the mention of the Kingdom occurs in this Gospel more than in the others, as in the parables respecting the Kingdom. And even in slighter points it may be shown, as in the giving of the keys of the Kingdom unto St. Peter, mentioned only in this Gospel; the question to St. Peter respecting "*the kings of the earth* paying tribute." It may be fanciful, but we cannot help noticing such points of coincidence in things more minute even than this, as for instance, "the disciples came unto Jesus, saying, Who is the greatest *in the Kingdom of heaven ?*" but in St. Luke, instead of this, we read, "there arose a reasoning among them which of them should be the greatest." In parables, moreover, not expressly concerning the kingdom, mention of the kingdom occasionally comes in. In that of the Vineyard, for instance, St. Matthew alone of the three inserts, "therefore shall the kingdom be taken from you." And again, we have the Lord's Prayer given us in both, but with this remarkable difference, that in St. Luke the Doxology is omitted, and the ascribing of *the kingdom and the power and the glory*, which had a place in St. Matthew's account of the same Prayer.

But still, in pursuing these points, we must remember, that it is not to be expected that the prevailing symbol should be indicated by such minute peculiarities, so much as by a general tone and spirit; and also, that it would be contrary to the description of these symbols themselves, or of the great truths indicated by them, to consider them in any way exclusively confined to each; for the King is one and the same in all; and so is the Son of Man; and the Priest is one and the same in all; and all are full of

D

our Lord's Divinity. The Lion and the Lamb are herein met together; the King and the Sacrifice. Therefore St. Matthew and St. Luke harmonize even in discrepancy, and are but different aspects of the same thing. He who is the King is also the Sacrifice; and therefore it is a kingdom indeed, but a kingdom of them that mourn; the sceptre of that kingdom is the reed of gentleness, and the throne is the Cross. Therefore in St. Matthew He speaks with authority indeed, but He who speaks is the perfect pattern of all meekness. And it is remarkable that our Lord sometimes speaks of Himself not as a king only, but as "*a man who was a king*⁹." Sovereignty is still secretly combined with Humanity.

And as we have compared the openings of the Gospels, let us compare also the last chapter of St. Matthew with those of St. Mark and St. Luke. Now in the first-named Gospel there is less reference to human feelings; great things are mentioned in a great way, rather generally than particularly,—collectively, not individually. Such is our Lord's appearing, not to St. Mary Magdalene, not to St. Peter, nor to St. Thomas, nor to the two disciples going to Emmaus, as in the other Gospel narratives; but to the women collectively, and afterwards to the assembled multitude of disciples at the mountain in Galilee ¹; on which occasion, moreover, our Lord is speaking of receiving His kingdom, and saying, "All power is given unto Me in Heaven and in earth." Such also is the authoritative injunction at the close, "Go ye and make disciples of all nations," and the solemn assurance of His Presence, "Lo, I am with you always, even unto the end." The other two Gospels, by the particular incidents and persons which they here introduce, bring it more home to human affec-

---

⁹ ἄνθρωπος βασιλεύς, as in Matt. xxii. 2. ¹ See p. 76, 77.

tions.   The striking way in which St. Mark here diverges
from St. Matthew, into the mention and description of
individuals, is more interesting but less majestic.

The 72nd Psalm, which describes our Lord's Kingdom,
may be found to express very closely the character, and
indeed the very incidents, of St. Matthew's Gospel ;—the
judgments of *the King*, and the righteousness given unto
the King's Son ; His coming down with extreme gentleness and peace, " like the rain into a fleece of wool ;" His
Kingdom being that of the poor ; *the kings* of Arabia and
Saba being there with gifts, and the termination of all—
the earth filled *with His Majesty.*   This is the prophetic
account of our Lord's Kingdom in that Psalm, and such
is the description of St. Matthew's Gospel as setting forth
the Kingdom.

Thus, in short, as St. Matthew's Gospel is peculiarly
addressed to Jews, it is of course more kingly, as the history of their King, being of their own Royal stock of the
line of David, and the Lion of the tribe of Judah.   But
as a Priest, our Lord is not of their own tribe of Levi, but
of the order of Melchizedec, and therefore is seen as coming
forward rather to all the world, than to the Jews alone ;
and, consequently, He speaks more in St. Luke to the
Gentiles also, and there not so much with the authority of
a King by precept, as by narrative, and by all things that
set forth especially the Great High Priest, and the One .
Great and only true Sacrifice.

SECTION V

THE MANHOOD OF OUR LORD IN ST. MARK'S GOSPEL

It has been observed, that those who consider St. Mark
to be represented by the Lion, apply the opening of this
Gospel to the fulfilment of that sign, and consider him as
the Lion whose " voice is in the wilderness ;"—words with
which St. Mark commences, as descriptive of St. John the
Baptist. Otherwise it appears difficult to conceive what
there can be found distinctive in this Gospel, to which
this emblem would apply. There is but little or nothing
in St. Mark purely his own, and in which the account is
confined to himself throughout ; scarcely any thing of instruction or discourse : discourses, indeed, he mostly
passes over, and records events. But still it may be observed, that those events, which have been noticed as
kingly in St. Matthew, St. Mark does not record. And
yet those events which he does mention, are generally the
same as those of St. Matthew ; often those of St. Luke :
and it can scarce be doubted that they are taken from
them, especially when we consider the multitude of circumstances, as St. John intimates, which might have
been selected for mention, and which have been left by all
unrecorded.

It may be observed, that St. Mark not only selects the
same subjects usually to narrate in our Lord's history, but
that he uses often the very same words ; that he not only
does this, but in so doing adheres sometimes to the order
of St. Matthew, when it clearly is not the order in which
the events occurred, but apparently arises from some association of circumstances in the mind of St. Matthew.

Such is the narrative of the anointing at Bethany, which both in St. Matthew and St. Mark is recorded on the Wednesday of the betrayal, instead of the preceding Saturday, on which day we find from St. John that it took place. But in using the same words, and recording the same transactions, St. Mark varies the account with little insertions, the result of personal knowledge, in very many cases such as appear to be peculiar indications of St. Peter; and sometimes such alteration arises from merely changing an expression to one better understood by the Gentile; as when he speaks of "the leaven of Herod²," instead of "the leaven of the Sadducees;" and of the "Greek woman of Syro-Phœnicia³," instead of the "Canaanite," as St. Matthew designates her. But what is very observable is, that perhaps there is not one single circumstance that he records, but that he incidentally shows that he is himself, either through the superhuman aid of express revelation, or by his own ocular testimony, a close observer and witness of the occasion. The latter, St. Jerome states, was not the case with St. Mark; for it is recorded that he had never seen our Lord; but this was the case beyond all others with St. Peter, to whom this Gospel has been always in some sense attributed. Whatever, therefore, is distinctive in this Gospel, so as to admit of a separate emblem, must be found in these little particulars.

There is a thought, indeed, that occurs to one, which might serve to account for the Lion representing St. Mark's Gospel; that we are to consider this Gospel as St. Peter's, and that St. Peter as the Apostle of the circumcision, and consequently St. Mark as the Evangelist of the circumcision, is to be termed the Lion of the tribe of Judah.

² Ch. viii. 15.　　　　　　　³ Ch. vii. 26.

But this reason does not appear sufficient to account for it, as there is nothing to support the individual character of St. Peter in this Gospel. He appears, throughout, as St. Peter watching the Son of Man : as when supported by *His hand, His look,* or *His voice,* never peculiarly in this Gospel as the Lion or the Rock ; never coming forth prominently in the express mention of himself, his own character and circumstances.

Now of these incidental particulars which characterize St. Mark, it must be observed that they do not introduce any thing of doctrine, or great principle, or important precept, any thing *humanly* speaking of consequence ; but have the effect of rendering the descriptions, what would be considered in poetry as graphic and picturesque, and setting them in an interesting manner before the eyes of the reader. They seem to indicate that St. Peter was himself watching with intense interest these circumstances, and especially our Lord's own Person, bearing, demeanour, countenance, feelings,—all that was human. And it would seem that it was but at a late period of our Lord's ministry that the full knowledge of our Lord's unspeakable Godhead was revealed to him. For the memorable Confession of St. Peter, which took place but a short time before our Lord's death, seems to prove that it was but then, or a little before, that St. Peter had come to this knowledge. It was indeed some months before that occasion, and at the termination of the second year, that St. John speaks of St. Peter as saying, " Lord, to whom shall we go ? Thou hast the words of eternal life. And we believe and are sure, that Thou art that Christ, the Son of the Living God." But then this declaration was not at that time accepted of our Lord, in the same manner as St. Peter's Confession afterwards was, which seems to indicate that

he had not yet come to the fulness of that belief. Up to
this period, therefore, if we may so venture to express
it with safety and caution, it was our Lord more especially
as the Son of Man, that he was watching; while the
radiations of our Lord's untold Divinity, as through His
earthly tabernacle, were by degrees breaking out more
fully and perfectly; as God the Father was revealing unto
him that which flesh and blood had not, and could not
disclose to him. And these are the circumstances which
it is wished especially to show in this Gospel,—namely,
these numberless little incidents and observations, which
indicate especially the Son of Man.

Now the points of difference in St. Mark being almost
entirely of a minute description, of course all our references
must be of that character; but if we trace this Gospel
together with the others, we shall find, I think, that
almost all the differences imply an eye-witness in close
attendance on our Lord; and that there is hardly any
incident in his narrative without instances of this kind.
And although we doubt not but that the most minute circumstances in the Gospels are the words of the Holy
Spirit, and therefore need not necessarily imply any personal testimony of the writer; yet when the peculiar
insertions in any Gospel do not apparently introduce any
doctrine or moral precept, but simply contain incidental
narrative, it seems not irreverent to suppose, that the immediate cause of the mention may be the personal circumstances of the writer himself. Nor is it on that account
at all less the words of the good Spirit, though apparently
incidental; for if not a sparrow falls to the ground without the knowledge of God, much more may we be sure
that not a word in Scripture respecting the Son of God can
drop by accident, or be without a Divine purpose. We

may therefore consider such points as indications of the writer, without derogating from the sanctity of inspiration.

Now many of these observations are (as we have noticed) such as intimate the inspired author to be in close attendance upon our Lord, and treasuring every thing with respect to His Person with deep interest. Some of these are such as merely introduce by the way an allusion to our Lord's *look*. And when we consider what to a thoughtful disciple must have been that look of the All-knowing God, which searcheth the reins and the heart ; and what especially to St. Peter must have been that look, which he always, doubtless, watched with earnest affection ; and which look on one occasion had power to save him ;—it is not unnatural that even this should have been expressly recorded by him. Thus when our Lord so severely rebuked him, saying, " Get thee behind me, Satan," St. Mark adds, that in saying these words He not only turned, but *" looked on his disciples* [4]." Again, on a very different occasion, when our Lord stretched forth His hand to His disciples, as being to Himself as " brother and sister and mother," St. Mark mentions the action of *" looking around upon them as they sat about Him* [5] :" a look and words never likely to be forgotten by them, when He was removed from them, and they thought of those words of ineffable endearment and condescension. In like manner, in expressing that terrible warning on the danger of riches, St. Mark inserts *" having looked round* He says to His disciples [6]," among whom, let it be remembered, was Judas, who might have been even then in the toils of the enemy, on account of that sin of covetousness. And a

[4] Ch. viii. 33.   [5] Ch. iii. 34.

[6] Ch. x. 23.

little before, on the same occasion, St. Mark speaks of His
" *looking on* " the rich young man[7].

And if the lively memory of even our Lord's *look* is ever
thus incidentally recorded, much more are those human
affections which are denoted by the external look and
demeanour.   Of this there are many remarkable instances,
—remarkable for the very natural and apparently casual
manner in which they occur.   Thus in the account of the
healing of the man with the withered hand in the Synagogue, although St. Mark otherwise uses the very words of
St. Matthew or St. Luke, yet he inserts, that when our
Lord looked round upon them, it was " *with anger*, being
grieved at the hardness of their hearts[8]."   Here one does
not see, humanly speaking, how this observation would
have been inserted in the narrative, but by a person who
stood close to our Blessed Lord, and fixed his eyes upon
His sacred countenance ; and who, like St. Peter, could
never forget even such things concerning Him.   In the
same incidental manner he mentions our Lord's *commiseration*[9] at the leper whom He healed, and His *very earnest
charge*[1] to the man not to divulge it.   In the conversation
with the rich young man, St. Mark alone gives us the interesting mention, that when our Lord looked upon him
" *He loved him ;*" which expression seems to imply something in our Lord's countenance, over and above His words,
and which the stander-by was able to interpret from
familiar knowledge.   In the other Gospels we may be
struck at the extraordinary want of faith which impeded
our Lord's mercies ; but in St. Mark we observe the superhuman charity breaking forth on His countenance, and the
very picture of distress in our Lord's manner in witnessing

---

[7] Ch. x. 21.   [8] Ch. iii. 5.
[9] σπλαγχνισθείς.   [1] ἐμβριμησάμενος. Ch. i. 43.

that unbelief, which alone occasioned his inability to help. Thus in working that difficult miracle on the man with an impediment in his speech, " *He looked up to Heaven and groaned*²," and when they asked for a sign, " *He groaned deeply in spirit*³." We find also attributed to our Blessed Lord, in St. Mark, that which is especially a human affection, viz. the feeling of wonder and surprise, that " *He marvelled on account of their unbelief*⁴." To these may be added that most amazing and touching picture on two occasions, of His taking the little children *into His arms;* it is in both cases entirely an insertion of St. Mark, and may be mentioned as an instance of affection shown in the external air and deportment.

Such intimations in St. Mark indicate a lively and deep interest in the Person of the Son of Man : and many more are there that imply a very close personal attendance in the writer, in many cases such as would denote a relation so intimate, as none but St. Peter and a very few others could have been admitted to. Perhaps one of the instances just mentioned of our Lord taking up the children into His arms, from a consideration of all its circumstances, may appear to be one of these ; for it seems to have been in a house with the disciples, and probably St. Peter's house at Capernaum, where the tribute was asked for. There is one of these little circumstances recorded on the commencement of our Lord's teaching; it was on the morning after the Sabbath when He had performed some of His first miracles, and which appears to have been that Sunday on which He may have delivered the Sermon on the Mount. Here, instead of the more general account of St. Luke that " the people sought Him," we have the par-

---

² Ch. vii. 34.   ³ Ch. viii. 12.

⁴ Ch. vi. 6.

ticular circumstances described in St. Mark, that " He was there praying, when Simon, and they that were with him, followed after Him, and when they found Him, they say unto Him, All men seek for Thee.[5]"   Such an assertion does certainly appear likely to have been by the hand of one of those few, probably three or four persons, included in the term, " Simon and they that were with him."   Such again is that expression of our Lord's being " *in the hinder part of the vessel asleep on a pillow;*" when it does not appear likely that any but disciples were present.   At the same time, in appeasing the storm, our Lord's very words are given in this Gospel alone ; " *Peace, be still; and the wind was still;*" and to His disciples, " *Why are ye so fearful?*"—a rebuke which we may well suppose St. Peter to have remembered, and which on another occasion he seemed desirous to avoid by attempting to walk on the sea, as if in order not to incur our Lord's former imputation of timidity.   And yet in the general narrative St. Mark seems to be transcribing the account of another. The same is the case on the other occasion also, when St. Mark adds the remarkable circumstance that our Lord "*was desirous to have passed by them;*" and that " *they all saw Him and were troubled.*"   And so also at another time he mentions, in addition to St. Matthew's account, that all " *they had in the boat was but one loaf;*" when it appears improbable that there were any there besides one. of the Twelve to have made such an observation.

There is, again, a very interesting incident of this kind in our Lord's conduct towards Jairus, when He was going with him to heal his daughter.   On news being brought the father that all natural hope was over, for his daughter was dead, St. Luke tells us that our Lord, on hearing it,

[5] Ch. i. 36, 37.

told the father not to fear; St. Mark, by inserting only two words, sets before us the very quick and instantaneous action of our Lord, in order to anticipate the father's unbelief: "*Jesus immediately as He heard the account, while it was being spoken, saith unto the ruler of the synagogue, Be not afraid, only believe*[6]." And afterwards at the restoration of the child, he incidentally introduces into the account, that "*He took the father and the mother of the child, and goeth in to where the child was laid out;*" and other little incidents are mentioned, on an occasion when only three disciples were admitted. Again, the case of the 'paralytic, in the first year of our Lord's ministry, partakes especially of this character in St. Mark, and the more so as it appears not improbable that it is St. Peter's own house where the miracle which is described takes place. It is full of the peculiarities of St. Mark. "*And again He entered into Capernaum in the day-time.*" "*And it was heard that He was in the house.*" As our Lord had not Himself where to lay His head, it appears probable that this the accustomed house of His sojourn at Capernaum should have been St. Peter's; that house into which we find our Lord entering on one occasion as He came from the Synagogue on the Sabbath-day, when He healed Peter's mother-in-law. And here we read the circumstantial mention, that "*immediately many were collected together, so that there was no room for them, not even about the door, and He spake the word unto them.*" And then we see the paralytic "*carried by four persons*" who "*were not able to approach Him.*" The writer, as it were unintentionally and unconsciously, gives us a picture of the very scene.

Again, at a later period in our Lord's ministry, in the

---

[6] Ch. v. 36, εὐθέως ἀκούσας τὸν λόγον λαλούμενον.

case of the Canaanitish woman, in St. Matthew we have some general statements of what seems to have occurred by the way,—of the woman crying after them, and the disciples being vexed at her importunity; but in St. Mark we read of what partakes of far more of *home* personal description, and what occurred apparently after the importunity which St. Matthew speaks of; that *"when He entered the house, He wished that no one should know it. But He could not be hid. For a woman who had heard concerning Him, whose little daughter had an unclean spirit, came and fell at His feet."* And this was an occasion when He had retired as privately as possible into the heathen parts, and therefore was not likely to have had any but His most intimate friends with Him. Although not of a nature so private, yet equally particular and descriptive, is the account of the healing of Bartimæus. Here alone have we his name recorded; here alone the account that he was *"begging;"*—we see the scene as if we had been present,—*"they call him, saying unto him, Be of good courage; arise, He calleth thee. And he, having cast aside his garment, rose up and came to Jesus."*

On other occasions how often does this Evangelist introduce the mention of little points, in themselves unimportant, but which, when we consider Who it is concerning Whom they are spoken, become of inestimable value! Thus we read, that *"when He was alone, they who were around Him, together with the Twelve, asked Him[7],"* or that, *"on that day, when it was evening, He saith unto them, Let us pass over to the other side[8];"* that when He could do no miracles, yet that *"He laid His hands on a few sick and healed them[9];"* and that of one kind of teach-

---

[7] Ch. iv. 10. [8] Ch. iv. 35.

[9] Ch. vi. 5.

ing "*He spake that saying openly*[1]." And on the same occasion, on delivering them these instructions of self-denial, St. Mark inserts the mention of this circumstance, that "*He called unto Him the multitude together with His disciples.*" It seems to one impossible to doubt in these accounts, either that he did not write from St. Matthew's Gospel (so close are his words in the general narrative), or that he did not himself witness what he records with the minute circumstantial accuracy of an eye-witness. Such observations are, many of them, not only those of a near and closely attendant disciple, but of one of the nearest.   •

Again, in St. Matthew we hear our Lord speaking in the Temple, but in St. Mark we see Him, as Son of Man, "*walking*" there[2]; in St. Luke we hear Him speaking of the widow's mite, but in St. Mark we see Him as He speaks, as if lingering about the Temple which He was about to leave "desolate," and "*sitting opposite the treasury*[3]." In the other Gospels we hear our Lord " questioning His disciples" "Who He was?" but by the insertion of "*by the way*[4]" in St. Mark we see them as in a picture, talking as they go, as our Lord is coming forth from prayer[5]. So also in that conversation of our Lord's respecting divorce, instead of the more general account in St. Matthew, we have the casual insertion, evidently of one intimately connected, "*and in the house again the disciples asked Him concerning the same matter*[6]." In like manner there occurs, in the same chapter in St. Mark[7], a remarkable description of their going up to Jeru-

---

[1] Ch. viii. 32. 34.   [2] Ch. xi. 27.
[3] Ch. xii. 41.   [4] ἐν τῇ ὁδῷ.
[5] Luke ix. 18.   [6] Mark x. 10.
[7] Ch. x. 32. 34.

salem with our Lord the last time, when He went with such earnest and fixed resolution to meet His death. "*And they were in the way going up to Jerusalem; and Jesus was going before them: and they were amazed, and were afraid, as they followed Him.*" Surely these are observations of a closely attending and very near disciple. As setting before us the very action and manner of our Blessed Lord, they are of very great value; and a lesson of instruction is often conveyed by such particulars, as much as by the repetition of words spoken.

Again, when our Lord sends two of His disciples to bring Him the colt, on which He rode into Jerusalem, it seems not unlikely that those who were sent might have been the same two who, as we learn from St. Luke, were afterwards sent to prepare for the Paschal supper—St. Peter and St. John. At all events, the description in St. Mark, where it differs from the others, is very like the observations of one of those two themselves who were sent, for it incidentally mentions that "*they found the colt tied at the door without, at a place where two roads met*[8]." And the mention of the very names of the four disciples, "Peter and James and John and Andrew," to whom the discourse was delivered concerning the Day of Judgment, would seem to indicate a probability that the writer himself was one of those four whom he mentions, as his other words are much the same as those of the other . Evangelists. One more instance may be added, that when our Lord comes to arouse His sleeping disciples in the garden of Gethsemane, St. Mark alone should insert the expostulatory address to St. Peter, "*Simon, sleepest thou*[9]?" This appears certainly as a touching evidence of that Apostle being the writer; this kind warn-

[8] Ch. xi. 4.   [9] Ch. xiv. 37.

ing from his Lord to himself by name he never could have
forgotten.

It may moreover be observed, that some of the
insertions made by St. Mark in his narrative seem to
indicate something of character and purpose in the writer
himself, as if he had an end in view in introducing them.
The following is an instance of this kind. The parable
of the Sower is given by St. Mark almost word for word
with the other Evangelists; but to the expression "and
yielded fruit[1]," which he repeats from St. Matthew, he
adds "*springing up and increasing*[2]." Thus informing us,
that our Lord even then used an expression which implied
the gradual increase and progressive development of the
good seed. We might at first sight have supposed this an
accidental insertion with no particular object in the mind
of the writer, but it is curious to observe, that St. Mark soon
after records one parable entirely his own, and mentioned
by no other, and the only one which he alone does mention; and this parable is an account of the gradual increase
of the good seed, of the seed "*springing and growing up,
he knoweth not how; first the blade, then the ear, after that
the full corn in the ear*[3]." Now the insertion of these two
circumstances, both intimating one and the same great
truth, evidently proves, that this writer considered that
both the expression in the former parable, and this other
entire parable, contained a doctrine too important to be
omitted. And it is observable that this gradual growing
in grace, unto the full knowledge of Christ, appears to have
been especially the case with St. Peter himself in the
history of his own conversion: and he particularly dwells
on the same continued and increasing advance in holiness

---

[1] καὶ ἐδίδου καρπόν.   [2] ἀναβαίνοντα καὶ αὐξάνοντα.

[3] Ch. iv. 27, 28.

in his Epistles, telling us to add to our "faith virtue, to
virtue knowledge," as the proof that we are "neither barren
nor unfruitful,"—and bidding us take heed "to the light
shining in a dark place, until the day dawn and the day-
star arise in our hearts."

Another instance of the same kind of definite purpose
and intention in the writer may be mentioned. In speaking of the good man receiving a hundred-fold in this
present time, St. Mark adds "*with persecutions*[4]," and
a little before, on our Lord's telling the young man to
follow Him, St. Mark says "*taking up the cross*[5]." Such
seem touching indications of St. Peter, as if he was ever
mindful of our Lord's rebuke, when He said "Get thee
behind me, Satan." And his own fall appeared to be in
consequence of his not apprehending that wholesome
truth—that persecutions, and the Cross, are the portion of
God's children. Therefore he preaches this doctrine more
particularly to all mankind, and says of this teaching, that
our Lord spake it openly to all[6]. This again bears on
the main subject of this argument; for sufferings and
humiliation in us speak especially of humanity and human
infirmity, and therefore such are characteristic of the Son
of Man;—and bring us near to our Lord as suffering Man,
and to His Cross, drawing us unto Him with the cords of
a man, the ties of human sympathy.

And such observations, which imply design in the
writer himself, would lead one to conclude that on other
occasions also his slight additions and variations, and
especially his marked discrepancies from the other Evangelists, had not only a Divine purport in the great Author
of inspiration, but were not accidental in the purpose of

[4] Ch. x. 30.   [5] Ch. x. 21.
[6] παῤῥησίᾳ τὸν λόγον ἐλάλει. viii. 32.

E

the human writer. As for instance, when in the Commission to the disciples, in the other accounts our Lord
forbids them to take staves or shoes.   St. Mark, on the
contrary, mentions the staff expressly as an exception,
saying "save a staff only';" and bids them be "shod
with sandals" on their feet, which sets before us even the
more strongly the same purport.   For we see the Apostles
without human aid, but with the pastoral staff, the symbol
of their office, and, like the children of Israel equipped for
their last journey, with sandals on their feet, and shod as
it were "with the preparation of the Gospel of peace."
The express exception in St. Mark of those things that
were typical and emblematic of their Pastoral and Evangelical commission, adds a weight to the general command
of their proceeding unprovided with all beside.

But further, not only does this writer delight to describe
the Son of Man in all that indicated human demeanour
and affections, but his brief insertions seems replete with
all the love and tenderness towards his Master, of one like
the good St. Peter.   Thus we have casual introductions
descriptive of bodily weakness and oppression in our
Blessed Lord, such as a disciple so deeply attached and
watchful would have noticed.

Thus, in speaking of His going to Golgotha, he incidentally changes the expression of His being led, and
says, "*they bear Him*⁸" to the place of execution.   In
like manner, on that occasion when he speaks of our Lord
sleeping on a pillow in the prow of the boat, he had said,
"*they take Him as He was into the boat*⁹;" words which
seem to indicate our Lord's fatigue and want of ease and

---

⁷ Ch. vi. 8, 9.
⁸ ἐξάγουσιν αὐτόν, ch. xv. 20; φέρουσιν αὐτόν, ver. 22.
⁹ Ch. iv. 36.

rest. · Again, at the miracle of the loaves and fishes in the desert of Bethsaida, we have in St. Mark an interesting account of the circumstances preceding it; that our Lord had said to His disciples, "Come ye privately into a desert place, and rest awhile; for there were many coming and retiring, and they had no opportunity even so much as to eat[1];" it was while in this need themselves of refreshment that our Lord, on being followed to His retreat by the multitude, came forth again, and, forgetful of His own great needs, and want of retirement, "*had compassion on them.*" All these things, and others of the kind, seem especially human, human in the feelings of the writer that notices them, human in the affections which they so deeply touch in us; human in the Person of our Blessed Lord, in His condescension to take upon Him the infirmities of mankind. The character of all this Evangelist's own observations, and of our Blessed Lord Himself as seen throughout this Gospel, seems so delineated, that if we might reverently apply it, we might characterize this Gospel by the line of the Latin Dramatic Poet:

"Homo sum; humani nihil in me alienum puto."

Moreover, it may be observed, that there are in St. Mark casual insertions or changes of expressions, which are not indeed exactly descriptive of our Lord's sacred person and demeanour, as from an eye-witness, yet do somehow in a remarkable manner allude to His Personal humiliations, as one who had made Himself subject to the infirmities of humanity. Thus, instead of saying—that He "was led by the Spirit" into the wilderness, he says "*the Spirit driveth Him,*" speaking of Him as if of a suffering creature. On the same occasion St. Mark adds that He was in the wilderness "*with the wild beasts*[2],"

---

[1] Ch. vi. 30—34. [2] Ch. i. 13.

E 2

where we see the Second Adam in the Son of Man, the companion of the wild beasts of the field, and reconciled to them: and as He may have been at His birth forty days with the beasts of the stall before His presentation in the Temple, so was He now forty days after His baptism with the beasts of the wild, before entering on His Kingdom and Ministry. Very remarkable, too, is that insertion, where our Lord says, when speaking of the Last Day, that the Father alone knoweth it, neither men nor angels; this Evangelist adds, "neither the Son [3]," words which would have presented a very serious difficulty as concerning the Son of God "equal to the Father as touching His Godhead," did we not interpret them to signify that our Lord is speaking of Himself, as the Son of Man, in the dispensation of His Kingdom, in which He is "inferior to the Father as touching His manhood." In like manner it may be observed that St. Mark alone speaks, on our Lord's coming down from the Mount of Transfiguration, of the astonishment of the people at beholding Him: it was perhaps in the same way as the Jews of old had been when they beheld Moses, and his face supernaturally illuminated with the rays of glory, on his returning from the Mount. But here it must be considered to have been the Person and radiant emanation of glory from the Son of Man, at which they were so struck with astonishment. For the Transfiguration appears to have been a typical representation, which set forth by anticipation the Resurrection and Regeneration of the Flesh, and which was shown in our Lord's glorified Body, as "the first-begotten of the Dead," "the first-born of many brethren."

The circumstances alluded to, as characteristics of this

[3] Ch. xiii. 32.

Gospel, have been mostly such as are contained in single expressions or short sentences; for the differences of St. Mark consist for the most part in these. But there are in St. Mark two entire actions of healing, which are confined to himself alone. It is curious therefore to inquire of what nature they are, and what, out of so great a variety, are the circumstances which this inspired Evangelist should have been led to select. They will be found to bear in the strongest manner upon the view here taken. "The Son of Man" condescending to human infirmities, and in some mysterious manner tied by our unbelief, and coming down to meet our weakness, is perhaps more strongly depicted in the instances of these cures which St. Mark alone records, than in any other throughout the Gospels.

"And they bring unto Him one that was deaf, and had an impediment in his speech; and they beseech Him to put His hands upon him. And He took him aside from the multitude, and put His fingers into his ears; and He spit, and touched his tongue; and looking up to Heaven, He sighed, and saith unto him, Ephphatha, that is, Be opened [4]." Now, this case is remarkable for the comparatively small extent of the evil, an impediment in his speech,—the smallness of the request, that "He would lay His hands upon him,"—and the circuitous mode—the pains and the trouble, so to speak,—which our Blessed Lord was pleased to take, in order graciously to meet the slowness of their faith.

The other instance occurs in the following chapter [5]. "And He cometh to Bethsaida, and they bring a blind man unto Him, and besought Him to touch him. And He took the blind man by the hand, and led him out of

[4] Ch. vii. 32. 34.   [5] Ch. viii. 22—25.

the town; and when He had spit on his eyes, and put His hands upon him, He asked him if he saw ought. And he looked up and said, I see men, as trees, walking. After that He put His hands again upon his eyes, and made him look up, and he was restored and saw every man clearly." Here surely He, at the word of Whose mouth the Heavens were made, was submitting Himself as the Son of Man, and withholding Almighty power in apparent difficulty, and under the bands of human infirmity. And both of these occasions are followed by the strict charge not to divulge them : a still further indication of the withholding and restraining the greatness of His Divine Presence on these occasions.

The slowness of cure in these cases, according to the analogy of other miracles, seems to imply slowness of faith ; and this would account for our Lord's *sighing*, as in pain, on working the former cure. In confirmation of this, it may be further observed, that in other places, from the insertions which he introduces, St. Mark appears especially alive to circumstances of this nature, where our Lord seems constrained and straitened by the unbelief and infirmities of mankind. Thus on one occasion, speaking of His teaching, he says it was *"as they were able to hear* [6]*."* Such, too, is that case of the father of the demoniac, struggling in an agony between faith and unbelief, and supported by our Lord, and when the father says *"if Thou art able* to help us," our Lord taking up his words, and using His accustomed expression *"if Thou art able* to believe [7]," and afterwards His taking hold of the hand of the child, and raising him up. All this indicates, that this Evangelist was especially observant of this weakness of mankind, whereby our Lord's power to

[6] Ch. iv. 33.   [7] τό, εἰ δύνασαι πιστεῦσαι.

help us was as it were bound, while it knew no other
bounds; for as the other two miracles are only mentioned
in St. Mark, so this cure of the demoniac, although it is
found in the other two Gospels, yet comes out in St.
Mark with such an absorbing interest of detail, as to
render the description peculiarly his own.

One instance more may be mentioned, selected from
amongst others of a similar character. It is in our Lord's
last teaching in the Temple, where St. Mark describes the
state of the Scribe's mind, and our Lord's expression to
him, that he was "not far from the kingdom," because he
discerned the force of that Divine precept of charity as
the whole of the Law; thereby showing us the gradual
growth of the Kingdom, and a state like that of the
Scribe where faith was incipient;—of one as it were at
the door of the Kingdom;—who had not yet entered in,
but in perceiving the Love of God had found Christ the
door; and had but to knock in order to enter in.

It will therefore, I think, be allowed, that if there is
any characteristic of this Gospel, it is that our Lord's
Incarnation breathes throughout; it is this which is set
before us, as it came before St. Peter, in a manner best
calculated to engage our affections, and most lively and
awful interest, respecting "the Son of Man," in wonderful
condescensions and indications of human affection. For
love of a human person is mostly formed, both from an
observation of character and moral qualities, and from
watching the development of them in the outer man until
it becomes familiar with the external expressions of them.
This Gospel has, therefore, the countenance of a Man.

Now, these peculiarities of St. Mark's Gospel are not
confined to our Lord's own Person and actions, but yet
in all things the same characteristic is displayed. There

prevails throughout the same casual insertion of circumstances of apparently little moment, which tends to give
an accuracy to the description, and brings things and
persons before the eyes of the reader. As a characteristic
of composition, this is not unlike something in great poets
by which they contrive by slight touches, and a mention
of some small characteristic marks, to give an individuality
to the objects they describe. And the reason, doubtless,
why it has this effect in poets is, because real feeling and
affection does always naturally express itself by means of
these distinctive points, avoiding generalities: for a person
naturally conveys to others that strong conception which
he himself entertains. Such, therefore, especially denote
human events, interests, and passions, and therefore may
be considered pre-eminently human. There is nothing in
these differences which are of the Lion, nor of the Calf,
nor of the Eagle; but there is in them essentially "the
likeness of a Man."

Many circumstances already alluded to would serve as
indications of this point, if shown at length,—as in the
detailed account of the cure of the paralytic, of the demoniac child, of our Lord's treatment of Jairus, of His conduct on many occasions towards His Apostles, and of their
disposition towards Him. Such are eminently descriptive
of human events and feelings. Of the same character is
St. Mark's well-known description of the Maniac in the
fifth chapter; "and no man could bind him, no, not with
chains: because that he had often been bound with fetters
and chains, and the chains had been plucked asunder by
him, and the fetters broken in pieces; neither could any
man tame him. And always night and day he was in the
mountains and in the tombs, crying, and cutting himself
with stones. But when he saw Jesus afar off, he ran and

worshipped Him." The same action of worshipping our Lord[8], St. Mark records of the rich young man; as if our Lord's acceptance of worship from His creatures was a point which now struck St. Peter, while he was gradually coming to the knowledge of His Divinity. Many other are the instances of this kind, full of interest, graphic, and affecting, from minuteness of circumstantial detail. As in the account of the woman with the issue of blood, "who had spent all that she had on physicians, and rather grew worse;" and in raising of Jairus's daughter, "putting them all out but the father and the mother of the child[9]," and that "she was twelve years old," and "walked immediately." These are all points which touch the chords of our natural affections and awaken our lively interest. If the Gospels themselves are all, by their very nature, of this character,—powerful to enlist our human sympathies, —the same kind of effect is greater in degree in St. Mark. And if our Lord's appearing to us as man is of such exceeding attractive force to our nature, all that brings Him, and the events in which He was engaged, more forcibly before us, is more particularly of this character. But notices of this kind are too numerous to enter into, or even to allude to, as that the disciples were "questioning one with another" the meaning of His words[1]; that as He walked on the sea, "they all saw Him and were troubled;" that the disciples in healing many of the sick "anointed them with oil[2];" that even the wicked Herod attended to John's preaching, and "heard him gladly[3]."

In all these circumstances we have little, if any thing, added of Divine Doctrine, or of what might expressly be said to be moral teaching; but instead of this the events

---

[8] γονυπετήσας, ch. x. 17.   [9] Ch. v. 26, and 40. 42.
[1] Ch. ix. 10.   [2] Ch. vi. 13.   [3] Ch. vi. 20.

and persons of that Sacred History are brought nearer to us: we are made to stand more in the place of spectators and witnesses; are brought more into company with those who saw and spoke to our Blessed Lord, and were the objects of His miracles and teaching; or had the inestimable privilege of His especial regard and favour: we are brought more nigh unto Apostles; we see the relative position in which they stand to our Lord and to each other: above all, we are brought to our Lord Himself, as to the Son of Man; we see His outward gesture and deed; we see the expression of His countenance on many occasions; we hear Him sigh at man's unbelief; we are led as it were to imagine the very eye and the ear of our ever Blessed Lord Himself; the peculiarity of His manner and expressions. Is it, therefore, unreasonable to suppose that in this Gospel we have "the likeness of a Man"?

One concluding observation may be made respecting this Gospel. It may be asked, why did not St. Peter (if this Gospel is to be considered as his) insert more of doctrine and precept? In the same manner it may be asked, —why did not St. Peter himself write a Gospel? Eusebius states as the reason for the latter, that he was too humble and modest to do so; and the same answer may be given to the former question. Increasing holiness is ever accompanied with increasing humility: nor is it to be wondered at, if the very chief of Apostles should have been so humbled from his near approach to Christ, as to shrink from doing that which ordinary men would have done: and that he who was so signally himself an "eye-witness of His Majesty," should have come more and more to this feeling, —" now mine eye seeth Thee; wherefore I abhor myself, and repent in dust and ashes." Nor need we be surprised if under this feeling he should have left it to others to hand down to the Church the written memorials of his Lord; and should have afforded us no notices of himself, but such as indicate his humilition and lowly affection, as of one who wished to be hid with God.

SECTION VI

OUR LORD'S ATONEMENT IN ST. LUKE'S GOSPEL

THE application of the symbol of "the Calf" to St. Luke is a matter more clear and decisive; inasmuch as the consent of the ancient writers is more strong on this point than on the two before mentioned. The thing intended by it is evident, that the "Calf" (or "the ox") is the sacerdotal animal; and it implies, according to St. Ambrose, either the Priest or the Victim. And throughout this consideration we should bear in mind the suggestion of the same writer, in applying these types not to the Evangelist, but rather to our Lord Himself as set forth in each Gospel. The subject, moreover, is not a little important in another point of view, viz. in the high and Divine light in which it sets before us the distinguishing differences of the Gospels; for these differences in the accounts of our Lord's actions and speeches do in no way, of course, detract from the strict fidelity of each, but imply that they were of such a character, so numerous, manifold, and varied, as to admit of this distinguishing selection, to suit the Divine purpose, in each inspired Evangelist.

The application, moreover, of this emblem to St. Luke throws a remarkable and interesting light on the whole of this Gospel. This sacerdotal animal implies Atonement and Propitiation; and this exactly corresponds with what is supposed to be the character of St. Luke's Gospel, as one which more especially conveys mercy to the Penitent. And we may observe, what a deep and mysterious view this consideration at once opens into the subject of this Gospel. For it seems to imply, that all the calls to humiliation which pervade it, the many incidents of mercy, and the miracles of peculiar compassionateness recorded in St. Luke, all arise out of, and have some close and peculiar connexion with, the Sacrifice of Christ. And doubtless all such, which may be considered the peculiar tenets of our Religion, are but streams which flow from this one great and secret fountain-head; all partake of their hue and character from this principle. All the parts indeed of this Gospel may be considered as varied manifestations of Christ Crucified.

And again, with respect to the place which St. Luke occupies in the four Gospels, as touching on one side on St. Mark, and touching on the other side on St. John: this also may be noticed as bearing on the description of this sacred figure. For this mutual relation which they have one with the other, seems to be implied in the emphatic expression, "two wings of every one were joined one to another." The King has the Son of Man attendant on Him, St. Matthew has St. Mark treading in his footsteps[*]; the King is further revealed in the Son of Man. And between the Son of Man in St. Mark, and the Son of God in St. John, is the Priest and Mediator between God and man in St. Luke. And with wings on each side he touches either; his position has a reference both to St. Mark and also to St. John, occupying a place between them both, and equally related to and connected with each

---

[*] Augustin, de Consen. Evan. lib. i. 6.

on either side, being in this Gospel set forth equally as Man and as God; being the Priest who has gone within the veil; and also the Advocate, One with the Spirit, Who "maketh intercession for us with groanings which cannot be uttered." Not but that even here in separation there is union, and in the nearest union there is also at the same time entire distinctness. Thus it may be observed, that St. Matthew, though separated from yet is one with St. Luke, and the King, though separate from is also one with the Priest, as David the king ate of the Shew-bread, which it was not lawful for any to partake of, but the Priests alone. And the Priest also, though one with the Son of Man, is not of the order of human lineage, or according to the generations of man, but "the King of Peace," "without descent, having neither beginning of days nor end of life, but made like unto the Son of God." So does the King of Salem disappear, and the Priest Melchizedec stands before us, till he also disappears in the Son of God[6]. Such mysterious adaptation and secrets of Divine wisdom appear to be indicated by the mere order of the Gospels.

With regard to the development of the Sacrificial animal in this Gospel, it may be observed, first of all, that it commences and terminates with this animal, or that which is represented by it, in a strongly marked and distinguishing manner. For it begins with the Priest, dwelling on the Priestly family of the Baptist; and ends with the Victim, in our Lord's death. And indeed the Victim and the Priest are one and the same throughout; the Priest, as St. Ambrose observes, "because Christ is our Propitiation and Advocate with the Father; the Calf or Victim, because by His own blood He hath washed and redeemed us." Thus,

[6] See Passion, p. 29.

first of all, we have this Gospel commencing, at its very opening, with something of a Sacerdotal character, as contrasted with the kingly of St. Matthew, "There was in the days of Herod, the king of Judæa, *a certain Priest*, named Zacharias, of the course of Abia; and *his wife was of the daughters of Aaron.*"   And afterwards, instead of the Wise men with their royal gifts and Herod the king, we have Zacharias the Priest standing at the Altar of Incense; and his high and spiritual prophecy afterwards of the Priestly child sent before, "to give knowledge of salvation unto His people for the remission of their sins."   Even at the commencement and vestibule we have the day itself, as it may be, of the Atonement, and the Priest in his white robes at the Altar; the Priest of the law in type and shadow, in like manner as at the termination we have the Antitype Himself of this High Priest, going up into Heaven, and there interceding for us; while we continue as the people without the vail, in the absence of the High Priest.   Thus, as it proceeds step by step, it may be observed that this Gospel is entirely of a Sacerdotal character, and appertaining to the Temple, both Jewish and Christian.

Here, in this Gospel alone, we have the three Hymns of the Church, the character of which is Sacerdotal.   Here we have the events occurring in the Temple, holy Simeon and Anna dwelling there.   Here we have the Circumcision, and the Purification and Presentation, and our Lord disputing with the doctors.   All these are Sacerdotal, and Hierarchical, and of the Temple.   And observe the distinction.   In St. Matthew, Christ is fleeing into Egypt; in St. Luke, coming to the Temple: in St. Mark, ever suffering; in St. Luke, ever atoning.   And even to the minutest points of expression does the Sacerdotal character extend: in St. Luke, Mary is the kinswoman of Elizabeth, of a priestly family; in St. Matthew there is no allusion to this secret connexion with the Sacerdotal line in the Mother of our Lord. "In St. Matthew, Joseph called His name Jesus" at His birth; in St. Luke, at the Circumcision, He is so named in compliance with the declaration of the Angel. The place, moreover, which the Genealogy holds in the two is remarkable; in St. Matthew it is introduced at the very first, as of one born the Son of a King; in St. Luke it is inserted after His baptism, when He is coming forth as from the Sanctuary, at the Priestly age, to fulfil His Ministry, and taking on Him His Sacerdotal office. In this, He is not pointed out to the Jews as "the Son of David" and "of Abraham," and therefore as their King; but He is set forth to all mankind as their High Priest;—set forth to them not on the Jewish claim of a Levitical descent, but as one of unknown lineage, and without parent, greater than either Abraham or his seed, and unto whom Abraham and all his seed bowed, to receive His blessing, in His type and representative Melchizedec. And again, if St. Matthew traces to David and Abraham, St. Luke ascends far higher, not to Adam only, the father of the human race, but in his genealogy connects man with God by the Sacerdotal bond of Christ, and traces Him to His origin, ascending up to God: not as St. Matthew, descending and bringing down Christ to the Jews; but ascending in the list, as showing the restoration of man to God; ascending up from Eli, the father of adoption, (who had adopted Joseph, as St. Augustin thinks,) to Adam, God's adopted child in Christ[6].

Surely it is more reverent and worthy to suppose the slightest discrepance in these genealogies to be ordained

[6] See Nativity, pp. 118, 119.

by some great and Divine purpose. And doubtless it is more philosophical also thus to consider it; for in the visible works of God the diversities of structure, in the smallest leaf or insect, are framed to meet some adequate design.

If, from the earlier parts of the Gospels we pass to the conclusion, there also shall we find the same diversity. In the last chapter of St. Luke, instead of the authoritative injunctions at the close of St. Matthew, our Lord is walking with two disciples, expounding the Scriptures respecting His own sufferings, and making Himself known to them in breaking of Bread; and with the assembled disciples, "opening their understanding, that they might understand the Scriptures" concerning Himself. While in St. Matthew our Lord's first meeting with the disciples is to say, "all power is given unto Me in heaven and in earth," which speaks of the kingdom: St. Luke records our Lord's saying to them, "Thus it is written, and thus it behoved Christ to suffer,"—"and that repentance and remission of sins should be preached among all nations." "And ye are witnesses of these things." Here we have the Priest and the Victim. At the same conversation in St. John all these things are omitted, and instead we read, "He breathed on them, and said, Receive ye the Holy Ghost:" which surely is Divine, where our Lord confers the Holy Spirit as God. Observe also, at the very close, our Lord's leaving them: in St. Luke He is—"lifting up His hands," as the Priests of old, and blessing them, and while in the act of blessing them, He is parted from them; —and they, in the last verse, are "continually in the Temple, praising and blessing God." All these things, so peculiar to St. Luke, are Sacerdotal.

But if, according to this Divine symbol, it is the Pro

pitiation and Atonement of our Lord, which is the leading attribute of this Gospel, it is more especially to be found in the characteristic spirit and tone which pervades the whole of it. If we were to select from the four Gospels, indiscriminately, those parables and those expressions which most of all speak of mercy, and remission of sins to the returning penitent, we should see that most of these would be found in the Gospel of St. Luke exclusively. Here we have the injured Father running to meet the returning prodigal son; and the lost sheep borne on the shoulders of the glad shepherd: here we have the woman rejoicing with her neighbours over the piece of money she had lost and found: here we have even the wicked judge relenting at prayer; and here we have the friend aroused at midnight from his rest and unwillingness by the importunity of a friend: here we have the good Samaritan bearing on his own beast his wounded neighbour, and pouring into his wounds the Sacerdotal oil and the Sacerdotal wine. Here we have the Publican Zaccheus restoring fourfold, and salvation come to his house; here we have Angels rejoicing over the penitent returning; here we have the sorrowful Publican accepted in prayer, rather than the self-congratulating Pharisee; here we have the Rich man condemned for want of mercy. The other three Evangelists record the act of Anointing in one who had "chosen the good part," and which good deed was to be "recorded as a memorial of her" throughout the world. But St. Luke, passing over this, has in the earlier part of our Lord's ministry detailed the similar action of a woman "who had been a sinner," and had "much to be forgiven."

Such are the many most touching incidents in St. Luke's Gospel of the abundant mercies which are with

F

God in Jesus Christ, and introduced in a manner best suited to instil those lessons of compassion : and these subjects, thus gently and affectingly insinuated, supply in St. Luke the place of those many parables of the Kingdom, and the awful warnings which are found throughout St. Matthew. Here indeed, throughout St. Luke, instead of precept and command we have parable and narrative ; and the parables also themselves, which are peculiar to St. Luke, may be in great measure narratives also,—narratives many of them respecting the unseen world. Here also, in the mention of the same persons, there is another and different side of their character introduced. Thus, for instance, the same thief in the other Evangelists is reviling, in St. Luke entreating. In St. Matthew, the Baptist preaches the coming of "the Kingdom of Heaven;" in St. Luke, "the remission of sins :" in the others, the disciples go forth to preach repentance ; in St. Luke, as bearing the Gospel of good tidings[7]. Here are more particularly the encouragements to importunate prayer ; and the various ways of leading men from high thoughts to compassionate lowliness[8]. Here on more than one occasion is our Lord Himself brought before us as "praying," as at His Baptism, when the Heavens were opened ; for St. Luke adds, that our Lord was "praying." And at the Transfiguration, as He became changed, St. Luke inserts that He was "praying." The same thing is mentioned by him at the Confession of St. Peter ; and also when the disciples came to Him to teach them how to pray[9]: and on another occasion St. Mark says[1], He was without in desert places, St. Luke adds, "and praying[2]."

---

[7] εὐαγγελιζόμενοι.

[9] Ch. xi. 1.

[2] Ch. v. 16, καὶ προσευχόμενος.

[8] See ix. 48; xii. 37.

[1] Ch. i. 45.

And this occurs on each of these occasions, when the other Evangelists do not mention it. Here we have the Mediator interceding for the barren fig-tree; here we have "the fatted Calf" with which the Father received the returning prodigal; here in the penitent thief we have the Atoning power of the One great Sacrifice and the true Priest entering within the veil: here at Emmaus we have the power of the Eucharistic Sacrifice and Sacramental grace in opening the eyes. In St. Mark, we had the Son of Man as bearing our sins, groaning deeply in spirit: in St. Luke, "there went virtue out of Him, and healed them all," as being God as well as Man. Here also especially break forth our Lord's most tender expressions of pity. Such is that His memorable thanksgiving to the Father—that He had hid these things from the wise and prudent, and had revealed them unto babes [3]; and "fear not, little flock, for it is My Father's good pleasure to give you the kingdom [4]." Here we have throughout the Healer of men, that great Physician from whose garments healing went forth; for every part of the narrative, as it drops from the pen of this gentle Evangelist, is, to use the expression of St. Jerome, "the medicine of the weakly and sick soul [5]."

Here on the approach to Jerusalem we have the King, who is coming to take His Kingdom, lost in the merciful High Priest, weeping over it at the sight of those miseries which should overtake it. And the same compassions also breaking forth at the Crucifixion, on the mournful lamentations of the women, and called forth by the same scene of their future distress in the prophetic eye of our Lord. Here also have we the most touching exhortations

[3] Ch. x. 21.   [4] Ch. xii. 32.

[5] Languentis animœ medicina.

F 2

to humility⁶; and His own humiliations as the example
to us⁷. In St. Matthew's Gospel we are commanded to
be " perfect, even as our Heavenly Father is perfect ;" but
it is very remarkable and striking to observe, that in St.
Luke there is a slight change of expression in the similar
passage, and we are told to be "merciful, even as our
Heavenly Father is merciful ;" showing us thereby that
this our very perfection and resemblance to God consists
in mercy.   Surely all these things are alike closely connected with the doctrine of Christ Crucified, the merciful
High Priest, and the compassionate self-devoted Victim ;
by resembling Whom in meekness and compassion, and
being made one with Him, we ourselves are to be rendered
Priests unto God, and our bodies living sacrifices unto
Him.

As, moreover, in this Gospel our Lord appears more
particularly as the Priest, who entered into the Holy of
Holies from the sight of men, and therefore in a manner
more unearthly and spiritual than in the former Gospel ;
so this Gospel does itself partake peculiarly throughout
of something unearthly and spiritual.   For instance, it
is but consistent with this character that this Evangelist
should speak of the beings of the unseen world, and of
things withdrawn from human testimony : and it may be
observed that there is often in this Gospel the mention of
supernatural circumstances, which could scarcely have
been the subjects of human communication.   Such is
the account of the conversation between Abraham and
the rich man in the unseen world : such is the appearance
of Angels on many occasions ; as of the Angel Gabriel to
Zacharias, the father of John the Baptist, and also of the
same Angel to the Virgin Mary.   Such too is the Hymn

⁶ Ch. xvii. 2.   ⁷ Ch. xxii. 27.

of the Angels heard by the Shepherds at Bethlehem ; such the appearance of the Angel in the garden of Gethsemane who appeared from Heaven strengthening our Lord : and such the conversation of our Lord with Moses and Elias at the Transfiguration ; when the disciples were weighed down with sleep, until they awoke, and "saw His glory, and two men standing with Him."

Of the same kind is the very early intimation, which this Gospel affords us, of the spiritual nature of Christ's Kingdom ; as acknowledged by persons speaking "in the Spirit" from the very beginning, very long before it was comprehended even by the disciples. Such is the case in the song of Zacharias, when he was "filled with the Spirit, and prophesied" of the tender mercy of our God, whereby "the day-spring from on high hath visited us :" and in that of the blessed Virgin, that His Church was to exalt the humble, and debase the proud. And such is the song of Simeon, of whom it is repeated that "the Holy Spirit was upon him —"that it was told him by the Spirit"—that he "came by the Spirit into the temple," and spoke clearly—that the Salvation of God was "before the face of *all people;*" that it was "a light to lighten the *Gentiles,*" and "the glory of Israel."

And of course all this, and the compassionate nature of this Gospel, is more particularly adapted to that teaching of the Gentiles which seems to have been its object. Hence this Evangelist proceeds immediately to detail matters of universal obligation, omitted by the others, rather than expressions more immediately referring to the Jews. As in the account of the Baptist, St. Luke adds the particular nature of his commission, that it was "to make low what was exalted, to make straight what was crooked, to exalt the low," in order that "all flesh should

see the Salvation of God." To which he adds the particular nature of the Baptist's precepts, as applying to all
mankind of every condition,—to the soldier, to the publican, and the like.

After this, at the very commencement of our Saviour's
teaching, St. Luke proceeds to speak of Him as declaring
the calling of the Gentiles, on His being rejected at
Nazareth, and bringing forward the prophetic instances
in the Old Testament, of Elias sent to the widow of
Sarepta, and of Elisha healing Naaman the Syrian, together with that remarkable declaration, so frequently
repeated, and so pregnant with deep and prophetic meaning, that "a Prophet is not received in his own country."
And we may observe how much all St. Luke's teaching is
of this character; the Sermon on the Plain, so similar to
the Sermon on the Mount, differs throughout, not only in
its compassionate character, but in this also, that it avoids
all those allusions to the Law, which in the discourse in
St. Matthew abound through the whole[8]. And, indeed,
in St. Luke the hearers of that discourse are expressly
mixed Gentiles, all the people from Judea, and Jerusalem,
and also from the sea-coast of Tyre and Sidon ; whether
it might have been that this discourse was selected by
St. Luke on that account, or that these expressions rather
than others were recorded by him. The higher expressions also in the Sermon on the Mount, as to disciples,
"Ye are the salt of the earth," and the like declarations,
are not in this.

It may here, by the way, be noticed as remarkable,
that as our Lord seems to have delivered two Sermons,
of which that on the mountain was more particularly
among His own countrymen, and that on the plain among

[8] As Ch. v. 17. 21. 23. 27, &c.

the Gentiles; so there appears to have been the same difference in the first and second miracle of the loaves, of which the latter appears to have been more among Gentiles, on the eastern side of the lake. As if thus by anticipation were set forth in figure the Preaching and the Sacraments, the spiritual light and spiritual food of the Kingdom; thus distributed alike to both whom that Kingdom comprises, the Kingdom which is composed of Jews and of Gentiles,—the two walls that meet together in Christ, the chief Corner-stone.

But when we speak of the compassionateness of this Gospel, another point in it must not be forgotten in which it differs from all human charity. It may be observed in St. Luke, that these consolations which abound in his Gospel are combined with great awfulness and severity; and that arising not so much from the authority with which they are declared, as from bringing to view the things that are unseen. Almost all the instances referred to will be found to combine these two points in a most remarkable manner. The very circumstance of the earnestness in prayer which has been referred to, and the poverty of spirit to which all its consolations are carefully confined, would indeed of themselves imply this, as showing the awful necessity of such prayers, and of such humiliations in the sight of God: as in the expression, "Watch ye therefore, and pray always, that ye may be accounted worthy to escape all these things that shall come to pass, and to stand before the Son of Man[*]." And sometimes they are both (i. e. tenderness and awfulness) combined, as in the parable of Lazarus and the rich man: and in the account of the days of the Son of Man. All this bears on two points which have been stated; the first of these

[*] Luke xxi. 36.

is, that this Gospel introduces so much what is unseen
and spiritual; and the second, that the compassions of
this Gospel are so much connected with the Sacrifice of
Christ, and the necessity of humility in man, as entitling
him to these consolations.

With regard to the introduction of the unseen world so
much in St. Luke, when this seems to occur in a parable,
as in the account of the rich man in torments, yet even
here it is to be considered perhaps not as parable or
allegory, but as true history or narrative. This appears
to be the more worthy mode of considering the words of
Him, in whose all-beholding eye both the seen and unseen
world were equally present,—things past or future, and
visible or invisible.

And as to the mention of things superhuman in this
Gospel—as in this instance, and in that of the Angel in
the Garden of Gethsemane,—it may be accounted for in
this way: that whereas the others contain accounts of
events which might be gathered by human observation
by the aid of the Holy Spirit teaching them, and bringing
to their recollection the things which had been said or
done, St. Luke, from His connexion with St. Paul, (whose
words, we know, on the Eucharist he closely adheres to,)
may have derived his Gospel from that Apostle. And
St. Paul tells us that he himself received the Gospel by
an express Revelation from God, and that he was himself
caught up into the third Heaven, and heard those unspeakable words which it is not lawful for man to utter!
This circumstance gives the same kind of interest to this
Gospel, which St. Mark's has from his being the companion of St. Peter.

It may further be observed by the way, that this circumstance of St. Luke introducing the unseen, may account

for his having been supposed to be a painter, if this supposition is grounded, as some have thought, on something picturesque in the character of his style; for it is not so picturesque from minuteness of detail, as St. Mark's style is. But the delineations in St. Luke do partake of the nature of painting, inasmuch as the poetry of painting consists in bringing out, and grouping, and setting before the eyes, those things which are expressive of the unseen, of feelings beyond every-day life, or common description ; and thus metaphorically he may be considered as a painter, as abounding in the graphic scenes of a painter or a poet.

But to return to the point in question, may we not in all the circumstances that have been detailed of St. Luke, venture to see the symbolical interpretation of this Gospel ? At all events, the authority of antiquity will excuse us from the charge of presumption, in considering "the Calf" as the representative of St. Luke. And as it is an engaging and profitable study to trace these differences, so is it especially so to trace them in connexion with these prophetic types. It gives a Divine meaning to things that might also be accounted for on grounds of human reason. For, humanly speaking, the compassionate character of St. Luke's Gospel may have arisen from this, that this Evangelist was but following the peculiar bent of his own temper, as "the beloved Physician ;" or it may have arisen from the circumstances of his life, as the companion of St. Paul in his preaching among the Gentiles, which might lead him to practical contemplations of this nature, respecting the unbounded compassions of the Gospel. But even in this consideration we are immediately led on to a Divine purpose ; for, as addressed to Gentiles, it partakes of that love and merciful spirit, with which our Saviour always addressed the publicans, and of His mode of speaking concerning and to the Gentiles. Whereas St. Matthew's Gospel partakes more of the tone in which our Saviour spoke to Pharisees; particularly in arguments drawn from the Old Testament; for our Lord's expostulations with the Pharisees, and St. Matthew's Gospel, both of them abound with appeals to what is written in the Law and in the Prophets.

And, indeed, it is sometimes curious to observe, how the different narratives of the same occurrence will partake of these indications, of more or less personal observation in the writer. An interesting instance of this kind may be seen in the account of the storm, as our Lord was going across the lake to the country of the Gadarenes. From St. Matthew's mode of speech, one might have supposed him to have witnessed the circumstance from the shore on that evening; for he says that "the vessel was being covered by the waves[1]." He was perhaps one of those on the land, who are said to have "gladly received," and to have been "all waiting for Him" on His return to that shore, for it was then that St. Matthew gave that memo-. rable feast to the mixed company in his house. But St. Mark, throughout the whole of that narrative, speaks, as St. Peter might have done, as if he had been himself in the boat, and one present in that excursion, saying that "the vessel was now filled to sinking[2],"—and our Lord's posture, as asleep, and the like. St. Luke writes as the narrator of what he had not himself witnessed, that "there came down a storm on the lake, and they were filled with water and were in danger[3]." These observations respecting the positions of the writers are all very interesting in them- selves. But the consideration of these things in connexion with the Prophetic emblems, induces us to lose sight of

[1] Ch. viii. 24.   [2] Ch. iv. 37.   [3] Ch. viii. 23.

the human agent in the Divine counsels; as in these
figures "the hands of a man" are hidden "under their
wings on their four sides." Under these Divine wings,
the emblems of inspiration, all that is human is concealed
from view. "Two wings of every one were joined one to
another, and two covered their bodies."

And as in St. Luke, so also in the other Evangelists, we
might see human ways of accounting for their diversities.
It is very evident how much the mind of St. John was
ever turned to things Divine and Heavenly, with such a
calm and deep love, that when he speaks of things transcending all that is earthly, he speaks as his own nature
itself seems to dictate. Nor is it difficult to perceive the
close adherence, and earnest gaze of St. Peter, watching
our Lord's actions, in St. Mark. It may not be so easy to
account for the characteristic complexion of St. Matthew's
Gospel; but his name of Levi may suggest that he was
himself acquainted with the Law, with the character of the
Pharisee and the Jew, and that he observed our Lord's
mode of conversing with them attentively. Why he
should select that which is Kingly may not be at once
perceptible. It might be, that as his calling lay amongst
the offices of a mighty empire, extending almost over the
world, his train of thought might run upon the kingdom
and its earthly grandeur: and this natural train of thought
might be raised to the conception and development of that
heavenly kingdom which is not of this world, and cometh
not with observation, yet which shall break in pieces the
rest, and survive them all. This may be more naturally
the subject of observation to St. Matthew, and especially
as to one conversant with both Romans and Jews. It is
in the strife between Gentiles and Jews that the kingdom
is especially brought out; for although the kingdom is of

Israel, and our Lord is King of the Jews, yet it is the Gentiles that point Him out as such; as the Wise men from the East at His birth, and Pilate's inscription on the cross at His death.

One little point more may be mentioned with respect to these the three first Gospels, that no manifestation of our Lord in Galilee after the Resurrection is recorded by either St. Mark or St. Luke; but St. Matthew dwells especially upon it. I do not know whether any reason can be assigned for this; but the object of these discourses in Galilee, when our Lord continued with His disciples after the Resurrection, seems to have been to speak to them of the things appertaining to the Kingdom of God. St. Matthew mentions no other appearance of our Lord at all to disciples, excepting that in Galilee, which is very remarkable; and the declaration there made to them is concerning the kingdom. And still more remarkable is it that the other appearance of our Lord, which St. Matthew narrates, to the women at Jerusalem, is apparently for no other purpose than that of declaring through them to the Apostles, that they are to go to see Him in Galilee: and the appearance of the Angel, which he records just before, seems to be for the same purpose, to announce Galilee unto them, as the place of our Lord's manifestation; although the most numerous and remarkable instances which are recorded are not in Galilee. And it is certainly to be observed, that the Kingdom is spoken of more than once as commencing from Galilee[4]. There was, perhaps, some peculiar fitness, that as "the Kingdom" belonged to "the poor in spirit," so it should go forth from the despised Galilee, as it is the kingdom of One Whose throne was on Calvary, and the title thereon was Jesus of Nazareth.

[4] As in Luke xxiii. 5. Acts x. 37.

But with regard to the whole character of these investigations, on the diversities that mark the Gospels, and so minute a mode of tracing the subject, it may be said again, that as in nature the more closely any subject is investigated the further is there seen to extend order, and variety, and distinctness of purpose, so may we suppose the same to exist in no less degree in the words of God in Revelation ; and that industry and attention, by the aid of the Holy Spirit, may be able to trace them even beyond what is usually supposed. The distinct classification, under which flowers are found to range themselves, is quite beyond the thoughts of any but a botanist. And the great beauty, and order, and exquisite nicety of construction, adapted to meet the peculiarities of its nature, are as strong an indication of present Divinity in the minutest flower, as in the greatest objects of the visible creation. In them we find as lively indications of Him who clothes the lilies of the field with beauty and glory far surpassing that of Solomon in his kingly attire ;— we discern indications of His moulding and ruling hand as much present in them, as we do in all the order and harmony of the heavenly bodies. Nor does there seem any reason, why a reverent and humble study of Scripture may not discover systems as great and perfect in the written Word and the Revelations it affords us, as the research and pursuits of later ages have done in the. material universe.

SECTION VII

THE DIVINITY OF OUR LORD SET FORTH IN ST. JOHN'S GOSPEL

WE have as yet considered those emblems which resemble each other in this point of view, that they all walk on earth. We now proceed to a consideration of the fourth, which differs from the others in this respect, that although its means of life and food are of the earth, yet its ways are above what is earthly ; it is ever on the wing, rising often beyond where human eye can follow, and is supposed to have the peculiar power of gazing with undazzled eyes on the very source of light [5].

These points will at once suggest to us the strongest case of analogy, and afford us some evident reasons why the Eagle has been considered by ancient writers to represent the Saints of God. It becomes therefore in the very highest manner applicable to St. John, both with respect to what we know of his personal history, as " the beloved disciple," and also on account of the peculiar character of his Gospel.

The account of the eagle in the Book of Job [6] may without impropriety be thus applied, as descriptive of the character of this Evangelist : She " maketh her nest on high ; she dwelleth and abideth in the rock, upon the crag of the rock and the strong place." Abiding in the rock, and the strong place, would anyhow serve well to describe those whose confidence is in God ; but we may

---

[5] See Augustin in Johan. Evan. Tract. xxxvi. 5, p. 2055, Benedict. Paris edition.

[6] Ch. xxxix. 28.

recognize in the words a still more definite sacred meaning
when we consider how often the Rock is in Holy Scripture the designation of our Lord Himself; and indeed it
seems especially to apply to the Divinity of our Lord ;
of a belief in which it seems to be said, " on this Rock
will I build My Church, and the gates of Hell shall not
prevail against it." Still more obvious is the explanation
of the preceding words in this passage, of " the eagle
mounting up at command, and making her nest on high."
But with a yet more peculiar adaptation may the application of some succeeding words be extended to St. John,
" her eyes behold afar off,"—" and where the slain is, there
is she." The meaning of this, as applied to St. John,
will be more apparent from setting it beside a passage in
the Gospels, which seems to have a reference to it ;
" where the Body is, there will the eagles be gathered
together." There is, I believe, something like a Catholic
consent for interpreting this text to signify, that where
our Lord's Body is, there will His Saints be gathered [7],
In the detailed explanation of this there is indeed a
diversity of opinion ; for some writers would refer it to
the Holy Eucharist ; others to the doctrine of Christ
Crucified ; others to the Saints meeting our Lord's Body
in the air at the last Day. We may therefore conclude
that it does in fact comprehend all these in that one application to our Lord's Body. Now if we look to St.
John's history, we find him alone, of all the disciples, at
the foot of the Cross, and therefore at once the literal
adaptation is evident—" Where the Slain is, there is he."
Or if we consider it with respect to his Gospel, it is
throughout especially Sacramental ; almost every thing
that St. John records seems to be full of some mysterious

[7] See Holy Week, pp. 281—285.

allusion to one of the two Sacraments, so that here again
in a higher sense is it fulfilled that "where the Slain is,
there is he." And thus that which was literally true of
St. John, might be spiritually applied to his Gospel, viz.
that his standing by the Cross was especially to bear
testimony to "the Water and the Blood." If indeed the
two Sacraments are contained in the words "light and
life [8]," so these words may be especially applied to St.
John's Gospel; it is throughout, in a very eminent
manner, "light and life," as he says at the opening of it,
"in Him was Life, and the Life was the Light of men:"
our Lord is through this Gospel especially seen as imparting Life and Light to men. And indeed, with regard
to this figurative interpretation generally, it may be
observed that birds of prey are to be found, from all
quarters of the Heavens, wherever their prey is, and that
in a manner quite beyond all human means of accounting
for, by some instinctive guidance; and so also the Saints
of God beyond all human reason are, instinctively as it
were and by the secret guidance of God, led to Christ
Crucified; and from thence, to use the expression of the
Psalmist, "their youth is renewed like the eagle [9]."

Moreover, it may be observed that, independently of
these particulars respecting the habits of the eagle, and
the Scriptural allusions to it, the mere natural motion
of this bird high on the wing, as poised in mid air, does
of itself afford a lively emblem or picture of faith, of faith
supporting itself under a sense of our Lord's Divinity;
such is the eagle as seen buoyant above earth and nearer
Heaven, from some internal elasticity or secret power
above sight. And thus "with wings as eagles" shall the

---

[8] φῶς καὶ ζωή.   [9] Ps. ciii. 5.

good mount up towards Heaven[1]; and God shall on eagle's wings bear them up unto Himself[2].

And if the Eagle does thus represent Divine Persons from their approaches to Christ, in a manner still more obvious and palpable does the Eagle represent our Lord's Divinity itself, which is the subject of St. John's Gospel. It is, indeed, that emblem by which God has chosen to speak of His Holy Spirit, Which led the Israelites in the wilderness, "As an eagle stirreth up her nest, fluttereth over her young, spreadeth abroad her wings, taketh them, beareth them on her wings : So the Lord alone did lead him. . . . He maketh him ride on the high places[3]."

St. John's Gospel does, we know, set forth especially our Lord's Godhead; and in this higher sense more particularly we wish to consider the Sacred Symbol, as expressive not of the character of the Evangelist alone, but of those attributes of Christ in His kingdom, which that Gospel more peculiarly sets forth. And the very words respecting this figure of the eagle, as described in Holy Scripture, may apply to our Lord Himself as revealed in this Gospel,—that He is therein bearing His people as it were on eagle's wings, and bringing them unto Himself; disclosing Himself therein as the Son of God, in whom alone we have access to the Father; lifting us aloft, as the eagle does her young, till in the sense of His Divine power we are able to sustain ourselves towards Heaven, and above terrestrial cares.

This indeed is a part of the argument on which it will be necessary to say but little, for the very reason that it is one on which obviously so much might be said, but which in fact needs no proof. For that the subject of St John's

---

[1] Isa. xl. 31. [2] Exod. xix. 4.
[3] Deut. xxxii. 13.

G

Gospel is especially that of our Lord's Divinity, is a point which will be at once allowed by all; for the highest and most mysterious doctrines of the Gospel are throughout the subject of this Evangelist. We have here but little or no mention of the Kingdom, none of our Lord's helpless infancy, little of human affections, no accounts of His being " moved by compassion," that " He wondered," that " He was angry;" nor is there here the mention of Angels and Priesthood; nor many incidents and narratives of great human tenderness and human compassions; but it is all of Him Who in the beginning was with God, and was God;—by Whom all things were made, and without Whom was not any thing made ;—Who was and is in the bosom of the Father, dwelling in Light that no man can approach unto ;—Who " came forth from God and went to God."

The Divinity, indeed, of our Lord being generally acknowledged as the pervading theme of this Gospel, the question for the discussion of modern writers has rather been, respecting the reasons why it should be so, than to prove the fact that it is so. And the circumstance is usually attributed to some inadequate human motives and occasions in the writer ; for surely it is but a very poor and inadequate way of speaking of a subject so vast and incomprehensible, to pretend to account for this, by saying that the Evangelist's object was to support the doctrine of our Lord's Divinity against rising Heresies ; though of course this may have been one point in the Divine dispensation, which marked the character of this Gospel, and the period of its appearing. If such things are to be traced to design and purpose at all, it is rather to that which is Divine and superhuman, so far as we may be allowed to perceive it, than to any object in

the mind of the human agent: such a mode of considering it, to which these sacred emblems lead us, is far
more worthy of inspiration; for of course the human
agents are but the instruments, in the hands of Him Who
creates and shapes and fashions them, to bring about the
objects of His own inscrutable will. With regard to the
purpose of the writer, we may well suppose that the
Disciple who lay on our Lord's bosom, and drank from
thence streams of Divine wisdom,—such as they only can
understand (as it has been said of old) who also lie on
His bosom by faith,—we may well suppose that this
Evangelist could no more have written a Gospel of a
different character, than the eagle could have lived on
earth; they who wait on the Lord, as this Evangelist,
must ever mount up on eagle's wings. Divine contemplation and Divine love, the perfection of what is morally
good in man, and which make up the character of St.
John, could have no other more appropriate topic than
that of our Lord's Divinity, so abundantly communicated
to him. These, as eagle's wings, ever bear him above earth.

Passages and words expressive of our Lord's Divinity in
this Gospel are familiar to us,—such as occur at the
very opening of this Evangelist. But it is not usually
observed what an extraordinary tendency there is in St.
John always to arise into the mention of Divine attributes,
to notice indications and emanations of Divinity, as ever
breaking through the veil of the flesh by which He
became visible to mortal eyes; and how thoroughly and
entirely this pervades, impregnates, enlightens this
Gospel, as the rays of light which transmuted our Lord's
clothing on the Mount of Transfiguration. As, for
instance, compare the testimony of the Baptist, recorded
by St. John, with the same testimony as recorded by the

other Evangelists, i. e. the circumstances in that testimony
which they have respectively selected to mention : " Of
His fulness have all we received, and grace for grace."
" No one hath seen God at any time ; the only-begotten
Son Who is in the bosom of the Father, He hath declared
Him." And so also in the Baptist's answer to the questions about purifying: "He that cometh from above is
above all; he that is of the earth is earthly, and speaketh
of the earth; He that cometh down from Heaven is above
all." " The Father loveth the Son, and hath given all
things into His hand. He that believeth on the Son
hath everlasting life." It would appear as unnatural, if
we may so express it, for this Evangelist to speak of
things merely human, as for the eagle to walk on earth.

Again, the very incidents which he first records have
about them something connected with the highest mysteries
of religion, in some Divine manner, which separates them
from actions more partaking of human incident ; such are
the events at the marriage in Cana of Galilee, and the
discourse with Nicodemus at Jerusalem, in which the two
great Sacraments are the subjects, in their most Divine
and mysterious import. There is something of the same
kind in the calling of Nathanael, which had been previously mentioned, where it is intimated that the man
without guile shall, like Israel of old, have the peculiar
faculty of discerning the Heavens opened, and "Angels
of God ascending and descending;" in other words, that
" the pure in heart" " shall see God." And these allusions so frequent to the two great Sacraments are, of
course, concerning the operations of the Holy Spirit, Who
gives and infuses life into these dead elements, and by
means of them ; and therefore the subject is especially of
Godhead, of the Spirit that brooded on the face of the

waters, and gave a new and hallowed life to material things.

It is indeed rarely considered how constantly these allusions pervade St. John's Gospel. The record of John the Baptist, the miracle at Cana of Galilee, the communication with Nicodemus, the conversation with the woman of Samaria, the miracle at the pool of Bethesda, the discourse on the pouring of the water at the feast of Tabernacles, the washing of the Disciples' feet, the testimony to the water and the Blood at the Crucifixion, the manifestation of Christ after the Resurrection by the lake of Gennesareth,—all connect with water the highest Divine blessings. And his allusions to the other Sacrament are not unfrequent. If we combine with these his constant introduction of what is Divine, of Light and of Life, perhaps we may express the subject of his Gospel in a few words of his own:—"There are Three that bear record in Heaven, the Father, the Word, and the Holy Ghost; and these Three are One. And there are Three that bear witness in earth, the Spirit, and the Water, and the Blood; and these Three agree in One." So full is this Evangelist (if we may venture thus to apply these very awful words) of the hidden and mysterious things of God, and so does he blend those most Divine doctrines with those Sacramental signs, the Water and the Blood.

Nor is it only when this Gospel is dwelling on discourses of high and great doctrine, that it is in its tone so Divine; even when it assumes the character of narrative and incident, it is still Divine: if the flight of the eagle appears for a while near the ground, yet it is in fact still on the wing, borne over the mountain-tops, and far aloof. Still, as the Prophet says, her "nest is on high," still "she dwelleth and abideth on the rock,—and the strong place.

From thence she seeketh her prey." Let us take, for
instance, the washing of the Disciples' feet, where, if ever,
He Who "thought it not robbery to be equal with God,—
made Himself of no reputation, and took upon Him the
form of a servant." Yet even in this transaction, this
Disciple sees as it were the fulness of the Godhead, and
every word that he records breathes intensely of Divine
dignity and love: "Jesus knowing that the Father had
given all things into His hands, and that He was come
from God and went to God,"—such is his mode of introducing the simplest narrative[4]. And again, in the apprehension of our Lord by the traitor Judas, in this Gospel
alone do we see the fulness of the Godhead. "Jesus,
therefore, knowing all things that should come upon Him,
went forth, and said unto them, Whom seek ye?" "As
soon then as He had said unto them, I am (He), they
went backward and fell to the ground[5]."

It may also be noticed, that the incidents, which this
Evangelist selects to record, are almost always for the
purpose of mentioning some Divine discourse to which
they gave rise, even if the incidents themselves are not
such as strongly mark His Divinity. Such is the discourse with the Samaritan woman, when our Lord speaks
of "the living water" flowing from His Divine nature,
as One with the Holy Spirit, to Whom this figure is by
Himself applied. There is a very remarkable instance of
this kind in the miracle of the five loaves and fishes,
and which is the more remarkable, as one does not see
at first sight why a miracle should be recorded, which
each of the other Evangelists had already given with such
accuracy and closeness of detail; but the reason is evident
from the introduction of that very long discourse which

---

[4] See Holy Week, Pt. iv. § iv.   [5] See Passion, pp. 52, 53.

ensued, respecting "the Bread that came down from Heaven," and which connects it with the Holy Eucharist. For this long and sublime conversation on the subject is evidently the reason why St. John introduces at all the account of that miracle, which had been already so circumstantially given; but that conversation brings forth in a striking manner that miracle itself as highly symbolical, and full of mysterious Divine significancy. And what is much to be observed on this subject is, that whereas this Evangelist is silent respecting the appointment of the Eucharist, as the narrative of a matter of fact, yet he records at length in this discourse its Divine import and character. Almost every incident, indeed, is of this nature, viz. an instance of connecting events that occurred with high and heavenly doctrine; such is that, in the fifth chapter, of the cure of the impotent man at the pool of Bethesda, which gave occasion to those great and mysterious declarations respecting the Resurrection, and the power of life which is in the Son, and His union with the Father. It seems as if when any thing earthly was mentioned, it was to introduce more at length that which is heavenly; whenever the eagle stoops to earth, it is but to renew his flight to the Heavens. The same may, perhaps, be said of the woman taken in adultery, in the eighth chapter; and the restoring of the blind man, in the following; both of which gave rise to discourses transcendental and mysterious, replete, to an attentive hearer, of our Lord's hidden Divinity;—to the indications of which we may suppose the heart, the ears, and eyes of the beloved disciple were especially open. The circumstances of our Lord's presence at the feast of Dedication, and at the feast of Tabernacles, and His raising of Lazarus from the dead, with all the discourses which are connected with it, are all highly of this character, as intimating especially His God-head, and the mode of arriving at the saving knowledge of it by obedience.

It must, moreover, be remembered, that those discourses in the thirteenth and following chapters in St. John, containing so much that is so deeply mysterious, and at the same time both awful and consolatory in doctrine, so far surpassing all that it has ever entered into the highest human philosophy to have conceived, were spoken in the hearing of the other disciples, and of one, and perhaps more, of the other Evangelists. That St. John, therefore, should have selected such discourses for distinct mention, is the more remarkable from the silence of the others respecting discourses so momentous: it marks the more strongly the predilection or purpose of his mind, to have so distinctly noticed and remembered what was of such solemn interest, and would not otherwise have been preserved from oblivion. Were we to consider the respective styles of the writers as a matter of human composition, St. Matthew's Gospel is characterized by precept, St. Luke's by narrative, St. Mark's by human incident and feeling, and St. John's by doctrine. But doctrine is as it were the very fountain-head from which precept and narrative and sentiment flow; to pass from the other Gospels to St. John is like passing up the streams to the head and source. Like the eagle, he turns from the effects and developments of light in objects below, to gaze on the sun itself.

Something, moreover, may be said with respect to the very composition itself of St. John. Soft and buoyant as is the flight of the eagle in the Heavens, such is the equable and gentle character of the style of this Gospel, —ever delighting to arise from the cares and incidents of life into the free and congenial atmosphere of its own skies, and that by a spontaneous and instinctive impulse, so spontaneous and instinctive as to have the appearance not of effort but of free motion; like the dove, which so often is the emblem of the good Spirit, among the haunts and houses of men it grieves, and is affrighted, and sad, till it escapes, and is seen as the eagle, winging its way into the clear expanse, and on its noiseless course is buoyed without effort on the wing[6]. Such is the style of this Gospel, that it appears no style at all. Soft as the dew that fell noiseless on the hill of Hermon; soft as the oil that came on the head of Aaron, and went to the skirts of his clothing. So full of the unction of Divine charity is the very style. A little child at the point of death has been known to ask to hear the reading of St. John's Gospel, mentioning, as a reason for it, the soothing and softening influence of that Evangelist. Of such little children is the kingdom of Heaven; something of that Divine wisdom which this Gospel contains is revealed even unto babes; it contains abundantly milk for babes, and at the same time in all its fulness, meat too strong for all but perfect men. The beloved Disciple writes alike "to little children," to "young men," and to "fathers[7]." This Gospel is that Divine stream wherein the elephant may swim, and yet a child may ford the same, and pass thereby to the heavenly Canaan. It flows equable and full and clear on the surface, on account of the depth of the stream beneath, and appears unruffled

---

[6] " Plausumque exterrita pennis
Dat tecto ingentem; mox aëre lapsa quieto
Radit iter liquidum, celeres neque commovet alas."
  Virg. Æneid. lib. v. 215.

[7] 1 St. John ii.

and motionless in the even tenor of its course, because of those deep waters below, wherein the footsteps of God are.

Indeed there appears great reason to suppose that the depth of this Gospel, what is mysterious and Sacramental and Divine in it, has been very little known; that the profoundest of men have rather indicated its depth than been able to sound it: those whose eyes have been most enlightened have been unable to follow the track of the eagle. To use the words of St. Augustin, " How sublime ought those things to be of which he treats who is compared unto the eagle ! and yet even we, who are so infirm and creep on the ground, venture to treat of those matters, and to expound them; and we think we are able to comprehend them ourselves when we think of them, or to be comprehended by others while we speak of them⁸."

Now, from what has been said, it will, I think, appear, that if we were to consider these emblematic representations merely in the light of metaphorical figures, or similes, without taking into consideration their Divine character, they would serve admirably to express the characteristics of the four Gospels. And this diversity also may, perhaps, be accounted for, humanly speaking, from the different disposition, situation, and circumstance of their authors. It is natural to suppose that "the beloved Physician" should select works of mercy to record, St. John the Divinity of our Lord; that a Jew writing to Jews should speak mostly of the promised Kingdom of the Messiah; that the interpreter of St. Peter should dwell affectionately on every incident respecting his Master and Lord. But we would rather consider it, not as arising out of these apparently accidental circumstances, but as in fact weighed long before in the secret counsels of God: we would look

⁸ In Johan. Evan. Tract. xxxvi. 5.

upon them as Divinely-ordered manifestations of our Lord; not only of His eternal Kingship, His Incarnation, His Atonement, and His Divinity, which His essential attributes are the subjects of these Gospels severally, but also as the various modes and reasons of His manifesting Himself to mankind;—to the Jew in judgment, to the Gentile in mercy; to the weak Christian as the Son of Man; to the perfect as God.

But there is always some danger when we confine our attention exclusively (as we often necessarily must) to one consideration alone. There is a danger in entering thus critically and closely on the structure of each of the Gospels; lest in examinations of the composition and nature of each particular part we lose the more general view, a sense of harmonious proportion and majesty, as a whole, of those four pillars upon which the Temple of God is constructed; lest in dwelling on the diversity and characteristic beauty of those Heavenly stones, on whose foundation the Temple is built,—the jasper, and the sapphire, and the chalcedony, and the emerald*,—we fail sufficiently to consider that "the Lord God Almighty and the Lamb are the Temple." And it must moreover be remembered, that in explaining these symbols, as closely applicable to the Evangelists, and as we think so intended of the Almighty, we do not confine them to these alone, or exclude other interpretations which tend the same way, and have one end and scope, as modes of God's revealing Himself to mankind. As of yore in His Church in the wilderness did He disclose His Divine presence in the midst of these significative Symbols, revealing Himself in a local habitation; so does He now manifest Himself in the Church, after a more spiritual manner, between these

* Rev. xxi. 19. 22.

living Cherubim; and hereafter for a third time may He manifest Himself to His Church in Heaven, from between these symbols in a manner that will equally defy all conjecture beforehand, "as eye hath not seen nor ear heard, neither hath it entered into the heart of man to understand."

PART II

Our Lord's Manifestation of Himself

SECTION I

VARIOUS DISPENSATIONS OF GOD

AS the four Gospels are but the history of our Blessed
Lord's life in the flesh, it is necessary that before
entering upon them, one should show at some length what
may be considered the rules under which our Lord acted,
in revealing among mankind His unapproachable Godhead. This is a subject indeed which has been discussed
in another place[1]; but it seems necessary to introduce it
here, both for the better understanding of the narrative of
the Gospel, and also as affording us principles of interpretation, and closely interwoven with other subjects which
it is expedient to introduce. Our Blessed Lord appears
therein to have acted according to the same laws which
He had done in previous dispensations with mankind, and
also as He continues to act in His providence, as now
witnessed and experienced among us. In all these He
withdraws Himself from the knowledge of men, except so
far as they are capable of receiving and acknowledging

[1] "Tracts for the Times," No. 80. Part I.

Him.   As the life of our souls does depend on our discerning Him, so He is ever exceeding desirous to reveal Himself to us.   But as our incalculable injury and destruction
does arise from His being manifested to us, and our not
being able, from unrepented sins and infirmities, to know
and adore Him as God; therefore is He ever withdrawing
Himself even in disclosing, and ever throwing about His
ways a veil of mysterious and inscrutable secrecy.   And
therefore it need occasion no surprise, if our Lord, as
revealed to our bodily eyes in the Gospels, does act in this
respect in a manner very similar to all other dealings of
God with mankind.

For, first of all, we may notice the phenomena, which
have become familiar to us, of the nations of the world
being so long involved in such great ignorance of God;
and therefore this His withdrawing Himself from the
knowledge of men, is not of itself a matter of surprise.
For of course the ignorance and darkness in which the
Heathen world were left, does at once indicate, that they
were both unworthy and incapable of receiving the knowledge of God; that after His Spirit had long strove in vain
with man, and they were not willing to retain God in their
knowledge, He gave them up to follow their own imaginations, and hid Himself from them,—hid Himself not
altogether, for that He never has done, but yet in great
measure.   And yet in the mean while whatever knowledge
of Truth the Heathens arrived at, was from Jesus Christ
manifesting Himself to them; for He is the true and only
Light "which lighteth every man that cometh into the
world."   In mercy as well as in judgment withdrawing
His presence, yet never leaving mankind altogether without witness of Himself.

Though very much less in degree, yet the same was in

some measure the case with the chosen people. In comparison with the Heathen they indeed had revealed to them the knowledge of God, Who was represented as nigh unto them, in a way that He was not to any other nation [2]. At the same time, in comparison with us in the Christian dispensation, they also were in darkness, and sitting under the shadow of death. The whole system under which God dealt with them was one of types and shadows, under which He veiled Himself from them; and that not only in the case of rites and ordinances, but throughout the whole of that dispensation, withholding from them the secrets [3] of His Kingdom, and giving them "laws which were not good [4]," and which could not give life; manifesting Himself rather as the God who would destroy their enemies in battle, and in temporal judgments, whereby children were punished for their fathers' sins, as in His natural providence.

And yet all this was in such a manner that good men could discern Him even through those shadows : and though He did not expressly reveal the nature of the mercies He had in store for them, nor even afford them any definite and clear assurance of any future state after death at all ; yet by obedience and preparation of the heart they were led to a kind of hidden knowledge, so much so as even to see afar off and rejoice in the day of Christ. By the Spirit ever illuminating the path of obedience, they were led to walk as strangers and pilgrims before Him ;—as looking, though almost indefinitely and unconsciously, to a city that hath foundations, whose Builder and Maker is God. "The secret things belong unto the Lord our God," said Moses ; for all was reserve and mystery : but the Psalmist added, "The secrets of the

---

[2] Deut. iv. 7.   [3] Deut. xxix. 29.   [4] Ezek. xx. 25.

Lord are with them that fear Him," and "He will show them His covenant;" for even in this mystery and reserve there was disclosure. And thus He spake to them indeed, but it was out of the cloudy pillar; but yet He spake to them; and His reason for doing so was their obedience; "He spake to them out of the cloudy pillar," and why? "for they kept His testimonies and the law that He gave them [5]." Even through these shadows He revealed Himself to those who had faith to discern Him; and thus were good men, seeing, as the Psalmist often expresses it, that there were wonderful things laid up in the Law of God beyond the letter, praying for eyes to see them; and, from the very light that was given them, only rendered the more sensible of their ignorance of God, So that great as was the light which the Jew enjoyed in comparison of the Gentile, yet it only served to bring him more to know that great attribute of God, which His Prophet has expressed, "Verily Thou art a God that hidest Thyself, O God of Israel, the Saviour [6]." "Out of Sion" indeed He is manifested, and "in perfect beauty;" yet so that "clouds and darkness are around about Him." The Christian indeed, "the true Israelite and without guile," even there among the clouds that surround Him in the Old Testament may say, "We have seen His glory;" but to the Israelite after the flesh, "He is without form or comeliness," and when they see Him there is "no beauty that" they "should desire Him."

Thus was it with the dispensations of old. And so is it now, that there is a very remarkable reserve and secrecy in the mode in which God does reveal Himself to mankind, as we witness His moral dealings with us, and the steps of His spiritual Providence. Without stopping to

[5] Ps. xcix. 7.   [6] Isa. xlv. 15.

point out the manifold ways in which this might be
shown, it is a point which will be readily allowed by all
considerate persons : and, indeed, independently of our
own experience and observation, it is a truth which no
Christian will think of denying, inasmuch as it is but the
fulfilment of our Lord's own prophetic declaration, or
rather perhaps of an universal law of His Providence,
which He has expressed in the promise,—that He will
manifest Himself unto those that seek Him, and do His
will, and not to the world. And no doubt there are some
in this and all ages of the Church, in whom those
mysterious words are fulfilled, "if any man will do the
will of God," that Christ will manifest Himself unto him,
and he shall know of the doctrine[7]; and if a man love
Him, Christ will manifest Himself unto him, and the
Father and the Son will come unto him, and make Their
abode with him[8]. And it is most certain that if Christ
is now in the world, yet it is not as manifested to all persons in a Christian country, but to various persons in
various degrees ; but in the higher and more blessed sense
which our Lord intimates, only to some few. There is
doubtless something most inscrutably and wonderfully
secret in the mode in which He discloses Himself; for
He is most certainly not seen or acknowledged in the
great places of popular resort, in the ways of the world, to
the persons who look after great place, or in the literature
of the day. Certainly if Christ is among us, it is after
some mode of singular privacy and reserve ; not in the
frequented places of Judea and Jerusalem, nor among the
ambition of the Pharisees, nor the learning of the Scribes,
but with some lowly persons in a retired Galilee. This
we may observe is the case now : for all will allow that

[7] John vii. 17.   [8] John xiv. 23.

H

Christ is not known and manifested abroad ; and therefore unless it is by some reserve of secrecy, it is not at all ;
and all good men will allow, and indeed most men under
the pressure of great calamities and needs, that He is revealed, if not constantly, yet occasionally, in secret—is
made known in Divine strength. And all persons who
act in any way as the Apostles of Christ did, who begin
by repentance, and then by self-denial, leave all to follow
Him : who wait and watch for Him, and continue with
Him in good and ill report :—there can be no doubt that
such persons have ever found Him. So will they confess,
and so doubtless will we believe : we cannot deny but that
He must be present with good men after some very intimate
and peculiar manner.

There is indeed in all this notion something of contradiction,—concealment and disclosure combined together.
There appears at first sight to some a palpable apparent
absurdity, when we speak of Revelation itself as founded
on a system of concealment ; and some persons would
at once hastily turn away from the very supposition, on
account of the contradiction implied in it. But the fact
is, that this circumstance is not at all unlike the ways of
God ; this very contradiction is a part of the mysteriousness of His ways, and is in itself one of the most remarkable peculiarities that pervade the Divine dispensations.
For thus it is that Holy Scripture itself is made up of
apparent contradictions and difficulties, such as are solved
by the life of faith, but in no other way, and therefore
must still appear to the world as difficulties and contradictions. Thus the Christian is not only differently described in different places of Scripture, but sometimes
even in one and the same sentence : thus he is spoken of
as "sorrowful yet" in sorrow "rejoicing ;" as "having

nothing and yet possessing all things ;" as all fear and trembling, and yet as all hope and confidence. Salvation is of faith only, and not of works ; and yet it is of works only, and not of faith ; it is of ourselves alone, and yet it is of God only. Thus is every thing in religion full of contradictions in the dispensation of Him, Who as Christ is perfect God, and yet perfect Man. And what is very remarkable is this, that the more we rightly realize either of these truths, the more have we the other also, and its opposite, revealed to us ; the more we fear, the more shall we hope ; the greater our love, the greater will be our fear ; the less we have, the more we possess ; in affliction we have most Christian joy. And this may be noticed through all the beatitudes—they are formed of contradictions ; the poor, for instance, have a kingdom, the meek have earthly inheritance. It is therefore not inconsistent with this, if the more under any dispensation God is revealed to us, the more do we become sen· sible how much He conceals Himself from us : the more light there is, the more visible does it render the obscurity ; the brighter is the sun, the darker becomes the shade ; the vista that opens but serves to show the depth that lies beyond. Nor is it therefore to be wondered at, if in the Gospel dispensation, where there is the greatest manifestation, we most of all observe this law of secrecy and concealment :—that the Gospels themselves, which are especially the light of the world, should be most replete with reserve ;—that of the four Gospels themselves, that of St. John, wherein our Blessed Lord is most fully revealed, should be most replete with mysteries ;—that in the spread of the Gospel through the world, those who are the commissioned heralds to communicate those good tidings, had to divulge the knowledge of good things, should be called "stewards of mysteries;"—that this should be the very title of God's ministers; implying that the very law of their disclosure should be marked by a name which implies the keeping in reserve, and the dealing out with judicious discretion, under a law of mystery.

But still all that is at present maintained is this, that the fact is perfectly analogous with the other dealings of God; that when it is observed that in our Lord's demeanour, actions, and words throughout the Gospels, there is a very remarkable reserve in the disclosure of Himself, this is but to say that when manifested in the flesh, He was pleased to act under the same laws, under which all will allow that He has always acted in the world, both in His dispensations towards the Heathen, and in the earlier revelation of Himself in the Law, and in His present dealings with mankind. He has made "His pavilion round about with dark water, and thick clouds to cover Him;" clouds and darkness are ever round about Him in all His appearances to men, excepting where perchance some bright ray of light breaks forth and falls on some favoured spot, bathing with light and warmth the footsteps of some few who have learned to value it.

But even that genial ray only tends to reveal that thick darkness wherein God is. Still every coming, as described throughout Holy Scripture, is with clouds: it was in a Cloud in the wilderness, it was amidst Clouds and thick darkness on mount Sinai, it was in a Cloud that God took possession of His Temple. He manifested Himself to Solomon under this especial· title; "Then spake Solomon, The Lord said that He would dwell in the thick darkness⁹." And so before, "The Lord said

⁹ 1 Kings viii. 12.

unto Moses, Speak unto Aaron thy brother, that he come not at all times into the holy place, within the vail before the mercy-seat, which is upon the ark, that he die not; for I will appear in the Cloud upon the mercy-seat [1]." It was from a Cloud at the Transfiguration that God spoke; and amidst Clouds shall He appear on the day of Judgment: but then alone "at the brightness of His presence shall the clouds remove," and "all eyes shall behold Him," and "we shall see Him as He is."

SECTION II

GENERAL CHARACTER OF OUR LORD'S LIFE AND MINISTRY

SINCE therefore there appears no improbability beforehand, we have now only to prove that through the whole of that dispensation in which, by the history of His Evangelists, He has become as it were visible to the eyes of flesh, our Lord's conduct was marked by an exceeding watchfulness and care,—not to reveal Himself too openly before mankind; but so contriving and controlling all things, to prepare the hearts of men, that they might be enabled to come to the knowledge of Him and to discern Him without danger to themselves. Thus was He ever concealing and withholding the secrets of His kingdom in a hand that was ever yearning and eager to impart them; and hiding the treasures of Divine wisdom, if I may so speak, in a heart overflowing with the aboundings of an expansive charity, but whose bowels of compassion were restrained, from a want of meet objects on which they could be bestowed.

[1] Lev. xvi. 2.

This Law of our Lord's dealing may be seen, even before He Himself appears in His own ministry and teaching, throughout the conduct of His great herald and forerunner, as preparatory to Himself, who is emphatically called "the Voice in the Wilderness." For this voice of the herald was so far from proclaiming aloud, or pointing out the Christ, that it was accompanied with a remarkable silence on that one subject. So much so that the Baptist had been for some time in the execution of his office, when serious doubts were entertained, whether he were himself the Christ or not; which evidently shows that an unreserved declaration of who the Christ was, or what was His character and office, was not the chief object of John's ministry. St. Luke has given us a particular description of his teaching, and has shown us, that it consisted in calling upon every person to amend what was amiss in his daily course of life : and that thus it was that in the hearts of men he was preparing that Royal road, under the figure of which the Prophet had described his teaching—by bringing down high thoughts, and making straight the crooked paths, in order that thus "all flesh might see the salvation of God."—And moreover, as if in perfect unison with our Lord's own subsequent conduct, over the person of the Baptist himself there was a mysterious veil of secrecy and reserve ; for whether he was or not the foretold Elijah, upon which point the authority of his mission depended, was wrapped up throughout in a strange incomprehensible doubt. He himself denied that he was, to those emissaries which were sent expressly to put this question to him. And when our Lord declared privately to His three disciples that the Baptist was that Elijah, He intimated at the same time, that it was a fact which could only be spiritually discerned, and depended upon the state of the heart, like the reception of a moral truth, adding to the declaration, "This is Elias *if ye are willing* to receive it.—He that hath ears to hear, let him hear."

For the Law had been, in fact, the "schoolmaster to bring them to Christ," and if they had believed Moses they would have believed Him, and therefore the object of the Baptist was to bring them back to the fulfilment of the Law, and to a sense of their failure in it, because by repentance they would- be led on more and more to the apprehension of Him ; to see, first of all, His holiness, and then His power, and then His Divine mission as one sent from God, and thus to come at length to a full knowledge of His infinite Godhead. For thus, in His power to remit bodily and spiritual evil, the prepared heart might see the Salvation of God ; so that being rendered merciful by the teaching of the great Forerunner, they might discern Him in his mercies ; being pure in heart they might see Him in His holiness ; that being penitent they might embrace His consolations : and thus, being poor in spirit, might enter into His kingdom.

And further, it may be observed that when indeed the Baptist did twice actually point out the Christ, and designate Him as "the Lamb of God that taketh away the sin of the world," it is said expressly on one of these occasions that it was to two of His disciples ; and we cannot but suppose that these two must have been among the most tried and faithful of that number ; they were, it seems, St. John and St. Andrew. And this is a stronger confirmation of the point than a complete silence would have been. For what is maintained is, not that the truth is entirely withdrawn or concealed, but that it is revealed only to persons capable of receiving it. And afterwards, when a more detailed and clear testimony to our Lord is afforded by the Baptist, it is to his own disciples; and the very occasion of their coming tends to a confirmation of this point; for they came to him on account of a dispute which had arisen between them and the Jews, on the subject of purifying,—with respect, it would appear, to the different powers of cleansing supposed to exist in our Lord's Baptism, as perfectly different in kind to that of the Baptist's[2]. This inquiry evidently shows that they had no very clear intimation of whom our Lord was. And again, at a subsequent period, when the Baptist was in prison, and sent his two disciples to our Lord, the occasion affords another clear indication of the nature of his teaching,—that it was to prepare his disciples by repentance in heart and life to receive, by observing and so acknowledging the Christ, rather than to attach them to our Lord as His disciples, by any express declaration of His greatness. And this is demonstrated, in a manner most full and deeply interesting, by our Lord's mode of receiving them[3]. For He pointed to His works. He put them in the position of others. He gave no direct reply to the question which they brought to Him, whether He were the Christ, or whether they were "to look for another." And indeed, not to dwell upon these particulars, it may be inferred from the very fact of the co-existence of disciples of the Baptist and disciples of our Lord ;—which we find was the case even at the middle of the second year of our Lord's ministry at the feast in Levi's house. For this is a proof that with the Baptist and with our Lord Himself there was a mysterious reserve respecting Himself; for otherwise this

[2] See Nativity, pp. 340, 341.
[3] See " Tracts for the Times," No. 80, p. 24.

distinction of separate disciples could no more have existed, than the morning star with its attendant satellites could continue to be visible in the full light of the sun.

Again, with regard to the history of our Lord Himself; we are so familiar with the narrative of His life in the flesh, that we can hardly hold it out as it were to contemplate it at a distance, and to notice the strong characteristics which accompany it;—otherwise we could not fail to observe how strongly it is characterized from His very Birth to His Ascension, by this circumstance of reserve in disclosing His Divinity. It is the point that the Prophet puts as the very motto in the foreground of his description of Him, "who hath believed our report, and to whom is the arm of the Lord revealed?" It is the circumstance respecting our Lord's birth and childhood, the most striking of all that appertain to it, viz., the extreme mysterious secrecy which surrounds it :—an adorable mixture of light and obscurity, where the light is the more remarkable for that veil of darkness with which it is enveloped; and the very darkness itself appears the more dark from the rays of light which emanate from it. It is much to be observed, how little an event so stupendous in its nature and its consequences, was known in the very place and nation where our Lord was born; for the space of thirty years the circumstances are so wonderful in this secrecy that we scarce realize the fact as we read—that the great and terrible God, whom "the Heaven of Heavens cannot contain," doth indeed dwell on the earth [4]; that it is He, the breath of Whose mouth made all the worlds, and which shall again destroy them, Who is thus in a manger unknown—a helpless infant; in the Temple received by His poor worshippers, and living among other

[4] 1 Kings viii. 27.

men, unnoticed but as they. Even then also when among them, when embraced in their arms, and held in their hands, and supported by a mother's care, yet was He even then, as in His Divine Providence, still incomprehensible to all the natural senses and highest faculties of man : He was present among them, as He is present with us now ; but still they might say with us,." I go forward, but He is not there; and backward, but I cannot perceive Him : on the left hand, where He doth work, but I cannot behold Him : He hideth Himself on the right hand, that I cannot see Him[5]." And blessed are they always who could thus feel their want, and bewail their ignorances of Him. As the riches of His grace are ever accompanied with a sense of our own deep poverty, so the knowledge of the wisest is rather indicated by the more fervent lamentations of their own blindness, than by any consciousness of having attained unto that knowledge. Wherever a ray of His Godhead is found among men, it "driveth him into the wilderness," or the inner chamber, into secrecy and solitude and silence, that he may listen the more attentively for that still and small voice in which God is,—not as if he had "already apprehended" Him, but "if haply he might find Him."

And throughout that period of our Lord's infancy, the little that becomes known respecting it, is such as to prove the exceeding danger of that knowledge to unprepared hearts, thus showing that even in His Swaddling-clothes, He is indeed that God Who is "a consuming fire." For to Simeon and Anna it is revealed, together with something of the spiritual nature and extent of that kingdom, and they are described as obscure persons of very holy and devout lives, to whom such a manifesta-

[5] Job xxiii. 8, 9.

tion could be made with profit; to Herod the king, the knowledge of One being born who was the subject of prophecy, and by his own confession the object of worship, was extremely prejudicial, and became the exciting cause that urged him on to a crime of almost unparalleled atrocity.

Again, our Lord's childhood is of the same character as His birth, that it is wrapped up in the same cloud of a holy and almost impenetrable reserve, through which there breaks forth on the world but one ray of light;—and that only such as to show more visibly the clouds with which He conceals His presence from the gaze of mankind. Once only is He seen, and then only to show how He is as one unknown among men. For the incident that is recorded of our Blessed Lord's childhood, when He was lost in the Temple at twelve years of age, seems to indicate that even His parents could have had but a faint sense of His inconceivable greatness and Godhead; and of course it may be that they would have been overwhelmed by that knowledge. And all that is recorded of the blessed Virgin indicates, that even she herself also came by degrees, as all the rest of mankind, to the right discernment of the Child of her miraculous birth; by "keeping His words," and "pondering them in her heart," and "comparing things spiritual with spiritual." And through all His childhood and His youth, up to the thirtieth year of His age, not only is God upon earth in a visible form, and yet unknown to the world, but not even upon those around Him, in the little household and village of Nazareth, did the rays of His inconceivable Godhead break forth. "For not even did His brethren believe on Him*." It was they who said "He is beside Himself[7]." They were His own fellow-townsmen at

* John vii. 5.   7 Mark iii. 21.

Nazareth who first attempted His life; it was at Nazareth, beyond all other places, where He could work no miracles, because of their unbelief. No one ever awoke up and said, "How dreadful is this place! surely God is in this place, and I knew it not." In all this there is a wonderful analogy to what is now going on in the fulfilment of our Lord's spiritual promises; there are instances where some few are coming more and more to the discernment of His presence,—such as keep His commandments, and to whom, therefore, according to His promise He is manifested; but to the rest He is not perceptible.

Again, when our Blessed Lord enters upon His public ministry, we cannot but observe how different His conduct is throughout, to that which would have been pursued by any mere human teacher; such as would have been desirous to obtain converts to impress mankind with a sense of his power and authority, and to be the Founder of a new kingdom or dispensation. Such a one would most of all have manifested himself in the most important places of resort; would have performed his most convincing miracles before those who most needed conviction; would have wished those attestations of his miraculous power should have been published abroad; would have spoken in a manner most clearly and decidedly in order to be understood; would have rendered all his teaching comprehensible to all; would not have checked and thrown back those who were apparently eager to follow him. It is therefore very remarkable how much the very opposite to this was the case with our Lord throughout. He appeared to be going about watching for opportunities to reveal Himself for the salvation of mankind, yet ever retiring from their view; charging earnestly that He might not be made known, as if there

was some great and peculiar danger in the manifestation
of Himself. And so also with regard to the disclosure
of all Divine truth and wisdom, He appears to have wrapt
and withdrawn it very much in the half teaching of
mysterious language;—yearning, labouring, watching to
reveal Himself, for the salvation of mankind depended on
the knowledge of Him, but shrinking, veiling, retiring,
lest they should be destroyed by His presence.

SECTION III

DARK SAYINGS AND PARABLES

OUR Lord had been pleased to reveal Himself to the
Jews of old in a dark and mysterious manner, speaking
to them through the medium of type and figure, and an
external ritual which they, to whom it was given, did
not understand; except that good men, here and there,
came by faith to the knowledge of what was contained in
them; seeing in temporal promises a better country, that
is, a heavenly;—that the legal cleansings signified hands
washed in innocency, wherewith alone we must approach
the altar of God;—that the hyssop implied spiritual purification, and the like; thus He spake to them indeed, but
it was "out of the cloudy pillar." So also in the Gospels
does our Lord frequently use dark sayings, and figures
which were not understood at the time by those to whom
He spoke. In the Gospels indeed He hath spoken to us,
in a more especial manner, from above the Mercy-seat,
more truly than He did under the Law, but still it has
been from the same cloud; "I will appear in the cloud

upon the Mercy-seat[8]." The words that are spoken by
the Son of Man, when appearing in the flesh, are as when
He spake by His prophets of old; when He spake by
them they were not understood, and so is it with Himself.
And what is most remarkable is this, that this circumstance does of itself partake of the nature of Divine com-
munications, and not of human. For among mankind
our object by conversation is to convey our meaning most
clearly or powerfully to others. But it is not so with
Almighty God; for as He is ever knowing and dealing
with the thoughts of the heart, His words have some
especial reference to them, nor can we ever be sure that
the object of Divine words is merely to impart knowledge;
they may have other objects which are better attained by
our difficulty of comprehending them, than they could
have been by their clear meaning.

Thus it is mentioned of our Blessed Lord, even when
He was a child, that His parents did not understand the
saying that He spake unto them; and the blessed Virgin
seems to have kept and cherished His words as a sacred
deposit, till the meaning should be revealed to her of
God; and such seems to have been the way with all good
persons, like the Psalmist, who says, "Thy words have I
hid within my heart, that I should not sin against Thee[9]."
They seem to have cherished His words, and compared
them with others, till they disclosed great truths unto
them. And as the way in which good men came to the
truth seems to have been by keeping in the heart, and
pondering on, what they had received, so it would seem
as if even with regard to our Lord's immediate followers,
that a great deal of what He said and did, must have been
to them as dark sayings, but cherished and preserved till

[8] Levit. xvi. 2.   [9] Ps. cxix. 11.

the meaning of them was afterwards disclosed to them by the Holy Spirit. Such must have been the case with very much that is recorded in the Gospels : of the repeated declarations of our Lord's sufferings and Resurrection it is said expressly, that they understood it not ; so also of our Lord's entering Jerusalem in that kingly manner on Palm Sunday, it is said that it was not until afterwards that they remembered the import of what they were doing. In like manner, when our Lord spake of the water at the feast of Tabernacles, they could not have known that He spake of the Holy Spirit, Which was not yet given ; or of the living water to the Samaritan woman ; or when He spake to St. Peter at the last supper of procuring a sword ; or to the Jews of the living Bread which came down from Heaven,.before the Eucharist was ordained ; or of His raising in three days the Temple which they should destroy,—words that could not have been intelligible beforehand. Many are the instances which occur, that incidentally intimate that it was our Lord's custom thus to speak ; and many must have been the circumstances which took place, of which the Divine import was not disclosed till afterwards, nor consequently our Lord's words respecting them capable of comprehension. As when He spake of the anointing at Bethany being for His burial, neither the circumstance nor the expression could have been properly understood till after His death.

The circumstance to be observed in all this is, not only that He spake darkly, and was not understood, but that these dark sayings were afterwards understood. And this is another point in which the case resembles that of the types and figurative language of the Old Testament ; not only that the Almighty has been pleased to use dark and incomprehended sayings and modes of action; but that time unlocks, and continues to unfold, their meanings to an obedient and attentive spirit. And something of this kind may possibly be signified in the circumstance, that Moses was not allowed to see the face of the Almighty, but was admitted only to behold His back parts and skirts afar off, when He passed, from the cleft in the rock where he was hid. It is spoken of as being especially the office of the Holy Spirit, that He should bring to mind things that were past, "He shall bring all things to your remembrance, whatsoever I have said unto you." So too our Lord said on an occasion very significative indeed, but darkly and mysteriously so at the time, "What I do thou knowest not now, but thou shalt know hereafter." There seems to be also something of the same kind in the events and occurrences of our life, wherein the providences and over-ruling intentions of God are not perceived at the time, but are, if we may so speak, like dark sayings to us, and are discerned afterwards when they have passed. Perhaps something of this nature may have been intended by the great and good Poet of heathen antiquity, when he represents his deities as not recognized at once in their converse with men, but in their retirings and departure to become evidently discernible as Divine. When therefore good men are spoken of as not understanding the words of Christ at the time, but as keeping them treasured in their hearts, and pondering over them, it is then that Wisdom meets them in every thought. And this may be the case in all God's dispensations, that we shall discern Him on looking back, shall discern Him when He is past; and that in the mean time it is the trial of faith and patience, while the ways or works of God are as dark sayings. And moreover, may it not be

that all this is a part of the great end of all things, and
anticipates the time when we shall look back, and behold
God in all those His dealings that now appear dark?

In the mean time, the discerning of the Hand and
intention of God in dark words and works, is not only
that in which our probation may greatly consist, but the
being offended at, or misapprehending those difficulties,
is of itself an indication of unbelief, or of weakness of
faith; as when our Lord spoke of His Body as a Temple,
it became to the Jews an offence; and they were dis-
pleased and angry at His speaking of giving them His
Flesh to eat. And in using dark and figurative sayings
to His disciples, it is evident that they did require at the
time, not intellectual, but moral and spiritual discernment
to comprehend them; so that they served to prove and
indicate the state of the heart and conscience. As when
our Lord spoke to the disciples of "the leaven of the
Pharisees," and on their not understanding the expression, He reproved them for it, and attributed it to the
hardness of their hearts; "He saith unto them, Why
reason ye, because ye have no bread: perceive ye
not, neither understand? Have ye your hearts yet
hardened[1]?"

Thus we observe this mode of speaking, so analogous to
the figures of the Old Testament, in our Lord's ordinary
discourse: and that the right understanding of these
figures was the proof of the moral state of the heart.
But much more than this, for we find that at length He
adopted a mode of teaching, characterized by the Prophet
as peculiarly His own, and described by Him as that of
dark speech, "I will open my mouth in *a parable*, I will
utter dark sayings of old[2]," and which the Evangelist

---

[1] Mark viii. 17.   [2] Ps. lxxviii. 2.

I

expressly tells us was spoken of Christ[3].   And thus in His teaching He confined to His disciples the more full and clear manifestations of His doctrines, and thereby appears to have been pursuing, under different circumstances, the same course of action as He had done of old. For when the world became corrupt, He confined to Abraham and to his seed the knowledge of His covenant; and in the wilderness, as it is said of Moses in distinction from others, he is "faithful in all Mine house.   With him will I speak mouth to mouth, even apparently, and not in dark speeches[4]."   As thus from the unworthy, whether nations or individuals, God of old withdrew the clearer revelation of His will, so now, in the Gospel narrative, He withdraws His free communication into the reserve of dark speech.

But the case here to be observed is, that our Lord adopted this mode of teaching by parables, as the history indicates, and as He Himself declared, on account of their slowness of belief, and impenitency.   For it was not till about the middle of the second year of our Lord's ministry,—when the hardness of heart of the Jews became strongly confirmed, and comes out more distinctly marked in the narrative,—when they had been attributing His miracles to Beelzebub, and had been warned by Him of their being on the very edge of the sin against the Holy Ghost, and approaching to that hardened and impenitent state, wherein the evil spirit would return with seven others worse than himself:—it was not till this state of obduracy, that our Lord begins to teach the multitude in parables.   And the first of these is a description of this variety of hearers, of which one only *understands* the Word, and so receives it into a good heart as to bring

. [3] Matt. xiii. 35.   [4] Numb. xii. 8.

forth fruit. On our Lord's disciples asking Him the reason for this His new mode of teaching by parables, He explains it to them on this principle, that on account of their hardness of heart He thus taught the people with dark sayings, such as they could not fully understand: "He said unto them, To you it is given to know the mysteries of the Kingdom of God; but to all others in parables, that seeing, they may not see, and hearing, they may not understand." St. Mark mentions in another place that He thus taught them, "as they were able to hear," and that "without a parable He spake not unto them." And all these things He expounded "privately" to His disciples, who, He said, had eyes to see, and ears to hear; in which respect this teaching was analogous to His disclosing Himself by miracles also, for that was in like manner in private. The expression that He taught the multitudes "as they were able to hear," serves of itself admirably to characterize that peculiarity of our Lord's teaching, which He Himself explained, as His not putting "the new wine into the old bottles," or the "new cloth upon the old garment."

There appears, therefore, to be all degrees of manifestation and also of concealment in the ways of Him, Who giveth to all "their meat in due season;" or "taketh away their breath and they die." Of the nations of the world of old,—of Saul when confirmed in his disobedience,—of the Jews at Jerusalem when utterly impenitent and unbelieving, it may be said alike that "He departed and did hide Himself from them." "When Saul inquired of the Lord, the Lord answered him not, neither by dreams, nor by Urim, nor by Prophets'." Then Saul went to the witch of Endor; and the Heathen

- * 1 Sam. xxviii. 6.

1 2

in like case went to their idolatrous oracles; and the Jews asked for a sign, and went after false prophets and Anti-christs. But there was a better state than this,—that of those to whom our Lord spake by parable, or by dark say-ings, and in the figurative language of His Prophets. Yet even this was on account of their hardness of heart and unbelief that He spake to them thus darkly; for to Moses of old, and to His twelve disciples now, He more fully and clearly revealed the secrets of His will, and explained unto them His parables.

But though His disciples were so far better than others, yet it would appear as if they were only comparatively so. And our Blessed Lord seems to have been excessively desirous, that His disciples should have come to the dis-cernment of those parables, without His explaining them, which would have been far better. For some time after-wards, when He had called the multitude unto Him, and told them the parable of "that which cometh out of the mouth defileth a man," and the disciples afterwards in-quired of Him the meaning of the parable, He complained of it with surprise, saying, "What, are ye also (or even yet) without understanding? Do ye not yet perceive[6]?" And it would appear that even to His disciples our Lord spake often darkly in parables; for on leaving them, and promising them greater and clearer light, He says, " These things have I spoken unto you in proverbs; but the hour cometh in which I shall no longer speak to you in proverbs, but shall tell you plainly of the Father[7]." And on understanding His words, His disciples, as if relieved, answer, " Behold, now speakest Thou openly, and speakest no proverbs." So synonymous was a proverb with a dark saying. And it is evident that this mode of speaking thus

[6] Matt. xv. 17.   [7] John xvi. 25. 29.

obscurely and reservedly was, because to have disclosed to them the truth more fully would have been prejudicial and injurious to them, until their hearts were more purified by faith to receive it. And, indeed, this His teaching and conduct often intimates. On one occasion He says expressly, "I have many things to say unto you, but ye cannot bear them now."

But these three cases will serve to indicate the general rule of His providential teaching;—the hard-hearted people He taught in parables; and these He expounded privately to His disciples, because they had ears to hear. So far, therefore, they were favoured and blessed above the multitude, that He explained things unto them. But from what is said on another occasion, we find that it was far better for them not to need such explanations, but to understand those His parables without[*]. Precisely the same was it in the manifestation of Himself by miracle. It was a singular favour to St. Peter that our Lord vouchsafed to show Himself unto him after the Resurrection, and not to others; and the same may be said of His condescending care of St. Thomas. But greater than either of these was the blessing of St. John, who needed no such manifestation, and without seeing believed. Thus in all things is Christ that good Shepherd, who carrieth the lambs in His bosom, and leadeth those that are with young:—blessed are they who are thus worthy of His support and care; but more blessed are they who need it not; those good sheep who know Him, and whom He knows, who hear His voice and follow Him!

And independently of this mode of speech by figure,

[*] " Aliquibus in signis et figuris dulciter appareo, quibusdam vero in multo lumine revelo mysteria . . . . Distribuens singulis sicut dignum judicavero." Thomas à Kempis, lib. iii. cap. 43.

metaphor, and parable, we find that our Lord was often in the habit of conversing with persons in a way to meet them in their ignorance, without fully disclosing the truth more than it was needful and good for them to know. One interesting instance of this kind might be mentioned: in that case of the Anointing, which is recorded in the seventh chapter of St. Luke[9], and the parable of the two debtors, which our Lord delivered to the Pharisee on that occasion; for in the statement of the two debtors, of whom one owed fifty pence and the other five hundred, when they were both forgiven by their lord, the Pharisee would readily have taken himself to be the debtor who owed but little, and the woman the one who owed much. Thus was he taken according to his own showing, and his own comparative standard of his own merits. But still the fact remained, that she loved much, and he loved but little; but now love is all in all: love is the very standard of all goodness, and all duties are measured by love. This consideration would have taught the Pharisee that he was himself "the sinner" above all; for he owed more especially the unmeasurable debt of love: and therefore if he had supposed that he had but little to be forgiven, it was but on account of the smallness of his love, which led him to think he owed but little. This will serve as one instance to show our Lord's custom, of meeting the thoughts of the heart in those with whom He conversed, and taking them according to their estimate of themselves. In like manner He said, " I am not come to call the righteous, but sinners to repentance," and " the whole need not a physician, but they that are sick." There is something of the same kind in our Lord's conversation with the rich young man, who called Him " good," and thought himself good, having

[9] See "Plain Sermons," Vol. II. Serm. xli.

altogether a low sense of goodness; whereon our Lord spoke almost, if one might say it, as if He were not Himself good, and were not Himself God. In all these cases it was this reserve of speech which would best serve to bring them to the full knowledge of themselves and of God.

SECTION IV

MIRACLES AND ATTESTATIONS OF DIVINE POWER

In strict accordance with these words of our Blessed Lord, and His mode of speech, were His works. They in like manner were withheld and restrained with a very wonderful and mysterious reserve. Thus we find that His miracles were always dealt out in exact proportion to the faith of those, on whom or for whom they were wrought; there was every variety in the degree of power that was exerted. Sometimes the miracle was wrought by a word, and at a distance, as in the case of the Centurion and the Canaanitish woman; sometimes by a word, without any other means taken, as in the case of the leper and the paralytic; sometimes by exacting of the persons some act of obedience as the exercise of their faith, as with the ten lepers who were sent to the Priest, or the blind man at Jerusalem to the pool of Siloam: sometimes by approaching our Lord's Person, as the woman with the issue of blood, and others who touched His garments; sometimes by our Lord's going to a distance, in order to perform the cure, as in the case of Jairus's daughter; sometimes by His taking manual and sensible means, as by His laying His hand on this person, and on Peter's wife's mother, and in the general expression of His laying His hands upon them;

sometimes by apparently difficult and laborious means, as
with the man in St. Mark[1], who had an impediment in
his speech, and the man whose eyes He anointed with
clay[2].   And, as far as we can discern, all these differences
were regulated according to one and the same analogy,—
by the faith of the persons.   " According to thy faith be
it unto thee," seems to have been alike the rule of all.
And this is often expressed by our Lord conferring the
request in the very words of the petition.   As when the
leper says, " If Thou wilt Thou canst make me clean[8];"
our Blessed Lord answers, " I will, be thou clean."   When
the Ruler says, " Come, and lay Thine hand upon her;"
our Lord proceeds for some distance in order to do so, and
then performs the cure by this very action of laying on
His hand; while by the way there takes place another
miracle, by means apparently far less adequate, on the
woman who touched the hem of His garment, and who was
healed immediately by the greater degree of her faith.   To
which may be added, that most touching account of the
father of the demoniac, in St. Mark, who says, " If Thou
art able, have pity on us, and help us; and our Lord's
answer is, " If *thou art able* to believe, he that believeth
is able to do all things."   When the Centurion said,
" Speak the word only, and my servant shall be healed;"
our Lord speaks the word, and his servant is healed.   In
all these narratives we have no request answered in a
manner less indicative of Divine power than was asked,
nor any display of greater power than they required.
All things seem illustrative of that great law of His providence, " Ask, and ye shall receive; seek, and ye shall
find:" which seems to indicate that what is not asked for

[1] Ch. vii. 32.   [2] John ix. 6.
          [8] Matt. Mark, Luke.

shall not be received; that the request made is the limit of power displayed. He will open the door, but requires that we should knock. And, indeed, as if to imply greater readiness on His part, and His gentle approaches to us, He Himself seeks access, and only requires that we should open to Him. "Behold, I stand at the door and knock; if any man hear My voice, and open the door, I will come in to him, and sup with him, and he with Me[4]."

In the very working of His miracles our Lord seems to take mankind, as it were, into league with Him, to combine in ineffable condescension their will with His will, in the works of His goodness. Thus in the miracle of the loaves and fishes, they take part and act together with Him in the performance of it; they in faith make the men to sit down, they distribute the bread in their hands; it is one of them, St. Philip, who is appealed to and taken as it were into council with Him by our Blessed Lord; it is one of them, St. Andrew, who commences as it were the mysterious miracle, by bringing the young lad with the five loaves and two small fishes[5]. In like manner is that healing of the paralytic, who "was carried of four," and "let down through the roof." These men thus appear by faith to become as it were accessaries with Him, and in a manner united with Him in that wonderful work of His goodness. And thus also is it in His Church: in all the operations of His grace He takes mankind into union with Him by faith, and acts by their instrumentality and concurrence, and through and by them, in continuing His Sacramental influences, and the marvellous blessings of His Kingdom. So also was it with all His miracles of healing: the sick, or the friends of the sick, became united with Him, in their desires for Him, and so became par-

---

[4] Rev. iii. 20.   [5] John vi. 8.

takers of His power; by importunity, and as it were by violence, they entered into the Kingdom of His promises, and by faith became the partakers of His treasures. They "came unto Him, having with them the lame, blind, dumb, maimed, and many others, and cast them down at Jesus' feet, and He healed them[6]." "He had healed many, insomuch that they pressed upon Him for to touch Him[7]."

Again, sometimes the cure was wrought with evident pain in our Lord Himself; when that pain appears to have been occasioned by the weakness of faith in the persons requiring it, as in the man with the impediment in his speech, in St. Mark; where, together with such difficult means, it is said that our Lord "looked up to Heaven and groaned," and at the same time that He put away the crowd, who appear to have been Gentiles. In the raising of Jairus's daughter the same Divine care is shown, in allowing no one to be present, but the three disciples whose faith was so pre-eminent, and the father who had the faith to ask for this cure, and had been carefully supported by our Lord, together with the mother. The crowd were all expressly excluded and put out, being evidently unworthy of witnessing such a manifestation of our Lord's inconceivable Godhead; for it is said that "they laughed Him to scorn." And in this respect this miracle was like that of His own Resurrection, not shown openly to all the people, but to certain "witnesses chosen of God," and hid from the sight of the unbelieving multitude. And so likewise in the raising of Lazarus from the grave, our Lord's personal deportment, so to speak, on that occasion, so indicative of distress, appears to proceed from the very fearful nature of such a miracle, to those who should witness it[8]. "Jesus therefore again groaning

6 Matt. xv. 29, 30.   7 Mark iii. 10.   8 John xi. 38.

in Himself cometh to the grave." We naturally watch
for some expression to give us some clue to the cause of
this distress, and in the next verse but one we read,
" Jesus saith unto her (Martha), Said I not unto thee,
that if thou wouldst believe, thou shouldst see the
glory of God ?" Accordingly one cannot but remark,
that the preparation, as it were, for this miracle, was a
gentle leading or drawing on of Martha, the weaker
sister, to this fulness of belief, which was necessary.
First of all, a confession of our Saviour's power is elicited
from her,—great indeed, but inadequate : " I know that
even now, whatsoever Thou wilt ask of God, God will
give it Thee." But our Lord proceeds afterwards to
declare to her His own inherent Divinity : " I am the
Resurrection and the Life." And a full confession is
required : " Believest thou this * ?" To this may be added
the case of the man with the withered hand on the Sabbath-
day in the Synagogue. For this miracle was unavoidably
in the presence of many, who showed themselves quite
unworthy of such a manifestation, when we find that our
Blessed Lord was strongly affected by the circumstance,
when He worked the miracle before them ; for it is said,
He looked about "with anger, being grieved for the hardness of their hearts[1]." And as some miracles were done
with exceeding ease and readiness, although of a portent-
ous magnitude, on account of the greatness of faith, and
others with extreme difficulty and anxiety, for a want of
sufficient faith,—so this difficulty and anxiety increased
into an actual inability, and withdrawal of all help, as at
Nazareth. " And He did not many mighty works there,
because of their unbelief[2];" and, " He could there do no

---

* See " Tracts for the Times," No. 80, p. 18.
[1] Mark iii. 5.   [2] Matt. xiii. 58.

mighty work, save that He laid His hands on a few sick folk, and healed them[3]."

Now all this pain and grief evinced by our Blessed Lord at persons not having faith, reminds us forcibly of the grief which He evinces, when persons do not comprehend His words. It would appear as if they both were in some degree of the same character; implying in one case a want of faith to discern Divine Power, and in the other a want of spiritual comprehension to understand Divine Wisdom. And so likewise our Lord's habit of so carefully removing persons when He wrought His miracles, who were, from weakness of faith, unfit to witness them, is very similar to His disclosing and revealing religious truths to a few, as distinct and apart from the multitude. Thus if He explained His parables expressly in secret to His disciples alone, so did He before them work many miracles. If to them alone He imparted the knowledge of His Divinity, most strictly enjoining them not to divulge that great truth; so to them alone was vouchsafed the miraculous attestation of His Divine presence. They only were witnesses of His solitary prayers; they only saw His miracles at midnight on the sea; they only (and, indeed, four of them only) heard our Lord's discourses on the destruction of Jerusalem and the day of Judgment; and they only saw His miracle on the barren fig-tree which portended it. And thus, I think, we shall find throughout, that slowness of faith and slowness of spiritual discernment appear to be received in the same manner. Thus the Scribe who perceived the beauty of our Lord's precept, when He explained the love of God as the first and great commandment, was highly approved of, and encouraged, almost as if he had done some work

[3] Mark vi. 5.

or made some confession of faith, and declared to be "not far from the Kingdom of Heaven." And when our Blessed Lord began to speak of the high and spiritual nature of the Eucharist, and many in consequence " went backward and walked no more with Him," He turns as if with mournful apprehension to His disciples, and says, "Will ye also go away?" And this very occasion does of itself bear much on this point; for here His hearers left Him because He spake of things mysterious and Divine: and on more occasions than one they were incensed against Him, because He worked some miracle in their presence which they were unfit to discern.

SECTION V

OUR LORD HIMSELF ALLUDING TO THIS LAW OF HIS CONDUCT

Now all this implies that there was very great danger to mankind in our Lord disclosing Himself, either in works or words, before them, unless they were prepared to receive Him worthily, and that their hearts were humbled before Him. And, agreeably to this, we find that the rays of joy and comfort, if we may so speak, which break forth from the troubled spirit of the Son of Man, are from the apprehension of His Divine Power and Godhead by persons untaught and unlearned. His expressions of grief and judgment are, on the contrary, on account of those who had what the world considers light without this humble faith: "If ye were blind," said He to the Jews at Jerusalem, " ye should not have sin: but ye say, We see; therefore your sin remaineth."

Hence it is that the most blessed of all things was to apprehend Divine things without their being seen, or heard, or revealed, from without. This is implied in our Lord's declaration of blessing on St. Peter, because he had of himself come to this knowledge, and it had not been revealed unto him by "flesh and blood;" and hence His high acceptance and admiring love of the Centurion, who saw in Him the power of God; His rejoicing in Spirit and thanksgiving to the Father, because He had "revealed these things unto babes;" His high approbation of the Canaanitish woman. In all these cases the ignorance of the Heathen enhanced the greatness of their faith; and such also were the blessings pronounced on the poor and simple, at the beginning of the Gospel, before He had been yet manifested. It would appear as if where there was, humanly speaking, the greatest degree of ignorance, that He received the persons the most graciously. He was going to a distance in compliance with the request of the Ruler to heal his daughter, taking so much trouble in compassion to the weakness of the rich (and probably learned) man's faith; when a poor superstitious creature (as we might suppose) received an instantaneous cure by merely touching His garment, and was received with most gracious approbation. The ignorant Heathen Pilate, the ignorant Heathen Centurion at the Crucifixion, and the (as we may well imagine) unenlightened thief on the Cross, could come in their various degrees to a sense of His Divine majesty, which the chief Priests and Scribes, most learned in the Law, could not.

And opposed to these blessings declared to the ignorant and poor, observe the "woes" so awfully pronounced in the Temple at last on those who had seen and heard so much. Observe too all the previous instances of our

Blessed Lord's conversations with the great and learned among them, who appear to have been highly instructed in the Law. Where He was the more revealed, there was there the more woe. Our Lord expressly declares that not the aggravation only, but the very reason of their sin, was on account of those works He had wrought, and the words He had spoken before them. "If I had not come and spoken unto them, they had not had sin." "If I had not done among them the works that no other man did, they had not had sin!" It was the very cause, our Blessed Lord declared, why Capernaum and Chorazin and Bethsaida were so bad that it would be more tolerable for Sodom and for Tyre and Sidon on the day of Judgment; for if the mighty works which have been done in them, had been done in Sodom, or in Tyre and Sidon, they would have repented long ago in sackcloth and ashes. And not only in the personal manifestation of our Lord Himself, but in the manifestation of His Kingdom by the Apostles also, would the like danger ensue. "Into whatsoever city ye enter, and they receive you not, shake off the dust from off your feet as a testimony against them; for I tell you that it shall be more tolerable for Sodom and Gomorrah in the day of Judgment than for that city." And above all things it may be especially observed, that it was to the Pharisees, and on their witnessing what appears to have been the highest of all His miracles,—that of casting out the demoniac,—that our Lord gave that the most solemn and fearful of all His warnings, of the sin against the Holy Ghost, on the very edge of which they now were; which hath no forgivness in the present world, nor in that which is to come. And certainly since their rejection of the Holy Spirit on the day of Pentecost, they have had no forgiveness in the present time, as their impenitence proves unto this day.

So thoroughly is it the case throughout the whole of this awful dispensation of Christianity, that however "knowledge" may "cover the world as the waters cover the sea," yet that "the wicked shall do wickedly, and none of the wicked shall understand[4];" and as the Prophet Hosea, "who is wise, and he shall understand these things,"—"but the transgressors shall fall therein[5]." And as St. John, "he that is unjust, let him be unjust still; and he which is filthy, let him be filthy still." That nothing shall be done, even in this last dispensation of God's gracious mercy, to do away with the determined propensities of the wicked.

And not only do these persons incur the charge of greater guilt, as rejecting greater light and knowledge in the sight of God, but by some very wonderful and mysterious law, they seem to have been actually rendered worse by the manifestation of Divine things, which they were incapable of receiving: which principle seems to be contained in that remarkable precept of our Lord, "give not that which is holy to the dogs, neither cast your pearls before swine;" for the consequence of this is not merely not doing them good, but it becomes evil to themselves and others; "lest they trample them under foot, and turn again and rend you." For beforehand there would have appeared no reason, why they should "turn again, and rend" those that cast precious things before them. And perhaps there is no instance on record of our Blessed Lord revealing Himself to the unworthy without ill consequences, and those persons being rendered apparently worse. Thus of the paralytic in the synagogue we read,

---

[4] Dan. xii. 10. [5] Hosea xiv. 9.

—what must appear to us in the highest degree astonishing,—"and he stretched forth his hand, and it was rendered whole as the other. But the Pharisees went out and took council against Him, to put Him to death." So also after the miracle among the Gadarenes it is said, that they besought Him to depart out of their coasts. And of the two miracles of casting out the demoniac, on both occasions our Lord required them to be kept secret[*]; but when these, apparently the most arduous of miracles, did come to the knowledge of the Pharisees, they then brought the dreadful charge of His casting out devils by the prince of the devils. And it may be observed, that the last year of our Lord's ministry, when His Divine works necessarily became more known, the Pharisees in a more fierce and determined manner seem pursuing Him from place to place, and thirsting for His blood. And more remarkable than all, the most astounding and public of all His miracles, the raising of Lazarus from the grave, appears to have been performed when the hope of their repentance seems almost to have ceased, when the things which should have been for their peace were become hidden from their eyes, and all things were hastening to the great consummation. So wonderful is this mystery of iniquity, whereby the things which should have been for their wealth were unto them the occasion of falling, that the greatest manifestation of love and mercy, accompanied with power to deliver from the greatest of all known evils, even from death, had but the effect of kindling in them the greatest malice and hatred. For this miracle itself became a subject of exasperation to them, wonderful as it seems. "But some of them went their way to the Pharisees, and told them what things Jesus had done.

[*] Matt. ix. 34; xii. 24.

K

Then gathered the Chief Priests and the Pharisees a council, and said, What do we? for this man doeth many miracles[7];" and this council was to put Him to death. To this may be added that which is, almost if not altogether, the only open and full declaration of our Lord's Divinity; which was by constraint, and forced upon Him by the adjuration of the High Priest, to which He was bound by the Law to answer, when He makes a full declaration that He was "the Son of God," "the Son of the Blessed." And that very confession was not only the immediate cause of His own ill-treatment and death, but the utter overthrow of all the Jewish Priesthood, as was mysteriously signified by the High Priest rending his clothes.

Now all this would seem to indicate that the knowledge of God, without suitable reverence and faith to receive that knowledge, makes mankind to approach to the state of lost spirits; as if, when the Blessed God puts us away far from Him, and comes to look upon us as with human eyes of compassion, under the veils of our humanity, it were with the hope that we may recover ourselves before He is revealed to us. In furtherance of this opinion, it appears, that as our Lord so carefully concealed the knowledge of His inconceivable greatness from mankind, so the confession of it is made by evil spirits, and that repeatedly, and in such a manner as requires all our Lord's authority over them to prevent their publication of it,—the publication of that truth which He had come on earth to reveal, and on the knowledge of which the Salvation of mankind depended. This is very wonderful, both as indicating that the knowledge of God, without the love of Him, is the property of evil spirits, and makes men to approach

[7] John xi. 47.

to their nature; and secondly as showing us the evil
spirits themselves desirous to disclose to mankind the Son
of God; and the most gracious Author of all good labouring to conceal and suppress it, and pained even to anguish
of soul at the necessity of revealing it before unprepared
hearts. Certainly the fact is very remarkable, especially
when we consider the known craft and subtlety of evil
spirits, that they were desirous to declare the ineffable
greatness of Christ to mankind; our Blessed Lord, to withdraw and forbear the full disclosure of it! And let us
connect these astonishing facts with our Lord's declarations, such as these, "If I had not come and spoken unto
them, they had not had sin;" and "If I had not done
among them the works which none other man did, they
had not had sin*."

Moreover it may be observed that our Lord's conduct
on the occasions we have spoken of, is often alluded to, by
St. Chrysostom and others, as an example to us of humility.
And thus it is that this reserve in concealing His greatness, whereby these great and Divine laws of His providence were carried out, does also co-operate to produce
another effect, and serve to render our Lord the peculiar
pattern of all meekness and forbearance to His creatures.
For thus is He ever doing good, but always, as it were,
desirous to conceal it; hiding His ineffable majesty and
greatness in the meanest human condition and actions;
ever meekly retiring from opposition and controversy, and
the pattern of inexpressible patience; forced by circumstances to confess Himself, and dying for that confession.
And thus the taking on Him the form of a servant, and
submitting to the death of a slave, becomes to us the
example of His humility; while in another point of view

* John xv. 22. 24.

K 2

it was, in our Blessed Lord, but one part of the mysterious concealment of His Godhead.   The humiliations of the Cross are a part of the Divine economy, whereby His God-head is withdrawn from view, but when those His humilia-tions become to us our example, they bring us to the secret knowledge of His Divinity; for it is by imitation of His humility, and a resemblance to His Cross, that mankind are brought near to the knowledge of Him.   Thus we find that, in the Gospel narrative, the highest acknowledgment of His Godhead is ever accompanied with the greatest humility.   In every instance of faith in His Divine power which is recorded, the expression and indications of humility are in exact proportion to the greatness of the faith; as in the Centurion, in the Canaanitish woman, in the leper who returned thanks, falling at His feet, and in the woman who touched the hem of His garment.   And the taking up the Cross, and following Christ, seems to have been the mode of arriving at the apprehension of the Godhead: thus the disciples seem to have attained to that great truth, on which the Church is built, and against which the gates of Hell shall not prevail.   It was by first of all renouncing all that they had, and following their Master from place to place in privation and hardship, while they witnessed His words and works, that thus after about three years they came to the knowledge of His Godhead, the very Rock of the faith.   And then this knowledge is not to be proclaimed aloud, but to be care-fully concealed ; while our Lord's mode of bringing others to that the living knowledge of Himself, is by calling *all men* to Him, and teaching them publicly to take up the Cross.   For thus when St. Peter's confession of our Lord's Godhead is made, it is followed by an earnest injunction not to disclose it, and the multitude are called together

and freely told to take up the Cross, as if that narrow
and straitened door had been the only entrance to the
Kingdom.

Now the rule which our Lord has given us, for the
discernment of false Prophets, is that by their fruits we
shall know them. We may well suppose, therefore, that
this rule, or something analogous to this rule, is that
which He hath laid down for us to bring us to the knowledge of Himself. Thus we find that He appeals continually to His works; and we may suppose that in so
doing, His appeal was not only to the power displayed in
them, but also to the Divine goodness. It was the power
of discerning this Divine goodness that the Pharisees
wanted; for they were not themselves merciful, and
therefore they could not discern the love of God, either
in the words of Holy Scripture, or in the works of Jesus
Christ. They felt no interest on the subject, their hearts
being occupied by very different matters; otherwise their
attention would have been arrested, their hearts would
have been opened, by His works; they would have known
Him to be powerful and merciful, and from thence, by
degrees, to be all-powerful, and all-merciful, infinite in
goodness and might, and therefore God. It was, in
discerning Him, as it would be in discerning His servants.
He that, on watching His works and words, received
Him as a righteous man, should receive a righteous man's
reward. He that received Him as a Prophet, should
receive a Prophet's reward, and thence should be led on
to the highest faith in His Godhead: and then held up
by the sense of His Divinity, buoyed up by that which
is infinite, as by an elastic power and breath of Heaven
within him, he shall rise above the world.

And, indeed, nothing can more fully explain the whole

law of our Blessed Lord's dealings, in all manifestations
of Himself to His sinful creatures, than what He Himself
pointed out to the Jews, when He was so visibly grieved
at the adulterous heart which was shown by the asking
for a sign ; He told them that they ought to have known
the signs of the times, i. e. the signs of His coming, in the
same manner that they became acquainted with the signs
of the weather.   And this is in fact precisely analogous
to the mode in which we become acquainted with religious
truth and doctrine, some more and some less.   For those
persons are capable of discerning and forming a judgment
of the weather, whose mode of life or occupation renders
it an object of interest to them to know ; they naturally
observe such indications, and from the recurrence of them,
or of similar signs, they obtain this knowledge.   In like
manner a faithful and loyal heart feels an interest and
desire to know the truths of God : and thus from its own
experience within, and from actions witnessed and words
spoken by holy men, it obtains an ever-accumulating
weight of unconscious evidence, which as the thoughts
are never at rest, when once it obtains an impulse, ever
continues to increase.   Thus the hearts of earnest men
are led on by God Himself to the knowledge of holy
words and the works of holy men, and at length by
observing His own words and works to the knowledge of
Himself.

Nay, further, the very nature of the kingdom itself did
require this spiritual discernment, this having eyes to see,
and ears to hear, and a heart to understand.   For this
reason, while our Lord was being manifested among them,
yet the Jews were far from His Kingdom ; for as He
repeatedly declared from the Prophets, God had blinded
their eyes, and made their ears dull of hearing, and hearts

incapable of understanding. On the contrary, when speaking of this moral discernment, to which the Kingdom was given, He said to His disciples privately, "But blessed are the eyes which see the things which ye see; for I say unto you that many Prophets and Kings have desired to see the things which ye see, and have not seen them." Therefore it is evident that the glowing description of the Kingdom in the Prophets was fulfilled, not in external change of condition, but in spiritual discernment, which could realize it, while hid from others. And indeed this our Lord Himself declared, that the Kingdom "cometh not with observation," but that "the Kingdom of God is within you;" it was within them as it consisted in righteousness, and peace, and joy in the Holy Ghost, in internal habits and qualities of the mind, and moral vision to apprehend. Thus our Lord said to the Scribe who was able to discern the spiritual nature of the legal commandments, in that they contained the love of God and one's neighbour, that he was "not far from the Kingdom." And what, in fact, is it to enter into the Kingdom but to come to that "life which is hid with Christ," the "knowledge of Christ crucified," "the treasures of darkness," the secret things of God? For on considering this mode in which our Lord concealed and disclosed Himself, we may, with a little attention, observe, that although He was thus ever withdrawing Himself from the carnal view, yet all our Lord's words and actions were replete with His Divinity, and with that Atonement which He wrought for us on the Cross, by which we are brought near to His ineffable Godhead. Thus we may observe, for instance, that all the Sermon on the Mount flows from the Atonement, insisting on poorness of spirit and forgiveness of injuries as the great qualifications for

the Kingdom. Throughout the whole of it, His secret
and awful Godhead, so carefully concealed, is yet apparent
to the watchful eye of faith ; for this is the point which
astonished all His hearers, that He spake with authority,
annulling or fulfilling by His power the Law of Moses,
speaking throughout as the sole independent Lawgiver
and Judge of all mankind, and as being One with the
Father. And this is very remarkable, that although His
manner was so meek and lowly, that the multitude
thronged and pressed on His sacred person, and the
Pharisees despised it, yet when He spake, this authority,
and as it were secret emanation of His Godhead, astonished
them equally as much as His miracles. Not but that also
the same latent Divinity and power of atoning for sin
were discernible in His miracles also. As when He took
on Himself the uncleanness and sins of the leper by
touching him, thus making Himself to bear our sins.
When in working all miracles He required persons to be
united to Him, and made one with Him by faith, and
thereby to partake of His atoning power ; and when, on
several occasions, He forgave sins, on His healing the
bodily malady, taking on Himself the expiation of those
sins which caused the bodily sicknesses, and pronouncing
by His own authoritative power that forgiveness of sins,
which no one but God alone could do.

So also in our Lord's extreme humiliation on the
Cross, to a devout faith His Divinity throughout is manifest, encircling the Cross itself with the rays of His
unutterable glory, as shown by the fulfilment of prophecy in every action then recorded or word uttered.
Every thing seems to sound of the unfathomable depths
of the Divine counsels. It is in fact deep calling unto
deep; while the waterfloods run over Him. And thus

in the contemplation of our Blessed Lord's humanity we are hid as it were in the hollow of the Rock, and are there sheltered by His hand, until our God in His dreadful majesty shall have passed by.

It did not therefore imply change of place, or circumstances, alone to be in or near the Kingdom, but this power of discerning the spirit in the letter. For every form of life, whether animal, intellectual, or moral and spiritual, depends on an adaptation of the inner frame to the outer world. Therefore it was that "the Kingdom" was not forced upon them, but they forced themselves into it: "the violent take it by force." And when our Lord spoke of actual impediment, that prevented the Pharisees from discerning Him, it was because of their " receiving honour one of another," instead of seeking for that "honour which cometh from God only," and therefore being incapable of perceiving Him. It would appear, therefore, not to have been our Lord's object to impart knowledge, but together with it an affection for that knowledge, in faith that could embrace and realize it. This was the cause, therefore, of His exceeding forbearance and gentleness in disclosing to them His unspeakable majesty : and this appears to have been the reason why He taught them in a manner which He Himself explains as the peculiarity of His own mode of teaching, in those parables of His not putting the new wine into old bottles : thus training them gradually and gently, and with extreme tenderness holding back in forbearance the fuller knowledge of Himself, Who is a consuming fire. The manifestation of Himself before the wicked was in judgment ; His retiring from them was in mercy. And thus it is, that when the Pharisees were incensed against Him, on account of a miracle He had per-

formed, He retired from them, and enjoined those whom
He healed not to make Him known ; and in doing this,
St. Matthew says that He was fulfilling the Prophet
Isaiah's account of His compassions : " Behold, My Child
whom I have chosen ; . . . . He shall not strive nor cry,
nor shall any one hear His voice in the streets.   A bruised
reed shall He not break, nor quench the smoking flax,
until He shall send forth judgment unto victory."

With regard to the personal manifestation of Himself,
He had said, " Blessed are they who have not seen, and
yet have believed ;" evidently implying, that, gracious and
merciful as was the manifestation of His visible presence
to the good, yet it was more blessed, to be so pure
in heart as to be able to discern God without such manifestation.   In like manner He had said to St. Peter that
he was on that account blessed, because flesh and blood
had not revealed unto him the Godhead of his Lord ; but
he had been brought to the knowledge of it by God the
Father Himself, Who ever blesses faith and obedience,
more and more, with the knowledge of Christ.   And it
seems to be on this principle that He welcomes with
delight and approbation every appearance of men embracing the love of Him, when " they to whom He was not
spoken of " perceive Him, " and they that have not heard
understand [9]."   It is with claim and pretension that the
false Christs will come, saying, " I am Christ," and " I am
Christ ;" and Antichrist himself will sit as with dignity
in the temple, and give out that he is God.   But not so
the meek Saviour Himself : He does not proclaim Himself,
neither shall any voice in the streets cry out, Here is
Christ ; but they that are of God will know Him : for the
Father Who is in Heaven will reveal Him unto them,

[9] Rom. xv. 21.

and His own sheep will know His voice and will follow Him. As He knoweth those that are His, so they that are His will know Him. Thus gently and softly in spirit does He walk before them, to ascertain whether there is that within them which can know and follow Him. As He now seems to walk by us in His Providences, trying our dim eyes and weak hands whether we have that Divine moving within us, that will lead us to behold and apprehend Him. So watchfully does He seem to wait for any approaches on the part of mankind, meaning to pass by them and leave them in darkness, unless they call to Him for help : as at midnight on the sea, when He would have passed by them, and they beheld Him in consternation walk on the deep ; but when they cried out to Him, then immediately was He talking with them, and supporting them by His presence and Godhead ; and He allowed Peter on another occasion to sink, until he cried out to Him, and then He supported him with His hand. And with the disciples going to Emmaus, He led them more and more to the knowledge of the Scriptures, so that their heart burned within them by the way. And then He was as if He would have gone further, and would have left them without the disclosure of Himself ; but when they constrained Him, then He went in and disclosed Himself unto them. Beautiful, indeed, and interesting, and full of awful and sublime thoughts, is this mysterious economy of God ; and the mode in which the actions of our Blessed Lord in the flesh harmonize with all His Spiritual dealings with us : preventing with gracious influence and co-operating with the efforts of men, but never superseding them, or acting independently of them. As if in the Redemption of mankind there was some especial need of their own consent and love. For it might be said of all the gifts of God, if they are good and beneficial to us, what need of our requests in prayer for the attainment of them ? but yet it seems a mysterious law of God that we should not receive them without. His hand is not shortened ; there is no limit to His power. But as man hath put forth his hand to evil, in taking of the forbidden tree ; and as ever since that time there is no spiritual evil which he is subject to, but he must put forth his hand, and take it to him, by his own connivance and consent, in order that he may be subject to the influence of it ;—so also is it with all good : he must put forth his hand and take it to him, he must lift up his voice for aid, or Christ will have passed by and will have left him,—perhaps never again to return.

SECTION VI

THE GREAT MANIFESTATION

IT would almost seem, if one might venture to say it, as if the disclosure of our Blessed Lord's Divinity was a part of the day of Judgment,—of His second coming ; and that although to those that are prepared for it, and are brought to the knowledge of it by faith, this is inconceivable blessedness, and indeed no less than eternal life, and that coming of the Kingdom for which as Christians we pray daily ;—yet to all others, that this manifestation of Himself in Godhead and Manhood is destruction.

It would seem as if the whole of our state of probation here was but a preparation for us, in order that we may be able to bear that last manifestation of God ; and that in the mean time, as to him "who knoweth and doeth

not, to him it is sin," therefore all possible pains and forbearance are used on the part of Almighty God, in order
to prevent the understanding from forestalling the will in
the knowledge of Divine truth. For of course, if such
knowledge of good, when not acted upon, of itself becomes
sin, it sets us the farther off from the Kingdom of God,
and therefore is actually of itself injurious. For the
knowledge of God can never be merely inefficient ; for the
Word of God, which hath gone forth, will accomplish that
for which it is intended and sent forth. To know God and
not to love Him, is sin ; and sin sets us afar from Him :
and therefore such knowledge sets us afar from Him, and
is in mercy withheld. Thus, as on the day of Judgment
the knowledge of God will be for life and for death, so is
this marked on every previous visitation of God, which
serves to typify that event. The cloudy pillar and the
fire in the wilderness is salvation to the Israelites, but destruction to the Egyptians ; the ark is full of judgments
to the Philistines, and to them that revered it not ; full of
grace to the Israelites, and to them who cherished it.
The Birth of Christ and the Death of Christ become salvation to the good, so far as the Cross is manifested ; and
destruction to the bad. The Cross was " set for the
falling and rising again of many." The preaching of the
Gospel " in every place is a savour of life, and also unto
death."

Now it is to be observed, that all nature and all the
course of time and Providence are replete with indications,
and types, and figures of the day of Judgment. All sudden
judgments, the coming in of every new order of things,
all new moons and new years, and calling of assemblies,
are as it were like movements, such as may be heard, of
the Heavenly armies advancing onward with the Great

Day ; like trumpet-sounds which prefigure the great trump of God. So also may all these circumstances alluded to be as gleams, or shadows, or forerunners, and parts of the day of Judgment. And therefore it is that from mercy and forbearance our Lord delays the great manifestation of Himself, doing in the mean time all that can be done to draw men unto Him with gentleness and long-suffering.

It is consequently the case, according to this great law of His Providence, that in every thing that relates to His manhood, His humiliation, and His sufferings, our Lord is most revealed to men ; but not in His Power, or His Glory. Throughout His Crucifixion He is a gazing-stock to all; but in His resurrection revealed only to few, and to a still smaller number at His Ascension, and to yet fewer in the manifestation of His Glory at the Transfiguration.

And it is to be observed, that those very circumstances which most endear the good unto their Lord, and draw them unto Him with the bands of a man, are the great stumbling-blocks to the wicked. As for instance, His taking upon Him our flesh, His infancy, His sorrows, and His humiliations. In this mysterious combination of light and obscurity that marks every revelation of God, the good are led over and won by those very things which blind and offend the others. In short, it would, I think, appear, as if every manifestation of our Lord, in this our period of probation, was but by anticipation of that great and last manifestation of Himself on the day of Judgment, and did therefore in some respect partake of those laws; and that, as He puts off the day of Judgment from His being " long-suffering to us-ward, not willing that any should perish, but that all should come to repentance [1]; " so did He on earth, and so does He now, in His Spiritual dealings with us, withhold the revelation of Himself, that He might " not break the bruised reed, nor quench the smoking flax." That when He has forborne to the utmost, and " the things that belong unto their peace " are, for their impenitence, "hidden from their eyes;" then does He draw near unto men, and reveal Himself, with blessings unspeakable to the good, but unspeakable confusion to the bad. Thus was it when our Lord drew near to them publicly, in His Holy City, at the close of His ministry, and taught them in the Temple at the last, more openly and fully than He had yet done. It was in judgment that He drew near, and "as a swift witness." And as this manifestation of Himself was so destructive to the wicked, it is wonderful with what care our Blessed Lord prepared the good to bear the disclosure. On this point one cannot but notice very much our Lord's treatment of His disciples, and with what exceeding forbearance He led them on, and trained them, by little and little, to the fuller revelation of His incomprehensible Godhead; and this He did up to the time of St. Peter's memorable Confession, and then pronounced him blessed, because it had not been revealed unto him by flesh and blood, but by the secret operation of the Father in his soul, by that good Spirit Who dwells with the contrite, Who discloses mysteries unto the meek, and reveals the kingdom unto babes. And it was exactly on that day week after the confession of St. Peter, by some mysterious, and no doubt important, connexion of the days, that some of them were permitted to behold His glory :— " the glory," as St. John says, " of the only-begotten of the Father, full of grace and truth; " and, as St. Peter

[1] 2 Peter iii. 9.

says, to be "eye-witnesses of His majesty [2]." And it is evident throughout the whole of the circumstances, that the Transfiguration and the disclosure of our Lord's hidden glory in His visible Person, has some typical connexion with His manifestation as Son of Man on the day of Judgment, and with the regeneration of our own bodies in Him. And it was apparently with reference to that event that our Lord said just previously, that some of them "should not taste of death until they should see the Son of Man coming in His Kingdom." For, in fact, those three, alone of all mankind, have seen that His inconceivable glory without having tasted of death. In which beatific and gracious sight Moses also, and Elias, were combined with them; they who, as types of Himself, had fasted for forty days, being supernaturally sustained of God, and of whom the one was translated, and the other was not found in death. Thus were these disciples led to the gradual knowledge of our Lord's Divinity, and then was that knowledge connected with the beholding Him in glory. And then earnestly did He impress on them the charge of concealing from others this knowledge of Him. So awful, and yet so gracious,— so terrible, and yet so blessed, was it to behold Him ; to behold Him, and yet to find that they were alive. And thus we read that they "were exceedingly afraid," and yet at the same time they could say, " It is good to be here." It was indeed to rejoice with trembling,— which is the best state of holiness here. And how do the very words bring before us the day of Judgment, "and they were weighed down with sleep, and when they woke they saw His glory, and two men standing

---

[2] 2 Peter i. 16.

with Him." The word that He had spoken, the Law and the Prophets—Moses and Elias are with Him.

There is indeed a sort of instinctive feeling in mankind, that the Most Holy God is a "consuming fire" to the unholy and those who are unprepared for His Presence; that no man can "see God and live." "We shall surely die, because we have seen God[3]," was the natural exclamation of Manoah; and his fear was only appeased by his wife's pious hope of God's graciousness towards them, in that He had received an offering at their hands. And the Patriarch observed, as with delightful surprise and astonishment, that he had "seen God face to face," and "*his life was preserved*" notwithstanding. It seems the same natural feeling in St. Peter, when, on the manifestation of our Lord's power, he fell down at His feet, entreating Him to depart from him; and such, perhaps, also, that of the Gadarenes, when "they were taken with great fear," and requested our Lord to depart from their coasts.

It may farther be observed, that on that remarkable occasion, when the impenitent Jews asked for a sign from Heaven, our Lord "groaned deeply" at the question, and, as St. Matthew twice records it, He said they should receive a sign, and that was the sign of the Prophet Jonah. And yet, according to St. Mark, He declared that no sign should be given them. Both which together must be capable of some interpretation. "He groaned deeply;" for the asking a sign was a proof of that adulterous or disloyal heart which would be their ruin. And because there should be a dreadful sign which this their unbelief would bring about in His death, when He, like Jonas, should be three days hid from sight, and then

[3] Judges xiii. 22.

L

should come forth again, like Jonas to the Ninevites, and His Spirit should preach to them,—not for forty days only, as Jonas to the Ninevites, but according to the gracious aboundings of the mercies of the Gospel for forty years. But He should not, like Jonas, bring their city to repentance; for the Holy Ghost should be given, and the Holy Ghost should be rejected, for which there is no forgiveness in the present time, nor in that which is to come; and therefore it should be worse for them than for the men of Nineveh[4]." So far, therefore, as St. Matthew says, should a sign be given them; and yet, as St. Mark says, no sign should be given unto them; for the Resurrection itself was hidden from them, and no sign to them, but to the good only. For, as Abraham himself had said of them, if they believe not Moses nor the Prophets, neither would they be persuaded though one rose from the dead. But another thought might have been in our Blessed Lord's mind, when He sighed so deeply, and spoke of the sign: perhaps He thought of the day of Judgment, when they shall have " the sign of the Son of Man in Heaven," and " look on Him whom they pierced." That was indeed the " sign from Heaven " for which they asked, as that which alone would satisfy them, and which they should indeed at length receive.

As the thoughts of His second coming seem so often blended and combined with the more immediate meaning of our gracious Lord's words, it was the thought of this, perhaps, that rendered Him so deeply sorrowful; when persons were not content to come to the knowledge of Him without such manifestation; and which rendered Him so inconceivably tender and forbearing in the disclosure of Himself, lest they should have light without life or love,

[4] Matt. xii. 41.

which is the state of lost spirits. But to be brought unto God the Father in faith, is indeed light, and life, and love; and is to be translated from the kingdom of Satan into that of His dear Son.

We must of course speak with caution, when we allude to any thing so infinitely beyond the reach of our faculties. But however this may be,—whether all these dispensations of God, and these laws in the disclosure of Himself, are but a part of the great system of His Revelations, and partake of the nature of the final manifestation of Himself, to which they are preparatory; yet of the fact itself there can remain no doubt, that there is something of the reserve we have spoken of, which very remarkably pervades the history of our Lord's dealings in the flesh. And now there is no truth which appears so important towards the right understanding of the Gospels as this,— of the manner of our Blessed Lord's disclosures of Himself; not only as it affords us a clue to a great deal of His conduct and teaching, but because it indicates this principle;—that we can never understand the Gospels themselves, but by taking those means which they did who were there mentioned as coming to the knowledge of our Lord—by relinquishing earthly affection, by watchfulness and prayer; as no one can approach the Son, excepting God the Father draw him. And immediately arising out of this principle, and closely connected with it, is another subject, which we must next discuss, viz., our Lord's own method of interpreting Holy Scripture.

PART III

The Rule of Scriptural Interpretation furnished by Our Lord

SECTION I

NOT LITERAL, BUT SPIRITUAL

THE mode of explaining the Gospels, adopted in the commentaries which it is intended to pursue, may appear to some not to adhere sufficiently to the first literal sense, but to require too much to be granted by faith; and I now proceed to show that something of this kind is the only right method of explaining the Scriptures, as being that mode which is furnished by our Lord Himself.

We have observed that our Lord often spoke in such a manner as not to be clearly understood, and that He often seemed so to speak designedly; and that to understand the meaning of His words depended on the moral character of the hearer, not on the intellect. So much was this the case, that He appeared to have been better understood upon the whole by the illiterate, and by those whom He termed "babes;" and the least of all by the Scribes, and those learned in the Scriptures, whom He termed "the wise and prudent." It is natural to suppose, therefore, that when He speaks to us in the Scriptures, by Prophets and Evangelists, He speaks to us in like manner, and is to be understood in like manner, as when He spake in the flesh. And this is confirmed by Himself in His use and application of the Scriptures.

For as our Lord did Himself often bring forward and explain the Scriptures, so we shall find in His own use of them the best rule of Scriptural interpretation. When speaking to the Scribes and Pharisees, He almost invariably appeals to the Scriptures; it is His peculiar mode of teaching them; and it may be observed, that in bringing forward the Scriptures, He interprets them in a different manner to what they do. They seem to have been themselves extremely well versed in the Scriptures, and to have been keen and correct in the interpretation of them, as far as the letter, and according to the natural reason (as may be shown hereafter), while they entirely failed in the right and spiritual understanding of them; and it will appear that our Lord did explain them after quite another mode of interpretation.

It is remarkable what a show of reason and knowledge the Scribes and Pharisees displayed in their application of Scripture, so as to have raised insuperable difficulties in the minds of humble believers. But it is evident, that in all these cases, good men came by degrees to understand the Scriptures rightly, and in the mean time to believe rightly, in spite of difficulties; while others were blinded, even as it may seem with reason and Scripture on their side. And this leads us to look with especial interest to our Lord's own mode of expounding the Scriptures. For it is very clear, that unless we have that faith which is of God, we may be deceived and entangled, not only by external circumstances, but even by the letter of Scripture itself, taking precepts and figures and prophecies, not according to the spirit, as unfolded to faith and obedience, but according to the false light of the natural reason.

Now there appear to be two modes of interpreting and understanding the Sacred Writings. Some persons with a scrupulous and religious jealousy would contend, that we should consider nothing as binding on the conscience, unless it can be supported by express warranty in the very words of Holy Scripture; or would perhaps allow as a great matter, that this acceptance and belief should be extended to deductions, legitimately and logically drawn from the sacred text. While others would consider that the whole of Scripture admits of higher and spiritual interpretations, whereby "mysteries are revealed unto the meek," who are led on by faith into all the treasures which are hid in Christ.

Now this latter we shall find sanctioned, I think, not only by the Church Catholic of all ages, and the practice of Fathers, and Apostles, and Evangelists, but even by the Divine authority of our Lord Himself. In all the instances in which He cites passages from the Old Testament, they are such as do not prove the point in question, in a manner to satisfy a rationalistic, curious, and captious inquirer. If we may venture so to speak of His Divine and awful sayings, the inferences to be granted cannot be logically deduced from the words referred to; they are rather appeals to the faith of the hearer than to his reason; arguments addressed to the heart more than to the head; being the tests of his own life and conscience, rather than submitting themselves in deference to his understanding; searchers and discerners of him, rather than to be searched and discerned by him.

It is not only to the Scribes and Pharisees that our

Lord appeals to the Scriptures; His language to all is, "Search the Scriptures; for in them ye think ye have eternal life, and they are they which testify of Me." Yet He no where implies, that unassisted reason was of itself sufficient to understand them: on the contrary, we find that even disciples could not, until Christ "expounded to them in all the Scriptures the things concerning Himself;" nor could the Apostles, until He "opened their minds that they should understand the Scriptures:" which very expressions would imply, that our Lord's proofs from the Old Testament were not of such a nature as to be palpably obvious to the intellect. And it seems reasonable to expect, in accordance with this, that He Himself (whether as infallibly residing in His Church, or as enlightening the individual conscience,) may furnish us with a key to unlock therein the things concerning Himself, which we should not otherwise arrive at. As when He sent the blind man to the pool of Siloam, He had Himself first anointed his eyes; in like manner, though He sends us to the Scriptures, He still requires a preparation of heart which is of God before we can perceive. "How can I understand except some man should guide me[1]?" is the exclamation of the natural man, although the words of Holy Scripture may be in his hands. And this natural exclamation was made in a case so approved of, that it was thought worthy of an especial mission of God's favour. And we find our Blessed Lord's disciples were reproved by Him for not perceiving the force of the Scriptures, in the same way as they were for not understanding His own words; not as implying in them slowness of reason, but of faith: "O simple ones, and slow of heart to believe all that the Prophets have

[1] Acts viii. 31.

spoken!" are our Lord's words to His two disciples who were going to Emmaus. Add to which, that as Divine knowledge is always spoken of, so emphatically, as the especial gift of God alone, and it is said that, "no man can come to Christ excepting the Father, which hath sent Him, draw him," this would lead us to suppose it probable that so great an avenue or access to knowledge as that of the Holy Scriptures, and so important a means of being brought to Christ, would depend for its interpretation on something of a higher nature than the mere reason; something more particularly to be considered of a Divine nature.

It is necessary to allude to this rule of Divine teaching, before we come to the particular instances to be referred to, that it may not appear a matter of offence to any one, or an ungracious task, as if we were derogating in some degree from the sanctity and certainty of our Lord's references, as not being satisfactory to the natural reason; whereas the effect of the argument will be found to be of a very different nature; as implying that in no way can we approach unto God, or understand His words, without purified affection illuminating and exalting the human intellect. The fact that our Lord's appeals to Scripture do not square with, or correspond to, the demands of a carnal mind, no more derogates from them, than it does from His Divine and mysterious majesty, as manifested in the humiliations of Christ Crucified, that it does not correspond with our natural ideas of greatness. In both instances it may be the case, that in the eyes of that "Wisdom which is from above," the apparent human weakness is Divine strength; for as the power and holiness and greatness of God are most seen in external circumstances of human degradation, so the wisdom of

God will be most seen in words which infinitely transcend the feeble demands of frail reason. All, therefore, that it is first necessary to allude to is the fact, that it is perfectly analogous with all the dealings of God's moral providence, both natural and revealed, that He should thus disclose to us Divine truths, concealing His wisdom in what may appear foolishness to the natural man. That the very inadequacy of the proof, humanly speaking, may be best calculated to attain those high ends for which it is Divinely intended. That the Holy Word of God, like the works of nature, and the dealings of a particular Providence, is as a sealed book to mankind till opened by faith, but to faith discloses all the treasures of the heavenly Kingdom.

At the same time it is not to be supposed that we derogate from the strict letter of Scripture, or allow of vague and fanciful interpretation ; for we of course maintain the Divine authority of Scripture even down to the very word and letter of it, as deeply and closely true, and full of Divine significations ; but that these are revealed rather to faith than to speculative reason. In short, that we must not do as men among us too often have done, when, for the sake of contending with unbelievers, they enter upon their ground, as if we could argue from reason only, giving up the armour in which alone we can trust, and forgetting that we ourselves stand only by faith. It is not that such evidence from Holy Scripture is against reason, or independent of reason, but that it requires faith together with reason to explain, and enter into the Divine fulness of its meaning. Faith is the essential and primary requisite, without which reason is quite unavailing, and unable to proceed one step. But with this accompaniment, so far from confining or limiting the powers of reason, we open to it the only scope and range through which it may freely expatiate, as leading through the infinity of boundless nature to the footstool of God.

Or it might be said, do you not leave each person to be the interpreter of Scripture according to the fancied secret sense of the Spirit? for if any one says he is led by the Spirit to attach such a meaning to the words of Holy Scripture, which is beyond the natural reason, you leave no appeal beyond the private interpretation of each. But this is not so; for we know that great essential truth is supported by adequate authority; that no truth which proceeds from the Spirit can be at variance with the Church, in which the Spirit resides, or to the general analogy of God's Word. But however, the point maintained is of itself to be proved, or disproved, merely as a matter of fact to be shown by instances; and all that is necessary is merely to beg on the outset a patient consideration, as to a point by no means contrary to religious reverence or natural piety.

SECTION II

THE GOD OF ABRAHAM, ISAAC, AND JACOB

LET us take, first of all, that instance, which at once occurs to us as the most remarkable one, of our Lord quoting the Old Testament, where He points out the doctrine of a future state as maintained in the words, "I am the God of Abraham, and the God of Isaac, and the God of Jacob[2]." Now let us set aside the knowledge we now have of the sacred meaning contained in this, and

[2] Matt. xxii. 32. Mark xii. 26. Luke xx. 37.

divesting ourselves of the half-unconscious interpretations of piety and Christian love, consider it only in the light of natural reason. It will hardly be too much to say that, unless our Lord had told us that these words do contain the doctrine, no one, from the beginning to this time, would ever have adduced them to an unbeliever as a proof of it; i. e. that it does not appear to the natural reason as obvious, that the expression, "I am the God of Abraham," &c., does of itself in any way prove, or is a substantial argument for, the immortality of the soul. Nor can we suppose, if adduced by mere human authority, that unbelieving reason would have allowed the argument; for it might be rudely said, and if we take not faith as the true expounder, perhaps rightly said, these words are such as would be at once understood by those to whom they are addressed, as a form of speech, as a condescending expression of favour and protection, as a promise of a continuance of that love which had been shown towards their forefathers, but that they could not be rightly supposed to contain any thing beyond their obvious and plain meaning: to suppose that they proved any thing more, might be said to border on something like the spiritual and mystical interpretation of the Fathers. So might natural reason have answered; it will therefore be extremely interesting to inquire, in what sense we are rightly to understand the full meaning of our Lord's words, and the principle of interpretation on which they are founded.

The Sadducees on this occasion had brought forward the instance of the woman with seven husbands. And the case, and the question founded upon it, seems to have partaken in some degree of a profane levity, such as characterizes that class of sensualists in all ages, whether

under the shape and name of Epicureans of old, or Uni-
tarians among ourselves, when they approach spiritual
and Divine subjects.   Our Lord in His answer goes immediately, as His custom was, rather to the state of their
hearts, and the source of that infidelity which gives rise
to the question, than to the mere captious inquiry itself :
telling them that they "erred," and repeating afterwards
that they "greatly erred ;" and this their error, their
great error, consisted in "not knowing the Scriptures nor
the power of God."   And yet the words with which they
came imply a studied appearance of respect for Scripture ;
they begin with saying, "Master, Moses wrote unto us :"
and what they required was express words and proof in
the text of Holy Scripture ; in answer to which our Lord
tells them, that they had the doctrine in the Books of
Moses.   There does not appear any just reason for supposing, that our Lord was adducing in these words the
strongest declaration of that doctrine which the Penta-
teuch could supply.   Might we not rather consider it as
an argument, that the doctrine did not require any such
express verbal proof at all?   For of course if it had been
needed, He could have at once supplied it in the fulness
and closeness of the written letter.   Or, if not there
already supplied, could have so spoken in the Old Testament, as to have met at once this occasion, things present
and future being equally one and the same to Him.   For
we must remember Who it is that explains and interprets;
it is He Who spake by the Prophets, and Who in so
speaking knew every circumstance on which the words
would be needed.   It were indeed something bordering
on profaneness to suppose any deficiency of proof, or
weakness of argument, such as fell short of what the
occasion required.   It must rather be considered as sup-

plying them with the law of Scriptural interpretation, and as furnishing the key that would admit them into the treasures of the Holy Writings, which they now knew not. Though they probably knew the letter, and were familiar with every argument to be adduced from it, yet our Lord says distinctly that they knew not the Scriptures. For Christ's answer seems to imply that the Patriarchs had not, and needed not, any express declaration of this doctrine ; for that an affectionate piety, and a due apprehension of God's power, had in these words the fullest assurance that it was capable of receiving. For when these expressions, of Divine approbation and care, were used with respect to those who were out of human sight, to any thing like an affectionate confidence in God it would have appeared almost impious to suppose, that such objects of God's love could have ceased to exist ; had lost their life and all, when God, in Whom there is life and no death, still spoke of them as of those who had obtained His peculiar favour. To a faithful Jew such an express intimation of God's love and care, would convey a stronger conviction of a future state, than any mere texts of Holy Writ which declared it ; as the whole of it depended on practical conviction, not on speculative proof. It was the very uncertainty of the proof on which the greatness of their faith depended. The higher the faith of the Patriarchs was, the more thoroughly would they have reposed on any expression of God's favour ; thinking not, and perhaps caring not for any distinct explanation of the mode in which that favour would be shown towards them.

If this be the method of explaining the passage, then our Lord's manner of quoting the Old Testament in this instance would be analogous to His other dealings with

men, when they demanded a sign or strong palpable indication: from which He ever turned them to that moral
proof which faith supplies.   The error of the inquirers
was (as Origen seems to think) their not seeing the deep
things of God contained in Scripture.

But what is very much to be observed is, that in all
these references not only is there nothing at all proved
without faith as the interpreter, but with that faith a great
deal more than reason could have desired, something more
concerning and sublime is taught, than any thing which
human conception could otherwise have attained to.   Thus
by the present instance something even far more than a
future life is inferred, a Divine life, something more truly
to be called life, and in God's present favour, something
contained in that very awful Name " I am," and in that of
" the God of the living."   It implied that the " righteous
are in the hand of God, and no torment shall touch them,"
or as our Blessed Saviour said, " no one shall pluck them
out of My hand."   Faith finds herein something infinitely
great and good; and love something infinitely touching
and consoling, with respect to the thought of death.   It is
somewhat like St. Paul's very high expression, that to
depart is " to be with Christ, which is far better."   This
is more than immortality.   It is to be with God.

SECTION III

DAVID CALLING CHRIST LORD

THIS case indeed which has been just stated was in answer
to the Sadducees.   But to the Jews in general, and those
critically studious of the Scriptures, our Blessed Lord

seems to afford the same law of interpretation. On the same occasion, during His teaching in the temple, there is another reference to the Old Testament. We should have supposed from St. Matthew that it was made to the Pharisees; from St. Mark, rather to the people; and therefore we may conclude made to both [3]. "How say the Scribes that Christ is the Son of David? for David himself hath said in the Holy Spirit, The Lord said to my Lord, Sit Thou on my Right hand, until I make Thy foes Thy footstool. David himself therefore calleth Him Lord; from whence then is He his son?"

Now those words do indeed to us intimate a great deal, of what has been since revealed, respecting our Lord and His spiritual Kingdom: but to understand the bearing of them on the present question, we must separate our own present knowledge from the case, and consider the occasion, and the persons to whom it was addressed. For although we indeed read in these words of the Divinity of our Lord; yet to them how little was the passage an argument to substantiate the truth of, or even to intimate our Lord's Divinity; or any evidence to them that He who now stood before them was the Messiah? If this had been all that was necessary, namely, to prove His Divinity by the written word, might we not suppose that our Blessed Lord might have adduced other places which would have asserted this more clearly? Might not the Scribes have said in answer, The Messiah, we all know, is always spoken of as a King far greater than David; of course therefore in prophesying concerning Him, David would with propriety call Him Lord? This might be said in the way of low, carnal, human interpretation, but such as is

[3] Matt. xxii. 43.   Mark xii. 35.   Luke xx. 41.

too often found, when men pare down the words of Holy Writ to their lowest and most literal meaning.

But to ascertain any thing like the full intent and purport of this reference to the Old Testament, we must consider the occasion upon which it was made. The Pharisees, Scribes, Herodians, and Sadducees, had been trying our Lord with questions, partly of an ensnaring kind, and partly with some sincere desire of knowledge; and were at length put to silence by His awful authority and indication of Divine wisdom [4]; in the presence of the people who were exceedingly eager to hear Him, and whose favour prevented His enemies from laying violent hands on Him. The state of feeling in the multitude at this time must have been such as St. John mentions, that of astonishment at our Lord's authority and majesty, blended with some degree of doubt from the Scribes and Pharisees not believing on Him. And the secret source of the unbelief, which filled these Pharisees, arose from a low sense of the Messiah, and from pride in a literal, but very superficial, knowledge of the Scriptures. This question therefore of our Lord's does not by the passage referred to solve any difficulty; but rather throws out a difficulty, which might arrest the attention of a Scribe desirous to know the truth, such as would lead him to see there was something far higher and more mysterious about the Messiah than he apprehended. To them all the reference, though dark at present, and full of obscurity, yet when explained by the events that were to follow, and recalled to their remembrance, would teach them the whole nature of Christ's Kingdom.

It is indeed much to be observed, that the lesson contained in the text appears to have been the great object of

[4] Mark xii. 34.

Revelation to instruct the Jews in at this present time. This we may infer from our Lord's answer to the adjuration of the High Priest, when the words containing this allusion were not absolutely required in answer; from the same words again used before the Council; from the same reference again made by St. Peter on the day of Pentecost[5]; from the dying words of St. Stephen, and the Revelation made to him at his death; from the subject of the Epistle to the Hebrews, the substance of which is "Jesus Christ sitting at the right hand of God, waiting till His enemies be made His footstool."

And here it may not be amiss to notice by the way, that when our Lord is spoken of, or speaks of Himself, as raised to the right hand of Power, and coming to Judgment, He is described as the Son of Man, as in the prophet Daniel, and in His own frequent declarations; and the reason is mentioned in the expression of St. John[6], that the Father "hath given Him authority to execute judgment also, because He is the Son of Man." Whereas when He speaks not of the Judgment alone, but of calling the dead from their graves, in a few verses preceding, it is said, "the dead shall hear the voice of *the Son of God*, and they that hear shall live." For as the Son of God, and as having "life in Himself," our Lord calls the dead into life. As the Son of Man, He executes judgment.

It was now, however, to this one point, which is contained in this text, of our Lord sitting at the right hand of God, to which the attention of the Jews was especially called; for if they would by faith have raised their thoughts to the contemplation of it, it would at once have disposed and enlightened their minds, to see the full

[5] Acts ii. 34   [6] Ch. v. 27.

M

meaning of all God's former and present dispensations.   It was not so much a matter to be proved by this or any other text, as a clue afforded, by which faith might apprehend the secret nature of the kingdom.   To reason it proved nothing, but to faith it opened transcendental views of the Divine economy in the Gospel, as far surpassing any thing that reason could have inferred, or earthly imagination conceive, as Heaven is above earth.

And I think it may be stated generally, that they who expect warrant in the words of Scripture, as respecting the doctrine of the Trinity and the like, will find nothing of this kind promised in our Lord's teaching; but on the contrary, dark insinuations thrown out, which He, by-and-by, in His Church, or in the ways of a particular Providence, will solve to those who will obey Him, and to them alone.   And in this respect it may be observed, that the Scriptures themselves are precisely similar in their purpose to our Lord's own words and dealings with His disciples.

SECTION IV

THE TESTIMONY OF TWO WITNESSES

On another occasion we find our Lord citing the Law, in a manner when the words quoted do not, to the natural understanding alone, bear at all decisively upon the subject: and in answer to which it might be said, that to require persons to admit the application, was to demand of them at once to grant all that was to be proved.   It is mentioned in St. John, when our Lord was speaking to the Jews at Jerusalem, with unusual openness and earnestness, respecting Himself:—" It is written in your Law, that the testimony of two men is true. I am One that bear witness of Myself, and the Father that sent Me beareth witness of Me[7]." The twofold testimony, therefore, was, first our Lord's own teaching and declarations concerning Himself; the second, that of the Father bearing witness by His miracles, according to our Lord's frequent intimation: "The works which My Father hath given Me to finish, they bear witness of Me." But might not unbelieving reason have replied to this appeal, that the second witness, the Father, bearing witness by His works, on which the whole force of the text depended, was not adduced by our Blessed Lord in a way to be allowed by His adversaries? And this our Lord's next words imply: "Then said they unto Him, Where is Thy Father? Jesus answered, Ye neither know Me nor My Father." The text, therefore, would prove nothing, unless faith could discern the two witnesses. And the truth is, that by an affectionate faith alone, under the guidance of Church teaching, can the reference be explained; and only then after a high, and what would perhaps be called by some, mystical manner, and which requires, as the very preliminary, a sense of our Lord's Divinity, and takes His words as extending beyond the reach of man's thought. We cannot but believe, that those words in the Law, respecting the two witnesses, did refer to the doctrine of the Trinity, and the twofold Witness of the Father and the Son, before the Holy Ghost was yet given, Who was the third Witness. For on referring to the passage in Deuteronomy, we find that it is said, "two or three witnesses." And may not the word *three* be here dropped in our Lord's statement for this reason assigned, viz. that the third witness had not yet been brought forward? For our atten-

7 John viii. 17, 18.

M 2

tion is attracted by our Lord's referring to the same words
on another occasion, and not omitting the full text, when,
with regard to an offending brother, He says, "Take
with thee one or two more, that in the mouth of two or
three witnesses every word may be established. And if
he shall neglect to hear them, tell it unto the Church;
but if he neglect to hear the Church, let him be unto thee
as an heathen." Now, it appears to be the case, that our
Lord's particular commands on moral subjects are oftentimes exemplified by subsequent actions of His own; so
that the precept is often best explained by His own conduct, and His own conduct best illustrated by a reference
to the command. It seems, therefore, not unreasonable
to suppose, that this religious injunction sets forth His
own conduct also; or, at all events, that His own conduct
may be very well described, as exactly corresponding with
this command, and that He was thereby Himself fulfilling
His own precept. For to the unrepenting Jew He
brought forward, first, His own Witness by His words,
then the Witness of the Father by His works, and then
the Witness of His Spirit after the Resurrection; and
when these Three were rejected, then were they condemned,—they were cut off from the Church, and are as
Heathens and Publicans. And this one thing is, indeed,
variously stated in different places, that this their condemnation did, in fact, consist in their rejection of the
Three Witnesses; of the first, for our Lord says, "If I
had not come and spoken unto them, they had not had
sin [8];" and of the second, for He says, "If I had not done
among them the works that no other man did, they had
not had sin." And St. Stephen declared that they "resisted
the Holy Ghost," Who our Lord said should "testify of

[8] John xv. 22.

Him ;" Who is, indeed, termed the Great Witness. And perhaps it was with a prophetic reference to this, that our Lord had cautioned them of the sin against the Holy Ghost, by which they would become excommunicate and cut off from His Church. And it is a remarkable confirmation of this secret reference being contained in the appeal to the three witnesses of the Law, that St. Paul, in his Epistle to the Hebrews, does so apply it :—" He that despised Moses' law died without mercy under two or three witnesses ; of how much sorer punishment, suppose ye, shall he be thought worthy, who hath trodden under foot the Son of God, and hath counted the blood of the covenant, wherewith he was sanctified, an unholy thing, and hath done despite unto the Spirit of grace [*] ?" Does it not, therefore, appear that this testimony, adduced from their own Law as being at that time fulfilled in Him, is such as to unbelieving reason proves nothing ; to the eyes of faith opens vast and mysterious views respecting the economy of God in man's Redemption ; and fills us with awe at the mysterious depth and breadth and height of Divine words, which man cannot fathom, though he be filled with a religious conviction of their truth and importance ? Intellectually, therefore, as well as morally, the parable of the seed is herein exemplified ;—to the natural man it lies on the surface of the ground which cannot receive it, being not understood ; but in the good ground of faith the Word bears thirty, sixty, or a hundredfold, as the soul is able to comprehend it. And thus in our Lord's references to the Scriptures, as well as in His miracles and parables, the prophecy of Daniel is fulfilled : " None of the wicked shall understand, but the wise shall understand."

[*] Heb. x. 28, 29.

SECTION V

AGAIN, perhaps there is no one who has not been at first struck with some feeling of surprise at the following instance, when our Lord quotes the Old Testament. For the obvious interpretation of it by unenlightened reason would rather be an offence, than lead to those treasures of wisdom which faith ever finds in Divine words. When accused of blasphemy for making Himself God, our Lord answers, " Is it not written in your Law, I said, Ye are gods ? If he called them gods unto whom the Word of God came, and the Scripture cannot be broken, say ye of Him whom the Father hath sanctified, and sent into the world, Thou blasphemest ; because I said, I am the Son of God ?" Now might not an unbeliever, who denied the Son, eagerly take hold of this, as if it implied that our Lord called Himself God in the same manner that the Judges of old were called gods ? And perhaps it might have been difficult for unassisted reason to prove the contrary. There appears in the passage an instance of the same sacred reserve, which our Lord always observed respecting His Divinity. To a dutiful and teachable spirit it contains all that gradual inculcation, which characterizes the manifestations of Him, Who "quenches not the smoking flax." And indeed both Origen and St. Chrysostom[1] make observations on the passage very much to this effect ;—

---

[1] St. Chrysostom says, τέως μὲν δεχθῆναι τὸν λόγον ταπεινότερον διελέχθη, ὕστερόνδε ἐπὶ τὸ μεῖζον αὐτὸν ἀνήγαγεν.

Origen also says, κατὰ τὴν ἑαυτοῦ φιλανθρωπίαν ἀπεκρίνατο.

they consider it an instance of our Lord's humiliation, and condescension to human infirmities, as wishing thereby to lead them on to the fuller knowledge of Himself.

He had taught them that a Prophet was to be known by his works: by His works, therefore, our Saviour required that He should be acknowledged as a Prophet of God; and adds, on this occasion, "If I do not the works of My Father, believe Me not: but if I do, though ye believe not Me, believe the works." From these, therefore, He required that He should be received as "Him Whom the Father hath sanctified and sent into the world." And now, if the Old Testament sanctioned those being called gods, unto whom the Word of God came; in that they were as such upon earth, in being His representatives, and as it were emanations from Him in some degree, and indications of the Divine Presence; how much more might He demand reverence and atten- tion Who gave such proofs that God was with Him? And such reverence and attention would lead them on to the fulness of Divine Truth; for if you attend reve- rently to Him, you will perceive that the Father is in Him, and He in the Father. For although to unbelief, and to unworthy thoughts of Christ, these words might be a stumbling-block, rather tending to disprove than to support our Lord's Divinity, and that except to faith they prove nothing; yet to faith how very much is inferred by this passage! That "powers ordained of God" may justly claim reverence as unto God, such as Prophet, and Priest, and King; and that such reverence towards them leads to the knowledge of the true Prophet, the true Priest, the true King. Nor only this, but that such are called Gods,—deriving some degree of

sanctity, and having as it were something of Divinity
around them (although, as the Psalmist adds, "they
shall die like men"); because they shadow forth and
represent Him whom, in a higher sense, the Father hath
anointed and sent into the world. They are called Gods,
because He whom they typify by their office was truly
God.

Would it not appear, from this passage alone, that there
is some essential difference in our low human use of
Scripture, to that of our Lord? Man seems desirous to
support Scripture, to prove it true, rational, and satisfactory. Scripture speaks concerning itself as if, like our
Lord Himself, it "received not honour of man," nor needed
his testimony, but "knoweth what is in man;" it speaks
of itself as perfectly independent of man, as needing not
his reception, nor his approbation and assent for its
support. It is infallible and Divine, though you understand it not. The matter is one that depends not on
Scripture or its sufficiency, but on yourselves: "He that
can receive it, let him receive it;"—"let the unholy
be unholy still." And it is perfectly analogous with all
God's dealings with mankind in Revelation, that any
given passage in Holy Writ should appeal to some
higher faculties of the soul than the intellectual reason;
for surely if that knowledge is so blessed as our Lord
declares, because it is revealed of His Father in Heaven,
He would not point out any inferior way of arriving at
it, by constraining evidence and the like,—any other way
which God has not so highly blessed. And it may be
observed, that the Jews not understanding the Scriptures,
and therefore not perceiving the Christ therein, is always
attributed to moral and not to intellectual causes.
"How can ye believe which receive honour one of

another ² ?"   They sought the first seats ³, but the
Kingdom belonged to "the poor in spirit," and therefore
they could not find the entrance into it.

SECTION VI

MERCY AND NOT SACRIFICE

BUT there is another instance which will serve still more
distinctly to set before us, that charity and faith, and
not human reason, are the laws of Scriptural interpretation which our Lord has sanctioned : and the more
forcibly, as it is found in the selection which He twice
has made of the same passage, "I will have mercy and
not sacrifice."   For although we find it was our Lord's
custom to repeat the same words and similar actions, yet
whenever these are so recorded, we may reasonably
conclude that it is on account of something, peculiarly
worthy of our attention, which they contain.   He twice
mentions this in St. Matthew's Gospel ⁴; first, on the
Pharisees murmuring at His eating with Publicans and
sinners, and at another time, on their accusing Him of
breaking the Sabbath.   He declares to them that they
did not understand the Scriptures; "Go ye and learn
what that meaneth," and "If ye had known what that
meaneth."   Now a person might be in the highest degree
critically and curiously wise in the Scriptures, without
ever perceiving that an incidental expression of this sort,
whether we take it in the Prophet Hosea, or in the
speech of Balaam, recorded in Micah, was to be set

² John v. 44.   ³ πρωτοκαθεδρίαν.
⁴ Ch. ix. 13; xii. 7.

before those numerous and weighty calls to observe the positive institutions of the Sacrifices. Natural reason, unenlightened and unillumined by the Spirit of God, would not of itself lead them to single out and select these expressions : nor would it ever have told them that this text was the clue that would lead them to, and the key that would open to them, all the secrets of the Divine Law. But this reference of our Blessed Lord does of itself teach us very much respecting the nature of Holy Writ. It seems to imply that these commands were the test of the character ; for that a good heart would in them see and receive the law of love : this is shown on many occasions, as in the case of the Scribe who saw that love was the first and great commandment, and before all burnt-offerings and sacrifices ; and was in consequence declared to be "not far from the Kingdom of God." And well might this be—for he would perceive not only the spiritual laws of Christ's Kingdom, but the very law itself by which our Lord acted ; for He had Himself set aside the burnt-offerings and sacrifices as unpleasing to God, in order that, in the redemption of mankind, He might act on the better law of love, —of ineffable love to God and man,—saying, "Burnt-offerings, and sacrifice for sin, hast thou not required : then said I, Lo, I come. In the volume of the book it is written of Me that I should fulfil Thy will, O my God : I am content to do it[5]." So that love is the key to open the Scriptures, and is that which the Scribes and Pharisees had not. Or again, it might be put in this way, that the end and object of all Scripture is to bring us to the knowledge of God ; and God is love ; so far therefore as it fails to bring to this knowledge, it fails of

[5] Ps. xl. 9, 10.

its purpose, and is not rightly understood. This knowledge of God is connected with the law of mercy in the
Prophet Hosea, " I desired mercy and not sacrifice, and
the knowledge of God more than burnt-offerings." So
far, therefore, as any one has come to the knowledge of
God, he will see that this law of mercy pervades, is
throughout interwoven with, and is the very foundation
of all the written Law : he alone will rightly have understood the Law, which would thus be unto him " the
Schoolmaster to bring him to Christ." So that had he
seen the Christ in His acts of mercy, he would have
acknowledged Him as God in His miracles of Divine
compassion ; and acknowledged Him as man also fulfilling the Law in its higher, better, and truer sense.

"The Scriptures," says St. Paul, " are able to make us
wise unto salvation :" but how? " through faith," he adds,
"which is in Christ Jesus." In all these passages it
actually requires " the faith which is in Christ Jesus,"
before any thing can be adduced from them ; but with
this they open of course the very highest wisdom which
is unto salvation. And therefore it is that when St. Paul
speaks of us, as being made by Grace " able ministers of
the New Testament," he adds, " not of the letter, but of
the Spirit; for the letter killeth, but the Spirit giveth
life."

SECTION VII

THE SABBATH REFERRED TO IN THE OLD TESTAMENT

AGAIN, much light may be thrown on this subject, and on
this general law of interpretation, by our Lord's miracles
on the Sabbath-day; and those appeals to Scripture by

which they are supported. Here again, I think, we must all have felt something like surprise, some difficulty to be cleared up; and the more thoughtful, some suspicion that there is far more in the matter than appears on the surface; that the performance of these miracles on this day, contained within it some great and mysterious significancy with respect to the Gospel dispensation. But all that is here necessary to notice is, that it appears from a consideration of all the circumstances, that such actions were not as it were by accident, but that our Lord, studiously and designedly, selected rather than avoided the Sabbath-day for the performance of His miracles of mercy. The five distinct instances recorded were probably but a few out of many. Add to which that they seemed, humanly speaking, to cause offence, which our Lord would have avoided, were it not for some great purpose or principle. On one occasion, that of the man with the withered hand[6], they watched Him, as if expecting Him to work the cure on the Sabbath-day, according to His custom. The circumstance, moreover, was not in private, but in the synagogue; and our Lord, so far from withdrawing from notice, which He so often did to prevent offence, took pains to arrest and draw attention to the circumstance, telling the man to come forth, and stand in the midst of them, and then introduced what He was going to do to their notice. A miracle, also, which is spoken of in St. John[7], appears incidentally to have been performed on the Sabbath-day, and which was one more particularly of a public character, as performed in Jerusalem and at the Feast, and at a time when our Lord thought it necessary studiously to retire from the Jews, because they were so highly incensed against Him. For

6 Luke vi. 6. 8.   7 Ch. vii. 22, 23.

it says, He went up "as it were in secret;" and by our Lord's expression, "I have done one work," it would appear that it was the only one that He had ventured to perform in their presence; and yet was this accompanied with this very aggravating circumstance, of the day being the Sabbath. In like manner, the miracle of restoring the blind man, recorded in St. John [8], which took place at Jerusalem, and attracted so much attention, was wrought on the Sabbath-day, to the great apparent detriment, at the moment, of its otherwise beneficial effects; for this is mentioned as the stumbling-block which prevented their belief: "Some of the Pharisees said, This Man is not of God, because He keepeth not the Sabbath." And yet of course nothing could have been easier than for our Saviour, who has times and seasons in His own power, to have had such occasions on other days.

To take another case, mentioned in St. Luke [9], the healing a man with the dropsy, on the Sabbath. It was at the house of a Pharisee, and at a time when they were jealously "watching Him." Such instances not only indicate that it was His usual custom, but that it was before those persons whom it would most of all offend. And here again, as on the former occasion, it is preceded by the very unusual circumstance of our Lord's inviting attention to the miracle. Nor does the miracle itself, under such circumstances, appear to benefit them, but to make them worse; in the former case, that of the man with the withered hand, they immediately took counsel to slay Him.

Moreover, on these occasions, our Lord took pains, as it were, to depart from the literal strictness of the written law, by doing those things which might have

[8] Ch. ix.   [9] Ch. xiv. 1.

been easily avoided, in order to draw their attention to the spiritual law of love;—conduct the more remarkable from His most religious care to observe the law in other matters. Thus, in one case recorded, He commanded the man to carry his bed [1]; which was, in fact, opposed to the letter of the Old Testament, for Nehemiah mentions it among his good deeds, that he would have no "burden brought in on the Sabbath-day [2]:" and it is commanded of God in the Prophet Jeremiah, "to bear no burden on the Sabbath-day [3]." And in the case of the blind man, the cure was accompanied with a work and manual means, which increased what they thought the breaking of the Sabbath. "It was the Sabbath-day when Jesus made the clay and opened his eyes [4]."

These circumstances are alluded to as containing in themselves a practical comment on the letter of the Old Testament; but the references themselves to the Scriptures, by which they are justified by our Lord, are more particularly to our purpose, as indicating our Lord's mode of interpreting the written Word. The first argument our Saviour uses, when His disciples were accused of plucking the ears of corn on the Sabbath, was taken from the example of David: "Have ye not read what David did when he was an hungred, and they that were with him; how he entered into the house of God, and did eat the shewbread, which was not lawful for him to eat, neither for them which were with him, but only for the Priests [5]?" Now, if this argument is to be addressed to unbelieving reason alone, one does not see how it could exculpate those who were charged by the Jews. For it is stated

---

[1] John v. 8. 10.   [2] Ch. xiii. 19.
[3] Ch. xvii. 21.   [4] John ix.
                    [5] Matt. xii. 3, 4.

that David did that which it was "not lawful" to do; and though indeed it was a case of extreme necessity, yet Holy Scripture had not sanctioned the action, nor mentioned it with approval; nor indeed does this appear to be a case of extreme necessity, as that of David's was. And moreover, that our Lord Himself was equal to David, was the very point which the Jews would not grant. It required faith to accept the application. Nor, again, will the next reference recorded by St. Matthew on this occasion, prove more satisfactory to an unbeliever, "Have ye not read in the Law, how that on the Sabbath-days the Priests in the Temple profane the Sabbath, and are blameless?" For it might be said in answer to this, that what was done in the Temple for God's service, by His express sanction, and for His worship, was very different from the actions of others without the Temple, which were so strongly restricted by that very law which allowed and required the former. There must, therefore, in these cases, be something far more than the letter. And the same may be said of another appeal which our Lord makes in St. John, to the case of Circumcision, "Moses gave unto you Circumcision, and ye on the Sabbath-day circumcise a man; if a man on the Sabbath-day receive Circumcision, that the law of Moses should not be broken, are ye angry at Me because I have made a man every whit whole on the Sabbath-day?" Now, if we may reverently say it, the instance alluded to does not bear the application according to a strong palpable logical inference, such as worldly men would require. For in this case the law, in a greater matter, was superseding another law of inferior importance, where one must necessarily give place to the other: the extreme necessity of Circumcision on

⁶ Ch. vii. 23.

the eighth day did not allow of its being postponed, whereas this work of healing, like all others, might equally as
well have been performed on any other day.   All these
references must either contain a vast deal indeed, after the
Patristic and Catholic mode of interpretation, or else they
must contain very little indeed, and next to nothing.
Again, another case which our Lord adduces seems to
refer to the law, by which they were required to lift the ox
or the sheep of a neighbour out of a pit, and which they
did on the Sabbath-day; but this does not appear, after
a human mode of speaking, strictly applicable, inasmuch
as the case of an animal fallen into a pit, and requiring
immediate extrication to save life, was not an answer to
the objection of the Pharisees, viz.—that it might be done
at another time,—that they should come to be healed on
other days.   Surely all this implies that there is a Divine
and heavenly mode of interpreting Scripture, to which
these Pharisees were strangers, because they received not
the love of the truth; and therefore, on this occasion
alone, it is said that our Lord "was angry," inasmuch
as it indicated great wrongness of heart.   The Psalmist
long before had implied that necessity of this spiritual
discernment, when he said, "Lord, open Thou mine eyes,
that I may see the wonderful things of Thy Law:" and
seeking this knowledge of God, from Whom alone it
cometh, he found it.   As Christ speaks of Himself as
the door, by which alone we enter into the kingdom of
Heaven, so is He the door, by which alone we enter into
the knowledge of God in Scripture.

As our Lord, when He preached in the Synagogue at
Nazareth on the opening of His ministry, explained that
the great year of release was then truly come and substantially fulfilled in Him, the great year of atonement

and jubilee, the Sabbath of Sabbaths, and Sabbath year; so His miracles on the Sabbath-day seem to imply that the Sabbath, which was but a shadow of good things to come, had now its true fulfilment in Him; in Him Who, in distinction from those rites, which were now departing, was Grace and Truth. For when our Lord performed the miracles on the Sabbath, of releasing the captive, of forgiving the debtor, and the like, He was in fact celebrating the jubilee, in the higher and diviner sense and reality; He was performing all that was needed of the Law, and fulfilling the prophecy. These works of mercy on the Sabbath struck at the very root of Jewish unbelief; they contained the whole of the Gospel, as the great revelation of Divine charity, arising out of the Law, which was now fulfilled and passing away. The true Sabbath had now arrived in Christ: the kingdom of Heaven had come, and the actions of Christians henceforth were to be all Sabbatized, as devoted to God, like actions in His Temple. Thus although God was said to rest on the seventh day; yet notwithstanding, as our Lord says, "the Father worketh hitherto, and I work;" and though the Christian Sabbath had arrived, yet acts of mercy must continue therein. Thus throughout the Old Testament this true Sabbath was foretold and signified by the Jewish Sabbath yielding to works of mercy, of which circumstance there were many indications, scattered through the law, even in things they thought not of. And these they would have read there, had they interpreted the Scriptures after a Divine and spiritual manner.

The Sabbath was a memorial of the rest of God, and so was it also of the rest of the children of Israel on coming out of Egypt; but fulfilled in the higher sense in Christians now, who were brought out by Christ from the house of

N

bondage : "thou wast a servant in the land of Egypt, and the Lord thy God brought thee out thence through a mighty hand and by a stretched-out arm; therefore the Lord thy God commanded thee to keep the Sabbath-day[7]." They found rest in the wilderness, but that rest was accompanied with the works of God's mercy, and the works of man's obedience; they had not yet attained the true rest; but we have, for the true rest is in Christ ;— rest in Christ now, by that faith which "worketh by love," and rest in Christ hereafter, when "we shall see Him as He is." In short, our Blessed Lord, Who taught as much by action as by word, was thereby teaching them the same lesson which St. Paul had so much to urge, viz. not to judge each other with respect to the Sabbath-days, "which are a shadow of things to come, but the Body is of Christ[8]."

The substance was now come, the true Sabbath, He in Whom man might find rest for his soul. He Who was now present, as the Son of Man, had power to dispense with, remodel, or mould to His great purposes all the ceremonial institutions, which did but wait on Him as the Son of Man, in Whom and in Whose kingdom they had their true fulfilment; for the Sabbath was made for man: it waited on the Son of Man. Thus the Law and the Prophets, if rightly understood, did but set forth Himself, His actions and people. Thus David as His type and emblem, when persecuted and driven from place to place, did receive from God's ministers, for those that were with Him, of that bread which was set apart for God, taking care only that they that were with Him should be pure and chaste ; and as such they did eat of that which belonged to the Priests alone ; for they together with Him, their future king, were typical of His own peculiar people, " the royal

[7] Deut. v. 15.   [8] Col. ii. 17.

priesthood," the people of Christ. In like manner would God support Christians in this His new kingdom or Sabbatical rest, allowing them still to work, but sanctifying their works, and accepting them as done unto Himself, in Himself, and by Himself, by the great law of charity. Though the letter of the old law did indeed itself condemn these practices; yet He who was now present did alone substantially fulfil that law in spirit and in truth.

And moreover, what the Priests did in the temple was a proof that the Law did itself, by requiring those sacrifices on the Sabbath-day, keep up a weekly memorial of that which should be done by the new Priesthood of Christ in His new Temple, or Christian Church; where they should have works to perform, but those should be hallowed works, offering up themselves and all their doings, as a continual spiritual sacrifice unto God. However, to see the force of these things required faith, in order to recognize the Son of God in these figures of the Law; and a good heart to understand the Divine meaning which set mercy above sacrifice: and declare the love of God and man to be better than whole burnt-offerings.

Again, in like manner Circumcision was but an external rite, which could but imply, but had no power to bestow that purity of which it was symbolical. It had no virtue to heal the soul, nor to remove those bodily diseases which were the external indications of its maladies. Yet even for this lifeless but mysterious rite the Sabbath was made to yield, on account of that great Sacrifice and that law of Christ's expiation which that rite implied, to which the Sabbath itself served but the place of a type, as representing that great Sabbatical rest. How much more therefore must it give way to that great power of atoning mercy, which implies the presence of God Himself, when by removing the maladies of the body He gave sufficient proof that He had " power to forgive sins also "? If it gave way to Circumcision the shadow, how much more to Christ the substance, for whom as Son of Man the Sabbath was made? "Judge not," our Lord adds, "according to the appearance, but judge righteous judgment ;" implying that the case was not to be considered according to the human appearances, nor to any mere rationalistic view of the argument used, but according to some other law—that of righteousness. Faith in Christ was the key to unlock the meaning of that Circumcision to which the Sabbath gave way ; and the Sabbath's giving way and yielding to that rite, was in itself a circumstance full of mystical and Divine signification.

In short, Circumcision did almost of itself imply the new and altered Sabbath, or the Lord's day, before which the Jewish Sabbath was to vanish away like a shadow ; for Circumcision was bound most strongly to the eighth day, inasmuch as the eighth day was the great day of our Lord's resurrection, and the coming in of the new covenant. If therefore the old Sabbath gave way to Circumcision on the eighth day, much more would it give way and depart before the Eighth day itself, the resurrection of Christ, and the coming of the Christian Sunday ; and before Christ Himself Who is the Resurrection.

And with regard to the case of an ox or an ass fallen into the pit on the Sabbath-day, which if it belonged to a neighbour, the law had commanded them to extricate, and which in their own case they did on the Sabbath ; would not all reverential piety exclaim with St. Paul, " Doth God take care for oxen? for our sakes no doubt it is written⁹." If God had so expressly provided for the ox

⁹ 1 Cor. ix. 9.

of our neighbour, in circumstances which, if our own, we
deemed more important than the Sabbath, how much
more when our neighbour himself was found in the pit;
with no one else but Jesus Christ to give him succour!

The natural prayer of a good man is that God will deliver
him from his own reason, and the deductions of his own
understanding, and would Himself lead him to that knowledge, which is always described as His own especial gift.
We may well suppose therefore that the right understanding of these passages would depend rather on the higher gift
of faith than that of human reason, a far inferior endow-
ment. And it shows the great necessity of a purified life,
great humility, and constant prayer, before we can expect
to understand the Gospels.

SECTION VIII

THE BILL OF DIVORCEMENT

AGAIN, the reference made by our Lord to the Old Testament respecting marriage and divorce is very remarkable[1].
"The Pharisees came unto Him and asked Him, Is it
lawful for a man to put away his wife? tempting Him.
But He answered and said unto them, What did Moses
command you? They said, Moses permitted to write a
bill of divorce and to put her away. And Jesus answered
and said unto them, For the hardness of your hearts he
wrote you this commandment." "Have ye not read that
He who made them from the beginning made male and
female, and said, For this cause shall a man leave his
father and his mother, and shall cleave unto his wife, and

[1] Matt. xix. Mark x.

they two shall be one flesh ?"   " What therefore God hath
joined together, let not man put asunder."   Here our
Lord sets aside the letter of Holy Scripture, in one case,
in the passage in Deuteronomy, (which He speaks of as
the command of Moses,) on account of the higher law of
Christian holiness and perfection, implying that the strict
letter of the Law itself was not a sufficient sanction ; and
establishes the point by a reference to another passage of
Holy Scripture, which does not at first sight indicate any
command, nor does of itself obviously, or in the literal
sense, prove divorce to be unallowable : for surely no one
would ever have adduced this passage in the book of
Genesis, to prove divorce to be forbidden, unless we had
Divine authority for doing so.

But it is to be observed, that our Lord does not speak
as giving a new law, but as enforcing an old one,—not as
superseding the law of Moses, but as interpreting it ; for
indeed He Himself declared, that not one jot or one tittle
of that Law shall fail.   And therefore this passage in the
book of Genesis not only is spoken, as St. Paul says it is,
of the Sacramental union betwixt Christ and His Church,
but does also signify that marriage is of itself of Divine
sanction, and the union formed of God, and necessarily
indissoluble as such.   True faith would have understood
this from that solemn declaration of God.   Nor does our
Lord's injunction appear to be any thing additional to
that declaration, but an enunciation of that law which
was contained within it ; and of a necessary consequence
to be inferred from it, for if God hath joined, man cannot
put asunder.

And surely if we attend to Divine words, with any
serious consideration of that holiness and depth which
they must contain, and that reverential spirit which they

must needs require in order to be apprehended, it were impossible to conceive any words that speak more strongly of the sanctity of marriage ; the awful and mysterious nature of that union ; the heinousness of adultery, or any thing else that can weaken and impair it, than those words in the book of Genesis. From which it follows that "they two shall be one flesh; so that they are no longer two, but one flesh." God hath weakened all other natural ties, in order to strengthen as His own this mystical, and as it were almost Sacramental bond ;—hallowed, by its resemblance to the great and true union of Christ with His Church, into a new and living import and mystery.

SECTION IX

CURSING FATHER OR MOTHER

Not altogether unconnected with this is the mode in which our Lord sanctions filial piety, by an appeal to the letter of the Old Testament, and to the law that he that curseth father or mother should be put to death. The passage is as follows : " God commanded saying, Honour thy father and mother; and, He that curseth father or mother, let him die the death. But ye say, Whosoever shall say to his father or his mother, It is a gift, by whatsoever thou mightest be profited by me, he shall be free²." The Jews to whom this was addressed appear to have now become liable to the condemnation of the Law, according to the passage in Deuteronomy, "Lest there should be among you a root that beareth gall and worm-

² Matt. xv. 4, 5.

wood : and it come to pass when he heareth the words of
this curse, that he bless himself in his heart, saying, I
shall have peace though I walk in the imagination of
mine heart[3]." And yet no mere human law could have
reached the case of these Pharisees, or proved that they
were liable to that curse of the Old Testament, or that
they had broken the fifth commandment, in putting piety
to God, as they would say, before duty to parents. We
can of course perfectly see the full force of our Blessed
Lord's words : the Pharisees in their hardness of heart
had fallen back even from natural piety, from that which
is the very foundation of all goodness, dutiful obedience
and reverence to parents, which is a part of that meekness
which inherits the kingdom ; and yet in doing this they
still observed the strict appearance of a holy severity.
And our Blessed Lord here brings out these precepts of
the Law, and kindles them up with the new light of
Divine charity, filling them with the genial life of faith
and goodness. We see that the command of not cursing
father or mother implies the greatest desire for their good ;
that the Law is spiritual and Divine, and extends therefore, like the eye of God, to all the heart, the thoughts
and actions ; making those letters of the written Law—
the phylacteries which are on the borders of the garment—
to be fragrant with the oil of the sanctuary, which is love.
We see that the very commandments themselves contain
all this ; but how do they contain it ? not surely in the mere
letter, not according to that strict interpretation which
the critical skill and wisdom of the carnal mind would
extract from them. It is only when we consider that the
words are Divine, that they appear, like the characters on
the wall, full of heavenly fire, so that he may run that

[3] Deut. xxix. 18, 19.

readeth them. The human reason fails before we attain to the Divine; the lion is dead first, before his carcase is filled with sweetness. It is the hard rock which opens its treasures, at the bidding of Him who hath said, "With honey out of the stony rock have I satisfied thee."

SECTION X

THE FORETOLD ELIJAH

THERE is another highly interesting department of Scriptural interpretation, in which the references made by our Lord may afford us the most sure and safe guidance, as furnishing us with a clue to the right mode of understanding the Scriptures: and this is on the very important subject of prophecy. Such is our Lord's explanation respecting the coming of Elijah;—" If ye can receive it, this is Elias which was for to come." As far as the literal expression of that prophecy went, and the argument which might have been founded upon it by mere reason alone, the Scribes might have urged a strong case: a circumstance which they took hold of to shake the belief of the disciples. They might have said that the Scriptures declare that Elijah the Prophet must first come; and that John the Baptist was not Elijah, as we all know; for a formal deputation was sent to him from Jerusalem to ask him that question, which he answered in the negative. But notwithstanding these strong arguments, the disciples had come to the full assurance that our Lord was the Messiah; and therefore were afterwards capable (by improved religious, not intellectual, discernment) of explaining that circumstance : for our Lord declared to them, that *if they would receive it, this was the foretold Elijah.* If, therefore, they had adopted the mere letter of Scripture alone, and acted upon it, they would never have come to that truth, which now they had done.

The circumstance may be applied to the interpretation of all prophecy, especially to those that refer to our Lord's second Coming. It is supposed, by various interpreters, that the event cannot take place until certain circumstances have been fulfilled, which have not yet occurred, and therefore cannot be without some time intervening. It is supposed, in consequence, that the Apostles were under a mistake respecting our Lord's speedy Coming, which they seemed to apprehend ; and yet we cannot but observe that, in this apprehension, they were but acting up to our Lord's command, Who had most solemnly enjoined them ever to watch, as not knowing the hour, whether at evening, at midnight, at cockcrowing, or in the morning. Further, it is supposed, as accounting for this mistake of the Apostles, that beforehand they took the approaching destruction of Jerusalem for the end of the world. And yet that evidently could not have been the case, as the Apostle who survived that event spoke, at the close of the Bible, in terms as strong, and indeed stronger, than any who had spoken before. But now if we take this instance of Elijah for our example, it is certainly reasonable to believe that the second Coming of our Lord, and the events which precede it, may in like manner be so mysterious, as to defy all previous supposition, grounded on the mere letter and words of Holy Scripture. It would seem that, somehow, this knowledge will depend on the disposition of the heart, and that he who adheres most closely to our Lord's commands, and in so doing expects it always, as the Apostles did, will find himself eventually to be nearest the truth; although in a manner we know not of, and perhaps such as is beyond human thought. For thus do we come to the mind of God, according to which it will be soon. We may certainly conclude something of this kind, from the analogy of the former case, and because we are expressly assured that the tokens of it will not be discerned; for on this last, as on previous and earlier occasions, that saying will be fulfilled,—that " the kingdom of God cometh not with observation," but that "the wise shall understand :" the good will be able to discern its approach, as the disciples recognized the Messiah. We are assured that it will be exceeding speedy, so as to be in the eye of God as already come ;—" The hour cometh, and now is," says our Lord Himself. And yet, notwithstanding, it shall appear otherwise to men; for He also says, that to the negligent servant He shall appear to be delaying His return; and St. Peter says of that Day, that to the scoffer of the last days it will seem long in coming. Therefore, prophecy is so put, that the intellect cannot of itself discern, or interpret it; but that obedience to Christ's commands does somehow, and as it were in some secret way, arrive at the truth. And this will receive additional confirmation from the fact, that the unbelieving Jews were ensnared and entangled by prophecies, which they (judging by reason, not by faith) considered unfulfilled; of which several instances occur. Thus they were right in requiring a sign equal to that of the Manna in the wilderness [4]; and it was given them, yet they had no faith to discern it. They had in their possession a great and Divine truth, when they said, " Howbeit we know this man

[4] John vi. 31.

whence He is ; but when Christ cometh, no man knoweth whence He is[5]." They were right in the Scriptural inference, but wrong in the fact ; for the latter part of this declaration was true, but not the former : for they knew not of our Saviour's supernatural and Divine birth, though they thought they knew whence He was. Again, perhaps they rightly said, " Search and look, for out of Galilee ariseth no prophet," and that Christ could not be from Galilee ; for the Scripture had said that He was to be of Bethlehem, the city of David. This was their answer to those who would have believed ; for they knew not that He was of Bethlehem. To others they said, that —none of the Pharisees had believed, and—that the people who knew not the Law were cursed. This also was in one sense true : they rightly declared the Scriptures ; but the people who believed in Christ knew the Law. These Pharisees were not aware that they themselves knew not the Law, and were therefore themselves under that curse. Thus were they ensnared by their own reason, while simple faith overcame the difficulties : for the guileless Nathanael thought like themselves, that no good could come out of Nazareth[6], but he notwithstanding instantly believed. And thus, what was hid from the prudent was revealed to babes:

SECTION XI

FULFILLED PROPHECIES

THERE is another most valuable rule of interpretation, which Christ Himself has supplied us with, respecting

[5] John vii. 27. [6] John i. 46.

prophecy, which would lead us to infer that prophecy pervaded, and was imperceptibly interwoven throughout the letter of the Old Testament, rather than that it was confined to distinct predictions and palpable declarations of things future. For He speaks of prophetical predictions as being fulfilled in that generation, which we do not find, on looking to the words in the Old Testament, were at all expressed as prophetical, or as in any way alluding to this period of our Lord's manifestation among them. Thus in St. Matthew we read, "Ye hypocrites, well did Esaias prophesy of you, saying, "This people draweth nigh unto Me with their mouth, and honoureth Me with their lips ; but their heart is far from Me [7]." Whereas in the passage referred to, it is not spoken in the future, but altogether of the Jews of that time before the captivity : "Forasmuch as this people draweth near Me with their mouth, and with their lips do honour Me, but have removed their heart far from Me [8]." Now to a considerate mind, a vast deal more is contained in this, and other such appeals of our Lord, than if they appeared in the Prophet Isaiah as a distinct prophecy, and were a simple fulfilment of it. For the Scribes might have denied that it was a prophecy at all respecting them ; whereas to faith it indicated that Isaiah as speaking by Christ, not to those of his day only, but to that nation generally, spoke prophetically, and warned them of those points in their conduct, which he foresaw in the Spirit would go on, till they were fully developed in their ruin. It gives to the warnings of God the character of prophecy : making admonition itself pregnant with the awful severity of the Judge's sentence, as coming from Him Who knoweth what is in man ; in like manner as our Lord's denuncia-

[7] Ch. xv. 7, 8.   [8] Isaiah xxix. 13.

tions of covetousness in the presence of Judas, and His earnest rebuke of St. Peter on his wishing Him to avoid the Cross, derive a peculiar force from the subsequent history of those two disciples. So too our Lord's warnings respecting those whose blood Pilate mingled with their sacrifices, and they on whom the tower of Siloam fell, were both a warning and also a prophecy, respecting the slaughter and fall of Jerusalem. This suggests to us, moreover, that all Scripture points to Christ and His day. In like manner, when our Lord so frequently alludes distinctly to the prophecy respecting the Jews of that generation, "that they should have no ears to hear, nor eyes to see;" we do not find in the Old Testament that it was spoken of as a future day; and yet St. John distinctly tells us, referring to those words, "These things said Esaias, when he saw His glory, and spake of Him [9]." In like manner when our Lord declares that it would be more tolerable for Sodom and Gomorrah in the Day of Judgment, than for that people : may we not conceive that He alludes to and explains the expression of Isaiah, when he called the Jews, "Ye rulers of Sodom, and ye people of Gomorrah"? And if this be the case, it will follow that single expressions, such as these appellations in the Old Testament, do not admit of any rationalistic human interpretation, but are, as the Fathers suppose, "full of eyes before and behind;" looking before and after, and pointing out mysteriously the way to great eventful destinies. This mode of interpretation proceeds every step, as if on holy ground, with this sentiment in the heart: "O Lord, Thy thoughts are very deep; an unwise man doth not well consider this,

[9] Compare also Matt. xiii. 14, with Isa. vi. 9 ; and Matt. iv. 16, with Isa. ix. 2.

and a fool doth not understand it." These instances are but few, but they are as the grapes of Eschol; sufficient to show the riches of this sacred land of Scripture, if we had but faith to attain unto them, and to enter into that inheritance.

Further, not expressions only in the Old Testament, but events also are pointed out by Christ, as being prophetical, and, like reflected rays of light, sent to precede great manifestations. Thus when our Lord read in Isaiah the Prophet the account of the Year of release, and said it was then fulfilled, He pointed out to them in the Old Testament indications of that great truth, viz.—"that a prophet is not received in his own country," as Elijah was sent to the widow of Sarepta, and Elisha healed the Syrian Naaman. These examples were slight intimations as it were going before of that great principle, prophetical indications bearing one way; in that secret manner in which single events are forerunners of great developments, such as could in no way prove or confirm the point, yet are clues, such as would lead a watchful and good man in that direction.

Again, on another occasion, when our Lord entered the Temple, and drove out the buyers and sellers, He referred to two expressions of the Old Testament: the one in the Prophet Isaiah [1]. "My house shall be called the house of prayer," and the other in the Prophet Jeremiah [2], "but. ye have made it a den of thieves." Now both of these are what would be called, by inconsiderate persons, applications; and what is said of Patristic writers is, that they use Scripture by way of application, rather than explanation or interpretation. But only let these expressions of our Lord's be duly considered. Among mankind,

[1] Ch. lvi. 7.   [2] Ch. vii. 11.

if any are wiser and holier than others, we earnestly take
hold of their words,—we retain them, and ponder them,
and find much more in them than first we thought for.
How much more must this be the case in Divine words!
And if we turn, as we naturally must, to these two Prophets, in order to understand the full and right meaning
of our Lord's words, we find that both of them form a
part of two most remarkable prophecies; and that both of
these prophecies bear, in the strongest manner, on the
time and occasion on which they were spoken by our
Lord; and that both of them, taken together, come in as
furnishing the interpretation of that most remarkable
action of His.   The first of these speaks of the calling of
those who were worthy from the Gentiles; the latter of
the rejection of the Jewish nation, as found unworthy:
and therefore are as comments on our Blessed Lord's conduct.   In the first it is said—that God will remember
the stranger and the eunuch who keep His covenant; that
He will bring them to His holy mountain, and make
them joyful in His house of prayer; that His house shall
be called an house of prayer for all nations; that He will
gather others unto Him there.   In the other Prophet,
Jeremiah, there is another passage, no less singularly
remarkable and emphatic, as bearing on this action of our
Lord's, in which it is said, that this House which was
called by His name was become a den of robbers; that He
would cast it out of His sight; that since when He was
rising up early and speaking (as Christ had now been
doing in His Temple), they had not heard; therefore He
would do to that house in which they trusted, and the
place which He had given unto them and their fathers, as
He had done to Shiloh;—that He would cast them out of
His sight;—that it was too late to pray for them.   We

are at first surprised that in one sentence our Lord should use words from two different Prophets; for, humanly speaking, it might appear as it is with mankind, when we blend together different quotations in one saying. But it was, in fact, no less than our Lord bringing forward the testimony of His two Prophets as His witnesses, responding to each other, and one taking up the allusion of the other, and both together speaking of Him on this occasion; both as His interpreters explaining the awful import of this His significant and mysterious action, when He came to His own Temple, as His Prophets had foretold, and men, as they had said, were not able to abide His coming.

SECTION XII

FIGURATIVE EXPRESSIONS

There is another subject in some respects akin to this, when our Blessed Lord alludes to expressions or events in the Old Testament, which might be considered figurative or allegorical; of which He has shown the fulfilment, not after a literal, but in a spiritual and high sense. He thus speaks to Nathanael: " Hereafter shall ye see Heaven open, and the Angels of God ascending and descending . on the Son of Man*." We do not know that at the Ascension, or any other time, Nathanael beheld this literally fulfilled; but if he did it was only in an inadequate sense, as the literal must ever be. We may suppose it to signify something of this kind,—" You are like Israel of old, simple of heart: and the privilege of

* John i. 51.

O

such is, that they shall see God, which your ready belief not only verifies, but hereafter you shall see the true fulfilment of the Patriarch's vision; you shall see the kingdom of Heaven upon earth, and such power bestowed upon the Son of Man, that it shall be no less than the heavens opening, and the Angels ascending and descending." Such the good centurion saw, when he spoke of Christ as having servants under Him, and being one in authority to command them. And it is very remarkable how much the Gospel dispensation throughout introduces the mention of Angels, from the Angelic hymn at our Saviour's birth, to those who are always said to attend on the Day of Judgment. Such a reference, therefore, to those words of the Old Testament teaches us, that such events and expressions contain within them deeply figurative meanings, to be fulfilled in the Gospels; that as Israel saw this vision, so in the Church visible upon earth the pure in heart should behold the true Kingdom of God, and "an innumerable company of Angels." May we not reverently suppose that here, again, a law of interpretation is furnished us, of which though none of us may be wise enough to follow it, yet we may see sufficient to show us that it *is* a law, and has the sanction of our Lord's example and authority?

To these may be added numerous instances, in which Christ makes use of the expressions of the Old Testament, and by so doing brings them out in a high and spiritual meaning, as if that object of bringing out the Old Testament was intended by Him. His parables are sometimes taken in their outline and framework from the Old Testament: as that of the Vineyard from Isaiah[4]. Thus, that the meek "shall inherit the earth," is explained in the

[4] Chap. v.

place from which it is taken, viz. that this inheritance will consist in their being "refreshed in the multitude of peace." And thus the expression, "out of Egypt have I called my Son," and that of "Rachel weeping for her children," bring out the passages themselves, from which they are taken, as full of new import. Thus the warning, "Remember Lot's wife," opens a great type, in that her looking back to the city of destruction. In the same way also, the song of the Virgin Mary throws a new light and interpretation on the hymn of Miriam and of Hannah.

Nor are these the only instances in which our Blessed Saviour points out figurative expressions in the Old Testament, as deeply full of Divine meaning. One of the most important prophecies of the Gospel is wrapped up in a figure of this kind;—that passage in the Psalms which our Lord pointed out, respecting the Stone which the builders had refused, which had become the head of the corner[5]. It could not have been, to those to whom it was addressed, any clear satisfactory proof adduced from the Scriptures; but must have been not only to the Jews in general, but even to Apostles, from their little knowledge at the time, perfectly a dark saying. It must have appeared at best not a proof, but an application, of an expression strongly figurative, and that application quite enigmatical. The expression, as used in the Psalms, seems either a proverbial saying, or an allusion to some well-known occurrence in a building at the time, which the Psalmist applied to himself and his own history. But that it spoke of the Messiah, or how it spoke of Him, time alone could explain; and even then not as any definite proof to reason, but to faith. Faith would afterwards, comparing things spiritual with

---

[5] Matt. xxi. 42.

spiritual, discern its wonderful fulfilment, as St. Peter did on the Day of Pentecost: then, but not till then, would faith perceive the "living Stone" of St. Peter; the Stone which Daniel saw, which should break to pieces the kingdoms of the world. Our Lord's reference is not an explanation of the passage, so much as a bringing it out to view, and leaving it in the eyes of all men as a dark prophecy; thereby rather to show hereafter that the things which would be so marvellous in their eyes were "the Lord's doing," than to afford any intellectual conviction beforehand, and at the time, by an appeal to Scriptural proof. Such passages continue to be as a dead letter, till found to be spirit and truth from being fulfilled in the Church. They are of the same nature as those numberless types, figures, and precepts, which may be and must be misunderstood, or not understood, by many; but which the life of some here and there may put to the proof, and thus verify, and show to be living words.

Nor is this mode of exposition, which our Lord uses, confined to the quotations of particular passages, but extends to the whole of the Old Testament, as if one perfect and entire system. We may observe the manner in which He explains who are the true children of Abraham. For, if we may venture to say it, He sets aside the lineal descendants of Abraham as not being the true sons, as in the expression, "If ye were the children of Abraham, ye would do the works of Abraham;" and claims the title for the Publican Zaccheus, "Salvation is come unto this house, since he also is a child of Abraham." And if the faithful were the children of Abraham in our Saviour's interpretation, the guileless were the true Israelites: "Behold an Israelite indeed, in whom there is no guile." Surely the Catholic custom of expounding Scripture is far more similar to this in its character, than that of modern interpreters.

Again, in like manner, the very commandments of the Law, which our Saviour has declared that He came to fulfil to the uttermost and to the least particle, and not to destroy, are according to His own interpretations, not literally taken, but spiritually. The unkind word and action is a breach of the commandment which only speaks of murder; the seventh commandment is broken by the evil look; the love of God and of our neighbour is the only true way of keeping the Decalogue; and to know and perceive this, is to be near unto the Kingdom. As faith alone can keep them, so faith alone can understand and interpret the full meaning of these commandments. Even the Heathen Philosopher says, that there is "an eye from experience by which men perceive principles[6];" that a man must lead a good life to understand the words of philosophy.

SECTION XIII

APPARENT EXCEPTIONS TO THIS RULE

THERE are three instances in which our Lord quotes the Old Testament, to which this law of interpretation may not appear to be applicable; but the occasion with which they are connected is so deeply mysterious, that one feels a natural fear and shrinking from entering upon it. They are all three made use of upon the same occasion; they are spoken to Satan in our Lord's temptation. Nor

[6] Διὰ γὰρ τὸ ἔχειν ἐκ τῆς ἐμπειρίας ὄμμα ὁρῶσι τὰς ἀρχάς. Arist. Ethics, lib. vi. ch. 11.

is it in any way requisite that these instances should bear the test, in order to support this rule of exposition; inasmuch as they are not made use of to mankind, who are to be directed how they are to use and search the Scriptures, but to those evil spirits who have not saving faith, and are incapable of profiting by them. They appear to me at first sight to militate against the general argument, but on considering the occasion of their occurrence, they seem to confirm, and rather to coincide with it, if on so inscrutable a subject one may say so: they sanction the general supposition that the letter of Scripture is for the disobedient. It is the letter that killeth, but the Spirit that giveth life: and it is to the Spirit that giveth life, within the letter, to which our Lord refers in teaching mankind, and points out to us the way to arrive at it. "The law is not made for a righteous man, but for the lawless and disobedient." To the Evil one, perhaps, alone therefore our Lord applies the very letter of the law, setting aside his temptation, with the solemn denial " *It is written.*"

Enough, perhaps, has been said to show that this subject of Scriptural exposition is an awful and mysterious one; that the saving knowledge of Scripture can only be learnt by a good life; that, notwithstanding any mistakes that individuals may make in particular instances of such exposition, this mode of interpretation is the true one; that the teaching of the Spirit alone can unfold the words of the Spirit. It might also be mentioned, that many important points of belief, not to say the whole of Church doctrine, comes to us as established by the same laws,— not palpable, and sensible, and strongly marked, but depending on a kind of indefinite and morally-received evidence; such, for instance, as enjoins the keeping of the Lord's day.

But now, if this be the law of interpreting Holy Scripture, not to be circumscribed by human reason, the question will occur to us, what are to be our guides and safeguards? How are we to know Divine affections and obedient piety, which are the true interpreters, from mere feeling and imagination? It may be shown by another instance. How is faith to be distinguished from superstition? for faith is doubtless characterized by an exceeding readiness to believe, and so is superstition. And yet they are as opposed as light and darkness; in one salvation consists, the other is the effect of a bad life and perverted conscience. The one may be seen in the woman who touched the hem of our Saviour's garment; in St. John, when he saw the grave-clothes wrapt up, and believed; in Nathanael, who acknowledged the Christ on hearing that He had seen him under the fig-tree. The other may be seen in Saul, when he went to consult the witch of Endor; in Herod, when he thought that John the Baptist had arisen from the dead; in the Jews, when they were so scrupulous of external observance, to the neglect of all moral duties. The one is the indication of a good heart, and is accompanied with a great reverence for the Divine power and goodness; the other the contrary. It may be difficult to lay down rules of distinction; but sufficient is it for all practical purposes, that one is the result of prayer and obedience, the other arises from an absence of both.

PART IV

Analogies of the Gospel

SECTION I

ANALOGIES OBSERVABLE IN NATURE

IT is, therefore, evident that Holy Scripture is not to be tied down to one human and literal interpretation, but discloses infinite meanings to the eye of faith, and that our Lord does Himself furnish us with this law of interpretation which the Church has always sanctioned. It is also evident, that this Divine knowledge, however attained, will be made up of analogies and correspondencies, such as faith will more and more reveal, pondering over and comparing intimations given, and thence from the laws of probable evidence proceeding to higher, and broader, and deeper views in the knowledge of Christ; and that there is something faulty in that moral discernment which is slow to perceive these spiritual analogies; as when our Lord reproved His disciples for not understanding that He spoke of subtilely-pervading doctrine, when He used the term "leaven;" and that He spake not of "the meat which perisheth" when He mentioned "bread;" and as when He taught us that we are to learn of Divine things as we dis-

cern signs of the weather. We are, therefore, to infer that
a knowledge of the Gospel will depend very much on our
spiritual discernment of analogies. The subject of Divine
knowledge is of course as infinite and incomprehensible as
is the nature of God; yet we may see in various branches
of religious knowledge one great law that pervades the
Scriptures, that of analogy.

Now there is in the human mind a tendency to be interested in and to rest in analogy; so much so, that
probability (which arises from a repetition of similar
observations) has been considered the very guide of life,
and the only means of arriving at practical and religious
knowledge. And this would lead one to suppose, that
there is something of analogy or sameness of operation in
the ways of God, as manifested in all His dealings with
mankind. For all knowledge that is worthy of the name
is the knowledge of God; and all progress in such knowledge consists almost in all cases, if not altogether, in
observing analogies, and rests upon the probability which is
founded on such similitudes.

And this observation is strongly confirmed by the facts
and instances which Holy Scripture itself supplies. The
cases of analogy which occur in it are so numerous, so
manifold, and so remarkable, that it seems to intimate
something of a vast system, of which these are but the
casual intimations; consequently, that greater light in
things Divine will consist in a fuller observation of these
analogies; and that to see more deeply into them, will
be to obtain a higher and greater knowledge of God.

Indeed, in many cases we are so familiarized with this
kind of evidence, that we take it for granted as satisfactory, and conclude and act upon it, as Bishop Butler
shows, and that almost instinctively, and as it were

unconsciously. But it seems desirable to show that this mode of arguing from analogy is so general, so sound and substantial, that we may reasonably pursue the same kind of interpretation in the Gospels, even into the higher and deeper things of God, as most safe and reverential, and perceive thereby some glimpses into those deeper treasures of knowledge which are hid in Christ.

Of course, such a method of reasoning, and the conclusions to which it may lead, will create great objections, and give offence ; inasmuch as it proceeds into things of a spiritual and what would be called mystical nature, and such abstract subjects as are more in the regions of contemplation than in practical and sensible life. For all moral subjects, when they are followed on into things heavenly and Divine, and such as require a preparation of the heart, are necessarily unpopular. As after the conversation at Capernaum, in which our Lord carried on the figure of the bread He had distributed miraculously, and of the manna in the wilderness, into the subject of His own Body and Blood ; "from that time many of His disciples went back and walked no more with Him. Jesus therefore," as if with mournful apprehension, "said unto the Twelve, Will ye also go away[1]?" And the reason of this effect is obvious, for this very knowledge is of faith. "I tried to understand this, but it was too hard for me, until I went into the sanctuary of God, then understood I the end—how foolish was I and ignorant ! even as it were a beast before Thee." Such is the difference of the natural and spiritual apprehension.

After all, it is a mode of reasoning which does not admit of demonstrative arguments, and is from its very nature more or less convincing to different minds. And this

[1] John vi. 67.

partly from constitutional differences; for some minds are naturally more quick in discerning resemblances than others, more apt to recognize them, and more ready to acquiesce in this mode of evidence. And to those who are not, the case is usually such as admits of no further proof which will carry conviction to them. Thus in human countenances one may perceive a resemblance which another may not; and to him that cannot, all argument to prove the resemblance is of course in vain; and yet to the mind of another the resemblance may be so strongly marked, as to indicate two persons to be of one and the same family, and be a sufficient evidence to act upon. And besides this constitutional diversity in various minds, there is also a vast difference in their degrees of moral and spiritual discernment; so that this mode of evidence appeals with an infinite variety in its degrees of acceptance to different minds, according to their habits, prepossessions, previous knowledge, attention, and interest in things Divine, and their various degrees of faith or charity. All that is here necessary to be shown is, that since Divine knowledge is attained by "comparing things spiritual with spiritual," it is beforehand probable, that there exists in "things spiritual" a mutual relation and analogy, as extensive and infinite as is the nature of that which is Divine.

First of all, as to natural providence, how far the whole. of it may be regulated by this order of analogy, may be gathered from a few palpable indications of it, which might be mentioned. For, in fact, natural philosophy does itself depend almost entirely on similarity or sameness in numerous facts, so as to admit of generalization; or inductions of numerous analogies, such as to denote a law. For instance, the course of time in which we are placed is entirely regulated by the law of analogy; every portion of it is but the return of similar periods: it consists in the development of days and nights recurring in similar order and succession, so certain and invariable as to afford a rule on which we act.   And so also of the longer durations with which we are acquainted, as in the returns of the year and its various seasons.   The analogy is so complete, and the resemblance so exact, that we naturally consider it as the greatest of certainties; viz. that the night, the day, the seasons of the year, will return in their appointed course.   And on this analogy in the periods of time depend an infinite variety of other analogies, by which the natures of all living creatures are regulated, the renewal, the decay, and changes of all creation; for all these are governed by, and depend upon, seasons of time.   And, moreover, this analogy of time in things natural is connected also with what is spiritual and Divine by Holy Scripture.   As for instance, in the appointment of the Sabbath :—the seventh day, the seventh year, the seven times seventh.   Nor is it possible to say, to what extent this may reach, or how far it may regulate the Divine proceedings; as was the case in the duration of the captivity being regulated by Sabbatical periods of time, "till the land had enjoyed her Sabbaths."   And many other instances might be mentioned, whereby some analogy in our religious life depends on analogous developments of the day.   So that as in nature the return of day and the return of spring prefigure the eternal morning, and the new year of the Resurrection : so do these returning Sabbaths, whether of days or of years or of a thousand years, prefigure the coming of the great eternal Sabbath : thus passing on into fulfilments even greater and higher, till lost in what is infinite and eternal.   And thus holiness on earth is as it were embodied, and heaven prefigured, in the recurrence of stated periods of time. For the Sabbath implies the heavenly kingdom, the Christian state now on earth and hereafter in heaven, and of itself represents the rest of heaven, its holiness and love. These things would lead one to apprehend that there may be some law of analogy throughout the spiritual and material world, whereby the development of certain events may be according to certain intervals of time: for here we observe first of all that nature has analogies of time, and then that Scripture falls in with and takes up these analogies. And we may be able to ascertain sufficient to intimate the existence of a system, although perfectly incapable of tracing out that system, from the infinite extent of spiritual worlds.

Again, naturalists observe a very remarkable analogy in the formation of animals: and that not only where similar ends are to be produced by similar means, but in many cases where they are not: yet they still seem to be controlled by one law. Thus where in the internal construction of creatures some organs are not needed, there is oftentimes a shadow or resemblance of them, as if even in variety the Author of nature was desirous to adhere to the same law of analogy or resemblance. These things indicate a love of order, harmony, and analogy, even beyond the requisites of apparent expediency ; so that it would be but according to the same law, if we find something of this resemblance in what is moral and spiritual. For even in matters apparently diverse in their nature and object there exists a certain likeness and relation to each other: so that what is found in one event may be looked for in another.

Another order of analogy may be observed throughout

things natural, in objects greatly differing in size and importance. The changes of day and night bear a certain analogy to the seasons of the year : the lesser circuit of time to the greater. Again, the natural day bears so obvious an analogy to the different periods of mortal life as to supply an usual metaphor, of the morning or evening of life ; and this extending to many particulars in the two. In the same manner it has been observed, that the periods of a state or nation form a resemblance to the four ages of human life, its infancy, gradual rise, completion, and decay. So also in the living creatures that come to our notice, small objects will appear to be formed after the model of larger ones, and in some degree to represent them in miniature ; or parts of the same object will be similar in formation to the whole, as the branch of a tree to the entire tree. So that if in Holy Scripture the history of a nation and an individual, or the Church and a Christian, are types of each other, it would appear to be according to the same law of analogy : or that the courses of events, as they proceed, should be developing similar circles, similar appearances, forms, or shadows of form, in matters infinitely differing in importance.

In short, it would seem as if in nature all things were made up of analogy and relation, as far as we can judge from the intimations of it which fall under the limited range of our view ; and therefore, why may not this be the case in Revelation also ?

SECTION II

GENERAL SCHEMES OF ANALOGY IN SCRIPTURE

AND now we proceed to show certain general forms or schemes of analogy throughout the Scriptures, after first premising by way of caution, that the reducing of things to scheme and system in religion is a practice of itself defective and liable to error. On subjects Divine, and therefore partaking of what is infinite, there is always a danger in attempting to class and separate into definite and human systems of division. The relations and dependencies of things are so great, that there is often much fallacy in marking out and distinguishing, and then arguing upon our own divisions and distinctions. As in ordinary gifts of the Spirit as distinguished from extraordinary, justification as distinguished from sanctification, faith as distinguished from works, the Church visible as distinguished from the Church invisible; these and many other such divisions and systems, however necessary in themselves, yet imperceptibly lead to manifold errors and misunderstandings. Nor indeed can they be strictly accurate, for things Divine, as things natural, blend with one another so imperceptibly, that no definite and accurate line can be drawn between them. Thus it is with the colours of the rainbow,—with the seasons of the year,—with the sea and shore,—they mutually recede and retire and blend into each other; so that it would be difficult and perhaps impossible to draw any strong line of demarcation. Allowing therefore that systems and divisions are liable to these errors, from the very infirmity of our human knowledge, which can in no way circumscribe the infinite; and therefore not depending too much on their exactness and accuracy in embracing the whole subject; we may still have recourse to them in order to arrange our ideas and facilitate our inquiries. And we may be perhaps allowed to throw these analogies into something of a scheme, being at the same time aware that they run into each other, and into other numerous and indefinable analogies not to be embraced in the same. Shallow minds alone can rest in systems, and be satisfied with the apparent ease and clearness with which they arrange great truths; their seeming clearness often arises from their passing over all the difficulties, without diving into their depths: for system is human, and squares out, delineates, and defines the surface: the subjects systematized are of a nature Divine and infinite, and contain within them unfathomable deeps.

Now first of all with regard to successive periods of time, there will be found in them analogous conditions or states; of which the first shadows forth, as in a glass darkly, another which is to ensue, and that which ensues again prefigures another which is to follow, until they are lost from our view in something which is infinite, which they also prefigure. As nights and days, and winters and summers, prefigure and promise the return of each other, till they are all lost in the night and winter of the grave, and the morning and summer of Resurrection.

Thus the Sabbath days followed each other, and had a higher fulfilment in the Sabbatical year; and the Sabbatical years followed each other, till they had a higher fulfilment in the year of the Jubilee: the great year of rest, of deliverance and release. But this itself was typical of the Christian kingdom; and the prophet Isaiah in describing that "the acceptable year²," is, by the very words

² Isa. lxi. 1—3.

which describe its observance, speaking of the coming in
of the Christian kingdom ; and our Lord's first preaching
in the synagogue at Nazareth, consisted in a declaration
that that "acceptable year" had come, in Himself and in
His kingdom[3]. Our Lord's Christian kingdom therefore
on earth is the great Sabbath, which all those Sabbatical
days and years presignified. And in this great Sabbath
our lot is cast ; that kingdom which consists in doing the
work of God, not our own, and in peace and joy in the
Holy Ghost. And yet this fulfilment is but an earnest,
and type, and figure of that "rest which remaineth for the
people of God" hereafter.

The number forty, as applied to days or years, may by
the way be mentioned as another instance of a mysterious
analogy contained in numbers and duration. It seems to
signify something of purgation and trial, and absence from
heaven. As in the forty days of the flood descending :
forty days of Moses fasting in the mount, and this twice
repeated[4]; forty days of Elijah fasting in the wilderness,
forty days in which he went in the strength of that
heavenly food ; forty days of purification from uncleanness before presentation in the Temple. Forty were the
days of our Lord's fasting and temptation[5], before angels
ministered unto Him ; forty were the days of our Lord's
stay on earth after His resurrection, speaking of the things
concerning the Kingdom ; and in like manner, forty days
had the spies been searching out the Holy Land, as it is
said expressly, "each day for a year[6]." The forty years
of the children of Israel in the wilderness is the subject of

---

[3] See Nativity, pp. 383, 384.

[4] "I fell down before the Lord forty days and forty nights, as I
fell down at the first."—Deut. ix. 25.

[5] See Nativity, p. 244. [6] Num. xiv. 34.

P

constant allusion and reference throughout the Scriptures ; for forty days did Jonah preach to the Ninevites ; and for forty years did the Holy Spirit plead with the guilty and blood-stained Jerusalem ; and forty years is the period of man's probation upon earth, whether it is considered as the average length of human life, or that period beyond which an entire conversion of character scarcely takes place, wherein for *forty years* long God stretched forth His hands.   Thus does that state of things which is revealed pass imperceptibly into that which is natural. In like manner, as may be seen in the number twelve, which, both in nature and revelation alike, seems to indicate something perfect in that which is finite : as the twelve hours [7] make up the day, twelve months the year, twelve tribes the Church, twelve disciples the Apostolic choir.   Or the same twofold, for again twenty-four hours make up the day, twenty-four courses the priests' order.   These three numbers, seven, and forty, and twelve, may serve as some slight indication of a hidden analogy of numbers, by which successive periods of time may be regulated.   But what has been said only affords a glimpse into a very vast and deep subject.

But to return ; the successive conditions of the Jewish nation were successive figures and analogies of the Christian state.   They were called out of Egypt as we are called out of the world, of which Egypt is the frequent type, to approach near to the holy mountain of God : and every part of their pilgrimage is, we know, but a lively exhibition of that of the Christian's course ;—the Red Sea being the figure of holy Baptism ; the Cloud and the Pillar of fire of the Holy Spirit that led them through that and from that Sea ; the Bread from Heaven, of the Holy

[7] See Passion, p. 62.

Eucharist; the Rock smitten, of Christ crucified; and the Water of His Spirit, the bitter waters of affliction sweetened by the Cross; Mount Sinai, of the Christian law; the tabernacle, of the guidance of the Church; Aaron's rod that budded, of the Christian priesthood; the oracle over the mercy seat, God's voice in the Gospels; the Urim and Thummim, of His voice in the Church. Their murmurings were the pictures and representations of our murmurings; their rebellions, of our rebellions; their distrust, of ours; their turning back to Egypt, of our worldly longings; their infidelity, of that which prevails in the Christian world. The very words in which their state is spoken of might equally well describe our own : He bore them to Himself "on eagles' wings;" He fed them " with angels' food;" " He led them through the deep as a horse in the wilderness, that they should not stumble; the Spirit of the Lord caused them to rest." And the very words which describe their disobedience are the account of ours also, as, " forty years was I grieved," and " all the day long" (as from the Cross) " have I stretched forth My hands to a disobedient and gainsaying people."

And the next dispensation in which we find the Israelites is again another mirror of the Christian condition. They are in their promised land and kingdom, like ourselves. But it is not the rest they anticipated; not from any deficiency in the land itself, for it is indeed, as they had been told, a land flowing with milk and honey; but on account of their own want of faith to expel their seven deadly enemies, who on this account continued in the land as thorns in their sides, but were made by the Almighty as means to humble them, "to try them, and to prove them, and to know what is in their heart." So is

It with us Christians, and with those seven [8] deadly sins that still prevail in the Christian state. Again, when they are distressed, and calling for aid, a Deliverer is ever raised up to succour them, as types and figures of that great Deliverer Who is with us; yet Who is often not sought or acknowledged till we are distressed by our enemies,—by those enemies whom our want of faith has left in our Christian inheritance. Many such points of resemblance will at once be recognized by all.

And these two instances are probably but indications of a far more extensive course of successive analogies. For, to mention no others, the age of David and that of Solomon have been well supposed to prefigure and shadow forth the two periods in the history of the Church; the first when the mould and pattern was set in the primitive age; and the second when it was afterwards more fully developed, and the riches of the world flowed into it.

It is in a manner precisely similar to this that the Christian kingdom, which was thus prefigured, does itself prefigure and set forth that which is to come; so much so, that perhaps there is scarcely any one expression used respecting one, but that it speaks of the other also; true

---

[8] Bishop Andrewes in his Devotions thus applies the seven nations to the seven mortal sins :—

τύφος,	'Αμορραῖος.
φθόνος,	'Εθαῖος.
ὀργιλότης,	Φερεζαῖος.
πλησμονὴ,	Γεργεσαῖος.
ἀσέλγεια,	Εὐαῖος.
περισπασμοὶ βιωτικοὶ,	Χαναναῖος.
τὸ χλιαρὸν τῆς ἀκηδίας,	'Ιεβουσαῖος.

Preces Privatæ, Dies quarta, p. 106.

in some sense now of that which is the earnest and pledge, true also in its fulness of the completion hereafter.

The Israelites were called, elected, preordained, and foretold, and were chosen out of all the world to be the people of God. It is said of all Christians also, that they are preordained, foretold, called, elected, the peculiar people of God. But all these terms, which are applied to Christians now, are also all of them applied in a higher and stricter sense to the immaculate Church invisible. There is an Ecclesia now throughout the earth, an election of God's people out of the world, the Church visible; but there is an Ecclesia also, the Church invisible, in a higher sense the election of God. There is a Regeneration, which is at Baptism, by which we are all made children of God; but there is another Regeneration, when the Son of Man shall sit on the throne of His Glory, when they that are accounted worthy shall in a higher sense become "the children of God," and "equal to the angels." The baptized are now clothed in white garments, which is the righteousness of Christ; but in a higher sense the redeemed walk with Him in Heaven in white robes, and are clothed with His righteousness. The riches of Christ's kingdom here on earth, such as eye hath not seen, nor ear heard, nor heart of man hath conceived, are revealed unto us, says St. Paul, by the Spirit; and yet doubtless these words can only receive their plenary fulfilment in Heaven. To show fully all these instances, would be to transcribe almost every page of the Gospels; and many errors have arisen from persons not observing this twofold sense almost throughout.

And again, as all these were but according to the pattern given in the Mount, so it will be found that all things in the Law have their fulfilment in the kingdom of God upon earth, and also in the kingdom of God in Heaven. For every thing in the Law bears onward,—is fulfilled now, and shall be fulfilled when Heaven and earth fail. At the sound of the trumpet the camp of Israel was moved[9], and the movement is mentioned from the four quarters, the East and West, and North and South: so also the Christian camp is moved to meet the new and heavenly coming of the Kingdom, at the sound of the Gospel, which is the trumpet; and is gathered by Christ's ministers, who are spoken of as His angels, from the four winds: and this which is now going on does further prefigure the time when the Son of man " shall send forth His angels with a great sound of a trumpet," and they shall " gather His elect from the four winds," from the East, and from the West, and from the North, and from the South.   There is One even now that walketh between the " seven golden candlesticks," which are the seven Churches; and there are also seven Spirits which are before the throne of God.   Of old there was eating and drinking for the Priests, or for those that were clean, and a feast upon the Sacrifice: frequent mention is made of their " eating, and drinking," and " rejoicing before the Lord[1];" of " eating those things wherewith the atonement was made[2]," and from which " the stranger" was expressly prohibited.   And in the Book of Exodus it is said of the people, " they saw God, and did eat and drink[3];" and the disciples " ate and drank" with our Lord after His resurrection.   So also now is there an Eucharistic feast upon our great Sacrifice: and very often, after some secret and mysterious resemblance, is Heaven itself spoken of under a like figure (as Origen has observed), " Blessed are they which are called unto the marriage Supper of the

[9] Num. x. 1—10.

[2] Exod. xxix. 33.

[1] Deut. xii. 7.

[3] Exod. xxiv. 11.

Lamb;" those that are found watching shall be made "to sit down to meat," and the Lord Himself shall "come forth and serve them."

It may be observed, that all these developments are not only successive, but also progressive; each of them advances onward into a higher and fuller dispensation, until lost in that which is infinite. Every thing is better than the preceding, as coming from that heavenly Bridegroom, of Whom it is said, that He hath kept the good wine until the last. Our present state, as Christians, being the intermediate state between the earthly and the heavenly, in all things combines the two. In the written word it has both the letter and the Spirit; whatever is historical is prophetical; whatever is typified is itself typical; in rites and ordinances every thing is Sacramental, combining the visible and the spiritual, nothing visible without a spiritual gift, no spiritual gift without a visible sign. Christian obedience has an external action to perform, but is also the exercise of an internal principle: the Church visible and Church invisible, so united and combined that neither can be conceived as disunited and of independent existence. To separate what is internal from what is external, the letter from the Spirit, the visible from the invisible, or the reverse, is in either case to depart from the Church Catholic into heresy (as they in whose system Baptism is separated from the Spirit, or the Spirit is acknowledged and Baptism rejected). Whereas in the previous dispensation they had the letter without the Spirit, the external rite without the accompanying internal gift, the Church was visible, and supported by visible signs, and the Church invisible was not disclosed therein. Works there were, but not of faith; external acts, but not the internal charity which connected them with Heaven. But again, in that which is to be hereafter, there will be the Spirit but not the letter of God's commands, for there will be perfect knowledge. There will be the spiritual gift without the Sacramental rite, for there is the beatific fruition of God; and we shall see "face to face," without the intervention of material veils.   Once the material veil alone; now the material veil, and Christ therein discerned by faith; there Christ Himself without the veil; the Church visible departing into the invisible.   Now the Word written, enlightening with knowledge; then the saving Word Himself, filling with the fulness of all truth.   Thus the Israelite walked in a system Divine and heavenly, encompassed with numberless signs of which he knew not the meaning, but which were closely interwoven and connected with the coming dispensation: much more is the Christian now encompassed with things heavenly, a supernatural world in which he is placed, but which is infinitely beyond his thought.

Numberless cases might be adduced of this varied and progressive fulfilment.   The Passover, for instance, spoke of what had occurred in Egypt, and of what was to come in the Christian Kingdom, being at the same time both commemorative and prophetic.   Another might be taken from the eighth Psalm, "What is man, that Thou art mindful of him; and the son of man, that Thou visitest him? Thou madest him lower than the angels, to crown him with glory and worship.   Thou makest him to have dominion of the works of Thy hands."   Now this is clearly spoken of mankind in Adam, it certainly was in him fulfilled; and yet no less certainly is it, we know, spoken of mankind in Christ, the second Adam; and doubtless was fulfilled at the Resurrection, when our Lord said, "All power is given Me" (i. e. as the Son of Man, not as God) "in Heaven and in earth."   And yet, certainly as it was

then fulfilled, no less certainly is it not fulfilled in a plenary sense till the end of the world; for St. Paul says, in
quoting the passage in his Epistle to the Hebrews, " In
that He put all in subjection under Him, He left nothing
that is not put under Him, but now we see not yet all
things put under Him." Again, another important instance
may be mentioned, of events going on in a course of
analogy, and being in themselves typical of a great and
future development. It would, I think, appear from Holy
Scripture, that all great and sudden judgments in the
order of God's Providence are typical and prophetical of
the general Judgment: and from this it follows that all
prophecies respecting a near and temporal judgment are
also descriptions of the final Judgment; and that all
accounts of the final Judgment may have a reference to
other previous visitations of God. The most remarkable
instance we have of this is our Lord's description of the
Day of Judgment; while at the same time the description
also applies in some mysterious manner to the destruction
of Jerusalem. The difficulties which have occurred in the
interpretation of this discourse have arisen from persons
limiting the account to one of these events only, and not
sufficiently perceiving that the description applies throughout to both, though it may break out into the more distinct
and marked description now of one of these, and now of
the other. And some, when they have perceived and
allowed this, yet appear to feel some difficulty from supposing such a case to be in some degree isolated and
peculiar, not sufficiently perceiving that it is according to
the rule of all prophecy. And other references of our
Lord to this great subject, as in His words on weeping
over Jerusalem, or in those addressed to the women that
lamented His sufferings, seem to combine both of these

events.   This judgment is that of destruction by war; but we have our Lord's own authority for perceiving in other judgments of God a type of the great Day: the destruction of the world by water at the deluge, and that of Sodom and Gomorrah by fire, He has Himself told us, are for their suddenness types of the great Judgment.   Other passages of Scripture will prove the same respecting other things; as for instance, the plague of locusts in the prophet Joel combines in its description a reference to the last great Day, nearly as much as our Lord's prophecy respecting Jerusalem.   It is evident that the taking of Babylon has the same most intimate and close analogy.   And in the Psalms the description of storms and earthquakes are found to have incidental references to the coming of God to judge the world.   The fall of Jericho at the sound of the trumpets, with all the circumstances of it, and innumerable other events of the kind, will at once suggest the same idea to a thoughtful mind.

All smaller events seem bound up in greater, as partaking of their character and of their laws ; especially therefore all lesser judgments in the great Judgment itself. And indeed they seem in some respects to be indications of the sentence already passed.   The cities which God hath destroyed, as Babylon, and Jerusalem, and Rome, still it may be observed long after their destruction continue to linger on, and even as it were after the declaration and execution of the sentence.   In all this, what are they but types of the world, on which death and the curse have passed, but which still lingers on alive in death, and as it were in a living death?

And in fact these things do but suggest to us, that in the moral and spiritual world the Almighty is pleased to work by invariable and immutable laws ; as in things natural, where all our knowledge arises from our observing that similar causes produce similar effects : although of course, in a system so vast as to extend into other worlds, and of which this earth is but a small part, we can only discern but a few broken links here and there of the chain.

Now things of this kind are numerous and manifold, and ever continue to increase upon us more and more on consideration and comparison; and this may afford us some mode of accounting for the interpretations of prophecies in Scripture. For they do certainly all appear to be fulfilled on many and manifold occasions, and yet still to wait for their full completion : inasmuch as the events themselves spoken of in prophecy are themselves typical of greater things hereafter : and it may be that all events in this mortal state of things are but shadows and figures of what is spiritual and eternal. Indeed, the cases alluded to in Scripture seem rather intended to convey to us an intimation of this circumstance, than to contain in themselves all we are to observe. So that the natural and moral government of God, and His present and visible Providence, serve the same office to His heavenly kingdom, which the ritual service of the Jews did of old ; the ritual and external to pass away, and the spiritual contained within it to remain : the visible and temporal state of things, in which we live, to depart, but at present to serve for schooling and training us, as the Israelites of old. And indeed one great object in the old dispensation appears to have been, to claim all the world for God's world, and to say that whatever is done upon earth God doeth it Himself.

The whole subject, so vast and incomprehensible, suggests another also still more so : whether the very nature of these analogies themselves may not arise from this, that they are various manifestations of Christ, or dispensations of Christ, and His dealings towards His people : and whether, as He is described as being " the same yesterday, and to-day, and for ever," this may not signify a sameness in all His ways towards His creatures, as His infinite attributes of perfection are shown in what is finite.   In the same manner as the sameness and analogy of nights and days, of months and seasons of the year, and the innumerable analogies of nature, depend on and arise from the circumstance of the earth coming under the same or different relations to the sun, while in itself it continues still the same and unvaried.   This may account for the analogy of events; viz. that they are all visitations of Christ, to cities, to nations, or to the world at large ;—to save or to destroy by the majesty of His awful presence, as they are found meet or unmeet to receive Him.

And there may be something deeply secret and mysterious in the very circumstance of repetition, from some unknown reference to the Unity in Three Persons.   Thus we find that the repetition of any thing in word or deed, especially a third time, has a great force in Scripture. And the number two is always considered incomplete till the third is added, inasmuch as three is the full and perfect number; so that, when any thing is repeated a second time, the mind is carried on to some third fulfilment.   Thus the driving the buyers and sellers from the Temple by our Lord, which twice took place, naturally carries on the mind to a third fulfilment in the destruction of Jerusalem ; and these to some higher spiritual development ; when at last the Lord shall again "suddenly come to His temple,"— " but who may abide the day of His coming?"   So also the two miracles of the loaves in the Gospel have their higher fulfilment in the Eucharist ; and that also may but precede some secret mystery in Heaven hereafter, which is now set forth by this great Sacrament. Thus the dream was repeated unto Pharaoh, implying confirmation[4]; and Samuel was thrice called in the Temple, before he heard and understood that it was the voice of God; when on the next time God's will was fully revealed to him.

It may further be noticed that these various fulfilments and progressive senses of prophecy, which we have spoken of, have generally some great coherence and mutual relation to each other. For instance, when in the Lord's Prayer we say "Thy kingdom come," we may signify the final kingdom hereafter in Heaven as distinguished from the present, for we are told to be "looking for and hastening unto" that day of Christ's appearing; and the Church in St. John prays for its coming. Or we may rather signify the present kingdom, the spread of the Gospel throughout the earth, as deeming ourselves unmeet for that great Day; or we may more particularly mean the kingdom being established in our own hearts; for our Lord says the "kingdom of Heaven is within you." But these are so mutually related, that in praying for it in one sense we are seeking for its fulfilment in the other also. For if we pray for the day of Judgment, we pray for the Gospel being spread upon earth, which must precede that time, for when we extend the Gospel we hasten the final kingdom: and we at the same time pray likewise that the kingdom be first established in ourselves, without which we are unprepared to meet the last. Or if we pray for the kingdom being established in ourselves, we take the most effectual means for its spread upon earth, and cannot but carry on our thoughts to its completion on the day of Judgment, without which it cannot fully be. Thus he who uses this

[4] See Passion, pp. 28. 54. 164.

prayer in one sense, does at the same time pray in the other also ; it is "as if a wheel had been in the midst of a wheel," and "the wheels were full of eyes round about." And wonderful as it proceeds is each of these evolutions of Providence, which the exclamation of the Prophet may well serve to indicate, "as for the wheels, it was cried unto them in my hearing, O wheel[5]."

SECTION III

ANALOGOUS MANIFESTATIONS OF CHRIST, IN HIS LIFE IN THE FLESH, IN HIS MEMBERS, IN HIS CHURCH

It has been observed that there are some analogies which may merely arise from the circumstance of their being various manifestations of Christ. The resemblance of the Jewish Church to the history of an individual, or to the Christian Church, may be nothing more than this, that in each of these Christ's image is reflected, and therefore each resembles the other, in that both of them mutually resemble Christ, and shadow forth His immutable glory. And hence another extensive course of analogy may be found in this, that whatever is fulfilled in Christ is found in some analogous form in His Church, and also in individual members of His Church. And this, if we may express it by the simile before used, is like the sun, which has his place in Heaven, and is imaged likewise and set forth throughout all his goings in every large body of water, and also in a manner equally distinct and full in each particular wave or drop below. This is the case very extensively

[5] Ezek. x. 13.

throughout all the Scriptures in psalm and prophecy, in parable and type.

It may be seen for instance in single typical expressions, nearly all of which appear to admit of a threefold sense ; being applicable first of all to our Lord Himself, and also to His Body which is the Church ; and likewise to individual members of that Body. For instance, the word *temple* our Lord Himself applies to His own Body, saying that He would raise it up in three days ; it often signifies the Church, into which individuals are built up as hewn stones "into a spiritual house :" and it is said of the particular members that their bodies are the *temples* of the Holy Ghost. Our Lord Himself is the " *stone* which the builders refused ;" the Church is " the *stone* cut out of the mountain without hands," to break in pieces the kingdoms of the world; and Christians also are spoken of as " living *stones ;*" and Christ in them hereafter is " the white *stone*," given to them who overcome. Again, our Lord Himself is " *the tree of life*," the true Vine ; the Church also is the *tree* " overshadowing the earth," the vine out of Egypt ; and the Christian is the " *tree* planted by the water side," the *tree* for which the husbandman intercedes in the parable. In like manner the *branch* is often put for our Lord Himself, as " the Man whose name is the *Branch ;*" sometimes for His Church, " the *Branch* which Thou madest so strong for Thyself," and " in that day shall the *Branch* of the Lord be beautiful ;" sometimes for individuals, as, " ye are the *branches*," he is " cast forth as a *branch*." And other instances of the same kind might be adduced. So also our Lord is often spoken of as the *sun*, " His face did shine as the *sun ;*" the Church also is the *sun*, and " clothed with the *sun ;*" and it is said of " the righteous," that they " shall shine forth as the *sun*," and " His seat is like as the *sun* before Me." Our Lord Himself also is the *star;* " I am the bright and morning *star*," and His indwelling in Christians is " the *day-star* arising in their hearts[6] ;" and " I will give him the morning *star*[7]." And surely it is of the Christian Church that it is said, "there shall come a *star* out of Jacob[8]." And the children of Abraham are often spoken of as the *stars*,—the stars which shall shine for ever and ever ;—separate as the *stars*, united as the *sun*. Single words will often indicate a system, for typical expressions are not used arbitrarily, but on a definite scheme, and according to great analogies.

But more than all this, the ever-blessed and adorable Name even of our Lord Himself, the Name of the *Christ*, is applied in this threefold manner. To Himself personally as the *Christ;* to His Church, the members of which " being many, are one Body, and so also is *Christ;*" and sometimes the same name is spoken of individuals, as " yet not I, but *Christ* that liveth in me," which St. Paul says of himself.

It is obvious again to us all, how far this threefold sense and application pervades the Psalms. So much is this the case, that passages and expressions blend with each other, and sometimes come forth alternately in such a way, that they will hardly admit of our applying them in a distinct manner to each, for any considerable time, without having our attention called to the other. For if we express our human wants and distresses in the Psalms, we are soon met with declarations of innocence and holiness which can only find a place in Christ, or in His Church, and in His members as found in Him. But again, if we recognize therein the Person of Christ as

---

[6] 2 Pet. i. 19.   [7] Rev. ii. 28; xxii. 16.

[8] Num. xxiv. 17.

speaking by His Prophet, we are soon met with confessions
of sin that can only find a place in our sinful human condition ; unless we consider Him therein coming before His
Father, as bearing our sins in His own person, and "numbered with transgressors." In other places, again, both
of these may be found, but in such a manner as to render
them in neither sense strictly applicable ; but alone truly
answering to the fortunes, the duration, the changes, the
sins, the righteousness, the miseries, and the triumphs, of
the Church of God. As, for instance, in that passage of
the 89th Psalm, which speaks of the Person of Christ, but
passes imperceptibly from Him to the mention of His
Church, "Thou hast overthrown all His hedges, and
broken down His strongholds ; Thou has put out His
glory, and cast His throne down to the ground." And
even in the 22nd Psalm, towards the close, the Psalmis'
passes from Christ's sufferings on the Cross to His presence
in His Church. These observations therefore necessarily
lead us to a third consideration—that there is something
analogous to be found in the history of Christ and of His
Church, and of His members ; and also in the prophecies
that speak of that history.

An obvious instance of this may be found in the beginning of the Gospels, where the Evangelist mentions that
our Lord's finding refuge in Egypt was the fulfilment of
the prophecy, "out of Egypt have I called my Son." But
that prophecy in Hosea [*], "when Israel was a child, then
I loved him, and called my son out of Egypt," is clearly
speaking historically of the Jewish nation in its infancy.
Yet, as the nation of Israel was itself typical of the
Messiah, therefore that which is said either historically
or prophetically of that nation, is also said more fully and

[*] Ch. xi. 1.

Q

truly of the Anti-type Himself, which is Christ.   But the same in the higher and spiritual sense is also true of the individual Christian, not literally of course, as coming out of Egypt, but out of that which Egypt mystically re-presents throughout the Scriptures, namely, the world, out of which, the house of bondage, the Christian is called, and, we may add, in his infancy.   Other senses also, of course, and mysterious references, may be contained in it, as of the Christian Church itself being called out of the Egypt of the world ; and these we cannot attempt to limit.   No one can definitely mention the various modes in which the sun may be reflected throughout the world at any given time.

We may take another instance, which occurs imme-diately after in the same history, when the Evangelist says, that in the destruction of the infants was fulfilled the prophecy of Jeremiah [1], concerning the weeping of Rachel at the tomb.   But the passage there referred to was clearly spoken in the Prophet of the Jewish nation going into captivity.   "A voice was heard in Ramah, lamentation, and bitter weeping ; Rachel weeping for her children refused to be comforted for her children, be-cause they were not.   Thus saith the Lord ; Refrain thy voice from weeping, and thine eyes from tears : for thy work shall be rewarded, saith the Lord ; and they shall come again from the land of the enemy.   And there is hope in thine end, saith the Lord, that thy children shall come again to their own border."   Now, the obvious explanation of this is, that the restoration of the Jews from captivity was itself a type of our restoration from death in Christ.   And therefore the consolation of these mothers was, that these infant martyrs, who were the

[1] Ch. xxxi. 15.

first-fruits to the Lamb, would in Christ "come again from *the land of the enemy*," for these infants represent all those who are born again in Christ, those "babes" to whom the kingdom is revealed. The restoration of Israel is to them a pledge that "there is hope in their end." And here again, what is fulfilled in Israel and in individual Christians, is also fulfilled in Christ, Who will bring them with Him "from the land of the enemy." For at His death more fully might it be said to Rachel, or the daughter of Sion, "Refrain thy voice from weeping, for He shall come again from the land of the enemy, and there is hope in His end."

The case may be seen still more clearly by the figure under which the return of Israel from captivity is shown in the Prophet Ezekiel[2], in the vision of the "dry bones" which are restored to life by the breath of the Spirit. For although the Prophet hereby represents the return of Israel from captivity, yet the figure is such that it bears an obvious application to the resurrection of our Lord from the grave, and the resurrection of all Christians at the last Day. So much is this the case, that the analogy is more close and full in the Anti-type, than it is in the more immediate application of the prophecy to the temporal Israel. And the circumstance arises from its being an instance of the same great system of analogy, of the sons of Abraham, according to the letter, being typical of the true sons of Abraham after the Spirit; so that the captivity and restoration of Israel was itself but a figure of death and resurrection. And here it may be observed, that it is in Israel alone, as a nation, that there is this power of recovery and restoration; of Egypt, Babylon, Tyre, Edom, and the like, it is otherwise; their

[2] Ch. xxxvii.

Q 2

end is, that they should "perish for ever;" but of Israel
it is said, "there is hope in thine end," and, "I will not
make a full end" of thee.   For Israel represents the true
children of God, who return from death; those other
nations, the children of the world, in whom there is no
power of restoration from death, as there is in those in
whom mystically and figuratively, or really and spiritually,
Christ dwells.

The whole subject may be connected with something of
this kind.   It may be that the Church of old typified the
history of our Lord; and our Lord's life the history of
His Church afterwards.   And into this may run another
analogy, that whatever occurred in our Lord, happens
also in His members.   And, therefore, we often see two
of these only; as the likeness in the people of Israel to
an individual Christian, or the likeness of Christ in the
history of the individual; when the fact is, that Christ is
Himself the Centre from which these shadows are thrown
before and after; or as He Who is "the First and the
Last," first shown in one and then in another.   And thus
it is that in Christ are all the treasures of wisdom,
for He is in fact All in All; and it may be that all the
acceptableness of our works arises from some resemblance
to His.   As our prayers, our intercessions, our works of
charity, derive all their efficacy from the prayers, intercessions, and charities of Christ, and also in the Church our
Priestly acts have all their power and value from His
Priestly acts, and the like: so, much that we perceive
may be but the casual indications of a principle infinitely
great and incomprehensible.   "Lo, these are parts of His
ways; but how little a portion is heard of Him[3]!"   It
may be all nothing more than casual observations of this,

[3] Job xxvi. 14.

Christ seen in nations or individuals, in His Church, or in His members, in their works, their histories, their characters, seen again and again, in such glimpses as reveal Him to mankind.

Take again the Parables of our Lord. They may be considered as prophetical, and to us as historical, and also as containing great principles of truth; and thus may be seen to contain in some degree these threefold meanings or more. But we know so little of the full explanation of them, that we can but explain the circumstance in a very small degree. Thus, "the kingdom of heaven is like unto *a grain of mustard seed, ...* which being the least of all seeds, when it has grown is the greatest of shrubs, and becometh a tree." Now we may easily recognize three interpretations of this parable. For we see the grain of mustard seed in the humiliation of Christ to the form of a servant; in the humility of a true Christian, which is the chief mark of true faith; and in the Church in her lowest beginnings. And this interpretation derives confirmation from another place, where we find faith represented under the figure of the grain of mustard seed. For this faith in a Christian during his sojourn on earth is scarce perceptible, in like manner as our Lord Himself was not known among men: but hereafter what is now so small will fill eternity. And so, likewise, the Church, which was once so small as to be scarce discernible, is now as the great tree which fills the earth. The latter application of the parable to the Church visible is, indeed, the most obvious interpretation of the three, and that probably because it is the most palpable and discernible, and in some degree the pledge of those fulfilments which are more spiritual and invisible, and are to be in Heaven.

In like manner in the next parable, that of the *leaven*, two of these interpretations readily suggest themselves. For as Christianity has leavened the whole state of civil society, so also does "the kingdom of heaven" in the heart of an individual, leaven, secretly and imperceptibly influence, the whole of the character. And this "kingdom of heaven" in both cases, of course is Christ, and was, perhaps, true in His personal history on earth also in the Flesh. These two parables, perhaps, differ from one another in this, that the former parable of the mustard seed applies more particularly to the *visible* development of faith in the three senses alluded to, and as seen in the Church visible; while that of the leaven signifies more particularly the *secret* operation of faith and Christian principle in those three senses, extending unseen itself, but traceable in its effects.

The same meaning is observable in many other parables. And something of the same kind may be seen in the developments and descriptions of evil also, as in the man out of whom was cast the evil spirit, who returns with seven other worse than himself. This is clearly applied in the first sense to the Jewish nation, who, after their partial repentance and recovery, fell away again into a state which was irreclaimable. But no one will doubt but that the same parable has its mysterious and manifold eye also on individuals, and on that state of the heart which, after the rejection of grace given, it is "impossible to renew again unto repentance."

These indications may serve as hints or glimpses of some great mystery, whereby our Lord's history is set forth in the whole body of His Church, and also in its separate members. And it may be observed merely with regard to His natural life, that what was fulfilled in Him is also to be fulfilled literally in us, His birth in our birth, His baptism in our baptism, His temptation in ours ; and His death, His resurrection, and His ascension, are all to be again acted in each of us. His very offices in some sense, though in a very inferior and subordinate one, yet in some sense, are to be spoken of us : as He was Priest and King, so are we termed "a Royal Priesthood ;" yea, as He was Prophet, so on all of us also of these latter days is to be poured forth the Spirit of prophecy ; and more than all, as He was, in the highest sense, truly and alone the Son of God, so are we all now, and to be more fully made hereafter, sons of God ; and in Him Who is Himself "the First-born from the dead," we also are "the children of the Resurrection."

And again, this analogy of our Lord's life to be found fulfilled in the Christian, is not to be confined to the literal fulfilment alone, but exists likewise in various spiritual senses ; and that so necessarily, as often to be expressed as a law and by a precept. Thus, for instance, the circumstances of our Lord's death, burial, and resurrection, are not only to find a literal fulfilment in the good Christian, in his own death, and burial, and resurrection, but also spiritually, by an imperative law of necessity. " If we die with Him, we shall also live with Him ;" "we are buried with Him by baptism into death ;" we must be "risen together with Christ" by seeking "those things which are above ;" we must be "ascended together with Him" by "having our conversation in Heaven," and in having our affections set on Heaven. He hath already, by His ascent, made us to "sit together with Him in heavenly places." It will be obvious on a little consideration, how many precepts and doctrines throughout the Epistles are founded on this principle, viz.—of the necessity of that being fulfilled spiritually in us, which has been literally fulfilled in Christ.

And, indeed, so readily and easily does this whole train of thought recommend itself to us, and descend to us through the stream of sacred tradition, that the Church itself seems naturally to fall into the same lesson, and herself represents in her yearly course of Services the same relation to the history of our Lord, which she is to represent and exhibit in things deeper and more extensive. For in her sacred round of Services she imitates her Lord, in being born with Him at Christmas, and bearing witness to His manifestation at the Epiphany, and fasting with Him at Lent, being crucified with Him, and rising together with Him at Easter, conversing with Him on earth, and then ascending with Him; celebrating the gifts of the Holy Spirit, and the full communication of three Persons in one God. All of which things, thus set forth in our Christian year, are mysteriously to be fulfilled in us, even to that awful and blissful consummation, when we shall be in soul thoroughly sanctified by the gifts of the Spirit; and the Father, and the Son, and the Holy Spirit shall come unto us, and make their abode with us.

SECTION IV

A THREEFOLD ANALOGY, IN THE OLD TESTAMENT IN GOD'S PROVIDENCE, AND IN THE GOSPELS

THERE is again another point of view in which we may observe a varied and extensive system of analogies—that whatever principle or mode of acting we can perceive in our Lord in the Gospels, we may observe the same in

His manner of dealing with the Jews in the Old Testament; and we may observe the same also in His mode of dealing now with mankind, i. e. in His providence and moral government.

For instance, one great peculiarity or characteristic of our Lord's teaching, consists in its being combined and made up of words and works. It has been observed, that all His actions and miracles are in themselves always a kind of teaching; and that they fall in with and carry on His words, explaining them, and being explained by them; so much so, that they blend together to make one system of instruction. His miracles speak a language as strong and emphatic as His parables; and often the same image is in both presented to our minds, and in a manner so similar that we might almost confuse one with the other. And, indeed, oftentimes a miracle is of itself a parable, and a parable of itself contains within it something equivalent to a miracle; either from the hidden knowledge it displays, so that the parable in the course of time becomes a miracle in its fulfilment to those who witness it, as an evidence of Divine knowledge; or that the very circumstance it speaks of is in itself miraculous. Oftentimes, again, a miracle and a parable stand in such a relation to each other, that the teaching of neither is complete without the other.

Thus our Lord spoke of His ministry, and of the Jewish nation, with whom He pleaded for three years, under the figure of a tree, about which the husbandman laboured for three years, and interceded for it, but on its being unfruitful at the expiration of that time, the command goes forth for it destruction. Now, when our Lord came at the expiration of the three years, and found the unfruitful fig-tree, and dried it up by His word, this action adds a living and peculiar force to the former figure, and is itself also explained and illustrated by it.

Again, certain parables must immediately, in the minds of the disciples, have taken the place of miracles, as that of the husbandmen in the vineyard slaying the Heir; for this in the course of a few days must have appeared miraculous, as an attestation of Divine knowledge and power.

And when our Lord wished to convey some great truth to His hearers, it is obvious that He often did it by a miracle instead of, or in addition to, His oral instruction. All the miracles evidently contain very great and Divine teaching : the very nature of the miracles was equivalent to preaching the Gospel, as our Lord, in answer to the two disciples from John, pointed to His works as setting forth His Gospel. Thus a miracle wrought upon the Sabbath-day contained within it, when considered, the whole of the Gospel, or kingdom of heaven. And on some occasions it would seem as if our Lord, being desirous to express some lesson, worked a miracle; as, for instance, by the miraculous draught of fishes in St. Luke[4], the disciples are instructed to give up their worldly callings by faith in Christ, and have set before them a lively figure of their further history, as apparently in vain for a long time " toiling" all night in the Gospel, and at last in the morning taking the miraculous draught, as "fishers of men." The same might have been set before them by a sermon. When He *touched* the leper on healing him, thereby taking on Himself the uncleanness, and standing before God as unclean Himself, according to the Law, instead of that leper, He taught us more than words could have done, that in forgiving our sins, and remitting their

[4] Ch. v. 1—10. See Nativity, p. 401.

consequences, He took them upon Himself before God, that He "bore our griefs, and carried our sorrows," and that "the chastisement of our peace was upon Him :" that His releasing us was not without suffering Himself in our stead. Again, the two miracles of the loaves and fishes were like an emphatic teaching respecting that Bread which came down from heaven, with which He would feed His Church. This, together with the marriage at Cana of Galilee, and many other miracles, as explained by the expositions of the Church, are to us equivalent to parables.

In addition to all this, it is to be noticed that the characteristic of our Lord's teaching was that of connecting His instruction with external events and objects, so as in fact to render them the instruments and vehicles of His instruction. By which circumstance, in addition to the immediate subject of His teaching, He evidently would instruct us to look upon all events and upon the objects of external nature, as conveying spiritual knowledge and instruction: and therefore not only sanctions our so doing, but urges upon us the necessity of thus interpreting all actions and events of external nature and providence.

Our Lord's teaching seems to have been so entirely made up of this combination,—appeals to external objects or actions of His own superseding or united with oral instruction,—that it would be difficult to separate the one from the other. On one occasion, pointing to the birds of the air and the lilies of the field ; on another, taking His lesson from the lowering sky, or the sheepfold, or the sowing of corn ; or from some passing event, as the destruction of the Galileans, or fall of the tower of Siloam ; or from some present object, as the cup and the platter, the contest for precedency of place ; or conveying the great principles of His Gospel by actions of His own, as that of taking the little children into His arms, of washing the disciples' feet ; or even by what would be considered, humanly speaking, an involuntary action, as the bearing of His Cross, and committing it to another to bear after Him.

All things with Him become immediately sanctified by His presence, hallowed by Divine associations, ennobled by lessons of things heavenly, full of warning or consolation, and thus minister to godly edifying.

And so mutually do our Lord's doings bear upon His sayings, that His own example often becomes the best and most lively interpreter of His teaching, His works of His words. His miracles often throw a force of reality and Divine emphasis upon His sayings. Thus when our Lord says, "ask, and it shall be given you," and, "every one that asketh receiveth," and, "all things, whatsoever ye shall ask in prayer, believing, ye shall receive," such expressions derive a very peculiar force, when we observe that our Lord in performing His miracles always conferred literally that which was asked, never once failing to do so, and always exactly according to the extent of the request, never more nor less, and when not asked not conferring, and without faith doing no miracle. So entirely was our Lord's mode of instruction made up of visible actions, or external works, and oral teaching.

Now we find that this characteristic of our Lord's teaching, when manifested visibly in the flesh, is precisely the same as His mode of teaching us now in His invisible providence. Whatever progress any one has made in the knowledge of religion, he will find has been made up of these two ; that is, of what he hears or reads, and also of what he observes in external objects : they both make up one teaching—one illustrates, exemplifies, and proves, the other. Even the course of time, day and night, speaks significantly and with Divine eloquence; "there is neither speech nor language, but their voices are heard among them :" to a person of thoughtful religious consideration, the events of life as they pass minister instruction; the whole in fact of his knowledge arises from a combination and comparison of circumstances that occur, together with that positive instruction which he gains from the written teaching of God. As, for instance, from the deaths of others we gain a sensible apprehension of our own, a deeper understanding of our condition; from observing the ill effects of pride or passion in the world, a more lively knowledge of the declarations of Scripture respecting them ; from the events that occur to ourselves, a more intimate knowledge and experience of God's ways. So much is this the case, that religious knowledge or wisdom does not depend on the great degree of study, but of study combined with these observations ; so that Holy Scripture in speaking of spiritual ignorance combines both the senses —the ears dull of hearing and the eyes being blinded,— and the meditative faculty within—the heart incapable of understanding. All this is indeed a very simple truth, obvious to any one, but it should be considered, that as all Divine knowledge is the especial gift from above, and Jesus Christ "the Light that lighteth every one that cometh into the world," therefore all this is to be looked upon in no other way than as the mode in which Jesus Christ instructs mankind, in that He is "the same yes-terday, and to-day, and for ever." And in all these His dealings with us now, there will be found something remarkably analogous to our Lord's dealing with mankind in the Gospels.

And we before stated that this analogy is threefold; and that as it is Jesus Christ who spake by the prophets, and dealt with the fathers of old, so we shall find this characteristic of His teaching throughout the Old Testament also; that is, a combination of oral teaching with external action. It is, indeed, if we may so venture to speak, the very peculiarity of the older dispensation. The greatest doctrines, and also the least, in apparent importance, are conveyed by external action and sign.

Thus we find at first no mention of an Atonement, but all things significative of it; we hear no express declaration, but find our first parents wearing the coverings of slaughtered animals, and making sacrifices. We do not read of Noah's express teaching in the book of Genesis, or preaching righteousness, but of his making an ark. And on the restoration of the world, after the deluge, all we read is of his offering an acceptable sacrifice, and of his seeing the bow in the clouds; and the "covenant" indeed, spoken of in connexion with it, but not explained. The peculiar people of God are afterwards taught throughout by action more than by word; every passage and event in their wanderings we have reason to believe was deeply significative in every part. The ceremonial Law consisted almost entirely of actions, which might be considered like the actions of every-day life, but were in fact replete with Divine teaching throughout. The frequent washings and sacrifices, the rite of circumcision expressly limited to the eighth day, clean and unclean animals, the putting away of leaven, and eating of bitter herbs, the Voice of God from the Mercy-seat, and God's oracle on the breast, and numberless other things, were all like a parable to those who had a heart to understand. So also was the appearance of God in the bush unconsumed; the angel appearing to

Joshua on his setting foot in the holy land. And again throughout the Prophets how much is conveyed by action and figures! The "wife of whoredoms" whom Jeremiah was to take; the "girdle" that was to be concealed by the river Euphrates; the king of Israel made by Elisha to shoot with the bow and arrows, and the like[5]: not to mention the whole character of the writings of the prophet Ezekiel. All these are cases palpable and obvious, to show that He, Who spoke by the prophets of old, thus spoke; pre-eminently and peculiarly spoke by action, by figure and sign.

Now this mode of instruction by means of external action, might be said to be the very characteristic of our Lord's teaching in the Gospels; and herein we find, if we may so speak, the God of the Old Testament, and also the God of that moral providence under which we live. The same analogy may be shown under other characteristics. The most astonishing circumstance, and perhaps the greatest stumbling-block to weak worldly minds, with respect to the Gospel, is this, that the Almighty God should be living among men so little known, perceived, or recognized: it is the same in the order of the world; the presence of God is as if He were not present: so also was it in the Old Testament; He was especially a "God that hideth Himself." The sacred nation is scarcely noticed or observed among the nations of the world. The extraordinary forbearance of our Lord with the wickedness of men, as that of Judas, submitting to be put in bonds by him, and treating him kindly to the last, this is unlike any thing human which we know, but the same is the forbearance of God in affording blessings to the wicked, and allowing them to prosper even to the last; in both cases to the

[5] 2 Kings xiii. 14.

astonishment of mankind. Such also is His revealing Himself in the Gospels, as men seek His presence and assistance, and retiring from those that seek Him not. Such also was our Lord's very remarkable silence,—it is analogous to the silence of God amidst the commotions of the world, while He is present but says nothing. Another very extraordinary and inexplicable circumstance in our Lord's history, is the hatred He met with from the world, notwithstanding His deeds of mercy and kindness; and the combination of all parties against Him. Yet to considerate and reflecting persons there is no more remarkable phenomenon in the world than this, that wherever the presence of God is among mankind, as shown by the maintenance of principle and the doctrines of holiness, it is met by the combined enmity of all the world, with a degree of intensity and universality that nothing can account for. It is a matter of fact open to observation, and to some minds one of the strongest confirmations of the truth of the Gospel that can be presented to them; viz. to observe this fulfilment of our Lord's prediction, the truth acknowledged by the world, yet hated and despised.

The strength and certainty of our faith depend a great deal on the strength and certainty of such analogy, so far as it brings home to our hearts the historical narrative of the Gospels. For the circumstance that affords those incidents so lively an interest to us, is the consideration that our Lord, as present in His Church, will afford to us precisely the same benefits under similar circumstances of our faith and the like.

To this it may be asked, is it certain that to the prayer of faith our Lord will afford the same instant remedy, in the case of any bodily malady, under the same circumstances now among us as He did of old? There seems no reason to doubt but that in fact it is so. It is not to be expected that the temporal malady should itself be precisely removed,—inasmuch as the Gospel has revealed to us that such temporal sufferings are in fact not evils but blessings: it is not therefore to be expected that the prayer of faith should remove that which is declared, and is known by faith, to be a blessing; but if it renders the sufferer resigned to it, and even desirous to retain it as good, it does in fact more fully and effectually answer the prayer. For the whole of the Gospel must be taken into account, both that our Lord infallibly hears and answers every prayer of faith, and also that temporal evils are the greatest blessings to the true Christian.

There exists therefore an analogy in the moral providence of God, as witnessed in the world; in the Old Testament; and in the history of our Lord's life; arising from the unchangeable nature of God. And the combination of these three forms that "threefold cord," which "is not quickly broken," and by which the soul is lifted up from earth to Heaven. And in fact, by observations of this nature, imperceptibly carried on in the heart, faith is matured and perfected. Hence it arises that a right understanding of the Gospels depends on the life; and a knowledge of all Scriptural truth is a matter of moral combined with intellectual discernment.

The Almighty appears to disclose Himself to mankind in His various attributes and perfections, according to that mode in which He is humbly sought for by faith; revealed in something of His different perfections according to that disposition in man which is most capable of apprehending the same. Yet not to each disposition independently of others; inasmuch as there is in the Divine perfections, and so also is there between all the Christian

R

graces, a correspondence and connexion, so that none can
be attained independently of the others in some degree.
To the merciful His mercy is revealed, to the meek His
inheritance of peace : to the devout and patient student
of Holy Scripture it is the knowledge of the Divine word,
which will be most fully vouchsafed ; if such knowledge
be pursued in the only way in which it can be innocently
by man, for the purposes of devotion, or as a guide to
practice, that is to say, to enlighten or to kindle the
natural conscience, which is "the candle of the Lord."
And the power to adduce or understand the facts by
which such knowledge is derived, depends on the moral
discernment ; i. e. is the gift of the good Spirit enlightening the path of obedience, or, if we might say it, prompting
and perfecting obedience, and then rewarding His own
works by this light, and insight into His word.

For instance, the knowledge that God heareth prayer
is a truth, the full extent and meaning of which is higher
than our best faculties can attain unto or understand.
But the rise and progress into higher degrees of this
Divine knowledge, and the right understanding of Scripture with respect to it, is something to the following
effect. The thought or conviction is first suggested to
the mind of each, more or less fully, by the natural conscience or spiritual light within. But the thoughts thus
suggested may be indefinitely enlarged, strengthened and
confirmed, into additional degrees of knowledge by a habit
of prayer : a knowledge supported and increased by a kind
of induction ; a secret process of unconscious reason,
founded on the repetition of frequent convictions that
prayer is heard and answered : and that in various degrees
according to its nature and character, of secrecy, of
reverence, of importunity, of fervency. A heart which

has thus obtained this secret and unconscious knowledge, derives the fullest confirmation from Holy Scripture, which declares by various expressions and proves by many examples, that prayer is thus answered : and itself also receives the Holy Writings with more or less conviction, according to this its own secret knowledge. But this knowledge assumes a peculiarly lively interest and character, not indeed higher in degree, but in its nature especially adapted to human affection, in the narrative of the Gospels ; where, though it be but in a glass darkly, yet visibly as it were, and sensibly, we behold the Almighty manifested in the flesh, answering the request of each without exception ;—and dispensing His gifts in proportion to the manner and disposition of His creatures that ask : and instances of these exhibited in every varied characteristic of prayer which we have before designated ; in one in humility, in another in fervency, in another in importunity. We find moreover the same declared in express words, as a law of God's dealing, universal in its extent and application, as "every one that asketh receiveth ; and he that seeketh findeth ; and to him that knocketh it shall be opened ;" and also explained and set forth in parables, which exemplify the same in its various forms.

Now all these passages of Scripture, which inculcate the duty, or express the privilege of prayer, by precept or example, are not in themselves capable of conveying or imparting this knowledge perhaps at all, to a conscience never exercised in that duty; but are as hieroglyphics to one that has never been taught the language. And what they do impart is to all in various degrees, according to the devout attention applied to the subject, and according to the knowledge that each person has before obtained by his own life of the power of prayer, i. e. by that evidence which he has unconsciously collected by long habit and induction. This it is that affords a power and cogency to all that is taught or narrated in Scripture, imparting a sort of Divine understanding of its meaning. Thus, as the heathen philosopher says, that the exercise of virtue and moral obedience afford an eye to the soul by which men see principles : so a religious life kindles and supports a light in the soul, by which men are able to read and interpret Divine words.

And if on a subject so mysterious and remarkable as that of prayer in general, and its efficacy, we thus arrive at a kind of supernatural knowledge : the same may be also shown in another branch of the same subject, in itself no less mysterious and remarkable, and opposed beforehand in some degree to natural reason, of the power of intercessory prayer. That the condition of any man, his future well-being, and the circumstances he is to meet with, should depend on the conduct of another, so as to be affected by another's prayers, may appear opposed to reason, and perhaps, in one point of view, may be so. And yet, as prayer is the suggestion of natural conscience, so also is prayer for others ; and this natural suggestion is by habit improved into a conviction, or some degree of moral certainty and knowledge, which acquires a fresh life and energy from the passages in the Gospels wherein the fact is expressed and exhibited, which perfectly establish and ratify the knowledge which a good life had brought to the understanding of. For it is observable, that although, as far as we can discern, benefits are conferred in the Gospels according to the prayer of faith, and in proportion always to its nature, kind, and extent, yet notwithstanding, there is a remarkable exception, or rather further development of that rule, that these benefits are not limited to the prayer of the individual who receives the benefit, but are extended also to others for whom these prayers were made. Here again we have this Divine knowledge imparted with a lively interest in compassion to our natural infirmities, in a manner that may be comprehended by a Divine life, so as to afford all the fulness of conviction in points that may appear opposed to natural wisdom.

And as the end and perfection of all knowledge is the knowledge of God manifested in Jesus Christ, so it may be shown that this suggestion of the natural conscience, improved and strengthened by habitual piety, and confirmed and enlarged by the facts and principles of Holy Scripture, proceeds thus progressively to the apprehension of Jesus Christ. For as we believe that the power and efficacy of prayer with God is owing entirely to the Blood of Christ, so may we suppose that the power of intercessory prayer in particular, has some connexion with the intercessions of Christ, by means of which, and from a resemblance to Whom, a virtue and efficacy is imparted to the intercessions of others who are the members of His body. Thus Noah, Daniel, and Job, thus Abraham, Elijah, and others, had power with God as intercessors beforehand, being therein types of Christ, and thus many in the Gospels were heard when they came in faith to entreat in behalf of others.

Again, another point of the same kind may be mentioned on this subject. It may appear in the narrative rather extraordinary, that our Lord should be so long in answering the requests of those whom He fully heard and approved of, and should have been as if He heard not, as in the case of the blind Bartimæus, and the Canaanitish woman, and the good Centurion. For it may be said, if He heard them, why did He not answer them, as men usually do? on the contrary, why did He suffer them to carry on their importunities, to the increase of their distress, and the inconvenience of others? But all this is as the ways of the Almighty God, which our Blessed Lord explained, as in His parables of the importunate widow, and of the friend who came to borrow three loaves at midnight. But the same is otherwise taught the good Christian by a life of devotion; for thus, through religious experience, he comes to know God, to know that He bears long, and is as if He heard not; but that it is in order that He may crown such delay with more abundant graciousness, that He hears and considers prayer, though forbearing and bearing long, and that His suppliants are the better for that delay. And thus taught by experience, the Christian recognizes the same God manifested in Jesus Christ in the narrative of the Gospel. The circumstances which are taught by spiritual experience and a religious life, are so analogous to those which the sacred history records, that either serves to explain the other. Add to which, that the parables alluded to are the explanations of our Blessed Lord concerning the dealings of God, and which thus tend to throw a Divine light upon both.

These are all points on which natural reason, without the illumination of a good life, might have speculated much in vain, and have come to very different conclusions; but the life of a good man discloses to him the dealings of God with the human soul, in which he finds this wonderful correspondence with His ways in revelation; and the result of which is, that he puts forth "both hands earnestly" to embrace Him Who is thus revealed to him. In points beforehand opposed to natural reason we have thus abundance of facts supplied by experience, so as to afford us a principle by induction on a subject so mysterious as that of prayer. The previous life reveals "the secret of God," and that secret is the crown of faith. This is expressed in the declaration of the man after God's own heart, on an occasion which is itself one of the highest instances of acceptable faith : He that "delivered me out of the paw of the lion and out of the paw of the bear, He will deliver me out of the hand of this Philistine*."

On other subjects innumerable our natural and moral life, of which experience affords us the knowledge, will afford us the highest testimony respecting that which is spiritually revealed. As, for instance, to take a case on the very threshold of Revelation, that our souls should be saved and supported by the death of another, may be surrounded with speculative difficulties; but nature supplies us with instances similar to it, for in the meanwhile our bodily lives are sustained by the deaths of innocent animals. Barren knowledge on these subjects, and intellectual inquiries, are oftentimes encompassed by speculative difficulties; but faith is able to supply sufficient evidence for practical obedience, by an ever increasing weight of analogy.

The apprehension of Christ, therefore, depends on spiritual knowledge, and that knowledge on facts sufficient to form an induction, and those facts on a religious life. The only knowledge which is of any value, arises from the moral discernment enlightening the natural understanding. Since, therefore, it must be among mankind so exceedingly weak, and inadequate to things Divine, it must be ever necessary to keep in mind the greatness of human ignorance. As Job has said of wisdom, "God

* 1 Sam. xvii. 37.

understandeth the way thereof, and He knoweth the place thereof." . . "And unto men He said, Behold, the fear of the Lord, that is wisdom ; and to depart from evil is understanding." Of the same Wisdom it is said, that she tries every man in crooked paths until she can trust his soul, and impart to him the knowledge of her secrets.

But it must be remembered, that all we speak of are only of certain effects in morals ; for as in nature we know nothing but of certain effects. The causes of things God hath hidden from us, and kept in His own power in the spiritual as well as in the natural world. But thus far we can see, that as God is revealed to us as being invariable and unchangeable in His own nature and attributes, although manifested to us under a variety of circumstances, so there is a wonderful analogy and correspondence in His ways, as far as we are capable of ascertaining them.

From hence it follows, that as analogous agreement and coincidence in our Lord's words and actions, as manifested in the flesh, or of others with relation to Him, appears to be the fullest confirmation we can derive of any separate evidence, so also does the same derive great additional weight, if it can be likewise supported by analogous circumstances throughout the rest of Holy Scripture, inasmuch as He is the same Who spake by the Prophets and Apostles. If to this we can add the correspondence of our Lord's present dealings with mankind, we shall have another kind of proof, great in itself, inasmuch as He Who reveals Himself in Holy Scripture is also "the Light that lighteth every man that cometh into the world." These, therefore, will together have the strength of threefold evidence, each in itself of the most satisfactory and highest nature, and the accumulative proof of each is added to that of the other. If to this threefold weight of analogy we can also, in the support of any opinion, adduce the testimony of the Church universal as consenting with us, such appears to be the fullest and strongest evidence which human nature is capable of in matters of religion.

SECTION V

ANALOGY BETWEEN THE MATERIAL AND SPIRITUAL WORLD

THE whole of this subject of analogy goes upon the supposition, that it is of a nature so intricate and so extensive, that we cannot attempt to do any thing more than to point out glimpses and indications of it;—sufficient to show that there does exist such analogy as far as it goes;—but with no idea of tracing out its infinite relations, and the mutual correspondence of various analogies ; or indeed any single one entire. A small part may be seen of a vast and complicated web, sufficient to indicate coherence, and adaptation in the texture, and a course of mechanism and design ; but not so much as to allow us to trace its various ramifications, nor the centre from which they are suspended, and to which they tend. The Divine wisdom may not be fully perceptible to man in the word of God any more than in His works; in both alike "she dwells in high places, and her throne is in a cloudy pillar. She alone compasses the circuit of the Heaven, and walks in the bottom of the deep." In both we doubt not but that there is the perfection of exquisite order, and arrangement of parts, and mutual adaptation, all variously harmonizing and combining to form a whole, which must infinitely surpass all comprehension of men : but casual developments may occasionally appear and come to view, and show themselves to be links of a chain, which extends to the throne of God. It may perhaps be sufficient if we can point out some indications of another course of analogy ; and we now proceed to inquire if there is not a correspondence to be observed in things bodily and spiritual ; and this but a part of a more extensive system of analogy between the external visible world and that which is internal and invisible; the invisible and eternal being comparatively real and true, and the visible and transient but shadowy, and typical of those things which are to endure for ever.

Now, first of all, let us take the case of *bodily and mental maladies.* And with this view let us consider our Lord's miracles of healing, in the light which is thrown upon them from the Old Testament ; or rather as if we ourselves had been previously schooled by the Law rightly to understand the actions of Christ when He came. Now one great preparation which the Old Testament was calculated to afford was this, to train mankind to look for spiritual lessons of wisdom in things sensible, material, and external : to connect something mental and internal with visible objects, and therefore of course implying some analogous relation between them. Thus the Tabernacle itself, being formed " according to the pattern showed in the mount," was but typical and emblematic of something unrevealed, and was in itself but as the centre of that vast system, whereby external representations set forth things Heavenly. To holy men thus educated, and taught to pass on from the letter to the spirit, from the body to the soul, from external cleansings to internal purifications ; consider how the miracles of our Lord, on the bodies of men, must have naturally tended to carry out and fulfil such intimations in the Jewish dispensation. For in this light they appear at once, not merely as indications of a Divine power, which had authority to command, but also as themselves the vehicles of spiritual instruction. For it was evident that the greater part of the ancient ritual, the distinctions of animals and external washings, and diseases considered legally unclean, must have contained some great moral and spiritual lessons, which were worthy of that Divine economy; and thus were they understood by the better part, who had eyes to see; and unconsciously suspected by others to do so. To the mind therefore of a Jew, instructed in these lessons of wisdom throughout the Old Testament, our Lord's miracles, when apprehended as Divine, must have appeared different from what they do to us, and been at once calculated to carry on his thoughts to something better beyond, on account of that religious discipline through the means of things sensible, to which he had been accustomed. Bodily diseases, and the removal of them by the power of Christ, would necessarily have suggested to a good man spiritual maladies, and the removal of them also in the new kingdom of Christ on the prayer of faith. And of this reference from bodily to spiritual maladies the Law itself had given distinct intimations, not only by its general character, but also by some express particulars; this was sufficiently indicated in the case of leprosy, which was inflicted in many instances, as in that of Miriam, of Gehazi, and king Uzziah, as the punishment of sacrilege; and was a disease which, having all the characteristic contagiousness of vice, bore the strongest mark of legal uncleanness. Add to which, our Lord Himself in His cures did sometimes studiously connect the external malady with the diseases of the soul; or we may say seemed earnestly to endeavour to turn the thoughts of the bystanders from the bodily disease to the sins that occasioned it, and were connected with it; as by using the words, " thy sins be forgiven thee," instead of merely dispelling the disease. And this too He did to the great offence of the Pharisees; and strongly reproved those who did not perceive, that His power of remitting the bodily disease implied His power of forgiving sin. And of course a good man would not limit the instruction, thus conveyed to those particular instances themselves; but would consider them rather as intimations of a great system, and of an extensive correspondence in the evils of the body and soul, which we know not how to limit, any more than we can limit the Divine order and arrangement of all things. But thus far we see, that the death of the body is but a figure and emblem of a worse death; and Christ's victory over the first death implied His victory over the other, of which it was but the emblem and figure : and all things respecting the first death tend to teach us a lively image of the second death,—the worm of the soul that never dies, and the fire consuming in death. And Christ declares Himself to be " the Resurrection and the Life," not of our bodies only, but also of our souls. From all this analogy, the thought will occur to one, whether every bodily distemper may not be but the analogy or figure of some corresponding malady of the soul, not of course existing in the same person, as they are often most free from any such connexion; but implying some resemblance in the diseases and distempers which prevail in the two worlds of matter and spirit. And this gives a very peculiar and forcible instructiveness to our Lord's miracles, as indicating that He who removed one on the prayer of faith, would also in His Church remove the other also on the prayer of faith; when we take into the account of course that difference which must arise from the relative importance of the two, and the greater difficulty of restoring the soul from those spiritual maladies which are, as it were, the paths that lead to the second death; and therefore such require greater perseverance and faith, to obtain their permanent removal; but the analogy may be complete and perfect, that to recover us from the vices or maladies of the soul, Christ is equally present, and faith equally powerful, to procure His aid. Now all this is indeed so obvious that it readily suggests itself, and is often appealed to in practical exhortations by way of illustration and practical comment. And yet at the same time it is not considered how substantially true this is, and how deeply founded in the philosophy of Divine wisdom, that what offers itself for illustration on the surface is but a casual indication of a vast system.

Now our Lord's expressions are such that they often necessarily indicate this connexion; that is to say, that they are such as suggest it to every reader. And this we cannot but suppose must have been foreseen, and therefore intended by our Lord, when He spoke the words, and had them recorded by His Evangelist. Such an allusion appears to be contained in that expression, "this kind goeth not forth but by prayer and fasting," when speaking of the possession of an unclean spirit. Perhaps there is no attentive reader, but would at once conclude this to be implied of a spirit of impurity [7]: whether it is spoken of a spirit of uncleanness going forth, or of the faith required to eject him, in either case we cannot confine the words to the immediate case of bodily possession, but we naturally pass on to the other. And in doing this

[7] See Quesnel's Commentaries, as on St. Mark v. 9; St. Luke iv. 33, &c. &c.

we necessarily infer, that this visible and sensible possession of the unclean spirit is but the figure of the evil
habit of impurity possessing the soul. For we have the
confirmation of our Lord's words, on another occasion,
telling us that what we call an evil habit is in fact the
possession of an evil spirit. And in this case the very
name [8] "unclean spirit" suggests the association, the
driving him through fire and water, the difficulty of the
expulsion, the dwelling among the tombs, are all most
closely applicable to that viciousness of heart which "will
not leave him till death [9]."

Again, the disease of the paralytic is so exact a figure
and resemblance of the infirmity of the human will, in
the case of the weak and irresolute, that Aristotle makes
use of this analogy to describe the state of mind of such a
person [1]. The case is exact in its correspondence throughout, and if the paralytic limb means that part of the soul
which has lost some power of good, some principle and
habit which it ought to recover, then the promises in the
Gospel, and its analogous miracles, are such as to promise,
that by the power of Christ it may be recovered. "I can
do all things through Christ which strengtheneth me;"
"lift up the faint hands and strengthen the feeble knees;"
the strength of Christ is "perfected in weakness;" all these
passages are spoken of the removal of diseases of the soul.
Therefore there is a power above nature in the kingdom
of Christ to restore such a limb of the soul, when it has
apparently lost all power. The case of the paralytic

---

[8] Πνεῦμα ἀκάθαρτον.   [9] Ecclus. xxiii. 17.

[1] Ethics, lib. i. ch. 13.—Καθάπερ τὰ παραλελυμένα τοῦ σώματος
μόρια εἰς τὰ δεξιὰ προαιρουμένων κινῆσαι, τοὐναντίον εἰς τὰ ἀριστερὰ
παραφέρεται, καὶ ἐπὶ τῆς ψυχῆς οὕτως· ἐπὶ τὰ ἐναντία γὰρ αἱ ὁρμαὶ τῶν
ἀκρατῶν. Ἀλλ' ἐν τοῖς σώμασι μὲν ὁρῶμεν τὸ παραφερόμενον, ἐπὶ δὲ
τῆς ψυχῆς οὐχ ὁρῶμεν.

would express this by a most lively figure. It is done also in the sight of all men (like that miracle in the Gospels [2]), when by some instance of God's grace in conversion, any one is observed to do those good things which before he did not perform, and was thought by all incapable of doing.

In like manner other cases of sickness, as that of the fever and of the dropsy, are so analogous to the fever of passion and the incurable swelling and weakness of the soul, accompanied with an ever craving thirst, that they afford an obvious and apt illustration to describe it in writers both sacred and profane [3]. And a reference to the bodily senses and their defection, is a mode of speech sanctified by the most constant use of it throughout the Scripture. Nothing is more frequent than the words of hearing and of seeing, and of deafness and blindness, as applied to the soul. Our Lord Himself repeatedly uses this figurative language; and on one remarkable occasion, connects the lesson of spiritual blindness with that of the bodily eye, and draws the attention from one to the other; for on healing the man that was blind from his birth He declared of the Pharisees, "I am come that they who see not may see, and that they who see may be made blind."

Much of this analogy may arise from the twofold nature of man, as composed of body and soul, and both of which have become so mysteriously and intimately connected with each other, by our Lord's taking upon Himself a

[2] Luke vi. 8.

[3] Aristotle, Ethics, lib. vii. ch. 3, where he likens the confirmed state of vice to dropsy or consumption, and the previous states to epilepsy. And Ovid, of covetousness,

"Sic quibus intumuit suffusâ venter ab undâ,
    Quo plus sunt potæ plus sitiuntur aquæ."

human Body and Soul; by His human Body becoming, as at the Transfiguration and at His Resurrection, glorified and changed: and by that great doctrine which flows from this, and is closely united with it, the resurrection of our flesh. Hence all the bodily senses are in an especial manner sanctified to Divine purpose, and represent, and also partake of, the illumination of the soul and all its qualities. The soul being filled with Divine knowledge, is spoken of as "the whole body being full of light, having no part darkened:" the conscience becoming insensible to spiritual things, is described as the "eyes being darkened, the ears made dull of hearing." And it is remarkable, as Tertullian has observed, that the future Resurrection is usually described by expressions which speak of the body: in whatever way they may be understood. The second death is accompanied with "weeping and gnashing of teeth," which expressions imply eyes and teeth: the guest who has not on the wedding garment is bound "hands and feet," which indicates bodily members. It may indeed be said that sufferings of the soul could not be expressed, but by these bodily images; this may be most true, and a very just and proper account of the matter, and yet notwithstanding this may not be all, and the case may be analogous to another we are about to state. The Almighty is spoken of, throughout the Old Testament, by expressions taken from bodily members and human affections; and it is said that by such references alone could the Almighty be represented to us; although they necessarily convey something like a contradiction when we speak of Him by expressions from things sensible, and at the same time declare Him invisible, and as moved by human affections when He is revealed to us as incapable of passion. But yet, notwithstanding all these things, we believe that these expressions set forth the incarnation of Christ. And so likewise it may be said in this case, such corporeal figures alluded to can alone represent the anguish of the soul: but still it may be the case, that they do set forth some great mystery, such as that of the Resurrection of the body. And, in fact, there may be some great impropriety in our thus speaking of Revelation, when we venture to state that things could not have been expressed but in this or that manner. Surely our thoughts are low and unworthy, when we speak of power with reference to Divine language and expression; for doubtless such power is infinite, infinitely capable to ascertain the means which may convey to us most suitably what it is fitting we should know: the Almighty could, we may suppose, represent Himself truly to us by other images than those of the human frame; and the future state by images other than those that are bodily. But we may reasonably suppose that there exists in these some peculiar and hidden fitness.

And this strict union between the soul and the body may be at the very foundation of far more extensive analogies, whereby things visible are made to represent things invisible. Bodily maladies set forth in figure mental maladies : there is a resurrection of the soul and a resurrection of the body ; there is a regeneration of both ; both are mutually dependent on, and connected with, each other; there is a washing of the body and a washing of the soul in Baptism, to separate either of which from the other, is to fail of the truth ; there is in Scripture the literal sense and the spiritual sense ; there is a visible Church and a Church invisible.

We may now proceed to consider a further development of the same kind of analogy between things sensible and things spiritual, *as seen in the symbolical charac-*

ter of single expressions. As the character of the legal dispensation prepared men's minds to consider material emblems as representative of Divine meanings, so we shall find throughout the Scriptures, that the signification attached to material things does not appear to be arbitrary, as the human use of illustration and metaphor ; but is usually the same throughout, and that sense often indicated by the Old Testament.

Indeed, with regard to sacred expressions, it does not seem reverential to suppose, that in Holy Scripture similes, metaphors, and figures of speech are used as by human writers, much less so in our Lord's own discourses. It may be very true that the corn was being sown in the fields, when the parable of the Sower was given ; or that the wine at the feast in Levi's house supplied the allusion to the wine in old bottles ; or the water at the Feast of Tabernacles, the type of the Holy Spirit ; but all these were thus applied by Him, by Whom they were made ; all their hidden qualities and their hidden resemblances were given them by Him, Who himself fully knew beforehand all that would happen, and what purposes they would answer. We cannot suppose that these should be used merely as men would use a metaphorical expression, but that there exists a depth of type and analogy, and an appropriate fitness and sacred language in the things themselves. When God speaks, objects and events are ready at hand, as instant and obedient as words, bearing with them sacred similitudes, that shadow forth the truth by an inherent and eternal adaptation. His Word, spoken long before, is often mentioned as the very creative cause of events that ensue ; much more may things created by that Word be ready to give forth the Divine senses of His kingdom. The wine, the bread, the oil, the salt, the

vine, and the fig-tree, come forth throughout the whole of
the Divine Scriptures to speak one language, the language
of the Son of Man, as readily as words range themselves
in order to form a sentence ; all things are at hand at the
will of Him that made them. As they obey Him in the
natural world, so are they obedient at His will to embody
the living language of His revelation ; He spake the word,
and the stars were created of old, and now " they shine in
their watches ; when He calleth them, they say, Here we
be, and so with cheerfulness they show light unto Him
that made them." He needeth not their light, but at His
bidding they come forth to give light to His creatures; so
do all His works, at His bidding, minister edification to
His children of the New Birth. All things in the Old
Testament are marked and stamped as being in God's
world, as belonging to Him ; but in the Old and New
Testament together all things are shown as belonging to
the God of our New Birth, as having a part in His kingdom in Whom all things are made new. The old creation
is itself become new, new in the significations which it
bears, as emblematical of things spiritual in the New
Kingdom ; and as the Church visible bears an analogy to
that which is invisible, why may not also the visible
creation throughout have a similar correspondence with
that which is invisible ? But the object at present is, to
show that single expressions are symbolical in the Gospels,
and their meaning often marked out by the use of them
under the Jewish dispensation ; so that things become
spiritual and full of grace, and containing the life-giving
Word, which were before but dead-letters or symbols.
And as our Lord has declared that not one jot or tittle of
the Law shall fail, and as He Himself reproved His
Disciples for not perceiving the spiritual meaning of such

s 2

His expressions, as of " bread " and of " leaven," it seems right that we should trace out in words these typical mysterious meanings. And where, on comparing things spiritual, and pondering Divine words, we find that the same expressions repeatedly occur in one and the same typical sense, and that such a spiritual import coincides also with other analogous senses, it would appear that such may be inferred to be the meaning of the Spirit.

To mention a few instances of this kind ; we find the word "leaven" applied by our Lord to any doctrine or principle of a secretly pervading and powerful nature ; and usually in a bad sense. It is applied to the principles of the Pharisees, called hypocrisy [4], a sort of self-deceit ; and to those of the Sadducees [5], a worldly temper ; and St. Paul says of permitted evil, that " a little leaven leaveneth the whole lump [6];" and in one place he says, with a more distinct reference to its sacred legal import [7], " Christ our Passover is sacrificed for us, therefore let us keep the feast, not with the old leaven, neither with the leaven of malice and wickedness, but with the unleavened bread of sincerity and truth." This passage more distinctly connects the expression with that import in its legal sense, which must have been familiar to the Jew ; and seems clearly to imply, that the putting away of the leaven in the Law, at the seven days of the Feast, signified, that in order for the Christian sacrifice and festival to be acceptable, all such evil principles must be set aside, which influence the whole man, and render him unmeet to keep the feast, or to inherit the final blessing. " There shall be no leaven in all your quarters."

---

[4] Luke xii. 1.   [5] Matt. xvi. 6.
[6] Gal. v. 9.   [7] 1 Cor. v. 8.

In one instance, I think, only, is the leaven used in a good sense, where the Kingdom of Heaven is itself likened to leaven; and this might appear, at first sight, to militate against the whole induction. But it may be that the word leaven is not here used in its sacrificial sense, but in another, from its domestic use—" a woman who took leaven." Or probably it might refer to another sacred and more acceptable use of leaven, as it was commanded in the Law to be offered " with the sacrifice of thanksgiving[8]." But, at all events, it would in both cases imply something so subtle, as not to be of itself perceptible, but powerfully to influence and change throughout that in which it was placed.

To take another instance; the expression " salt," seems to signify that sound principle which alone keeps from corruption. In the Law it was divinely ordered that " salt" should be used in all sacrifices[9]. On infants also, salt was used, "as for thy nativity, thou wast not salted at all[1];" which use of it seems to import, that man is born without any good in himself. And " salt" was thrown into the waters to heal them by Elisha, the type of Christ in His Church. These are sufficient to indicate the use of it in the New Testament—that " salt which hath lost its savour" cannot be recovered[2], i. e. that good principle, when lost, cannot be restored, nor have any thing substituted for it. Our " conversation". is to be " seasoned with salt," i. e. with sound Christian principle[3]. And in St. Mark[4] the allusion is carried on from the Law to some mysterious and higher fulfilment in the soul, and to her final probation. The passage seems to allude to the custom

[8] Lev. vii. 13.   Amos iv. 5.
[9] Lev. ii. 13.
[1] Ezek. xvi. 4.
[2] Matt. v. 13.
[3] Col. iv. 6.
[4] Ch. ix. 49.

mentioned in Ezekiel[5], that "fire" and "salt" must be applied to "each sacrifice," such sacrifice being itself without blemish; perhaps implying that the Holy Spirit, or the Word, denoted by fire, and true principle signified by salt, will try men at last, and render the sacrifice acceptable:—that as fire came of old from heaven to consume the sacrifice, so the fire of the Holy Ghost will descend to make a good Christian an offering meet for God; but it will not be a fire to consume; for as in the burning bush this fire consumes not, so the sacrifice will be "salted" and kept from corruption by that "fire" which sanctifies it. As this sacrifice of the Christian soul will be hallowed by "fire," i. e. by the Holy Spirit, so will it also be "salted" and kept from corruption by sound Christian principle. The Christian who is not thus made a sacrifice to God, will be, as the preceding verses imply, cast away to Tophet, or that place of death and corruption, " where the worm dieth not, and the fire is not quenched."

Thus, likewise, the "oil" throughout the Scriptures is obviously and extensively typical of the Holy Spirit, and especially of His gifts as connected with sacred offices. It is the widow's oil multiplied by Elisha, which failed not, and thus serves to represent those spiritual blessings which fail not in the Church of Christ; it is the "oil" which the foolish virgins had not in their lamps; it is that which tempered the unleavened bread[6], the Spirit which relieves and sanctifies works of mortification. It was poured on the pillar, on the altar, and on every thing sanctified to Divine use. It was the "oil" which was like charity, when it came on the head of Aaron, and went down to the skirts of his clothing; or the Spirit that was poured upon our Head, and descended from Him to all

[5] Ch. xliii. 24.　　　　　　[6] Exod. xxix. 2.

His Priesthood and members unto the end of the world. And this was carried on into the Evangelical dispensation, by the oil which was used in miraculous healings of the sick. In all things it appears to be sanctification connected with the great Anointed of God.

Again, as "wine," which represents in Scripture the Blood of Christ, is connected with the gifts of the Spirit, so "oil and wine" are frequently combined together. "Oil and wine" the good Samaritan pours into the wounds; the command in the Revelation is, not to touch "the oil and the wine:" the "oil" in the Psalms is placed between the table and the cup, "Thou hast prepared a table before me, Thou hast anointed my head with oil, and my cup shall be full." The gift of the Spirit is with the Bread and the Wine. It is the oil that gives "the cheerful countenance," i.e. it is the Spirit that gives joy, when the Wine refreshes, and the Bread strengthens man's heart.

This is that "new wine" which, if received into the old bottles, will burst them, the Gospel which will be the destruction of the unregenerate man. It is "the good wine" which the Bridegroom hath kept to the last; and the fruit of the Living Vine, which is Christ, when bruised in the wine-press of the wrath of God. And the signification of bread, also, is so obvious, as to need no induction to prove it, passing so readily from the food of our bodies to the staff of our spiritual life; and to Him Who has declared Himself to be "the true Bread," "the Bread that came down from heaven and giveth life unto the world." He Who is Himself our "life," "our daily bread," for which we pray daily, passing from dead legal symbols into living Sacramental emblems, and from thence into the spiritual gifts conveyed thereby. So that the voice of the Church, as represented by Wisdom, which is Christ, ever has been, "Come, eat of my bread, and drink of the wine which I have mingled[7]." It is seen in Melchizedec, bringing forth the "bread and wine" to Abraham, the father and figure of the faithful; or as the manna in the wilderness—bread indeed, but prepared for us not by the instrumentality of man, but by God only. It is seen in the miracles of our Blessed Lord in the wilderness of Bethsaida, and His earnest discourse which ensued, warning us, that we think not therein only of "the meat that perisheth," but that we pass on from these to the Sacramental Bread, and to that which is spiritual in the Church of God. It is bread, and yet it is not bread; it is mysteriously something far more, and we must not ask or explain what it is, for it must ever continue a question, for its name is manna, i. e. "what is it[8]?" And that we may not dwell on the bread alone, our Lord varies it often with the expression of "My flesh," saying, "He that eateth this Bread," and then, "He that eateth My flesh[9]." And in the Law the sacrifice is sometimes the "meat-offering" of flour, sometimes the flesh of the slain victim. Thus ever is Holy Scripture connecting bread with the animal sacrifice; and the flesh of the slain with the bread of life.

The Kingdom of Heaven, therefore, is that Marriage feast at which there is no lack of the oil, and the bread, and the wine, until the Bridegroom Himself shall come to see the guests. And here it may be observed, that not in the single objects themselves, but in their various uses and connexions, does the analogy hold good, so as to indicate, even in this little department of so vast a subject, something of system.

Perhaps one or two more single and detached instances may be mentioned, to show the interpretation which the

---

[7] Prov. ix. 5.　　　　[8] Exod. xvi. 15.　　　　[9] John vi.

Gospel affords us of the symbols of the Law, and from thence furnishes us with a clue to the interpretation of external nature. Such was the distinction of animals into clean and unclean, which seems to indicate that separation between the good and the bad which is to be made hereafter. Whereas, into the Ark of Christ's Church now, which is borne on the waters of Baptism, both the clean and the unclean are admitted, as into the ark of Noah which figuratively represented it of old. Yet, into that Holy City of the new Jerusalem, which is above, it will not be so, for the catalogue of those who are excluded from its walls commences with the emblems of legal uncleanness, "*without are dogs*, and sorcerers, and whoremongers, and murderers, and idolaters, and whosoever loveth and maketh a lie [1]." The Jews, indeed, themselves seem to have understood this distinction of animals to have signified a distinction in the human race, for we know that they considered the heathen as dogs and the like. And our Blessed Lord seems Himself to have sanctioned their notion, that some such distinction was intended by it; as when He sent the devils into the herd of swine among the Gentiles, and when He said to the Canaanitish woman, that it was "not meet to take the chidren's bread, and to cast it to dogs." But in both cases our Lord seems to carry it on to that final moral distinction, of which the privileges and distinctions of the Jewish nation were themselves but types, and to that ultimate separation which the Day of Judgment will make. The destruction of the herd of swine in the former case, as it sanctions the opinions of the Jew, so it evidently implies the power that evil spirits have in the wicked, in urging them to self-destruction, when God

[1] Rev. xxii. 15.

gives them up to a reprobate mind, "to work all uncleanness with greediness." This moral and not mere natural
distinction is signified in other places, as "give not that
which is holy to the dogs, and cast not your pearls
before swine:" and "the dog hath returned to his vomit
again, and the sow that was washed to her wallowing in
the mire."

To take another instance perfectly different in kind.
The application of fire to the Holy Ghost is frequent, and
found often in the shape either of doctrine or of precept.
It implies the divinity of the Holy Ghost, for "our God
is a consuming fire:" and appeared as "a pillar of fire,"
and as a "bush of fire;" and the Lord descended from
Mount Sinai in "fire;" and the Holy Ghost is in the
baptism "of fire:" and in the "tongues like as of fire:"
and "the fire comes forth from the Lord:" and "upon
earth He showed thee His fire:" and fire from God is
needful for every sacrifice: and "the Lord God answereth
by fire:" and fire purifies, for Christ shall be "as a
refiner's fire:" and the fire is seen in God's ministers,
"I looked, and behold a fire enfolding itself:" and pro-
tects them, for He will be unto them "a wall of fire
round about:" and in heaven He is "the Seven Lamps
of fire burning before the throne:" and the full revelation
of God will be the destruction of the wicked, for "He
will burn them with unquenchable fire:" and "the
breath of the Lord, like a stream as of fire, doth kindle
Tophet:" and Jesus Christ came to "send fire upon
earth:" and in His Church His "face is as the sun, and
His feet as pillars of fire:" and the Church is "clothed
with the sun." Fire, therefore, is the visible living
emblem of that fire which is invisible and spiritual. All
things are double, "one thing set against another."

And the most awful and fearful of all elements, the most comforting, the most purifying, the most life-giving, is the emblem which God hath given to speak of Himself.

But here we must remember, that the same which appeared as a Pillar of fire, was also the Cloud over-shadowing; and this teaches us to pass from one emblem to another, though apparently of a different nature. For the Holy Spirit is ever seen in Holy Scripture in the Cloud also; and the Cloud is ever passing into Water. Water is the emblem of the Holy Spirit also, and thus the Cloud falls to the earth and is found in water, and replenishes the earth in every shape of Baptismal blessings, and the dews of God's grace.

When thus we pass from one point to others, on this most extensive and complicated subject, there seem indications, not only that the signs and emblems are in themselves definite and fixed, as representing things spiritual and invisible, but also that they fall in with others and with each other, so as to form a system. And it seems not unreasonable to suppose that one object in the Law itself was thus to sanctify external nature by intimating this circumstance: and this coincides with other apparent intentions in the Old Testament to mark the presence of God in temporal reverses in judicial blindness of heart, and to speak of all His creatures as waiting on Him: and, in short, to declare the world to be God's world, and all dispensations to be His; and why, therefore, may it not have been its object to teach us to look also on external and visible nature, as the shadow of something better and more Divine?

If we take separate emblems in Holy Scripture, and find them frequently used in one sense, so as to indicate and mark some definite meaning, and that this our opinion of its mystical sense is confirmed by the opinion of great and good writers, so as to be sure that we are using it in a reasonable and safe manner : and if we put many of these together, as thus explained, we shall find, I think, that they will afford something like a system, as if all external nature was systematically expressive of things spiritual and invisible, through a very extensive analogy. Thus the sun is a very usual emblem for our Blessed Lord Himself, but Who in distinction from it is "*the true* Light;" as if the sun were but an image of Him Who is the true Light, setting forth, as it were, visibly Him whom no one can approach unto and live ; Who is Himself unchangeable, yet giving light and life to all things. In numberless instances and connexions the sun is emblematical of Christ ; the centre, and mover, and life, and light, of all visible things, regulating their changes by His approaches to them. And in like manner is the moon of His Church ; the stars of His saints ; the successive changes of light and darkness, of the conflict of good and evil in His kingdom. While the moon has no light of its own, but borrows all from the sun in order to light us through the darkness, so in the night of this world is the Church with no light of her own, but bright with that of Christ, while He Himself, the true Fountain of light, is unseen by us. Ever renewed by persecutions and troubles at intervals of waning or increasing lustre. Again, the flowing water is a figure of the Holy Spirit, as connected with baptism ; dews and rains, of His gracious influences ; winds are the signs of His unseen power; clouds of His visible agents—the stewards of His grace which attend Him. Again, the wood is ever the emblem of Christ's passion, and the tree of the same, bearing life like Aaron's rod; night is the emblem of death, and morning of resurrection; serpents, of evil spirits; the lamb, of Christ and His followers; the sheep and goats are both sacrificial, both in covenant with God, but the one the more worthy, the other the less approved; the one is set on His right hand, the other on His left. Or, to take another class of analogies, the Bridegroom is Christ, and the Bride is His Church; and the marriage Feast, the good things He has prepared for them that love Him, in His kingdom now, and in Heaven hereafter. Or again, Christ is the true Vine, and Christians the branches, and its fruits are good works, and the leaves, external professions; and the fig-tree, that Jewish Church which has a great show of leaves, indeed, but is found unprofitable, though that also, as the Vine, is in the garden of the Lord, and planted by His hand, they are both in covenant with God; but the Vine is the more worthy and acceptable, and though the fruit of the fig-tree be good, yet in Scripture it is too often found barren. And the Church is Christ's robe, and our clothing is the righteousness of Christ, which God hath given us instead of our own self-sought covering of the fig-leaves [2]; and our daily washings indicate our need of constant renovations of the Spirit. These may not, in every instance, be rightly applied or interpreted; but, on a full investigation, they will be found to have some such definite meaning, and one spiritual sense. Some of these interpretations which are here mentioned, are such as naturally offer themselves as the most obvious; some of them are thus taken by ancient writers of high authority; and some of them of such frequent use in Scripture, as to mark them as applicable to one sense.

[2] Gen. iii. 7. Matt. xxi. 19.

All this is not intended fully to exhibit or to explain so comprehensive a subject, but merely to indicate something of its nature and extent. And the inference to be adduced from all these analogies is, that in reading the Gospels we must not be satisfied with only a limited or superficial interpretation ; but are to consider the various modes in which these analogies may be connected with any one event or expression ; and to remember that one simple and manifest interpretation is no reason why manifold others may not be equally true ; and that a more deep and extensive knowledge of Scripture might be able to elicit them in a manner to satisfy any reasonable mind of their truth. What has been here said may serve rather as notices and indications of analogy, than any thing further.

OUR STATE SIMILAR TO THAT OF THE JEWS

THE Israelite of old walked in an external world of rites, and ceremonies, and ordinances, a ritual minutely described, and frequent and continual duties connected with it; and yet he was himself all the while unconscious of the great and spiritual world with which all these were connected; was in general ignorant of their bearings, their significations, and their importance. Whatever was disclosed of these was only revealed to persons of great holiness of life; and intimated by occasional commands scattered here and there which prescribed the great law of charity, like a heavenly underchime which could be heard by those alone who had ears attuned to things heavenly. And yet full and pregnant was every particle of those laws, not only such as were moral, or seemed to have a moral end in view, but such also as might appear ceremonial or natural;—replete with great things in Christ's Kingdom, of which not the slightest point or tittle shall fail.   And to us it is already evident in many things, that such circumstances respecting the temporal Israel were but shadows of something more substantial, and such as have been or are now being fulfilled.   For those institutions were, as St. Paul tells us, but images of the "true Tabernacle which God hath pitched and not man," according to that pattern of things invisible which is with God, and was seen on the Mount. In like manner, we also ourselves are living in a dispensation which is but the figure and shadow of a future one, hereafter to be developed: and the things which are now prescribed to us have their reference to and have their fulfilment in that Kingdom.

Whatever state is foretold seems, as we have observed, to be prefigured by an earnest and shadow of it.   The Jews were servants, and we are sons.   They knew not the reasons of the commands which were given them; but we know, and this is the state of sonship, "for the servant knoweth not what his Lord doeth."   But then again the state which is to come is more particularly that of sonship; and we, in comparison of those who shall be deemed worthy to inherit it, are still servants, for we know nothing now as we ought to know, and if we see, it is but "through a glass darkly."   For "the servant abideth not in the house for ever, but the son abideth ever," and our present Kingdom is in some sense to pass away.   With regard to the past we are sons; with respect to the future we are servants; the two states are now combined in us; we are in a state of servitude, but that our "service" is a state of "perfect freedom."   We enjoy the full revelation of God: but that revelation is full of mysteries: it is emphatically and expressively called the "wisdom of God in a mystery[3]." We have wisdom given us to lead us on by obedience unto things higher and better, to teach us love and thankfulness: but it is in a mystery, that we may learn humility, and "not to be high-minded, but fear."

Now all these various schemes and orders of analogy it does not seem possible to reduce to any definite system; and perhaps it is not at all desirable that we should be able to comprehend them; but the great object to be derived from the study of them is, that we should have such a sense of the greatness and wisdom of those things among which we live upon our minds, as to lead us to walk with reverence on holy ground; and such things are best and most profitably learned by faith, by which we are led on to a practical sense of the mysterious presence of God.

[3] 1 Cor. ii. 7.

PART V

Mention of Angels in the Gospels

SECTION I

THE UNSEEN WORLD COMING TO VIEW

IT has been shown that every dispensation of God towards mankind, as it is the fulfilment of previous prophecy, so does it tend to foreshadow and prefigure, and to afford a foretaste of that which is to come;—containing within it previous and preparatory rays of light, or preliminary anticipations of that which follows, set forth in incidents recorded or words spoken. This may be seen in our own dispensation in a remarkable circumstance;—the manner in which the unseen world is introduced throughout the Gospels, as if it were blended with the things that are seen. It is our present object to notice it with respect to the mention and intervention of those spiritual beings, which are known to us under the name of Angels.

A person who has imbibed his impressions of Christianity from the tone and sentiments which have of late ages prevailed in literature and religion, cannot fail to be struck with this circumstance, when he comes to substantiate as it were and realize to himself incidents recorded,

T

and words spoken in Holy Scripture.   So far as he gives himself up to a meek and acquiescing faith, unbiassed by the world, he can scarce fail to derive a strong and lively sense, not merely of the existence of Angels, but of their presence and active employment in the Christian Church: as if the Christian dispensation were in some higher and more intimate sense under the ministering agency of Angels.

The present object is merely to enter into the subject so far as it is expedient for the fuller understanding of the Gospels, not as a topic of curious speculation, or from any idle indulgence of the imagination; nor to consider what has been or may be said respecting the nature, orders, and offices of Angels; nor to guard against any practical corruptions which may have, or do exist on the subject, in making Angels the objects of religious worship; a practice condemned by the Council of Laodicea, and the consent of primitive antiquity.   But the present object is merely an endeavour to know what sense of these things a person should have on his mind, who wished to study the Scriptures for the amendment of his own heart and the regulation of his thoughts.   What we speak of is a certain general practical impression, which a right study of the Gospels is calculated to convey; and if it is suited to convey such an impression, we do not know how far such an impression may be beneficial, and indeed perhaps necessary, for us. It may be conducive to that tone of mind which most rightly and reverently receives great doctrine; it may be that it affords a sense of reality to the unseen world; that there may be something of strength and consolation in the feeling of heavenly society which it introduces; for we are naturally much affected by the consciousness of sympathy; or there may be something of wholesome awe in the consideration of watchful witnesses of conduct: or, as the Lord's Prayer would suggest, in the thoughts of perfect patterns of obedience being constantly brought before us, with the prayer that we may do God's will as it is done by them in Heaven; and it no doubt raises us in the scale of being, to consider ourselves as acting our part among creatures superior to ourselves, and higher and better in their nature than any thing we see. And it will be, moreover, satisfactory to perceive, that the mode in which the ancient Liturgies introduce the mention of Angels, and in which the earlier Writers are in the habit of alluding to them, is quite in accordance with the Holy Scriptures, so as to intimate something of the same spirit in both. And this tends to corroborate the high authority we afford to the interpretations of the Fathers, as opposed to those of a later age, such as partake of the spirit of the world, which is governed by sense and not by faith.

It is obvious, as has been before shown, that as the land of Canaan was a type of the Gospel, or the Christian dispensation, so the Christian state itself is made throughout to be a type of the future Heavenly kingdom. The visible Church is made to be a type of the invisible, and words that are applicable in a higher sense to the latter are applied to the former also, in some lower and subordinate signification. They are both spoken of as the " regeneration," the state of " election," " the kingdom of Heaven." The members of both are termed the " called," the " elect," " saints," and " citizens of Heaven," and " sons of God." It is not therefore to be wondered at, that both should so much at once introduce mankind into the society of Angels. That they should be incidentally but constantly alluded to in the Gospels, as really but essentially and peculiarly present with Christians who have entered into the Kingdom. But such a sense of their presence can now be only known by faith: but on the last Day may be known by their coming visibly and sensibly to sight.

We hardly realize what it is to have the unseen world open upon us, as it does in the Christian kingdom; we do not adequately contemplate, or consider them as events which have actually taken place, when we read of the appearing of beings from the other world. Throughout the narrative of the Gospels, and also in the expressions made use of, we find Angelic beings are continually introduced, in the same manner that human beings would occur in a mere human story, as taking part in it as well as mankind. The actions attending and preceding our Saviour's birth are carried on by Angels as much as by men. On opening the Gospel, on entering within the portals of the Heavenly Jerusalem, of the kingdom of Heaven, we at once find ourselves in the company of Angels. It is at the very vestibule that we find the Angel Gabriel, announcing the birth of John the Baptist, and immediately after appearing to the blessed Virgin Mary. Still, in the simplicity of the sacred narrative, the wonderful nature of the things recorded is not put forth for effect, and therefore we pass on unconsciously, and are slow to consider what it is to have one of the Heavenly inmates conversing upon earth as man to man. Again, it is an Angel in a dream who informs Joseph of the mysterious conception. And if this may be considered as the vestibule, surely the entrance is when our Lord is born. And how is His birth celebrated? It is by a mixed company of Angels and of shepherds. It brings as it were the unseen world near to us; the floor of Heaven stoops down, and that of earth is lifted up to meet it: Heaven and earth both blend together as forming one Church. As St. Chrysostom says, "What could be ever equal to these good tidings? God on earth, man in Heaven, and all became mingled together, Angels joined the choirs of men, men had fellowship with the Angels, and with the other powers above[1]." Mankind is not left to feel isolated and alone. For as the brute creature partakes of the suffering and labour which man hath brought upon the world, so does he with man partake of his Sabbath of rest from that labour. So was it in the older dispensation, which had a reference more strongly to things temporal and to this world: but the Christian state, as bringing in things Heavenly, associates with man the higher creation. Thus, therefore, as the lower creation is linked with man in the ease and rest which is afforded to brute animals in the law of the Sabbath, and in the many other references to them in the Mosaic dispensation; so is the higher creation associated with him in the Christian kingdom. And as at the commencement of our Lord's life on earth, Angels are thus introduced foretelling, announcing, and celebrating it; saving Him from death, and directing His course into Egypt: so are they throughout. Angels ministered to Him after the temptation; an Angel strengthened Him in His agony; more than twelve legions of Angels were ready to assist Him at His betrayal; Angels were visible at His resurrection; and Angels at the Ascension announced His return. From the short and casual notices that are given of them, how may one suppose Angels to have thronged invisibly round His tomb? appearing now in one spot, then in another, now one and then two being seen; and these disclosed to one and concealed from another; and all this in a manner that may seem unaccountable to the human reader, as if they were but the casual disclosures of the outskirts of countless hosts

[1] Comm. in Matt.

attending; one or two manifestations only, and rare and far between, like the appearances of our Blessed Lord Himself, though every where and ever present.

SECTION II

ANGELS AT THE LAST DAY

But further, as every introduction, as it may be considered, of the Christian kingdom is marked more particularly by the introduction of Angels, and if thus at the commencement of the Christian dispensation, Angels come to view throughout the Gospels, no less so do they at its full completion or termination, or rather as it may be considered at the coming in of "the new Heavens and the new earth wherein dwelleth righteousness." For it is remarkable that the Day of Judgment is hardly ever described or mentioned without the mention of Angels. As on entering the tomb of Christ, an Angel meets us in the vestibule, so before the Gospel commences do we find the Angel Gabriel. And afterwards as we enter in we find an Angel at the Head, and another at the Feet, where the Body of Jesus had lain : in like manner at the opening and at the close of the·Gospel, of the Church visible, which is as it were the Body of the Son of Man here below, do we find Angels; at our Saviour's coming and at His departing : at the first announcement of the Gospel to mankind, and at its full termination upon earth on the Day of Judgment.

It is really much to be observed how variously, yet consistently and constantly, it is the case in all the Evangelists and in other parts of Scripture, whenever that great Day is spoken of, that the mention of Angels is introduced. Thus it is said, "Then shall they see the Son of Man coming in the clouds of Heaven with power and great glory,"—these very words alone might of themselves have implied the Heavenly Host; but it is added, "and He shall send forth His Angels with a great sound of a trumpet, and they shall gather together His elect from the four winds, from the one end of Heaven to the other[2]." And so incidentally in other places when that Day is mentioned, "For the Son of Man is about to come in the glory of the Father, together with His Angels; then shall He give unto every man according to his work[3]." And such expressions are repeated in the other Evangelists. The mention of Angels is in the same manner introduced in the parables that speak of that awful Day, in which they are described not as mere spectators, or unconcerned witnesses of those events which are then to take place, but as taking a most active part in them. I think we are not used to consider what a strong and visible reality there is in our Lord's words respecting them. In one parable the Angels are the reapers, for in speaking of the harvest where the tares are found mixed with the corn, it is said, "the Son of Man shall send forth His Angels, and they shall gather from His kingdom all things that offend[4]." In another parable, wherein the Kingdom is described as a net which gathered of every kind, they are expressly introduced as going forth and bringing the net to shore, and separating the good from the bad[5]. And whatever the Trumpet may signify which is to usher in the great Day, as is so often mentioned by name, this which appears to be the means of

[2] Matt. xxiv. 31.   [3] Matt. xvi. 27.
[4] Matt. xiii. 41.   [5] Matt. xiii. 49.

collecting, and the sign of that great gathering, is connected with Angels, "And He shall send His Angels with
a great sound of a trumpet[6]." And St. Paul mentions
the trump in the same connexion with the Angelic voice,
"The Lord Himself shall descend from Heaven with a
shout, with the voice of the Archangel and the trump of
God[7]." There is therefore express and frequent mention on that day of Angels appearing with the Son of
Man, of their active employment in bringing together all
mankind, and of the sound of an Archangel's voice being
heard.

But it is not only as agents in the scenes of that day
that Angels are mentioned : but their presence as witnesses is spoken of as something awful and impressive,
even beyond that of the Saints of God, and of the eyes of
all mankind. For our Lord says, "Whosoever shall confess Me before men, him shall the Son of Man also confess before the Angels of God : but he that denieth Me
before men shall be denied before the Angels of God[8]."
And He repeats similar expressions on other occasions, as
"Whosoever shall be ashamed of Me and of My words, of
him shall the Son of Man be ashamed, when He shall
come in His own glory, and in His Father's, and of the
holy Angels[9]." And in the Revelation also our Lord says
of His faithful servant, "I will confess his name before
My Father, and before His Angels[1]." In connexion with
these expressions, we cannot moreover but remember the
solemn charge of St. Paul to Timothy, "I charge thee before
God, and the Lord Jesus Christ, and the elect Angels[2]."
In perfect accordance with all this the same Apostle speaks
of Christians being made even now in this present time

---

[6] Matt. xxiv. 31.   [7] 1 Thess. iv. 16.   [8] Luke xii. 8, 9.
[9] Luke ix. 26 .   [1] Rev. iii. 5.   [2] 1 Tim. v. 21.

"a spectacle unto Angels[a]." "All the Angels," says St. Chrysostom, "will be present together with Him to bear witness, and themselves to testify of how much they, by the mission of God, have administered unto the salvation of man."

Now, when we consider what it is to appear in the presence of God, the thought itself is one that admits of no comparison or increase. It is in depth and awfulness so profound, that the introduction of Angels to add to the solemnity is not of itself such as we would, humanly speaking, have expected ; and if left to our own thoughts concerning that great manifestation, it is rather, I think, the eyes of our fellow creatures and fellow Christians that our imaginations would suggest to us. But there may be something in our moral nature, which this manifestation before Angels is peculiarly adapted to meet. There are no more powerful feelings in our nature than the dread of shame, and the desire of praise, especially from those above us ; nor are there any motives of conduct in mankind which moralists are more at a loss either to regulate or to account for. Bishop Butler seems to consider the final cause and the only legitimate end of the love of honour, to be a desire of being approved of by the unerring judgment of God, and the dread of His disapproval. But may there not also be something more in it besides this and in addition to this ? May it not have a reference to the circumstance of that approbation or disapproval of the Almighty being expressed before a multitude of superior Beings ? And would not the expressions of our Lord which have been referred to, lead us, even now in this present time, to act with a view to that "honour which cometh" indeed "from God only," but is in the

[a] 1 Cor. iv. 9.

presence of His creatures ; when the Master of the feast shall say, "Friend, go up higher ;" but he to whom it is spoken "shall have worship *in the presence of them* that sit at meat" with him⁴? In the passage, indeed, in the Old Testament on which our Blessed Lord's words are founded⁵, it is "in the presence of the Prince whom thine eyes have seen ;" but our Lord, in His infinite condescension, brings forward the presence of others, His creatures, in the application of it, and not His own. For speaking, indeed, of Himself on such occasions, He says, "He shall come forth and serve them." But it is sufficient for our purpose merely to notice the fact, that Angels are thus introduced in this manner, so appalling yet full of interest, on the Day of Judgment; and perhaps to this the Psalmist alludes in such expressions as, "He shall call the Heaven from above, and the earth, that He may judge His people⁶," and "the heavens shall declare His righteousness, for God is Judge Himself⁷." For the Heavens being called to attend the Judgment seems, of course, to imply the Angels being summoned. And it will be found, as has been before observed, that scarcely ever is the Judgment and the Advent of our Lord mentioned, without this distinct allusion to Angels; the manifestation of our Lord on that day is, in the words of St. Paul, the "Lord Jesus being revealed from heaven with His mighty Angels⁸." Nor is it only on the Day of Judgment that Angels are spoken of as actively engaged in the charge of human souls throughout the Gospels, but at death also. When Lazarus died, he was "carried by the Angels into Abraham's bosom⁹." And even where Angels are not mentioned, it appears to be mysteriously

---

⁴ Luke xiv. 10.   ⁵ Prov. xxv. 7.   ⁶ Ps. l. 4.
⁷ Ps. l. 6.   ⁸ 2 Thess. i. 7.   ⁹ Luke xvi. 22.

implied by the use of the plural, as "this night thy soul
do they require of thee[1]." And in another place[2], that
"they may receive you into everlasting habitations,"
where it is difficult to supply any other nominative case
but that of Angels: and in another passage we find the
same, where it is said, that the eagles will be gathered
together wherever their prey falls[3]; so would it seem to
be intimated (in addition to any deeper mysteries which
the words may contain[4]), that where the body falls, the
Angels are at hand to carry the soul to its destination.

SECTION III

ANGELS IN THE PRESENT KINGDOM

THIS circumstance of Angels so frequently taking a part
in the Gospel history, and coming sensibly to view on the
last Day, will prepare our minds for that constant introduction of them throughout the Christian state, which is
often alluded to in the New Testament. So that we are
brought thereby, as St. Paul says, to "the heavenly Jerusalem, and to an innumerable company of Angels[5]." And
in the same Epistle, St. Paul speaks of Angels as being
"all ministering spirits, sent forth to minister for them
who shall be heirs of salvation[6];" which very expression,
the "heirs of salvation," appears more particularly to
signify baptized Christians. And it may occur to every
one, in how great a degree all this is realized by the
many appearances of Angels, in the short and cursory
history of the early Church, which we have in the Acts

[1] Luke xii. 20. [2] Luke xvi. 9. [3] Luke xvii. 37.
[4] See page 79. [5] Heb. xii. 22. [6] Ch. i. 14.

of the Apostles;—an Angel releases St. Peter, an Angel commissions Philip, an Angel directs Cornelius, an Angel comforts St. Paul, an Angel smites Herod. Nor is it unreasonable to suppose, that the term "the kingdom of heaven" upon earth may have some reference to this active operation of Angels in the Christian dispensation. It is remarkable, that in the Lord's Prayer, after the expression of "Thy kingdom," the words immediately occur of doing God's "will in earth, as it is in heaven;" and the bringing of these together in this connexion naturally suggests their mutual relation,—men among Angels by obedience, Angels among men by love; both inhabitants of the kingdom, and subjects of the King, Whose laws to both are Divine love. And we also know that the Angels feel an intense and earnest interest respecting the mysteries of Redemption, a longing desire or holy curiosity to dive into the wonders of God as therein disclosed; for St. Peter, speaking of such mysteries, says, "which things the Angels desire to look into[7]." And St. Paul speaks of it as one of the very objects of revelation, to make known such things to Angelic beings, "to the intent that now unto the principalities and powers in heavenly places might be known by the Church the manifold wisdom of God[8]." From which expression the Fathers seem to have supposed that the Angels themselves were instructed by means of the Church.

And here it may be observed that it may be the case, that even the revelations of God to mankind, particularly with regard to the limitations and extent of them, may be regulated with respect to unseen Beings as well as to men; for we know, that not only do good Angels desire

---

[7] 1 Peter i. 12.   [8] Eph. iii. 10.

to look into the things of redemption, but " if the princes of this world had known it, they would not have crucified the Lord of Glory." And this may account for the mysterious silence of Holy Scripture on many occasions; for the birth of our Saviour from a Virgin seems to have been a secret not made known either to spirits or men for some time, and His Divine nature also. And the Fathers supposed that the Virgin's miraculous conception was on this account so mysteriously concealed, in order that it might not be known to evil spirits. This consideration seems to open to us something of the vastness of Holy Scripture, and its deep mysterious divinity, as much in what it conceals as in what it discloses. For it is evident that the subjects it reveals are matters of contemplation to unseen beings, and, therefore, may we not suppose that they watch its significations with more intense interest than we do ? And, perhaps, this is partly the cause why the mode in which prophecies are fulfilled is so dark beforehand, and defying previous comprehension; inasmuch as by these means evil spirits as well as evil men are deceived, or kept in ignorance.

Nor does this lively interest and sympathy of Angels extend merely to the Church at large, but we are told expressly that each individual is to those heavenly inhabitants an occasion of the same most earnest regard. We are too familiarized with the expression to consider all that it imports, that there is "joy in the presence of the Angels of God over one sinner that repenteth *;" for these words of course imply, that among those spiritual beings, however distant they may appear from us, there is a more close and intimate sympathy felt towards mankind than among men towards each other. And that this

* Luke xv. 10.

strong interest felt towards mankind among the Angels of heaven, is a circumstance to be considered by us, in a way to influence our own feelings towards each other, is evident from our Lord's admonition, "Take heed that ye despise not one of these little ones ; for I say unto you, that in heaven their Angels do always behold the face of My Father which is in heaven[1]." And I would dwell particularly on this expression of our Lord's, as a proof that it is designed that we should have on our hearts a practical devout expression respecting those unseen beings, such as to operate on our conduct towards our fellow Christians ; being, as it were, an additional bond of union, arising from the connexion of Christians with their Lord, by which we are all made as brethren ; for it is implied that we should look with attention and respect on the Christian who most humbles himself, as being the especial favourite of highest Angels, and in the court of Heaven.

SECTION IV

ANGELS ATTENDANT ON THE SON OF MAN

THE reason why Angels are thus more especially introduced in the Christian dispensation, may be on account of their attendance on Jesus Christ as the Son of Man. For as God is every where present in the natural world, and Angels are supposed to carry on the operations of nature : so where our Lord is present in some higher and more especial manner in the Christian Church, it might be reasonably supposed, that Angels also, as attendant upon Him, should also be present in some higher and

[1] Matt. xviii. 10.

more peculiar manner. For instance, our Lord has vouch-safed His presence in a house of prayer, "where two or three are gathered together in His name." And St. Paul speaks of the Angels being there present as a cause for especial reverence, and it has ever been the belief of the Church that Angels are there assembled, as attendant on the nearer presence of Christ. In like manner may it be the case in the Christian dispensation upon earth, in which Christ is revealed and manifested, and is more parti-cularly present, as in His own kingdom. It is of course a mystery perfectly inexplicable to us how God should be in a more especial manner present in some places rather than in others; for of course He is in some sense every where present, and it may be that Angelic beings also are every where present; but the thing to be observed is, that where His presence is more particularly vouch-safed, there also there appears to be more particularly the attendance of spiritual hosts.

And indeed the sight of our Lord upon earth, as mani-fested in the flesh, accomplishing the Redemption of man-kind, is spoken of as a spectacle to those Angelic beings. It is recorded as a great and important part of the dispen-sation, from among the things which were wrought in the great mystery of godliness, St. Paul enumerates that He "was seen of Angels [2]." And although the narrative little requires any mention at all of their unseen ministrations to our Lord in the flesh, yet on more than one occasion are they mentioned; as that "Angels came and ministered unto Him" after the temptation, and that in the garden of Gethsemane an Angel from Heaven was seen "strengthen-ing Him." And the expression of the good Centurion was much approved of by our Lord, when he intimated that as

[2] 1 Tim. iii. 16.

he had servants under him, and he said to this man, "do
this, and he doeth it," so our Lord had ever present with
Him those who at a distance would execute His commands;—an expression which would seem to indicate
that our Lord's miracles also were performed by means
of Angelic ministries.   At all events, the expression,
could I not now pray to My Father, and He would pre-
sently give Me "more than twelve legions of Angels,"
seems to be spoken by our Saviour as the Son of Man [3],
for as such only did He need Angels to be afforded Him
for His support, being Himself, as God, the Creator, the
Supporter and Life of them.   And the declaration of
the Psalmist is of course said of Christ in some high
and peculiar sense, when he says, " He shall give His
Angels charge over Thee," and "they shall bear Thee
in their hands, that Thou hurt not Thy foot against a
stone [4]."

Moreover, that it is as attendants on the Son of Man,
that Angels have the great prerogative and privilege of
taking part in the Christian dispensation, would appear
from this; that whatever is said of them, is as being
allowed to have a share in the charities and humiliations
of the Son of Man ; as reflecting in themselves His loving
kindness to the children of mankind !   If they have "joy
over one sinner that repenteth," it is but participating in
the joy and triumph of Him who had gone forth to seek
the one sheep that was lost: if the highest among them
watch over the humblest of Christ's little ones, it is but
that as Christ humbled Himself beyond all, and that the
humblest of men is the highest in His kingdom, therefore
the highest of His Angels feel the greatest joy over the
humblest Christians.   And it may be observed, that in

[3] See Passion, p. 69.   [4] Ps. xci. 11, 12.

those three parables in the fifteenth chapter of St Luke, our Lord speaks of Himself as rejoicing together with the Angels, and calling upon them to rejoice with Him [*] over the recovery of lost mankind. Thus in the parable of the lost sheep it is added, "he layeth it on his shoulders rejoicing. And when he cometh home, he calleth together his friends and neighbours, saying unto them, Rejoice with me." And in the succeeding parable of the woman and the lost money it is also again added, "and when she hath found it, she calleth her friends and her neighbours together, saying, Rejoice with me;" and to both of these our Lord repeats, "Likewise I say unto you, there is joy in the presence of the Angels of God." And on the return of the Prodigal son the father calls on his household to rejoice with him.

Nay, so closely and intimately do the Angels seem to be allied to and made one with their Lord, that they seem only to act and speak and feel, as He Himself acts and speaks and feels. Indeed they use on some occasions His very expressions, and so "hearken to the voice of His words," though unspoken and unheard, that they seem to execute (if one may so express it) His minutest sympathies, "Go, and tell the disciples and Peter," said the Angel to the women, as if already expressing their Lord's compassion to that penitent disciple to whom He first appeared ; and, "Woman, why weepest thou ?" were the compassionate words addressed by the angel to Mary Magdalene, before the very same gracious words were spoken to her by our Lord Himself. But of course this touches on that inscrutable mystery, which we must not venture to speculate upon, of the nature of Angels, how far they act spontaneously of their own free will, how far

[*] Ver. 6. 9. 23.

U

they are but " the eyes of the Lord running to and fro
throughout the whole earth, to show themselves strong in
the behalf of him whose heart is perfect towards Him [6],"
being as it were but like the lightnings which "fulfil the
voice of His words ;"—from the perfect union of their wills
with His will. And indeed it seems to have been the
opinion of some, that the knowledge of Angels does not
arise from what they discern in objects themselves ; but
from what they behold, as it were in a mirror, in the
Divine mind, in the beatific vision of God. Which
opinion is only mentioned to show how perfectly mysterious and inscrutable such a subject must be.

But that some peculiar authority and dominion over
Angels is given to Christ as the Son of Man, i.e. in His
kingdom of Heaven upon earth, is evident from many expressions. His sitting on the Right hand of God, in His
victory over sin, is frequently connected with it. Thus
St. Peter, in speaking of the Ascension, ascribes to it the
gift of some especial authority over Angels, evidently in
some distinct and peculiar, although to us perfectly unknown sense ; as if they were made at that time subject to
Christ in a manner different to what they were before.
He is spoken of by St. Peter as from that time being " on
the right hand of God, angels and authorities and powers
being made subject unto Him [7] ;" and by St. Paul as being
" set in the heavenly places, far above all principality and
power [8]." And the description of the Ascension in the
sixty-eighth Psalm is connected with the same circumstance, " the chariots of God are twenty thousand, even
thousands of Angels, and the Lord is among them as in
the holy place of Sinai. Thou art gone up on high ;

[6] 2 Chron. xvi. 9. [7] 1 Pet. iii. 22.

[8] Eph. i. 21.

Thou hast led captivity captive." Our Lord's being made a " little lower than the Angels " in His humiliations, is in order " to crown Him with glory and worship," which expression of glory and worship being given Him, of His being set over principalities and powers, and all things being made subject unto Him, in consequence of His passion and humiliations, must signify of course these things being done in the Christian Church ; for otherwise as God, One with and equal to the Father, they are of course at all times subject unto Him from the beginning, and have their life and being only in Him. Expressions also of the same kind seem also to have a reference to our Lord's Resurrection : thus it is said, " when He bringeth the First-begotten into the world He saith, And let all the Angels of God worship Him[9]." For the expressions, " the First-born," " this day have I begotten Thee," and the like, seem to refer, as in St. Paul's discourse in the Acts [1], to our Lord's Resurrection. And all this is confirmed by our Lord's own words, for they seem in some manner to include both Angels and mankind : "All power," said our Lord to the Eleven, " All power is given unto Me in Heaven and in earth [2] ;" whereby it seems implied that, in consequence of His victory over sin and death, spirits also minister unto Him in order to carry on His designs respecting His Church. Add to which the remarkable salutation in the book of the Revelation, "from *Him* which is, and which was, and which is to come, and from the seven Spirits which are before His throne." For infinitely high and mysterious as the words are, applying as we may suppose to the Ever-blessed Spirit of God, yet this mention of Spirits before the throne in the Christian

[9] Heb. i. 6.   [1] Ch. xiii. 33.

[2] Matt. xxviii. 18.

u 2

kingdom is remarkable : as the form of expression which is used to signify the sevenfold and infinite power of the Holy Ghost.

And moreover, the circumstance of Christians being in some especial manner objects of interest and care to Angels, arises from their very close and most intimate connexion with our Lord Himself. For if to us the assurance is given, that what we do to the humblest of mankind, we do to Christ Himself ; and if this is an expression which our Lord will repeat in the presence of Angels at the last ; much more may we suppose this touching declaration to be considered by Angels themselves—that what they do unto us they do unto Christ. And therefore, what is said in the Psalms of our Lord Himself, " they shall bear Thee in their hands that Thou hurt not Thy foot against a stone [3]," would for this very reason be said of every Christian, also, in whom Christ dwells ; forasmuch as the care which they can bestow upon the least of those whom Christ terms His brethren, is done unto Himself.

Our Lord Himself seems to imply this active ministration of Angels in the Christian Church in His words to Nathanael, whereby He explains to him, that this in fact was the true interpretation and fulfilment of the Patriarch's vision, " Hereafter shall ye see heaven open, and the Angels of God ascending and descending upon the Son of Man [4]:" which vision, that Nathanael was to behold, was of course to be by faith seen in the Christian Church, by the guileless Israelite—by the pure in heart, whose peculiar privilege it is to see God. And, indeed, the visions of Angels and of God's host, seen by the Patriarch Jacob, were themselves, perhaps, but prophetic intimations of the same in the

---

[3] Ps. xci. 12.   [4] John i. 51.

Christian Church, of which Israel was the type, in distinction from his brother Esau, who represented the Jewish dispensation which was set aside. And in like manner we may, I think, conclude that the case of the Christian's having Angelic aids set around him, and his having by faith eyes given him to discern them, is the very thing which was signified and represented in that action of the Prophet Elisha; for this Prophet is, it has been supposed, the type of Christ or His Holy Spirit *in the Church.* "Fear not," said Elisha [5]: "for they that be with us are more than they that be with them. And Elisha prayed, and said, Lord, I pray Thee, open his eyes, that he may see. And the Lord opened the eyes of the young man; and he saw: and, behold, the mountain was full of horses and chariots of fire round about Elisha."

It is probably, indeed, the case, that on most occasions the introduction of Angelic visions in the Old Testament is significant of the future Christian dispensation. Thus it was the vision of these the latter days, and of that great Day yet to be revealed, which the Prophet Daniel beheld, when "the Ancient of days did sit," when "thousand thousands ministered unto Him, and ten thousand times ten thousand stood before Him, the judgment was set, and the books were opened [6]." And in that memorable vision of the Prophet Isaiah, when "the train" of the Lord "filled the temple," and he beheld the Seraphim, and heard their voices [7], and his "eyes saw the King, the Lord of Hosts,"—it was of Christ, as St. John expressly tells us, that the Prophet spake, and "the glory" of Christ that he saw [8].

And if in the vision of Isaiah, "the train" of the

[5] 2 Kings vi. 16.
[7] Ch. vi.
[6] Ch. vii. 10.
[8] Ch. xii. 41.

Lord which "filled the temple," was, as the Evangelist says, "the glory of Christ," who is especially "the Lord of hosts,"· so is it no doubt of Christ's coming that the Prophet Haggai speaks in that glowing prophetic promise, "I will shake all nations, and the Desire of all nations shall come; and I will fill this house with glory, saith the Lord of hosts⁹." Nor is it unreasonable to suppose, that to these Divine ministries allusion was made in the Prophet Haggai, when we consider it in connexion with this passage of Isaiah, and many others which blend heaven with earth, and Angels with men, in the glories of the Christian Church, as attendant on the Son of Man.

It is also to be observed, that the expression "the Lord of hosts," does not occur in the earlier Scriptures; but when the Prophets come to speak more distinctly of the Christian Church, and to look more nearly to it, it is repeated with a remarkable frequency, as the term by which the Almighty is pleased to designate Himself, especially in the Prophets Haggai and Zachariah; in the latter the expression occurs as often as fourteen times in one chapter of twenty-three verses. The term has, indeed, been supposed to have a reference to the idolatrous objects of worship which they witnessed in their Captivity, and which thus ascribes to God the dominion over those hosts of heaven which others worshipped: but this or any other such allusion to passing events, would not at all interfere with this Divine purpose here ascribed to the use of it, as the kingdom of Christ becomes more and more visibly manifested in the Prophets. For all passing events and worldly incidents, with their subordinate pur-

⁹ Ch. ii. 7.

poses, are moulded by their Almighty Disposer to serve the higher objects of His kingdom.

The term "host," indeed, as applied to the Angels of God, does occur early in Scripture, for the Patriarch Jacob says, "this is God's host," when "the Angels of God met him" on his return to Canaan. And the Angel, or more than Angel, who appeared to Joshua on his entering the holy land, says, "as Captain of the host of the Lord am I now come [1]." But it is obvious to any one that both these visions were typical, and prophetical of our entering on the Christian Canaan, and, therefore, rather tend to mark the significancy we have here attributed to the subsequent appellation of Almighty God, as "the Lord of hosts," when we consider it to contain an allusion to Christ in His Church and His Christian kingdom.

It is also to be noticed, that these Prophets in the Old Testament, as they approach nearer to the opening of the Christian Church, do more especially introduce Angels into their prophecies. Indeed, in the Prophet Zechariah, the description is mostly carried on through the conversation of Angels; and they, too, are mentioned as speaking with the same interest and lively pity for the Christian Church, which our Lord describes to be the case with the ninety and nine whom He left in Heaven, when He came to seek for the sheep that was lost. "Then the Angel of the Lord answered and said, O Lord of hosts, how long wilt Thou not have mercy on Jerusalem?" . . . . . . "And the Lord answered the Angel that talked with me, with good words and comfortable words [2]."

All these things seem to prepare the way for a more

---

[1] Ch. v. 14.　　　　　　　　[2] Zech. i. 12, 13.

distinct and marked interference of Angels in the affairs of earth, and for the appearance of the Angel to the father of the Baptist, and to the mother of Christ, and for that "multitude of the heavenly host" which took the shepherds into union and concert with themselves, in that celestial song which they, together with the redeemed of God, will never cease to sing.

These Angelic ministrations in the later Prophets are more fully and strongly carried on in the Book of the Revelation, which being the description of the Christian Church, both now and at its final consummation at the Day of Judgment, bring before us more particularly the instrumentality of Angels. They thus seem to carry out more fully the parables and expressions of our Lord, inasmuch as they are represented as engaged in the fulfilment of those events which are spoken of in the parables, and are to happen to the Church. The mention of Bishops under the term of Angels, as commissioned by Christ to superintend His kingdom, in the beginning of that Book, when taken together with the same appellation subsequently given to the ministering spirits of God, appears again to be another circumstance which combines together in one the operations of Angelic and human ministers, as attendant on Christ in carrying on His kingdom. And if here His ministers are spoken of under the term of Angels, so are the same figurative expressions applied to both in the Gospels; for our Lord speaks of His ministers as "reapers" sent forth into the harvest, and also as fishermen who are to "catch men;" and in His parables He applies both of these terms to the Angels. Both alike, though in different senses, gather "from the four winds [3]" and collect the heavenly harvest; both alike,

[3] See page 214.

though in different senses, draw the net to shore ; one in the kingdom now on earth, the other in the kingdom hereafter. The high appellation which at the Resurrection our Saviour bestows on mankind as " His brethren," and as having His God and Father for their God and Father, will render these remarks not presumptuous, though they seem so much to elevate the dignity of mankind in Christ to a kind of fellowship with Angels.

The Angels indeed themselves speak of this their union with us for Christ's sake in the Christian Church, as the bond of sympathy which holds us and them together. "I fell down," says St. John, when he was shown the vision of the city of God, "to worship before the feet of the Angel which showed me these things. Then saith he unto me, See thou do it not ; for I am thy fellow-servant, and of thy brethren the prophets, and of them which keep the sayings of this book: worship God[4]." And in another place, where a similar circumstance occurs on his being shown the supper of the Lamb, the Angel, in the same rejection of worship, says, " I am thy fellow-servant; and of thy brethren that have the testimony of Jesus; worship God: for the testimony of Jesus is the spirit of prophecy[5]."

In the same book the Angel is described as evincing the same kind of interest in disclosing to the Evangelist the circumstances respecting the kingdom, which other expressions of Scripture intimate that they entertain towards us. As for instance[6]: "And there came unto me one of the seven Angels . . . and talked with me, saying, Come hither, I will show thee the Bride, the Lamb's wife. And he carried me away in the spirit to a great and high mountain, and showed me that great city, the holy Jerusalem,

[4] Rev. xxii. 9.   [5] Rev. xix. 10.
[6] Rev. xxi. 9.

descending out of Heaven from God, having the glory of God."

We cannot fail to observe how lively a picture these words afford us, if we might so with reverence speak, of one of those Angels, which always behold the face of God, yet watch over one of Christ's little ones,—of those good spirits who minister unto the heirs of salvation.

SECTION V

HOW FAR NATURE COINCIDES WITH THIS SPIRITUAL ACCOUNT

WHEN it is stated that there is so peculiar an introduction and intervention of Angels in the Christian dispensation, it is not of course implied that all mention of Angels is exclusively confined to the kingdom of Heaven upon earth. A circumstance true in itself, often loses the attention and credit due to it by an over-statement. Nature itself would suggest to us that the physical world is replete with spiritual beings; it is confirmed by the belief of all nations: the feeling which every one has in solitary places seems to be an instinctive consciousness of their presence, which the presence of mankind as being more palpable serves to put out of the mind. And when we find that the material world is replete and animate with living beings, as far as we can descend into the minutest observations by the aid of artificial sight—discovering to us that what we considered laws of matter is carried on by means of living agents—we necessarily conclude that what is above us also in the moral and spiritual world is conducted likewise, not by dead laws, but by living agencies.

So that what the microscope does for us in the material world beneath us, in disclosing to us all things carried on by living agents beyond our natural sight, is something similar to what Holy Scripture does for us in the invisible world above us, in manifesting all the creation of God as replete with life, and acting living beings. And it is this natural common-sense view, of an unseen world existing around us, that the Gospel so thoroughly confirms and sanctions. Scripture as in all other matters takes up, carries out, and extends, ennobles and hallows these our natural feelings with reference to Christ's new kingdom, of which nature presented us with indistinct glimpses and shadows. As the invisible things of God become revealed to us, we find that the instinctive imaginations of our nature, and the fables of old, which they gave rise to, contained within them images and reflections of Divine truths. Like the gathering of water, but a few inches deep, by chance collected between the stones in the street, of which the poet says, that it furnishes us with a mirror of the skies extending below us, and within it contains the vast circuit of the Heavens and Heavenly bodies ; as in a world beneath us [7]. Thus the wonderful mysteries of the Christian Church, and its unearthly companies, find a correspondence and reflection in the longings and imaginings of our lower earthly nature,—in the things which we see as it were beneath our feet. And they of old who

[7] " Ut conlectus aquæ digitum non altior unum,
　　Qui lapides inter sistit per prata viarum ;
　　Despectum præbet sub terras impete tanto,
　　A terris quantum cœli patet altus hiatus ;
　　Nubila despicere, et cœlum ut videare videre, et
　　Corpora mirando sub terras abdita cœlo."
　　　　　　　　　　　　　　　Lucretius, iv. 418.

peopled all things with living spirits, may be nearer the truth in their ignorance, than we in our knowledge without faith and fear.

Nor, again, is it maintained that all mention of Angels in the Old Testament has an exclusive reference to the Gospel dispensation ; but only that it is sufficient to intimate a remarkable and peculiar connexion of Angels with the kingdom of Christ.   It may be merely throughout a matter of comparison in various dispensations, that as the kingdom of Heaven becomes more distinctly revealed, so do Angels become more visible.   First of all, in the older dispensation as preparatory to and prophetical of the Gospel, and then in the Gospel itself: and lastly, still more strongly and distinctly do unseen beings come to view at its consummation on the Day of Judgment.   But here it might be objected, that it is the old dispensation itself which is spoken of as being carried on by means of Angels ; it is said of the Law, that it was given "by the disposition of Angels[8]," that it was "ordained by Angels[9]," that "it was spoken by Angels[1]."   These accounts of course imply, that the older dispensation was in some peculiar manner conducted by Angelic ministrations : but all this is thus spoken of in distinction from the manifestation of God in His Son, the Son of Man.   It is not that Angels were more especially made use of under the Old Testament; but that it was through them as inferior to the Son of God, appearing in the New. .If the word conveyed by servants was so sure and weighty, what must be that of the Lord Himself, Who comes down to us in the Gospel,—Who comes down to us, we may add, attended by them ?

[8] Acts vii. 53.   [9] Gal. iii. 19.

[1] Heb. ii. 2.

Add to which, that the appearance of Angels in the Old Testament is often explained as being that of the Lord Himself appearing by them. Thus, for instance, when Jacob speaks of the Angel which redeemed " him from all evil," it is evident (as St. Athanasius observes) that it is the Lord Himself who is spoken of; and in the former verse He is mentioned as the " God before whom my fathers Abraham and Isaac did walk². " In other instances it has been usually observed, that it is the Lord Himself, Who appears by His Angel, as St. Augustin notices of the Angel who appeared to Manoah, that it was Christ³; and also to Abraham and Sarah⁴, and to Jacob⁵. For as " no man hath seen God at any time," when He spoke to the Jews of old, He spoke through His Angels. When, therefore, God is said to speak, it is through His Angels He speaks: and when His Angels are said to appear and to speak, it is He Who appears and speaks in them. But the Christian dispensation is ever described as very different from this of the Jews, for therein God is manifest, and Christ is ever present, and Angels are ever present together with Him. Not indeed as appearing visibly and sensibly to bodily eyes, for such is not the nature of the present Kingdom, but as discerned by faith, which is the spiritual eye of the soul; and hereafter to be beheld, as it were sensibly and visibly, when " we shall be changed;" —when " we shall see Him as He is,"—when " He shall come in His glory, and all the holy Angels with Him."

Moreover, it may not be amiss to notice the manner in which spiritual agency is spoken of in Scripture. One cannot but observe how much in the revealed Word is attributed to living agents, which we should consider as

---

² Gen. xlviii. 15, 16. ³ iii. 963.
⁴ iii. 615, 616. ⁵ v. 46.

natural or moral consequences, and the result of certain necessary laws. So much so as to make it highly probable that spiritual agents, as well as human and animal, act under certain general laws, and carry on some great systems, while they still continue free agents; though such systems are quite beyond our comprehension. To take, for instance, the effect of evil spirits on our minds; it is clear from Scripture that they have the power of conveying impressions and unworthy thoughts into our minds, as in the case of David, when it is said, that he was tempted by Satan to number the people; and in the remark of St. Peter when our Lord said to him, " get thee behind Me, Satan:" and they have also the power of removing good thoughts, as when Satan takes the good seed out of the heart. And when bad thoughts are settled into a confirmed bad resolution, as in the case of Judas, it is called the entering in of Satan. And this entering in is spoken of at different times of the same person, as if, when the habit or purpose of evil became more and more confirmed, the evil spirit took possession with greater degrees of fulness or intensity,—for it is said of Judas, a year before, that he was a devil[6]; it is said of him, when the intention of betrayal had taken possession of his mind[7]; and yet, when receiving the sop at the last supper, and going out to execute his purpose, it is again said, as if for the first time, that " Satan entered into him[8]." And yet in all these cases, these impressions, and the settled resolution arising from them, may be often accounted for, humanly speaking, in the way of natural effect, constitutional tendency or passion, accidental circumstance, and the like. Again, what we consider an evil habit,—the necessary consequence of the repetition of certain acts,—is, in Holy Scripture, the

---

[6] John vi. 70.   [7] Luke xxii. 3.   [8] John xiii. 27.

possession of an evil spirit. Again, we naturally observe, and explain by known maxims of moral philosophy, how liable an evil habit is to return, after it has been once for a time subdued. Holy Scripture tells us that it is an evil spirit, who, being cast out, is ever seeking for an opportunity to enter into his former abode or dwelling place, the evil heart of man. And the same rule still goes on to apply to all moral laws; ethical philosophy speaks of the extreme difficulty of restoring one who has relapsed into vice after repentance: our Lord tells us that the evil spirit, when he gains admission a second time, takes possession with seven other spirits worse than himself. And in this very expression, there is something perhaps a little different from what our own preconceived notion might have been in such a case, for we should have thought of one spirit possessing the heart of a man with more or less degrees of strength and entireness; but this expression of a man being possessed, not by one only, but by many spirits of evil, is remarkable. And not only are we certain that such words of our Lord must be literally and closely accurate and true, but a vivid reality and palpable force is given them by the coincidence of events recorded, which bring to view the unseen world; for we have an actual instance of this possession of one person by many evil spirits, in the case of the man among the Gadarenes, out of whom were cast a "legion" of devils. The whole of such narratives derive a very intense interest from their bringing to view, as it were accidentally, that unseen state of things, of the existence of which Scripture speaks, with all the substantial reality which there is about actual events: as, for instance, in the conversations which our Lord held with those evil spirits, and the expressions which break out from them in the most abrupt and natural

manner, such as "I know Thee who Thou art, the Holy
One of God[1]," and "what have we to do with Thee,
Jesus, Thou Son of God; art Thou come hither to torment us before the time[2]?" Such also is their entreaty
that our Lord would not "command them to go out into
the deep." All these are indirect proofs from the spiritual
world of some of the highest doctrines of our faith. For
they acknowledge our Lord as the Saviour, as the Holy
One, as the Son of God; and the coming to torment them
"before the time," indicates either some knowledge of the
mystery of the Gospel being preached to the Gentiles,
and the evil spirits cast out from them; or else the final
Judgment committed to the Son of Man. So interesting
and remarkable is the manner in which the Gospel brings
before us, as actually going on, what were otherwise matter
of natural induction from known religious truths, or comprehended in some precept. In like manner, the permission given to the evil spirits to enter into the swine, and
the commands of our Lord to them "not to divulge Him,"
are living and palpable proofs that their power of evil is
entirely limited by Divine permission, and that they are
still entirely subject to Divine command. Now all these
things, it is reasonable to suppose, are but indications of a
vast and incomprehensible system, carried on by spiritual
agents, where we behold nothing but what we consider
physical or moral causes. And indeed it seems probable
that physical evil, as well as moral, may be carried on by
the instrumentality of spirits, as the plague in the time of
David; and the case of bodily infirmity spoken of by our
Lord as the woman "whom Satan had bound[3]." St. Paul
speaks of bodily inflictions and sufferings as the being
given up to Satan; and his own infirmity as "a messenger

---

[1] Mark i. 24.   [2] .Matt. viii. 29.   [3] Luke xiii. 16.

of Satan to buffet" him[4]; as if all the evil which God permits or sends, even in temporal suffering, was done by means of the author of all evil. Although in inflicting these chastisements he is made, against his will, subservient to our spiritual well-being and the glory of God. And perhaps the cases of demoniacs in the Gospel were not very different, excepting in · degree, from such as are now to be found in instances of insanity, which are treated as medical cases, and as depending on medicinal treatment, like other bodily diseases, so as not to be in kind essentially distinguished from them. It is very evident that there are states of bodily ailment or disorder, capable of being removed by medical treatment, and arising from obvious physical causes, which are closely connected with spiritual sins. Such are thoughts of gloominess, discontent, unkindness, which mere bodily disarrangement gives rise to. And yet those very thoughts are also doubtless from the evil spirit. In like manner other states of body give rise to other thoughts of sin, which are clearly from the Evil one. So that it is impossible to say how intimate the connexion may be between bodily temperament and spiritual influences. As things in the material universe, which were supposed to be fortuitous, are found to be regulated by vast, and fixed, and general laws, in like manner the little that is mentioned to us of spiritual agencies may be but the casual appearances of a system, infinitely great, and more incomprehensible than that of the material Heavens.

And herein the poets of heathenism may have touched on greater truths than their philosophers ventured to suggest. For the progressive effects of vice are described in Aristotle's Ethics as corrupting, enslaving, and darkening the whole man by the power of evil habit; and

[4] 2 Cor. xii. 7.

x

Socrates, in the Gorgias of Plato, speaks very beautifully
to the same effect; but they may not be nearer the truth
than were Homer and Æschylus, when they speak of the
Evil spirit, or Ate, that principle of evil which they
describe under various personifications, as attaching herself
to individuals, and families, and carrying on the effect of
crimes; while crime unrepented of instigates to fresh
crime, and infatuation, and woes; and the criminals themselves, as Helen and Clytemnestra, attribute their crimes
to the possession of an evil demon or god [5]. It is as if
they felt the chain which they had wrought for themselves,
and attributed it almost unconsciously to a power without,
and beyond themselves, wishing thereby to overcome and
throw off the sense of responsibility;—feeling, but not
liking to confess, the self-induced slavery of sin, which is
no less than the toils of the devil.

There is a question closely connected with this subject,
which may be here mentioned,—whether spirits have
any inherent power of discerning the thoughts of men?
At first sight we might suppose that they had, as they
evidently have the power of inspiring bad thoughts and
removing good; and good Angels are supposed to convey
our prayers to God : they have also frequently appeared to
men and conveyed God's commands to them in dreams,
which is of course by means of the mental vision, when
the outward senses are closed; and Scripture itself
sanctions the belief of all nations, that sleep and dreams
bring us into some nearer connexion with the unseen
world. Add to which, saving thoughts in sudden contingencies, remarkable presentiments, and the like, and even

---

[5] As Æschyl. Agamem. lin. 1477, &c.

φανταζόμενος δὲ γυναικὶ νεκροῦ
τοῦδ', ὁ παλαιὸς δριμῦς ἀλάστωρ, &c.

holy inspirations have been considered, as by Bishop Bull, to be instances of their operation and assistance ; to which we might add simultaneous coincidences of thought in persons at a distance from each other. And yet even these things are not sufficient to establish such an inference, for some of these things imply no more than such influences as we have over the thoughts of each other. The whole of the subject is one so perfectly dark and mysterious, that we cannot support any inference beyond what Scripture and the Church warrant.

But now it may be observed in Holy Scripture, that although Angels are so often appealed to as witnesses, introduced as anxious spectators, as affectionate ministers, and watchful guardians,—yet they are not ever spoken of in Scripture, that I am aware of, as knowing the thoughts of our hearts. But it would appear as if the Almighty had kept to Himself that, as His own peculiar attribute, speaking of Himself as " the heart-searching God," as " knowing the thoughts long before," as " trying the reins," " a discerner of the thoughts and intents of the heart," and in the prayer of Solomon, " for Thou, even Thou only, knowest the hearts of all the children of men[6]." And indeed Petavius[7] maintains, and proves by various passages from the Fathers, that this was their opinion,—that the thoughts of men are not known to spiritual beings, excepting so far as they are made known by external act or expression ; something in the same way as they are among ourselves. But St. Augustin thinks that this is the case to a very great degree, that spiritual beings do thus become acquainted with our feelings. But to say that they are incapable of reading our thoughts would not of course

---

[6] Kings viii. 39. [7] Lib. i. c. vii.

imply that they are incapable of conveying thoughts and impressions to our minds, for this we do to each other, and men commonly do to men, although they have no power of discerning each other's hearts. Those therefore would not be opposed to this opinion, who speak of Angels, with Bishop Andrewes, as "suggesting thoughts of salvation," or with Bishop Bull, when he says that "Good Angels suggest to the faithful good thoughts and affections, and excite them to good works and actions [8];" or with Bishop Ken, in his Evening Hymn, when he speaks of his Guardian Angel as instilling "love angelical," and stopping "the avenues of ill," rehearsing "celestial joy," and conversing with him "thought to thought."

SECTION V

THESE OPINIONS CONFIRMED BY CHURCH WRITERS

Now all that has been here maintained in this treatise is, I think, the teaching of Holy Scripture respecting Angels, in itself highly edifying and impressive, and remarkably unlike the tone and spirit of the religious notions of the present age. And it is very well known that the mode in which ancient writers are continually introducing the mention of Angels is quite of this character. It is not merely that this is their mode of speaking of them in set discourses, in which they are introduced more at large, as in St. Augustin's City of God;—but their casual and consistent allusions to them, with reference to those things spoken of them in Scripture, indicate

[8] Sermon x.

that they had on their minds a strong impression respecting them, of their existence, their presence, their ministrations, and active co-operation in the Christian warfare on earth, and triumph hereafter. The circumstance itself hardly needs any proof, or examples to point it out, for it is perhaps chiefly shown in casual mention or allusion. Thus, for instance, St. Clement of Rome, urging the necessity of a devout life, adds, "He exhorteth us to turn to Him with all our heart, and not to be slothful nor negligent to every good work: let our boast and confidence be in Him; let us subject ourselves to His will: let us consider the whole multitude of His Angels, how they stand before Him, and minister unto His will. For the Scripture saith, 'thousand times ten thousand stand before Him'.'" And Clement of Alexandria, speaking of a good man, says, "Moreover, he prayeth with Angels, as one who already is made equal unto the angels, and is never out of their sacred custody, and if he pray alone he hath a choir of Angels standing together with him [1]." Origen speaks full often to the same effect; as in his Treatise against Celsus [2]: "We confidently affirm, and have experience of the fact, that those who, according to the Christian religion, worship the God of all through Jesus, and live according to His Gospel, with regularity and earnestness, using their appointed prayers, are not assailable either by magic or devils. For of a truth, 'the Angel of the Lord encampeth round about them that fear Him, and delivereth them from every evil.' And the Angels of the little ones in the Church, and who are appointed to protect them, are said always to behold the face of our Heavenly Father, whatever that beholding His face may signify." And St.

[3] Cor. Epist. xxxiv. p. 142.   [1] Strom. vii. 317.
[2] Lib. vi. p. 302.

Basil, " An Angel is ever by the side of one that believeth in the Lord, if we drive them not away by evil works."—— " If thou hast in thy soul works worthy of angelic custody, and a mind rich in thoughts of truth dwells within thee, God doth necessarily set by thy side watchers and guardians, and walleth thee round with a guard of Angels. And consider how great is the nature of Angels, that one is compared to a whole army[3]." And St. Augustin, " From so great blessedness, which is in the Heavenly Jerusalem, from which we have wandered afar, they attend us in our wanderings, and pity us, and assist us at the command of the Lord, that we return to that our common country[4]." St. Gregory Nazianzen says, " The finding the drachma makes the heavenly Powers partakers of the joy, as they had been made the ministers of the dispensation[5]." And St. Cyprian, " Unity and concord affordeth delight, not only to faithful men, but even to celestial Angels themselves, with whom, saith the Divine Word, there is joy over one sinner that repenteth and returneth to the Lord of unity, which indeed would not be said of Angels, who have their conversation in heaven, unless they also were united with us, and rejoice in our unity[6]." St. Cyril, speaking to the Catechumens of Baptism, says, " You must approach it solemnly. You are each of you on the point of being presented to God, before innumerable hosts of Angels[7]." " Angels," says St. Hilary, " daily offer to God the prayers of those who are to be saved in Christ ; dangerous therefore must it be to despise him, whose requests and desires are carried to the eternal and invisi-

[3] Vol. i. p. 148.   [4] Tom. iv. 869.   [5] 34. ad locum.
[6] Epist. lxxv. 341.   [7] Lect. iii. 3.

ble God by the service and ministry of Angels[8]." St.
Jerome also speaks of the great dignity of souls, each of
which has an Angel assigned to him from his birth to guide
him[9]. St. Ambrose, St. Chrysostom, and others, might
easily be quoted to the same effect. It is well known,
indeed, how common such allusions are amongst ancient
writers, of Angels as guardians, assigned to individuals
at birth or Baptism; of their presence in Churches; of
their conveying the prayers of the faithful. Unconsciously,
as it were, but continually do they blend with their practical exhortations or devout studies, the mention of Angels,
as motives to piety, which they felt and were used to.
Their general opinions indeed on the subject of Angels
seemed to be merely such as were contained in the very
words of Holy Scripture, or necessarily flow from them;
such impressions as faith would necessarily imply in a
hearty adoption of the statements of Scripture. Nor do
they appear to go beyond these statements of Scripture,
as far as any general consent goes, but only to carry out
the same into their own impressions and feelings respecting them. So fully does the Catholic Church harmonize
with Holy Scripture; it is one and the same system in
both; expanded, but not added to; not developed, but
realized; not improved upon or enlarged, but the tone
and spirit preserved; and sometimes, as it were, embodied
in particular forms.

And if it thus pervades their writings, we may find it
in a still more distinct shape in those sources from which
their devotional tempers were in some degree moulded;
viz. in the ancient Liturgies. Without entering more
particularly into these, we may just refer to the Liturgical

---

[8] Comm. Matt. lib. iii. c. 8.   [9] Com. Matt. c. 1.

prayer in the Constitutions[1]. " It is very meet, and right above all things to praise Thee, the true God, who art before all creatures ; of whom the whole family in Heaven and Earth is named."—And afterwards, " O God, and Father of Thy only begotten Son, who by Him didst create the cherubims and seraphims, the ages and hosts, the dominions and powers, the principalities and thrones, the archangels and angels ; and after them didst by Him create this visible world."—And again, at the end of the same prayer, " The innumerable armies of angels adore Thee ; the archangels, thrones, dominions, principalities, dignities, powers, hosts, and ages ; the cherubims and seraphims also with six wings, with two of which they cover their feet, and with two their faces, and with two they fly, saying, with thousand thousands of archangels, and ten thousand times ten thousand angels, all crying out without rest and intermission : and let all the people say together with them, Holy, Holy, Holy, Lord of Hosts ; Heaven and earth are full of Thy Glory."

To our own Liturgy also there has descended some remains of the same Catholic spirit, as speaking the language of those who " have come to the Mount Sion, the City of the living God, and an innumerable company of Angels." In the first Book of Edward, in the Communion Service, were the words, " Command these our prayers and supplications by the ministry of the holy Angels, to be brought up into Thy holy tabernacle, before the sight of Thy Divine Majesty." And in the Te Deum we have still supported, in inspiring language, the connexion of the Church of God in heaven with the Church of God on earth : "To Thee all angels cry aloud, the heavens and all the powers therein. To Thee cherubim and seraphim continually do

[1] Lib. viii. cap. 12, quoted in Bingham.

cry, Holy, Holy, Holy, Lord God of Sabaoth. Heaven and earth are full of the Majesty of Thy glory." And surely in language no less beautiful do we, in the Communion Service, join "with angels and archangels, and with all the company of heaven," to "laud and magnify 'God's' glorious name." So intimately connected are these sentiments with that which is most transcendental and Divine in doctrine. Nor on this subject can we forget the ancient Collect, which we have still retained for St. Michael's day. Nor is it to be wondered at, that, together with the Liturgies, those most sacred safeguards of Divine truth, there should have descended also to the divines of our Church something of the same ancient spirit; that they should have imbibed the same Evangelical feeling,— of their having been admitted to the Mount Sion of Angels and of Saints, and should have given vent to those feelings in similar language. We need not allude to larger and more distinct accounts of them, as in that beautiful one in the Ecclesiastical Polity, and in the two Sermons of Bishop Bull. In order to observe this tone of thought and reflection, it is only sufficient to remind ourselves of Hooker's memorable expression, in his last dying contemplations, on "the number and nature of Angels, and their blessed obedience and order, without which peace could not be in heaven:" and in the Morning Hymn of Bishop Ken, lifting up his heart to take part with Angels, "who all night long unwearied sing;" and the Morning Prayer of Bishop Andrewes, that God would "grant him an Angel of peace," (or meaning, perhaps, more than an Angel,) "as a faithful guide, the guardian of souls and bodies, encamping round about, and suggesting saving thoughts:" and the prayer of Bishop Taylor, that God would afford his friends "the guard of Angels to preserve them from evil, and the

conduct of His Holy Spirit to lead them unto all good ?"
and the thanksgiving of Bishop Wilson, for "the guard
God's holy Angels keep over him," and his Evening
Prayer, that God would take us "under His gracious protection : give His holy Angels charge concerning us." Of
the same kind was the expression of one who was lately
among ourselves,—"My aim for the future shall be to conduct myself in the presence of men with such humility,
that to Angels I may be an object rather of pity than
concern[2]."

In conclusion it may be observed, that at the same time
that the Almighty has impressed us with an instinctive
consciousness of the existence of Angels, and by His
Revelation has greatly increased and heightened this
natural feeling ; yet He has so mercifully provided, that
the Angels are, as it were, purposely excluded from our
view : as if it were for this reason, viz. that we could not
bear their lustre, without forgetting Him, who is their
and our own Creator.　We know nothing of their nature,
or of their properties ; they come to our knowledge only
as *messengers* of the Most High, and beyond that name
we know nothing of them ; as spirits we know them not,
but only as angels or messengers.　If indeed their Orders
are mentioned, yet it is nothing but the names, there is
nothing to gratify the curiosity ; and how little do those
nine names, which are supposed by sacred writers to designate their different ranks, convey to us of "the ninety-
nine left in the wilderness," the unfallen creations of
God ?　Even those names of their Orders seem given them
more in relation to mankind, as in the subjects of contemplation which Bishop Andrewes assigns them, than as

[2] Froude's Remains, vol. i. 211.　See also Mr. Newman's Sermons,
especially that on the Feast of St. Michael, vol. ii. ser. 29.

designating their distinctness of nature. And it is observable, that those three Angels, who are known by name in the Holy Scripture, have rather a name by which God is known in them, than any descriptive or distinguishing appellation of their own; such as Michael, Gabriel, and Raphael: that is to say, "who is as God," "the fortitude of God," and "the medicine of God." As in the more general terms Angels and Archangels, so likewise in those personal appellations, they are not themselves beheld, but the messages of God in them. It is not indeed revealed to us that they have even thoughts or designs of their own, as separate from those of God: they have no will but His; yea, it is even He, as St. Augustin says, that hears and speaks in them. We may well therefore adore the silence of Scripture in such a case: for where it is silent, human imagination cannot lead us. And well indeed it is so. Neither creatures in Heaven nor in earth are objects for the soul to rest in; and yet so far as they partake of any thing worthy of our regard, there doubtless is a danger of such regard being turned too exclusively toward them. For even among mankind, if there is any thing that we admire and love, which may be either naturally or morally formed to excite veneration and regard, and particularly if closely united to ourselves, by use, good offices, and sympathy, it may be difficult altogether to avoid the snare of an idolatrous regard. And if a human friend may become dangerous to us to contemplate, how much more an Angelic guide? There is also another point in which we cannot but thankfully acknowledge the Divine goodness. For it would appear as if it were an instance of singular mercifulness towards mankind, that the Almighty has been pleased, during our probation, to keep our hearts in His own hand alone.

Something of this kind may be signified in the many places in Holy Scripture, where it is said that God is "a place to hide in :" that He hides good men in the hollow of His hand, and the like. For it is a consideration especially calculated to produce both love and confidence, that the very secrets of our hearts are known to Him alone : that as He alone knows our infirmities, as we are His creatures, He has made us, and knows whereof we are made : so He has been pleased to keep the secrets of our hearts (excepting so far as we choose to reveal them) to Himself alone : that in the infirmities and silent wants of our hearts we may turn only to Himself. "If our heart condemn us, He is greater than our heart, and knoweth all things." For however deeply interested other creatures may be respecting us, and actively engaged for our welfare, yet all that concerns the renovation and restoration of our souls is the work of God alone.

"Whom have I in Heaven but Thee? and there is none upon earth that I desire in comparison of Thee. My flesh and my heart faileth ; but God is the strength of my heart and my portion for ever."

PART VI

Places of our Lord's Abode and Ministry

SECTION I

FLIGHT FROM PERSECUTION

SINCE in a former part of this volume an attempt has been made to point out one law of our Lord's conduct in the manifestation of His Godhead; and since there is always a danger in Divine subjects of confining the attention too exclusively to one point of view; it may be well to mention some other laws and principles, which appear to have regulated our Lord's movements and actions. Both of these are indeed such as will be found to harmonize and fall in with each other, but yet they are such as may appear to be distinct reasons for the same line of conduct.

Thus with regard to our Lord's so constantly withdrawing Himself,—and, consequently, withdrawing the scenes of His abode and ministry,—from the gaze of mankind, from places of greater importance and more public resort; this has been shown to have been owing, in great measure, to His concealing from the worldly view the knowledge of His awful Godhead; but in the same line of conduct there may be profitably traced out other motives and principles of action. The former was a rule of conduct which, as God, He always has observed in His dealings with mankind, and therefore to be looked on with awful adoration and regard ; there is another also in which we may study and imitate the meekness of the Son of Man, as our example, and perfect pattern of humility. In the same line of conduct there may have been motives which admit of a separate consideration ; the one connected more particularly with our Lord's Godhead, the other with His manhood. In the same action our Lord may appear as God withdrawing Himself from view ; as Man fleeing from persecution : as God concealing in mercy His most awful Presence : as Man affording us an example of that lowliness which loves to conceal itself from mankind. And these principles, though in themselves distinct, yet may have some necessary connexion with each other ; thus to intimate the meekness of the Son of Man is the only mode of arriving at the knowledge of His Godhead ; and, again, the knowledge of God will humble us and make us desirous to conceal ourselves among mankind. And thus our Lord may state both principles, when He says at one time, "no man cometh unto the Father but by Me [1]," i.e. that no man can come to the knowledge of God but by the Son of Man ; and at another time, "no man can come to Me, except the Father which hath sent Me draw him [2];" i.e. that no man can perceive God in Christ, or that Christ is God, except it is revealed to him by the Father.

As Christ was "perfect God," therefore He acted perfectly as God does in all His dispensations and providences : as He was also "perfect Man," He there-

[1] John xiv. 6.   [2] John vi. 44.

fore was perfect in human submission, as the pattern of suffering humanity. So mysteriously did He, as Man, subject Himself to all those accidents of our suffering nature, and the laws and conditions of our earthly state, any of which He might, as God, have suspended if He had so pleased. For it may be asked, why was the ignoble Galilee the chief place of our Lord's abode and ministry? Or, again, what was the reason of His being born in a stable? Or of Egypt, the very type of worldliness and idolatry, being the country of His childhood and nurture? or why Nazareth should have been His home, rather than a place of higher name? It may of course be said it was the Divine will and purpose: but can these circumstances be explained by being resolved into any rule of conduct or principle which regulated our Lord's actions: or can any law of His proceedings be learned, which would account for these things as human actions are accounted for? One law can, I think, be traced throughout them all, that of submission to human evils and casualties, as opposed to the free choice of the natural will. And it is very remarkable, that the very temptation of Satan was a temptation to suspend those evils to which His suffering humanity was subject, by an act of His Divine power: " If Thou be the Son of God, command that these stones be made bread [1]."

To take, in the first place, the very circumstances of our Lord's birth. It has been shown that the concealment and obscurity thrown around it was such as ever characterized the dealings of Him, " Whose paths are in the great waters, and Whose footsteps are not known," Who hideth Himself on the right hand and on the left,

[1] Matt. iv. 3.

so that we feel for Him, yet perceive Him not.   But setting aside this view of the subject, which has been so fully considered, let us contemplate all those points in Him as the Son of Man, and we shall find that sorrow and humiliation ever went side by side with Him, were the cause of all His movements, and coincided with all His actions, while He ever lived adhering to the calls of duty under suffering and abasement.   This is the law which is developed through the course of His earthly conduct—the rule we may extract from His ways.

As our Lord in becoming Man, submitted Himself to all the bonds and infirmities of our fleshly nature, so did He especially in the accidents which, as men, we are subject to.   As He came into the world to be a sacrifice, so it appears that His life was so as well as His death, a continual living sacrifice ; so unceasingly did He live in a state of persecution, that the places of His sojourn seem to have been chiefly regulated by this circumstance. The rule for the places in which we find Him were, for the most part, twofold, operating opposite ways ; that of duty taking Him into the midst of His enemies ; and where duty did not require this, a continued flight from them.

This principle will explain the very place and circumstances of His birth.   For His being born at Bethlehem, instead of at a home, was accompanied with circumstances of peculiar humiliation and distress to His parents ; but occasioned partly as a duteous fulfilment of prophecy ; for the circumstances of His birth, as well as those of His death, were in the act of fulfilling prophecy ; and also on account of the oppressive exaction of the Roman Emperor, imposing a penalty, in itself so severe, on the subjects of a conquered state ; and which was doubly severe on our

Lord's parents by occurring at such a time. The power of Rome represents worldly tyranny; and thus were the circumstances of our Lord's birth marked by the suffering of worldly oppression: nor did the Royal lineage which brought them to Bethlehem add any thing of worldly dignity to their humiliations; for it evidently brought nothing to them of respect from others; and, humanly speaking, would only have enhanced, by the contrast, their condition of privation and poverty.

While at Bethlehem, their first movement from the place of the lowly manger was at the call of duty, which led them forth to the presentation in the Temple: and all the circumstances of which were those of the meanest human estate and lowly privacy; and this was in itself not without danger, so far as it did not partake of that privacy. St. Augustin indeed has supposed that the rumour, spoken of as occasioned by this their appearance in the Temple, was the exciting cause of Herod's cruelty, when he slew the infants.

And their change of place is now again occasioned by the circumstance of persecution: immediately is our Lord seen as one persecuted and fleeing; as that scape-goat which must flee from men, for on His Head are laid the sins of us all. Circumcision had already marked the Victim, and shed the Victim's blood, and He is henceforth to live as a Sacrifice. For the next occurrence which is mentioned is the flight into Egypt. The hardships and privations during such a journey, for a family so poor and in a condition so helpless, must have been great, though Holy Scripture has passed over them in silence. And if the flight was itself so severe to a poor mother and helpless infant, not more inviting was the place of refuge itself to which they were fleeing. For

Y

Egypt was that country which Scripture had spoken of. as
the very proverbial designation of idolatry and iniquity,
as the sink of the world. If, humanly speaking, it was a
comfort to be poor in the Holy Land, and to be taken to
the Holy City ; yet that comfort was converted into sorrow when that City and that Land was their enemy, and
that which was the refuse of the world opened its arms to
receive them.

The next circumstance of which we read, implying
change of abode, is the return of the Holy Family to their
native country.   And here it appears that, for some
reason or other which is not explained, Judea would have
been the place of their choice, and to which they would
naturally have returned ; whether as to the more sacred
or honoured land, or because Bethlehem was the place of
their family, or, as St. Augustin supposes, on account of
the Divine intimation, which spake of Israel[4], not being
perfectly understood. For whatever reasons it might have
been the purpose of the Holy Parents, they are diverted
and prevented from this their intention by the fears of
persecution, which they might reasonably have anticipated
from the son of Herod, against the long-promised and
expected Heir of the kingdom, appearing in Judea itself.
No reasons of that kind would have operated with respect
to Herod Antipas and Galilee ; and we read that Joseph
came into the land of Israel, according to the command of
the Angel, "but when he heard that Archelaus did reign
in Judea in the room of his father Herod, he was afraid
to go thither : notwithstanding being warned of God in a
dream, he turned aside into the parts of Galilee." It is
therefore persecution, or the fear of persecution, which
again marks out and regulates the place of our Lord's

[4] Matt. ii. 20. See Nativity, p. 169.

earthly sojourn. It is this that is the occasion that the ignoble and despised Galilee becomes the place of our Lord's early abode, rather than any other place in human eyes more eligible. And certainly this is of itself a point of inquiry of great interest, when we find at last that Galilee is so strongly designated by our Lord Himself, and by His Angels, as the place wherein, after His resurrection, He would teach His Apostles the things concerning His kingdom. For we naturally ask how it came to pass that Galilee should become thus signally honoured? And this circumstance supplies the answer, that it formed a part of Christ's cross. Nor is it only the ignoble and despised Galilee, but Nazareth, which, even in Galilee, was the most ignoble and despised place, becomes the scene of our Lord's abode. For if Galilee was despised at Jerusalem, so that a Pharisee should say contemptuously, " Art thou also of Galilee ?" and " Out of Galilee ariseth no Prophet ;" yet Nazareth was itself despised by a Galilean, so that the simple-hearted Nathanael naturally exclaimed, " Can there any good thing come out of Nazareth ?"

From this time our Blessed Lord's early life is hid in silence from our view, with the exception of one circumstance only, during His childhood and youth, which has become very memorable, from the fact of its being the only one recorded of Him, and is in itself highly interesting and mysterious. The event is that which is recorded of Him when He was twelve years of age ; and which bears on the present question, as implying change of place and departure from home ; and which tends to confirm the view that has been here taken, inasmuch as the occasion was, it may be observed, at the call of duty ; for He was now at that age when the young were first of all required to appear in the Temple at Jerusalem. And thus it happens that even this change of place, and the appearance of our Lord in Judea, and all the circumstances attending it, and our Lord's separation from His parents to continue alone in Jerusalem; slight as these circumstances are in themselves, yet they tend, as far as they go, to indicate the same great law or principle which regulated our Lord's movements, that of submission to the appointed order of things in which He was placed as suffering man. As the narrative mentions upon this occasion His obedience and subjection to His earthly parents, or supposed earthly parents, so was He also with the same piety submitting Himself to the painful requirements of His mother, or supposed mother, the Jewish Church.

After this occurrence, we find nothing more recorded of our Blessed Lord's habitation, or of His movements, until after eighteen years of silence : but as on the last occasion of His mention, we found Him coming up at twelve years of age to stand before God in His Temple, as the Law required, so do we now meet Him on the banks of the Jordan, in Judea, coming "to fulfil all righteousness" by the baptism of John. Here again there is indeed no persecution, nor fear of persecution, but yet it harmonizes with the general view here taken, inasmuch as it is in obedience to the Law and at the call of duty, for the humiliating purpose of receiving washing, as if He had been one who needed cleansing, from the hands of a creature. But no sooner is His Divine character declared at His baptism, than the fire of persecution is kindled, by the breath of which He is driven from place to place to suffer, and to testify as a suffering creature ; not indeed yet persecution on the part of man, to whom His goodness is not yet known, but of evil spirits, to whom He has become manifested by the declaration from Heaven, as " the Holy One of God," and "the Son of the Most High God," as the evil spirits afterwards call Him. For immediately we read, "the Spirit driveth Him into the wilderness to be tempted of the devil :" the very word " driveth Him," given emphatically by the Evangelist, seems to intimate that it was under a constraining power from on high that He was forced upon this state of painful suffering, not of His own human choice, but as a sufferer. The same law of obedience which had brought Him into the wilderness of this world, to share the years of mankind's probation and pilgrimage, now brings upon Him a new abode of forty days into the waste and howling wilderness: and the mountains of Judah behold their God. As He had been for forty days in the stable and in the cave with the tamer animals of the stall, so is He now for forty days in the wilderness with those animals whose subtle or cruel nature, loving the darkness of the night and waste places, suggests them as external emblems of those worse enemies He had to encounter there in the evil spirits. Without attempting to enter further into a subject so awful and inscrutable, yet thus far one may venture to observe, that our Lord's dwelling in the wilderness was not indeed to flee from, but to meet persecution, and that as it were by some mysterious forcible constraint.

We afterwards find our Lord again in the scene of the Baptist's ministry, as if there abiding among the penitents, He Who "shall not break the bruised reed nor quench the smoking flax ;" and there watching for the effect of that stern preaching of repentance, which might dispose the hearts of some of them to receive Him, and to look with welcome to "the Lamb of God which taketh away the sin of the world ;"—that He might take away those sins which the baptism of John could not, though it brought men to the sense of their weight. For it is here that the disciples St. Andrew, St. John, St. Peter, St. Philip, and Nathanael, are first brought to Him. Here little more than this is known of Him, but He is soon after in Cana of Galilee, in company perhaps with these the same, His future disciples. Such is the interval between our Lord's baptism and His public teaching.

SECTION II

THE FIRST YEAR OF OUR LORD'S MINISTRY

But it is from His appearance at the ensuing Passover in Jerusalem that we usually date the commencement of His ministry, the first act of which appears to be when He drives the buyers and sellers out of the Temple, fulfilling the Psalmist's expression, "The zeal of Thine house hath eaten me up," and "the reproaches of them that reproached Thee are fallen upon Me[5]." For that even at this time He bore heavily the reproach of God, the reproach which the world lays on those who are with God, is evident from that interview at this festival with Nicodemus by night. As bearing upon our present point of consideration, the circumstance is in itself interesting and important, as an evidence of the condition of our Lord, and of the estimation in which He was held, even at this time; it was such as to render an eminent Jew ashamed of Him; so much so, that to profess Him openly would subject him to reproach, and require some courage.

And now we should naturally suppose, if circumstances

[5] Ps. lxix. 9.

would have allowed it, that Judea and Jerusalem, the Holy Land and Holy City, would have been the place of our Lord's ministry. It is, if looked upon in a mere human point of view, the more worthy and honourable course for the Founder of a new religion and kingdom,— that He should come forth among the more honourable men, and in a place more honoured. And it is the course of conduct, which we should most of all have expected would have been that of our Lord's adoption, for it is most like the regulation given to His Apostles, and to His own practice,—to go first to the lost sheep of the House of Israel, and to enter first into the Synagogue. It seems natural that He should chiefly and in the first place go to the more glorious and true seat of the sacred nation, the chosen place of the Temple ; and it is written that "out of Zion shall go forth the Law[6];" and more than once it is said, "Judah is my Lawgiver[7]." It seems reasonable, therefore, to expect that our Lord should commence and continue there ; and so, in fact, we find that His first teaching was so, and the commencement of His ministry was there : as if this would have been His wish and purpose, that the Lawgiver might not only proceed from, but continue in Judah. For He appears to have continued at Jerusalem in the work of His ministry, so far as to have created some sensation there, as St. John states ; and very much, doubtless, must have occurred there, although not mentioned in detail, and only thus intimated, "Now, when He was in Jerusalem at the Passover in the feast, many believed in His Name when they saw the miracles which He did." And St. John afterwards casually mentions the report of these miracles in Galilee : "The Galileans received Him, having seen all the things that He did

[6] Isa. ii. 3. [7] Ps. lx. 7 ; cviii. 9.

at Jerusalem at the feast[8]." It is evident too that on leaving Jerusalem He continued for some time in Judea, as is expressly mentioned in St. John: "After these things came Jesus and His disciples into the land of Judea; and there He tarried with them[9]," which expression of His tarrying there seems to imply some lapse of time. And, indeed, His continuance there was sufficient to have caused a very considerable impression; so much so, as to have thrown into the shade the Baptist himself, respecting whom all the Pharisees and the people had been moved: for we find that the Jews had a dispute with the disciples of John respecting the comparative value of the two Baptisms, and that the Baptist's disciples, when they came to state this to him, spoke of the numbers who attended our Lord, saying, "All men come to Him[1]." And afterwards, as our Lord is passing from Judea into Galilee, through Samaria, an incidental expression indicates that a considerable part of the first year of His ministry must have then elapsed, for our Lord says, "Say not ye, there are yet four months, and then cometh harvest[2]?" which expression must signify, that it was only four months before the Passover of the second year, and therefore our Lord must then have already spent eight months of that year in Jerusalem and Judea.

We may conclude, therefore, that not only was it reasonable in itself, but that it appears also our Lord's intention, humanly speaking, to have made Judea the place of manifesting Himself; and, therefore, it may fairly give rise to the question, what the reasons or circumstances were that should have induced Him to retire from thence, and that the Gospel should have gone forth from Galilee. We

[8] Ch. iv. 45.   [9] John iii. 22.
[1] John iii. 26.   [2] John iv. 35.

are expressly furnished with the cause of it; it was from fear of the Jews; this is clearly intimated in the following simple words of St. John: "When therefore the Lord knew how the Pharisees had heard that Jesus made and baptized more disciples than John, He left Judea, and departed again into Galilee³." So that our Lord is forced, as it were, by fear of persecution, to withdraw from Judea, which would have been otherwise the natural scene of His miracles, and to take up His abode in Galilee, as the chief place of His future ministrations.

But in the mean time there is a country still more ignoble than Galilee, where His Divine presence is vouchsafed, and that from the same constraining necessity which leads Him to retire to Galilee, for "He must needs go through Samaria⁴," where He makes that disclosure of Himself which St. John records at Sychar by the well, where He had sat down from painful weariness. And to Galilee He went from thence as to no place of honour or expected success, but of unwelcome ministry ;—"He departed thence, and went into Galilee, for Jesus Himself testified that a Prophet hath no honour in his own country."

And now that our Blessed Lord retires into the obscure Galilee, there is one spot there beyond any other that claims His peculiar regard, one that might naturally become the scene of His abode and ministry, that of His own native place and village of Nazareth. If He is not to teach in the sacred ground of His own Jerusalem and Judea, this is the spot in which next of all He would be disposed to lift up the light of His gracious countenance. We are therefore immediately led to inquire how it is that He should select a new place of abode, and be found

³ John iv. 1. 3.   ⁴ John iv. 4.

living at Capernaum, for we read at once that, "leaving
Nazareth, He came and dwelt in Capernaum, which is
upon the sea coast in the borders of Zabulon and
Nephthalim⁵." And we find from St. Luke that Nazareth was indeed the first place of His choice, and for
opening the door of His kingdom. It was here that He
went into the Synagogue and unfolded the book of Prophecy, and declared that the true Sabbath, the acceptable
Year of the Lord, had now come. It is only, therefore,
before the violence of persecution that He relinquishes
the favoured spot of His nativity, and seat of His childhood; for He is taken by His countrymen to the brow of
a hill in order to be cast down, and is obliged to escape
for His life. "They were filled with wrath, and rose up
and thrust Him out of the city, and led Him unto the
brow of the hill whereon their city was built, that they
might cast Him down headlong⁶." Nor does our Lord
venture again to return to this His home, till near the
second year of His ministry had expired, when He again
ventures to try the recovery and restoration of His own
maternal village, but in vain. His attempts served only
to bear a new testimony to that frequently-declared truth,
that "a Prophet is not received in his own country."

It was this circumstance of His forcible expulsion that
occasions our Lord to bear the Gospel to the borders of
the Heathen, so that, as usual, the rejection of His
countrymen and His chosen people becomes the light of
the stranger. It is ever thus in Divine dealings; that
grace is not lost, but transferred to the more worthy: the
birthright which Esau rejects is established in Jacob; the
crown of the faithless Saul is given to the faithful son of
Jesse; the talent which is taken from the unprofitable

⁵ Matt. iv. 13.   ⁶ Luke iv. 28, 29.

servant is not lost, but bestowed on another [7]. And thus, when Nazareth puts far away from her the Sun of righteousness, who was rising upon her with healing on His wings, "The land of Zabulon and the land of Nephthalim, by the way of the sea, beyond Jordan, Galilee of the Gentiles; the people which sat in darkness saw a great light [8]."

After this we find our Lord having His residence at Capernaum, and entering more formally on His ministry, one of the first steps of which is, that as He walks by the sea-side He there sees the four disciples who had before been with Him, and gives them a more solemn and definite call to follow Him [9]. Then do we read of Him teaching in the synagogue on the Sabbath-day [1], instead of the synagogue of Nazareth; "healing all sickness and disease among the people," with a great sensation attending His miracles and extensive report: "preaching in their synagogues," and persons from all parts flocking unto Him; while He continues teaching and healing among their cities. But still, as far as it was possible, He Himself kept withdrawing from these crowds and retiring, and continuing in the deserts in prayer; of which St. John probably explains the cause, for when speaking of the miracles He had wrought at Jerusalem, and the sensation that He had occasioned, he said that "Jesus did not commit Himself unto them, because He knew all men," and "knew what was in man [2]." And from this His retirement, when He entered into the city of Capernaum, we find Him thronged with vast numbers of people. It does not appear, from any mention in the Gospels, that our Lord had any home of His own in Capernaum, but

[7] Matt. xxv. 28.   [8] Matt. iv. 15, 16.   [9] Matt. iv. 18. 21.
[1] Mark i. 21.   [2] John ii. 24, 25.

probably, literally, had not a place " where to lay His head ;" perhaps He spent the night out of doors, as we find it expressly mentioned on some occasions that He did ; and He might, more or less, have made St. Peter's house His home.   Thus we may observe on the first Sabbath-day that is mentioned, it is said that on retiring from the synagogue it is to St. Peter's house that He goes : and in the last year of His ministry, on returning after some absence to Capernaum, He is asked for the tribute, together with St. Peter, whom they asked respecting Him ; and St. Peter, by his Evangelist, speaks of their being " *in the house* " as if it were his own[3] ; and he had spoken in a similar manner before, when our Lord " returned to Capernaum, and it was rumoured that He was in the house, and straightway many were gathered together, insomuch that there was no room to receive them, no, not so much as about the door[4];" one might suppose it was St. Peter speaking of his own house, and of that position about the door which he was familiar with.

But our Lord had been now but a short time in the exercise of His ministry at Capernaum, for most of the first year had, as it has been observed, probably elapsed before He arrived there, and it was now nearly at its termination. It is on the occasion of the last miracle recorded that we find the first intimation of the envy and ill will of the Jews.   It is that of the higher classes, the Pharisees and Teachers of the Law, who at that time, it is said, had come down from every village in Galilee and Judea, and even from Jerusalem[5].   Their disposition and purpose is shown by their very posture, while the multitude are thronging Him with every sign of " amazement" and " fear," of importunity and wonder, they are "sitting down " and

[3] Mark ix. 33.   [4] Mark ii. 1.   [5] Luke v. 17.

watching Him. But even here their ill will is not yet openly expressed, but rather shown by their secret murmurings and reasonings at the fuller display of that ἐξουσία, that awful and commanding Divinity in the power and authority of His words, which had so forcibly struck the people, as distinguishing our Lord's teaching from that of the Scribes. It is on the occasion of the Paralytic, who is let down through the roof in the midst of them, and whom our Lord absolves from his sins, at the same time that He restores him the use of his bodily limbs.

But still as yet, through these few months of our Lord's teaching at the close of the first year of His ministry, these appearances are for the most part favourable and full of promise, excepting for this secret intimation of ill will; and it seems, as it was with the Baptist, that they "were willing for a season to rejoice in His light." More than once He goes down expressly to the sea-side and teaches them, or to their villages, or to the mountain; not upbraiding and warning them, as afterwards, but with beatitudes; not darkly with parables, as in the next year, but openly: and accompanying His teaching with numerous gracious miracles; so that every form of malady was brought before Him to seek for His aid: and the eagerness, the astonishment, the thanksgiving, and adoration of the people are several times spoken of, and of their "giving glory to God." Their observations are, "we have never seen it on this fashion," "we have seen strange things to-day." On first coming into these parts, our Lord had called the four disciples who were previously known to Him, and they had instantly obeyed the call; and now the last circumstance that is mentioned this year is His seeing Levi at his gainful post by the lake, and from the despised order of the Publicans He summons him also as a true son of

Abraham.   But the selection of one from a state so despised, by Him who knew what was in man, seems already to intimate something of what was to follow,—we have a Ruler coming by night—the Pharisees sitting apart and thinking evil, a Publican leaving all things and following. And here the first year terminates, for our Lord has again to appear at Jerusalem at the passover.

SECTION III

THE SECOND YEAR

WE might have again supposed that our Lord would make the Holy City and the Holy Land the seat of His ministry; and by His working at least one remarkable miracle there, and the long conversation which ensues with the Jews, it might appear as if He attempted to make it so. But the enmity of the Jews is now showing itself more distinctly and openly; and on our Lord's healing the impotent man at the pool of Bethesda, we find that they attempt to kill Him[6].   St. John alone records the circumstance, and thus furnishes us at once with the reasons why He should no longer continue in Jerusalem, or indeed in Judea.   And an additional reason is now incidentally mentioned, which indicates the danger of His continuance any longer in Judea, and our Lord's reason for departing from that country, viz. His hearing that the Baptist was now cast into prison[7].   The natural enmity of the world at that which is good, will always assume to itself the appearance of principle, and take hold of some point apparently open to objection, by which it conceals its real

[6] John v. 16.   [7] Matt. iv. 12.

character and motives; and this is but one part of that great truth, that Satan will transform himself into an Angel of light. For it is now for the first time that the charge of breaking the Sabbath is brought forward, on the cure of this impotent man; but when an occasion has once been found of fastening a charge on one so blameless, a charge which has so much appearance of truth in it as to render it suitable for their purpose, it will not be readily lost sight of. Soon therefore, after being once taken hold of, it occurs a second time, but on an occasion of a very different nature, for it is again mentioned at what appears to be the season of Pentecost that next ensued, for the Sabbath at the Pentecost is probably meant by the expression[8], "The second Sabbath after the first," when the disciples are plucking the ears of corn[9]. This circumstance, from the occasion and the season, we naturally conclude takes place in Judea; but from recording this the Evangelists proceed, in the order of association and connexion rather than that of time and place, to mention another instance of the same cavilling and ill will in a Synagogue, apparently in Galilee. The charge now put forth, of His breaking the Sabbath, would soon have found its way from Judea to Galilee from the persons that attended the feast, and probably from these very Pharisees. It occurs on healing the man with the withered hand[1], and the consequence of which miracle was, that they immediately meditate His destruction. And as it was now in the jurisdiction of Herod, we find the Pharisees immediately going out, and combining with the Herodians for this purpose[2]. We may here reasonably conclude, in confirmation of the general argument, that it is in consequence

---

[8] Σαββάτῳ δευτεροπρώτῳ.
[1] Matt. xii. 9. Mark iii. 1. Luke vi. 6.
[9] Luke vi. 1.
[2] Mark iii. 6.

of these determined and combined attempts against His life that our Lord retired towards the sea, together with His disciples, charging those that followed Him not to make Him known. And it is on this occasion that St. Matthew speaks of the character given of our Lord in Isaiah being fulfilled, which describes His preaching to the Gentiles, and His meekness being seen in this His retiring from opposition, that "He shall not strive, nor cry; neither shall any man hear His voice in the streets³." Which proves that this was a remarkable occasion of His meek retiring from persecution. To this it must be added, that if the Sermon on the Plain in St. Luke is not the same as the Sermon on the Mount in St. Matthew, it must occur about this time, and differ from the earlier discourse in St. Matthew in this respect, that it is more addressed to a mixed multitude, and to Gentiles, many of them from Tyre and Sidon, and that neighbourhood: a circumstance which serves as an additional indication that our Lord was at this time obliged, for fear of persecution, to be withdrawing from His Jewish enemies.

It is at this period in the sacred narrative, and about the middle of the second Year, that our Lord retires to a certain mountain, where He was probably used to go, and, after spending the night in prayer, called His disciples unto Him, and out of their number selected the Twelve, and gave them the name of Apostles. After this He Himself returns to Capernaum, and it is from henceforth, I think, that we may observe a marked difference already commencing in our Lord's teaching among the Jews, in a more deep and severe tone of warning and reproof. It is soon after this that, for the first time, He begins to denounce these Jewish cities, wherein His wonderful works

³ Matt. xii. 19.

had been done, and to contrast them with the better states
even of those heathen cities of Tyre and Sidon in their
neighbourhood, on which they looked with contempt; and
even with that of Sodom, whose wickedness had become
so proverbial, and whose ruin was still as it were before
their eyes, and its sound in their ears. "Then began He
to upbraid those cities in which most of His mighty works
had been done, because they repented not. Woe unto
thee, Chorazin! woe unto thee, Bethsaida! for if the
mighty works which have been done in thee had been
done in Tyre and Sidon, they had repented long ago in
sackcloth and ashes. But I say unto you, that it shall be
more tolerable for Tyre and Sidon at the Day of judgment,
than for you. And thou, Capernaum, which art exalted
unto Heaven, shalt be brought down to hell; for if the
mighty works which have been done in thee had been
done in Sodom, it would have remained until this day.
But I say unto you, that it shall be more tolerable for the
land of Sodom in the Day of judgment, than for thee[4]."
But still there is not so much opposition raised as actually
to impede His ministry, for He proceeds still preaching
the Gospel through their cities; and the meek, and the
mourner, and those whom He terms babes, receive Him,
and are brought into His kingdom. For these little ones
He gives thanks to the Father; these He invites to take
His gentle yoke upon them.

But soon after we find that charge brought forward by
the Pharisees, who had come down from Jerusalem, which,
more than any other circumstance, appeared to grieve His
gracious Spirit, that of casting out devils by Beelzebub the
prince of the devils. They had before, indeed, sought to
kill Him under a show of jealousy for the keeping of the

[4] Matt. xi. 21—24.

z

Law, on account of His breaking the Sabbath; but this charge was new, and of a different kind. If He had indeed acted profanely in breaking the Sabbath, it would go to prove Him no Divine teacher; and therefore to speak evil of Him was to speak against the Son of Man. But to admit the actual performance of the highest of all miracles, and to say that such things were by the power and instrumentality of the Evil One, was a crime of a very different complexion; for what more could be done to recall those, who could see the power and goodness of God manifested, and yet would blaspheme? It is upon this that our Lord so solemnly warns them of the precipice to which they had thus approached, the danger of sin against the Holy Ghost, which remains for ever unpardonable; and of that corrupt temper of heart from which such words must flow, for "from the abundance of the heart the mouth speaketh:" these words were fruits that indicated the tree[5], that had its root in bitterness, and the fruits whereof were gall and wormwood. Here it is that our Lord, in consequence, commences His awful "woes" on the Pharisees, for their ambitious and covetous lives, with manifold hypocrisies deceiving themselves and others, while they seemed to be seeking the high places in God's Church, which appeared then, as now, but an innocent and laudable ambition; and holds up to them the dreadful end they were coming to. To all of which our Lord adds that warning parable respecting the state of the old Jewish nation,—the parable of the man out of whom the unclean spirit had been cast, and who returned and entered again with seven other spirits worse than himself.

It is now, therefore, under these circumstances, when these indications of irreclaimable impenitence began to take

[5] Matt. xii. 33.

the place of better feelings, and of that curiosity which was at first excited, that our Lord begins to adopt a new mode of teaching, and to instruct the promiscuous multitudes, which now flocked to Him, by parables. And the reason for this, which He assigned to His disciples, was their incorrigible hardness of heart. For thus, by His parabolical method of instruction, He overcame the immediate difficulty that presented itself, from multitudes of bad and hardened men flocking around Him, to whom He did not reveal the mysteries of His kingdom; for this would have been against His own precept, of not casting pearls before swine; while others were among them teachable and attentive, who would ascertain the meaning of those parables. Thus did He adopt that language with which He always speaks to the world; for all nature, and all natural and moral Providence, is a parable, which some understand, but others do not. These parables appear to have been delivered, for the most part, from a boat by the sea-side; a mode of addressing the multitude which our Lord frequently adopted, for reasons which are not altogether apparent, but chiefly, as it is stated, because the people thronged Him; and this might imply danger as well as inconvenience. Immediately afterwards, while these indications of evil, together with eagerness to approach Him, seem to gain ground in Galilee, our Lord crosses the lake to the Heathens. Fatigued, as it would appear, and weary as He was[6], He was taken into the boat, and there, from exhaustion and weariness, He lay asleep on a pillow. This change of place, therefore, was in suffering and in privation ;—not dictated by choice, but by constraint ;— not in ease, but in hardship. His going away was to escape from the multitude that thronged Him, and proba-

6 Mark iv. 36.

z 2

bly because, in addition to His weariness, and want of a
home to which He could retire, He could not trust Himself
to them.   St. Matthew, in mentioning the circumstance,
introduces our Lord's answer to the Scribe that offered to
follow Him, when He says, "the foxes have holes, and the
birds of the air have nests ; but the Son of Man hath not
where to lay His head'." It would, indeed, appear from
St. Luke, that this observation to the Scribe takes place
a year later ; St. Matthew, therefore, here introduces it in
the thread of his narrative, to explain the feelings and the
condition of our Blessed Lord when He thus withdrew ;
thus inserting the incident respecting the Scribe, and our
Lord's reply to him, in order to explain His conduct of
avoiding, rather than inviting, such earnest but weak followers.

And if thus, as one patient and passive, and having no
place of protection, or of rest, in which to lay His head,
our Lord now seeks the Gentile coast, it is from a similar
reason, as one acquiescing, and not holding out against
opposition, that our Lord again returns from them : for
"the whole multitude of the country of the Gadarenes
round about besought Him to depart from them;" and He
entered into a vessel and returned⁸. The country seems
to rise up to shake Him from them.   Thus is He taken
from place to place at the call of duty, and as one already
bearing the Cross on which He was to suffer ; and driven
from every place of His choice by men who rejected Him.
"They that sought My life laid snares for Me, and they
that went about to do Me evil talked of wickedness."
" As for Me, I was like a deaf man, and heard not : and
as one that is dumb, who doth not open his mouth.   I

7 Matt. viii. 20.   8 Luke viii. 37.

became even as a man that heareth not, and in whose mouth are no reproofs[9]."

And now, indeed, there are many waiting to receive Him on the shore of Galilee[1]; and He is entertained on His arrival at the great feast in the house of Levi. It is indeed no feast of peace and harmony, for His enemies, the Pharisees, are there, and are actively engaged in endeavouring to set the disciples of the Baptist, and His own disciples, against Him; and He is summoned away from it, in the midst of that entertainment, at the call of duty and charity. For while He is in the midst of His discourse, there comes the request of Jairus respecting his daughter, and He immediately leaves the company to proceed to the Ruler's house: submitting to that trouble which the weakness of their faith occasioned Him, while He might by His word have healed her, or by a mere act of His will.

These changes of place may appear unimportant in themselves, yet are not so, as furnishing us with the principle of our Lord's movements. They seem to indicate that His ministry is not to be considered as formed of certain preconceived, defined, and extensive circuits of preaching, as of one acting with free choice and control, independent of human circumstances, but as of one submitting to, rather than commanding, occasions and events; as of one watching for opportunities of good, and educing good out of evil; of one undergoing, as Man, all the temptations, and persecutions, and infirmities, with which His servants are encompassed, rather than of one Who had the power to command events as God;—or as a superhuman Teacher, marking out for Himself fields of usefulness in a systematic course of conduct, dependant only on

[9] Ps. xxxviii. 12. 14.   [1] Luke viii. 40.

His own choice. He was always, during His life and ministry, as He Who preached to the women that lamented Him while He was being led to execution, and sinking under the weight of the Cross: Who on the Cross was watching for the salvation of a fellow-sufferer ; Who was submitting Himself to be put in bonds while He healed the ear of His enemy. All the works of His life, including His teaching and His miracles, were like those of His death. Thus was He ever not making for Himself occasions of good, which His own Omnipotent will could command, but rather finding occasions of good under the pressure of His own calamities. It was so in many remarkable instances ; and as the Cross itself was the excellency of Divine Wisdom, but the apparent result, not of choice, but of submission to sorrow, in what seemed human foolishness and weakness : so do even the circumstances appear of our Lord's life and ministry. " Behold the Man !" behold the instance of human suffering, of submission to human contingencies, and the victim of oppression ! All this may be applied to Him in His life as well as in His death. In both He was wearing the crown of thorns. " Behold the Man !" in weakness of perfect Manhood to human eyes, but to Divine eyes in strength of perfect Godhead.

Another circumstance at this time occurs, which shows the same constraint laid on our Lord's charities ; and which seemed to regulate His actions and movements as bonds of human weakness laid on His Divine compassions, from the weakness, or ill-will and wickedness, of others. It is at this time that He proceeds once more to visit again His country Nazareth, which it appears from the narrative He had not seen since the effort He had made to convert them on the first opening of His ministry, and which was followed by the attempt upon His life. During the eighteen months which had probably elapsed since His absence, we may naturally conclude that, with both human and Divine affection, He was still yearning towards the place of His earlier abode, and that of His parents ; and that He would be ever turning with anxious regret to His home and His countrymen ; for in taking our flesh He had compassed Himself about in a remarkable degree with all human tenderness and affection. And now neglected by Heathens, and not received by strangers, once more He attempts to return to them, and reclaim them. But we read, that " they were offended at Him," that " He did not many mighty works there, because of their unbelief[2]." And St. Mark adds the extraordinary expression, that " He marvelled because of their unbelief[3]." So entirely, and in such manifold senses was it fulfilled in Him, that " He came unto His own, but His own received Him not ;" and it is His own pathetic lament in the Psalms, that His " kinsmen stood afar off[4]."

And now, towards the close of the second Year, our Lord sends forth the Twelve, under circumstances hereafter to be considered ; but all that is needful towards the present argument is, to notice that it is with lessons respecting the hardships they are to endure ; and when these things attract the notice of Herod, our Lord retires with them apart into the desert of Bethsaida, both in order to escape from the effects of this sensation that had been produced, and also from being wearied with the multitudes, and hungry. " And He said unto them, Come ye yourselves apart into a desert place, and rest awhile : for there were many coming and going, and they had no leisure so much

[2] Matt. xiii. 58.   [3] Mark vi. 6.

[4] Ps. xxxviii. 11.

as to eat ; and they departed into a desert place by ship privately[5]." And here a circumstance occurs which will serve as an additional proof, and a very remarkable one, of the apparently accidental contingencies, and the constraint and pressure of external events, out of which our Lord's mightiest works took their rise. For here one of the chief and most memorable of His miracles takes place, on account of a circumstance which to all human eyes would seem fortuitous, and that forced upon Him by others. For hungry and fatigued as He was, He is drawn out from His place of refuge by the multitude which followed Him by the land, and had overtaken Him ; He performs this great miracle in spite of His own weariness and want of repose, being led to do so under the constraints of His own yearning compassions over them ; for it is in order that they might not faint by the way, and as it was now growing late, that our Lord feeds them all with the five loaves and fishes. Here the second Year closes with the conversation which ensued on the subject of this miracle at Capernaum ; a conversation which speaks in words so awfully impressive, and deeply melancholy, of unbelief and desertion ; and of something worse than both, even among his own[6].

SECTION IV

THE THIRD YEAR

It is now that our Lord's life becomes, in a still more marked manner, a continued flight from persecution from place to place. No mention is made of this Passover ; but we may conclude, I think, without hesitation, that

[5] Mark vi. 31, 32.   [6] John vi. 70.

our Lord was present at it in Jerusalem, as the Law required : and a single verse in St. John seems to indicate
that He was obliged to withdraw from Judea, which
otherwise, therefore, would have been the natural seat of
His ministry, if circumstances had not prevented. For
after the discourse at Capernaum, on the miracle that had
just occurred, at the end of the preceding year, St. John
continues, "and Jesus after these things walked in Galilee,
for He could not walk in Judea, because the Jews were
seeking to kill Him[7]." And this passage in St. John
seems of itself an indication that our Lord had been at the
Feast. For as the preceding narrative had been in Galilee,
there appears no reason for this mention of Judea, were it
not that the Lord had been there on some occasion between
the preceding narrative and that which follows, and
would have continued there if He could have done so in
safety. But the first circumstance of which distinct mention is made, occurs apparently in Galilee, and intimates a
determined persecution, on the part of the Jews, more
fierce and settled in design than any thing which had
preceded. For the Scribes and Pharisees seem to be
gathering around Him, and to have come down from
Jerusalem with the purpose of watching Him[8]. Mention,
indeed occurs, before this, of there having been Jews
present who were come from Jerusalem[9]: and as the
Chief Priests had, at the very first, sent a formal deputation to the Baptist, it seems probable that, with no less
circumspection, though in a different manner, they would
be watching the movements of Christ Himself. And
though no doubt the intensity of hatred with which they
were actuated was no other than that mysterious hatred of

[7] Ch. vii. 1.   [8] Mark vii. 1.

[9] Luke v. 17.

goodness, which exists in the natural heart of man, yet here again, as usual, it assumes to itself the appearance of religious zeal. The first occasion which presents itself is that of the disciples not "washing before dinner," when they begin to find fault at the time, and after our Lord's remonstrance with them, and His full inculcation to the whole multitude whom He calls around Him, of what is truly pure and good, their indignation increases; they "are offended." We read that the disciples brought intimation of this to our Lord, and immediately after we find that "He rises up from thence, and departed into the coasts of Tyre and Sidon[1]." It was perhaps partly for this reason, that that heathen neighbourhood, being in the dominions of Philip, would be more a place of security, in addition to the circumstance of its being so retired.

But we need not discover reasons of this kind, for, indeed, where else had He to go? He had no place where to lay His head, not only not in comfort, but not even in safety. He had fled from Jerusalem, and there is no spot in Judea which is a place of refuge or of security to Him. Can He go to His own country? can He go to His native abode and home? It was there where, of all places, His life was most in danger. Can He return to the friendly roof of a disciple at Capernaum? Here were His determined foes at this very time lying in wait for Him. Well might they tauntingly say of Him, "Whither will He go, that we shall not find Him? Will He go to the dispersed among the Gentiles?" More truly of Him than of David, or any of His Saints, is it said, "I had no place to flee unto, and no man cared for My soul." It is evident that, of all countries which the map of the Holy Land presents to our eye, an escape towards the Mediterranean, and the

[1] Mark vii. 24.

infamous cities of Tyre and Sidon alone remained. And here, indeed, an incident, perhaps as touching and as edifying as any in the Gospel, has gone forth to the world, respecting our Lord's interview with the Canaan-itish woman; but this is, as it were, forced from Him under the influence of a constraining necessity, when He was seeking a place of refuge, and wished to be hid. No where, indeed, can we find a more instructive instance of that Divine commiseration which hears every word of complaint, though it seems to bear long with it: and of that Divine love, which, when trampled on and broken, sends forth to all the world its heavenly sweetness and fragrancy, "for the healing of the nations."

From this time and place, if we trace the few intimations that are afforded us of our Lord's course, it will appear to be regulated by the same Laws. His circuits, and His ministry, and His preaching, were doubtless in all things controlled by Divine Wisdom, and every thing dispensed in order, and weight, and measure, most supremely good and perfect. But what is in all to be observed is, that the law of our Lord's teaching was not that of unrestrained design, and to be spoken of like actions of human wisdom, and contrivance, and expediency: but, as has been said, like the Cross itself, the strength of God manifested in human weakness. Indeed, the Cross, as it indicates God's strength in human weakness, may be, as it were, the key to all the Divine dispensations, containing within it a proverbial principle which may unlock the secret rules of His counsels. It is, indeed, no other than that circumstance which may be seen in all His ways, wherein He manifests His mighty arm in our infirmities, and His Saints and servants in Him achieve victories over the world, when most bereft of human aid and counte-

nance. So was it in the Old Testament, when Christ was
tabernacled in the temporal Israel, it was ever under the
pressure of worldly evil that the hand and the salvation
of God was seen; every revelation of miraculous power
was when Israel was in distress and in much trembling.
Thus was it that, under the severities of Egyptian bondage, the wonders of God were seen; when the sea was
before and the chariots of Pharoah behind, God opened
the way. It was only on occasions of distress that God
manifested His miraculous power under the Judges; it
was on the destruction of Judah and Israel that the
Evangelical Prophets appeared; it was in the Babylonian
captivity that the wonderful works of Daniel, and of the
three Children, were manifested. So, also, in the Christian
Church, it was in consequence of persecution at Jerusalem
that the truth spread through the world; it was the captivity of St. Paul that chiefly set forth the Gospel in
Rome, and his bonds were the furtherance of it. This
point, therefore, in our Lord's life which we are endeavouring to establish, is but analogous to His operations in
the Old Testament, and in the Christian Church, as has
been shown in so many other matters[2]. He is now in
the flesh as of old in type and shadow; but the temporal
Israel has taken the place of oppressing Egypt and of
enslaving Babylon, and Christ is as the spiritual Israel,
mighty through suffering, and Divinely wise in what
appears folly to the world: while the fierceness of man
turns to His praise. "The arm of the Lord" is in Him
"revealed," but He is "a Man of sorrows, and acquainted
with grief."

It will, I think, appear, that the line of our Lord's proceedings lay now among the Heathen; and if we trace

[2] See Part IV. Section 4.

His course we shall find that, for some time, He continued to keep aloof among the more Gentile parts, as if from the same motives that had now led Him to them.—viz. for fear of persecution from the Jews. For we read, "and again having gone forth from the borders of Tyre and Sidon, He came to the sea of Galilee, through the midst of the coast of Decapolis³." It was this same town of Decapolis in which the demoniac was said to have preached of his miraculous cure some time before, and that, too, at the express injunction of our Lord⁴, during that short stay He had made among the Gadarenes. From which it is evident, in the first place, that this city was in the Heathen parts; and secondly, that they might have been prepared for Him by that event of the preceding year; and His foreseeing this may have been the reason why our Lord on that occasion enjoined the demoniac to go and preach instead of concealing His wonderful works. Another reason which shows that our Lord's course was now among heathens, is, that when the multitudes came in great numbers, with persons to be healed, another Evangelist adds, "and they glorified the God of Israel⁵," words which clearly indicate that the persons were Gentiles; in the same manner as when our Lord used the expression, "I have not found so great faith, no not in Israel," it was of the Roman Centurion that He spoke. And this circumstance not only marks the fact that our Lord was keeping aloof from the Jews; but affords a reason for the repetition of the miracle of the loaves and fishes, which He now performed; viz. that the former of these two miracles, with all its teaching, its typical and prophetical significations, was among the Jews; and this second one, so similar in its character, was among another people, the Gentiles.

³ Mark vii. 31.　　⁴ Mark v. 20.　　⁵ Matt. xv. 31.

This is the more observable, as although the teaching of the Gentiles is only usually by constraint, yet it runs parallel, and is coincident with that of the Jews. As for instance, the Magi are taught by a star, and the shepherds by the Angels; Judea by the Birth and the Presentation, and Egypt by the reception of the Christ: and so it had been of old; Moab had the prophet Balaam, when Israel was being taught in the wilderness: when Elijah was in Israel, the widow of Sarepta was the witness to Sidon, and Naaman to Syria in the days of Elisha; Daniel was in Babylon, and Moses was in Egypt, bearing testimoney to the heathen, while God was dealing with His own people: and thus is it now in the narrative of the Gospels, for together with all the teaching and preaching to the Jews, there are incidental miracles and instructions of the Gentiles. This consideration affords a new and interesting character to this miracle, which is so similar to the preceding. But what is at present to be observed is, that this incident is again followed by a suddenness and apparent haste in our Lord's movement, such as to indicate a desire to be hid from pursuers; for it is added, " and immediately He embarked into a boat with His disciples, and came to the parts of Dalmanutha⁶," or " the coasts of Magdala⁷;" and these appear to be cities of the heathens on the south-east side of Galilee. Our Lord's ministry at this time seems confined to that side of the Lake, and marked by a rapid change of place, and on this and on other occasions, contiguity to the sea appears to afford Him His usual means of escape. And no sooner does He arrive at these places by crossing the sea, than the Pharisees and Sadducees appear to be there also, coming there apparently in pursuit of Him: for they would shortly have learned

⁶ Mark viii. 10.　　　　⁷ Matt. xv. 39.

of His passing from place to place, and of the spots where
He might be; and although this is not mentioned, yet the
circumstance of finding them there, and the evident ill-
will with which they are actuated, readily suggests the
thought that they are there in pursuit of our Lord. And
although this is not expressly stated by the Evangelists,
yet their words incidentally rather confirm it, than otherwise. St. Matthew says "they come to Him," St. Mark
"they went forth;" they came to Him evidently with
hostile intentions, demanding a sign. And after a few
words of warning to them, it is added, that "He left them
again, entered the boat, and passed over to the other side[8];"
i. e. not to the opposite side of the Lake, but from one
side of the bay to the other, not westward but northward.
And here an incident is mentioned, which indicates the
haste, on account of some absorbing interest, with which
they departed, for it is said, "they had forgotten to take
bread, and excepting one loaf, they had nothing with
them in the boat[9]." And from the conversation that
ensued, and a variety of expression in St. Mark[1], it
would seem that the Sadducees who were joined with the
Pharisees, were of Herod's party, for instead of the term
"the leaven of the Sadducees," which we find in St.
Matthew, he adds, "the leaven of Herod." From which
it would appear, that the Pharisees from Jerusalem had
combined with the government of Galilee against Him;
and this would account for His retiring from the dominions
of Herod. The whole therefore of these movements of
our Lord are now on the east of the Lake, since He came
from the parts of Tyre and Sidon, and keeping aloof
above the Lake, had passed down that eastern side; and

[8] Mark viii. 13.   [9] Mark viii. 14.

[1] viii. 15.

now, at length, we find them at the extreme point of the Lake, at Bethsaida[2]. This village perhaps is mentioned, as being contiguous to the place where they landed; for one would have thought that they did not enter the village itself, from the circumstance which is there recorded; for it is said, that when our Lord cured the person with an impediment in his speech—the only miracle there mentioned—He charged him "not to enter into the village, nor to mention it to any one in the village[3]."

It is immediately after this, in the sacred narrative, that we find our Lord with His disciples in a place very far out of the way, up towards the mountains of the North, and apart from all His usual resort, or that of the Jews. And St. Mark in speaking of it, says, "He went out," or "went forth;" as if to imply that His going thither was a departing or retiring; this Evangelist had used the same term of the Pharisees, who came to Him to Dalmanutha, as if they had *gone out* thither with the purpose; and so also, when our Lord departed from the coasts of Tyre, he said, "He went forth[4];"—where the word seems to indicate a considerable change of place, and a departure from that neighbourhood which had been before spoken of. And now "Jesus and His disciples *went forth* unto the village of Cæsarea Philippi." It is here that the ever memorable confession of St. Peter takes place; and every thing indicates it to have been an event of very great importance in the sacred history. It is far from the scene of any other action, nothing else is recorded as having occurred in those parts; and the conversation is not such, as that it should be connected with that or

  [2] Mark viii. 22.   [3] Mark viii. 26.
  [4] Mark viii. 27, ἐξῆλθεν. verse 11, ἐξῆλθον οἱ Φαρισαῖοι. vii. 31, ἐξελθὼν ἐκ τῶν ὁρίων.

any other local event. The circumstances of that journey, and all that led to it, are entirely passed over in silence, as if to give the greater weight and prominence to this one and only circumstance. It is preceded, moreover, by the express mention of our Lord's praying, which mention usually precedes some event of unusual importance to His Church, "and it came to pass, when He was alone praying, His disciples came unto Him. And He asked them[s]." All which is to be noticed, as the sacred writers usually introduce matters of the very greatest moment and magnitude, without any direct allusion to their importance.

Henceforth, from this day it appears to me, that our Lord's conduct assumes a very decided change : and that He no further holds aloof from the Jews, and from persecution. It is remarkable, that from this time, it is said that He began to teach His disciples of His approaching sufferings ; it is the subject to which He is constantly recurring, not three times only, but thrice three times, for as many as nine instances are spoken of, and it is a subject which He had not before mentioned. Independently, therefore, of the facts, it would not be unreasonable to suppose, that together with this circumstance of His teaching, our Lord's whole demeanour also, and proceedings, might be altered ; for now He found from their confession of that great doctrine, that they were able to endure all things, and in the strength of that faith, were able to meet whatever man could do. They had been with Him in all His sufferings of oppression, persecution, and privation, and had partaken with Him of the hate of the world, and now they are to be made one with Him, by being taken into sympathy with His sufferings and His cross, and strengthened to drink of His cup. " Ye are they that

[s] Luke ix. 18.

A a

have continued with Me in My temptations," said our Lord, and there is no more hallowed bond among men than that of common sufferings : " the world hath hated them, because they are not of the world, as I am not of the world," was His own testimony concerning them unto the Father. After this gradual preparation, therefore, when their faith in His Godhead was confirmed, He strengthens and humbles them by persecution and by teaching. Thus it is that from this distant position we find that on that day week, they are in the very heart of Galilee, if, as it is supposed, it was on Mount Tabor on which the Transfiguration took place. Here we find Him at once returning to Capernaum, where, on entering the house, He is asked for the tribute money together with St. Peter, as one who had been for some time unseen and absent, and was now returning to His accustomed abode in the house of His disciple. And the circumstance seems of itself to indicate that our Lord had no house of His own, that the question should be put to Him on entering the house of St. Peter.

That His thus subjecting them to persecution together with Himself was in consequence of their having come to knowledge so exalted and heavenly, is confirmed by this circumstance ; that these instances in which our Lord impresses on His disciples His coming sufferings, seem often connected with something that would otherwise lead them to high thoughts and exaltation ; at first, on the confession of His Godhead ; at the second time, on witnessing His Transfiguration ; at the third time, on all men marvelling at His mighty works. " And when all men were wondering at all the things which Jesus did, He said unto His disciples, let these words sink down into your ears[6]." The principle, therefore, on which this is founded, is the same

[6] Luke ix. 43, 44.

as that which now alters our Lord's line of conduct and
the course of His progress, namely, that their strength and
exaltation were now to be tempered and proved by trials
of persecution, and by a preparation for humiliating suffering : His conduct, which is new in its character, and the
new subject of His teaching, mutually explain each other.
It may be observed, that as persecution and the blessings
attending it come the last in the Beatitudes, this circumstance seems to presuppose a person trained already in the
more domestic virtues, and those of daily life ; the highest
crown being that attained in persecution ; so that persecution comes the last thing in the course of probation, when
persons have been already formed and disciplined to sustain it.   And perhaps, persecution does then more naturally arise in the course of God's providence ; for if
persecution follows on holiness, as the shadow which
accompanies the earthly side of that on which God's light
shines ; such persecution will not arise till habits of self-
denying goodness and faith are now in some measure
already formed : for as " all who will live godly in Christ
Jesus shall suffer persecution[7]," the godly life in Christ
Jesus must precede and be somehow first seen or known
before the persecution arises.

It is sufficient to observe that now our Lord's manner and
the place of His ministry seem to undergo a change ; the
portion of history which ensues, consists of all those events
and conversations at Jerusalem, which St. John records ;
or those circumstances of His last progress and public
approach to Jerusalem, through the cities of Galilee and
Samaria, which occupy so much space in the narrative of
St. Luke, and which St. Luke alone records ; whether, with
some harmonists, we place the narrative of St. Luke first

[7] 2 Tim. iii. 12.

A a 2

or, with others, consider that the stay of our Lord in or
about Jerusalem, as St. John mentions, preceded the circumstances in St. Luke. Not that this change of demeanour implies that our Lord now courted persecution,
for that He never did : and indeed, after the Transfiguration, while preparing His disciples for His sufferings, it is
said, that as He proceeded through Galilee, He would not
that any should know[8] ; and to the feast of Tabernacles,
He went up, as it were in secret[9] ; and while continuing
at Jerusalem, He still kept withdrawing from it to avoid
the ebullitions of violence[1]. But still we find that our
Lord is much more mixed up with the danger, and openly
faces it more than He had done, to the astonishment, more
than once expressed, of His Apostles and of the Jews.
Thus in St. John, we find that surprise is expressed at
His open and bold speech ; " Is not this He whom they
seek to kill, and behold, He speaketh openly, and they
say nothing unto Him[2]." And " His disciples say unto
Him, Master, the Jews of late sought to slay Thee, and
goest Thou thither again[3]?" The scene of His teaching
too is in the Temple, or on the banks of the Jordan, the
most open and public places of resort. And all the narrative which has been spoken of in St. Luke, embracing this
period of the sacred history, is, it may be observed, of a
peculiar complexion ; on this, His last leaving of Galilee,
instead of going secretly from city to city, He sends the
Seventy to prepare the way before Him, in every city
where He Himself would come ; and when He is told of
the danger to be apprehended from Herod, He speaks of
His death and sufferings as approaching and not to be

[8] Mark ix. 30.   [9] John vii. 10.
[1] John xi. 54.   [2] John vii. 25, 26.
            [3] John xi. 8.

shrunk from, which now gave this new and martyrlike character, so to speak, to our Lord's proceeding ; it was all of the same nature as His last entrance and approach to Jerusalem ; not as formerly in secret, but courting attention, and publicly proclaimed. His deportment, too, throughout the journey was remarkable : He appeared to those whose city he approached, as one whose face was as if He were going to Jerusalem[4]. " He set His face stedfastly " as He proceeded : and He advanced before His disciples with a boldness in His manner, which amazed and alarmed them : " they were astonished, and as they followed Him were afraid[5]," is the short and emphatic description of St. Peter's Evangelist. His discourses also now, it may be observed, assume a different character ; and indeed, perhaps, all His doctrine is more high and severe ever since the confession of St. Peter. Not only His words to His Apostles in secret, but His parables also which were more public, now assume a tone preparatory to the great events that are to follow ; many of them such as intimate the calling of the Gentiles, and the rejection of the Jews ; while all His very manner indicated that the kingdom was now about to be established. From the Galileans that Pilate had slain, He clearly warns them of the destruction of Jerusalem ; of which that event and the fall of the tower of Siloam were the parallels, and served as typical representations of it. And He adds the parable of the unfruitful fig-tree, spared for three years of trial, which are now at their close,—and other parables and expressions, and incidents, which cannot be read with reference to this subject, without perceiving the great and striking force which they bear upon it ; of the difficulty of being saved, —of the necessity of taking up the cross,—of sitting down

[4] Luke ix. 53.   [5] Mark x. 32.

first to count the cost,—of the reckoning taken with the servants at the Lord's return. And all this high and warning tone of instruction has its full completion and consummation in our Lord's last teaching publicly in the Temple during the week of His Passion ; and in the more private, but most awful discourses at its close, concerning the Day of judgment.

It appears probable that all our Lord's conduct which has been here noticed, may have been regulated by more than one consideration ; with regard to Himself, it was a course of meek resignation to all those sufferings which were prepared for Him, while He thus proceeded willingly to lay down His life. With regard to the Jews, it appears from our Lord's words on entering Jerusalem, that the time of their visitation was now passed, and the things that had belonged to their peace were "hidden from their eyes[6]." He had therefore been dealing gently with them, till this was the case, in retiring from them ; but there was now no farther need of forbearance, for they were not to be reclaimed. And so likewise with regard to the Apostles ; they had had their time of visitation and probation also, when driven about with Him from place to place, until the things that belonged unto their peace were gradually revealed to them ; and now that they were strengthened and confirmed by faith and the knowledge of His Godhead, He takes them to meet their great trial. With both of these parties, though so opposed to each other, yet in His Divine Wisdom He had dealt gently and gradually until they were both confirmed and fixed ; the Jews in unbelief ; the disciples in that faith on the confession of which His Church was to be built, and which as a rock would defy all the storms of the world.

[6] Luke xix. 42.

PART VII

Our Lord's Mode of Dealing with His Apostles

SECTION I

THEIR FIRST PREPARATION AND CALLING

IN pursuing the former subject, it was observed, that a remarkable change, which takes place in our Lord's conduct, was connected with the training of His Apostles; so much so, that He seems to have altered His mode of action with a peculiar reference to them. The conduct of our Blessed Lord towards His more intimate disciples, may well form the subject of a separate consideration. It is in more than one point of view highly instructive and important. Even as an object of human interest, if there is any one whom we greatly love and revere, we are desirous to know what passes between him and those most intimate with him; and since, moreover, the former subject indicated our Lord's conduct towards His enemies, and those from whom He withdrew His presence, it is well to observe what His conduct was with reference to those whom He called His friends, and the various ways in which He disclosed Himself to them : but more than all, as our Lord's

stay on earth, and ministry, was in order to lay the foundations of His Church, it is natural for us to look with
especial regard to those in whom its foundations were to be
laid, the " Twelve Stones " on which His Church was to
be built, taken from the floods of Jordan ; the chosen few,
who not only shared His most intimate society in the flesh,
but who were commissioned, as it were, to stand in His
own place upon earth when He departed from it.

And it so happens, that a great part of what we read in
the Gospels, is the account of what thus occurred, not
publicly before all the people, but privately between our
Lord and His Apostles ; and though there is but little
express mention of this purpose, yet it is sufficient to
indicate, that much of our Lord's conduct may have had
an especial reference to this object, of training His disciples for their great work.   It is, indeed, highly interesting and instructive to trace out how our Blessed Lord
dealt with them ; the manner in which He first drew
them to the society and knowledge of Himself: the
different ways in which He dealt with each of them,
according to their characters ; His long forbearance with
them in their ignorance and slowness of faith ; His
gradual preparation of them for the high trust He was
about to commit to their charge ; and many other particulars which will from time to time occur to us, as
we trace out the account of His gracious intimacy with
them.

The first object of interest, which naturally arrests our
attention in the sacred history, is our Lord's first and
sudden call of the four disciples by the Lake, and their
instant obedience to the call.   And our minds are naturally engaged in the reflection, whether any previous
intercourse may have existed between them and their

Divine Master; and if so, to what extent, and of what nature it may have been. The three earlier Evangelists supply us with no allusion to this having been the case; but notwithstanding their silence, our Lord's usual mode of dealing with mankind, and the providential ways of God in His Church, would have led one to suppose that they must beforehand have had some evidence set before them, on which their ready faith was founded; some knowledge, either from previous experience or hearsay, of His holiness and of His power. And the last Evangelist has been graciously allowed to supply us with some intimation of this, which is such as quite falls in with this usual analogy of God's ways, wherein He gradually draws men to Himself by His own appointed means.

The means which God's wisdom had designed to bring men to Christ, appear to have been the preaching of His forerunner, the Baptist, the object of whose ministry was to prepare the minds of men to receive the Christ; and, perhaps, to those who were capable of discerning Him, to point out "the Lamb of God." And we might well have supposed, that this method of God's dispensation had its end fulfilled in those who did embrace the Christ, especially in His most favoured disciples. Now the narrative of St. John acquaints us with the fact that it was so: from which we find, that St. Andrew and another, whom we take it for granted was the beloved Evangelist, were disciples of the Baptist: true disciples no doubt, such as pre-eminently practised the repentance he taught, and thereby obtained spiritual eyes to discern "the salvation of God;" for it was to them he pointed out "the Lamb of God that taketh away the sin of the world." And Christ, as in His moral providence, was watching for them, but waiting that they might seek and inquire for Him first. "The two disciples heard Him speak, and followed Jesus. And Jesus turned, and beholding them following Him, saith unto them, What seek ye? They said unto Him, Rabbi, which is being interpreted Master, where dwellest Thou? He saith unto them, Come and see[1]." They went with Him, and continued with Him, it would appear, nearly a whole day, for it was the tenth hour, or ten o'clock in the morning; and though there is no record afforded us of the conversation which took place between them and their Divine Master, we cannot doubt but that to hearts thus prepared, that discourse must have revealed something of His infinite holiness and wisdom; and that this must have been related, or the impression of it conveyed by St. Andrew to his brother St. Peter, whom he immediately finds, and brings to Jesus, with a declaration no less than this, "we have found the Messiah." It is at the same place, and therefore probably as being present there for the same purpose, i. e. as disciples of the Baptist, that on the next day, our Lord calls Philip to Him, and through Philip Nathanael. From the conversation between Philip and Nathanael, it seems that they were acquainted with Nazareth, and with our Lord's family, and especially Philip, but not intimately so with our Lord Himself, before that time. Our Lord is then on the point of returning to Galilee, and immediately after this occurrence we find the disciples are with Him at Cana of Galilee, and witness that first miracle which there occurred, by which it is said "He manifested forth His glory, and His disciples believed on Him[2]." It appears, also, from the saying at Nazareth, on our Lord's teaching there for the first time, that He had been performing

[1] John i. 37—40.   [2] John ii. 11.

miracles at Capernaum, which probably took place at this time in presence of His disciples; for after the miracle at Cana, it is said, that "He went down and stayed a few days at Capernaum," with His own Mother and family and His disciples. It would appear, therefore, that our Lord's stay in Judea among the disciples of the Baptist, and that His first and preliminary miracle at Cana, and perhaps those at Capernaum, had an especial view to this object,—that of drawing unto Him those disciples on whom the teaching of the Baptist had had its legitimate and intended effect.

When, therefore, on our Lord's taking upon Him more formally His public ministry, St. Matthew and St. Mark record His calling of those four disciples by the Lake, He had been already for some time preparing them to obey this call. The incident recorded in the fifth chapter of St. Luke, so similar to this as to be often taken for the same circumstance, appears to have been but another instance of our Lord's preparing them for their entire abandonment of all things for His sake, and the execution of their great work. The miraculous draught of fishes was in all its circumstances signally and singularly calculated to convey all that lesson to them, more than words could have done[3].

As in the instance of these four disciples it appears evident that there was some preparatory teaching, and probably much more than is mentioned; so it leads one to infer that the same was the case also in the instance of the other disciple, whose call is distinctly mentioned, that of Levi the publican. This takes place while he is sitting at the receipt of custom, at the close of this first Year of our Lord's ministry. It appears like the good providence of

[3] See p. 234; and Tracts for the Times, No. 80, p. 20.

God, lying in wait to catch men, and incidentally manifested, as taking hold of them at last, and bringing them forth for His high purposes. And thus were they probably all of them first prepared to be disciples, and then all of them prepared as disciples to be made Apostles also; for now we find them in close attendance on Him, before they are selected as Apostles, and we may conclude, instructed much by word and work. Doubtless, now that "they had left all" to follow their poor and houseless Master, the trial of their faith was great; and an incident which is mentioned early in the following year, of their plucking the ears of corn and eating them as they passed, was probably in some degree owing to their poverty. The allowance of such a custom by the Law, like the privilege of gleaning corn-fields, seems a law of charity and mercy; and therefore intended more particularly for those who were in need and poverty. And this incidentally indicates that the period of their discipleship was in itself a high exercise of faith.

This consideration gives a peculiar force to many of our Lord's expressions concerning the blessing of poverty, as addressed in the presence of those whose poverty was so great a trial to them. While it may be observed that our Lord never held out any prospect of alleviation from temporal evils to His followers, but the contrary: but always taught them that such evils were not to be dreaded or deprecated.

There is of course something of an awful character in our Lord's demeanour towards them: but one little incident may be mentioned out of many, which intimates with what ineffable sweetness and touching beauty He suggested to His disciples, how He Himself would be to them all that they had relinquished. It was upon the occasion when our Lord was told, that "His mother and brethren were without, desirous to speak with Him. But He answered and said unto him that told Him, Who is My mother; and who are My brethren? and He stretched forth His hand toward His disciples, and said, Behold My mother and My brethren! For whosoever shall do the will of My Father which is in Heaven, the same is My brother, and sister, and mother[4]." Now independently of other more general references and significations contained in this incident, it is evident, that if our Lord had shown how strongly He Himself felt the weight and force of those domestic ties, so far would He have been discouraging His own disciples, who had forfeited and relinquished all those home ties for His sake. For He had said to them, "Whosoever hateth not his father and mother cannot be My disciple;" and they had therefore at His word readily foregone them. A circumstance, therefore, which might have turned to their discouragement, He converts to an occasion of unspeakable comfort to them. And this passage derives a great additional interest, when set in juxtaposition with another of similar import addressed to His disciples, and either of which serves to explain the other: "there is no one who hath left houses, or brethren, or sisters, or father, or mother, or wife, or children, or lands, for My sake and the Gospel's, but he shall receive an hundredfold now in this time, houses, and brethren, and sisters, and mothers, and children, and lands, with persecutions[5]." This latter passage seems a remarkable confirmation of the former, and the former explains the latter. It was the new relationship, in which our Lord Himself would stand towards them, which would more than supply to them the very things they had relinquished.

[4] Matt. xii. 46 – 50.   [5] Mark x. 29, 30.

For it is not only that they shall receive an hundredfold, but that they shall also receive brother, and sister, and mother; expressions, indeed, which some explain of new spiritual relations, or of Angels; but how far greater and peculiar a force does it derive from the consideration of our Lord Himself, and from His promise to them on the other occasion—that He would be to them as brother, and sister, and mother. In all these cases, it may be observed, that much as our Lord encourages them, yet He does not flatter nor unduly elevate them. It is by the way remarkable that in neither case does He speak of "Father;" in the latter, indeed, He pointedly drops that expression, when He takes up and repeats those of the other relationships.

In this manner did our Lord gradually train them to the humility of His kingdom, and faith in Him; and much do we find, even to the last, that they needed these lessons. We cannot but observe what may appear an almost unaccountable slowness of perception in the disciples long after these things;—their difficulty in comprehending the humiliations of our Lord, the humbling doctrines of His kingdom, and the call of the heathen into it. Several times we meet with our Lord's reproofs and expressions of disappointment at the slowness of their faith and spiritual perception. Yet notwithstanding all this, our Lord does at other times appear pleased with their spiritual progress and discernment, which indeed is the great consolation of His sorrowful spirit: as in that thanksgiving to the Father, "I thank Thee, O Father, Lord of Heaven and earth, that Thou hast hid these things from the wise and prudent, and hast revealed them unto babes[6]." And on the occasion just spoked of, when our Lord says, that they who do the will of God, shall be

[6] Matt. xi. 25.

brought into that near relationship to Himself, He stretches forth His hand to His disciples, implying that they were the persons of whom He thus spake; "bearing testimony," says Origen, "to His disciples, that they did the will of His Father." And when He adopted His teaching by parables, He expresses His sense of their religious discernment, and blesses them for it, "But blessed are your eyes for they see!" And here we may observe their progress;—He had blessed them because they were poor, because they mourned, and hungered for righteousness, and were hated; He blesses them now because they have spiritual discernment; and afterwards because God had revealed to them, or to St. Peter as their chief, that doctrine on which His Church was to be built, the confession that He was the Son of God. At the same time progress in Divine things may be infinite, as God is, and as are the blessings of Heaven, and therefore we often find that they are spoken of as in possession of that which they have, in one sense, still to attain. Thus they are said to have eyes to see[7], and yet they are afterwards reproved, because they have not[8]; St. Peter makes confession of the faith, and yet our Lord speaks of him afterwards as not yet converted, "When thou are converted, strengthen thy brethren[9]."

Thus does their gracious Lord, by little and little, warn and console, subdue and support them; and perhaps, the whole of His demeanour towards them and treatment of them, cannot be better set before us, than by that incident which occurred at the feast in St. Matthew's house, and the circumstance which gave rise to our Lord's explanation. For on the Pharisees objecting that His dis-

[7] Matt. xiii. 16.   [8] Matt. xv. 16.
[9] Luke xxii. 32.

ciples did not fast like those of the Baptist, our Lord set before them His gentle mode of dealing with them, by the parables of the new wine not being put into old bottles, nor new cloth on an old garment. From which it is evident, that while He was with them He drew them unto Him thus mildly; taking them from place to place with Him; teaching them privately; admitting them to witness miracles which none else beheld; and above all things, His own unspeakable holiness in His private life; thus with exceeding gentleness, leading them by degrees to have faith in Him. And, indeed, the very nature of that intimacy must have been of a character edifying and instructive, very far beyond what the miracles and teaching of our Lord could have been to the multitude. For even among ourselves, how different do the words and actions of an intimate friend appear, to what the same do to strangers? and our Lord's words and actions must have contained a great deal which they only could know; they in whose company He performed them, would have seen a great deal in the repetition of sayings and of miracles, which they would not who saw or heard but single circumstances.

SECTION II

THEIR APOSTLESHIP

THUS did our Lord first of all previously instruct and prepare them, before they were called to be disciples; thus did He as disciples instruct and prepare them to be Apostles: and when by a solemn act of selection, and dedication; and after continuing the whole night in prayer,

He had, about the middle of the second Year appointed them as Apostles : yet still He keeps them with Him after they have received this authority, and continues by little and little still to train them to trust in His Almighty power. It is some time after, and as it were gradually, that He sends them forth, thus exercising them to know Him, and to be without Him, and still when absent to trust in His unfailing support[1]. As of old "when Israel was a child, then I loved him, and called My son out of Egypt. I taught Ephraim also to go, taking them by their arms : I drew them with cords of a man, with bands of love[2]." " He led him about, He instructed him, He kept him as the apple of His eye. As an eagle stirreth up her nest, fluttereth over her young, spreadeth abroad her wings, taketh them, beareth them on her wings ; so the Lord alone did lead them[3];" "bearing them on eagle's wings, and bringing them unto Himself[4]."

Thus St. Mark, in recording their nomination to be Apostles, not only says it was that He might send them forth to preach, but adds, also, " that they might be with Him[5]." Not only to be with Him, for that they were before as disciples, but to be with Him in some new capacity and with some appropriate nearness as Apostles. For it appears some months later, when He sends them forth with authority to cast out evil spirits, and to heal. It seems probable that, either at the nomination, or at the subsequent sending forth of the Twelve (for these are combined in St. Matthew's description), our Lord gives that injunction, which He does also previously to His sending forth the Seventy[6], the foundation of the practice ever

[1] Luke ix. 2.   [2] Hosea xi. 1—4.   [3] Deut. xxxii. 11, 12.
[4] Exod. xix. 4.   [5] Mark iii. 14.
[6] Compare Matt. ix. 38, with Luke x. 2.

since observed in the Ember Weeks ; when He calls upon His disciples to " pray the Lord of the harvest, that He would send forth labourers into His harvest."

Now this mission of the Apostles, when they are sent forth to preach during our Lord's lifetime, appears to have been in an especial manner a preparation of them, that they may have faith in Him, while they are out of His sight and immediate protection. Their commission at this time is accompanied with all the instructions and directions of their last mission into the world, but had two circumstances in it, which had the especial tendency of exercising their faith in Him, towards those subsequent missions. The first of these, was a power afforded them to work miracles, and to heal the sick in His Name. The second was an injunction to relinquish all their natural means of support, and to depend alone on His power and *the staff* [7] of His commission, which they were to bear : a circumstance which our Lord afterwards alludes to as a ground of their confidence, when He was about to be removed from them : —" And He said unto them, When I sent you without scrip, and purse, and sandals, were ye in want of any thing? And they said, Nothing[8]." Where He appears to allude to that mission having been accompanied with some supernatural supports, such as they were not afterwards to expect.

This period was not only marked with this previous essay or trial of their ministry, but was followed also by a circumstance, which seemed to represent, in figure, the exercise of a sort of sacramental power. For on the Apostles returning with the account of what they had done, our Lord takes them apart into the wilderness, and there, when the multitudes assembled, through and by

7 Mark vi. 8 : see p. 50.   8 Luke xxii. 35.

their hands performs that miracle of the loaves, which is in many points so evidently figurative of the Holy Eucharist. We do not read of His performing any miracle for the multitude, before this, through the instrumentality of His Apostles, but on this occasion, it is expressly stated by each of the four Evangelists, that it was through the medium of their hands that He did it. Thus by anticipation and prophetic type did our Lord, as it were, set forth His Church, as it was to be unto the end; exhibiting its Apostolic powers and doctrine, when He sent them forth to preach and to heal:—and the stewardship of Mysteries, when He communicated the bread of natural life through their hands. And thus far have they advanced at the close of the second year.

It has been already shown, that the earlier part of the third Year was to our Blessed Lord a continual flight from persecution; and the circumstance seemed to indicate that the cause of our Lord's thus retiring, had an especial reference to His disciples. For when after fleeing from His enemies for some time, He had led His disciples out of the way into the parts of Cæsarea Philippi, and had there received the assurance of their faith in His Godhead; when they had now been prepared by His miracles to trust in His power, and by His sufferings to suffer together with Him; from henceforth He appears to alter His mode of acting; He proceeds at once into the heart of Galilee, and before three of the Twelve He manifests His unconceivable Majesty and Glory. And this change in our Lord's outward demeanour and conduct towards them, is accompanied with a circumstance which, we are expressly told, takes its date from the same time; viz. that from that day forward He is continually foretelling them, again and again, of His approaching sufferings; which, notwithstanding, they understand not. It is moreover connected with another point, which confirms this view of the principles on which this change in our Lord's conduct is founded ; viz. that the occasions, which our Lord takes, for instilling into them a sense of His coming humiliations and death are, when any thing has occurred which leads them to high thoughts, from a sense of His power. The first time when He does so is, after He had confirmed them in the full knowledge of His Godhead, at the confession of St. Peter ; the second time, when He thus forewarns them, is after the Transfiguration ; the third time, is on an occasion when it is said expressly, that "all were amazed at the mighty power of God," and "while they wondered, every one, at all things which Jesus did[9] ;"—it is then that He, the more deeply and earnestly, brought before them His sufferings. The same period is also marked with a constant struggle for precedence among the Apostles,. which appears now to show itself for the first time ; and it is remarkable that the occasions on which it breaks out, are when our Lord has been thus warning them of His own humiliations. The consideration that our Lord appears at all times to be speaking to the hearts and thoughts of those whom He addresses, gives an additional force to the many instances, in which He graciously takes pains to correct this temper in them. Such is that of His setting the little child before them on His return to Capernaum ; and at the last Supper, when the same contest for precedency takes place, by His washing their feet. Other occasions, at this period, are marked with the same lesson, and arise out of the same feelings in the disciples[1].

But it is to be observed, not from these indications

[9] Luke ix. 43.   [1] As Mark ix. 42, and Matt. xx. 25—28.

alone, but from the thread of the whole history, how much our Lord's conduct was confined to His disciples; how much of what He said and did had an especial reference to them. Such are many of the conversations, and many of the incidents, which take place in Galilee; and still more evidently so as His ministry is drawing more near to its close. Such is that long and awful discourse on the Mount of Olives, respecting the Day of judgment; such are all the circumstances and conversations at the last Supper; and such the mysterious Agony in the garden, the knowledge of which was confined to some of them alone; all these things are full of instruction and peculiar adaptation to them; and such as suggest to us very much more, which must have taken place, in our Lord's daily private intercourse with them, and His nightly stay with them at the Mount of Olives. And, indeed, throughout the whole of our Lord's ministry, considering the private and confidential mode of His revealing Himself;—and the very necessity for constant intercourse between Him and them who were His constant companions;—their travelling with Him from place to place; their staying in the same house;—being with Him in mountains and deserts alone;—His crossing the sea from time to time with them alone; and so often fleeing from all men to conceal Himself with them apart: all these things prove that of necessity a great part of the three years of our Lord's ministry must have been spent in forming, converting, instructing, and training the Twelve. Full is it of inspiring contemplations, to behold God on earth, with a chosen few; but it is almost dangerous to dwell on the magnitude of their privileges, which they themselves were scarce allowed to know till He was gone.

This argument might be farther carried out into a great many points which seem especially to indicate an immediate reference to their Apostleship, their training for that purpose, their nomination, their preparatory mission, their subsequent consecration. Thus it seems probable that a great deal of what took place at the last Supper, had a reference to their Apostleship and ministry: The Washing of their feet, over and above its mysterious and instructive significations with respect to them and to all mankind, had probably a reference to that washing which according to the Law was to precede Consecration[2]; and so also the Prayer of Sanctification which ensued,—a prayer that they might be One after some mysterious resemblance to the Godhead, and the Three in One,— seems to contain a peculiar reference to the Apostles[3]. In some manner they also were to be Twelve in One, and One in Twelve, representing the Apostleship of Jesus Christ continued on earth. In like manner after the Resurrection, the forty days which our Lord spent with them upon earth, are comprised in the short mention of His "being seen of them forty days, and speaking of the things pertaining to the kingdom of God[4]."

In all these respects, our Blessed Lord was in some measure perhaps setting forth a great principle, which He has also exemplified in His own saints and good men of all ages, if we may say it with reverence; inasmuch as their own direct and more immediate influence was often confined to their own circle, but the effects of it, through and by them, operated on mankind.

[2] See Exod. xxix. 4. 9.   [3] John xvii. 18—23.
[4] Acts i. 3.

SECTION III

THE LAKE OF GENNESARETH

A CIRCUMSTANCE may here be noticed, which has probably struck most persons, viz. how much the Lake of Gennesareth finds a place in the sacred narrative. We are not in the habit of considering such things; and yet all particulars with respect to our Blessed Lord must be well worthy of thoughtful reflection; although they appear merely to relate to the most common contingencies of time and place. Our Lord's first call of the disciples, and one of His last recorded discourses with them, were on the shore of that Lake: and so much besides, that it cannot be thought merely fanciful on such a subject, to consider the history of our Lord's intercourse with His disciples, in connexion with it. It may be said, indeed, that all this may have arisen from the fact, that the chief of our Lord's disciples had their home and occupation on that sea: but this only gives rise to a further question, why the four who were first called were fishermen; why fishermen should be thus singled out for such a pre-eminence: whether there might have been some secret reason, as for instance, that thus our Lord did not take those who derived their sustenance from that disobedient land, or more extensively from that ground which God had cursed: or whether their calling rendered them more suitable, as being in some degree separated from the world, and one that tended more to contemplation: or whether some symbolical meaning was contained in the fish and the fishermen, in their being fishers of men, while their net, which is the Church, gathers of every kind; or whether it might have been by mere accident, as it were, and in an indiscriminate selection from all classes irrespectively. However that may be, their history, in connexion with our Lord, on that Lake, may stand for an epitome of the view which has been taken of our Lord's dealings with them.

Our Lord first of all calls them when they are on the land mending their nets, when He is walking on the shore, and, as it were, apart from them[5]. This may well serve to represent, figuratively, our Lord's first invitation of them, of which He said, "Ye have not chosen Me, but I have chosen you, and ordained you, that ye should go and bring forth fruit[6];" such was the case when He stood watching for them, where the Baptist was with his disciples, and invited them to Him. The next occasion, when we find our Lord and His disciples by the Lake, is on that occurrence mentioned by St. Luke[7], when He Himself gets into the boat with them, and teaches the multitude from thence; then He launches forth into the deep together with them, when by the power of His word and of His presence, they take the miraculous draught of fishes. Thus was it when He sent them forth during the time of His own ministry, and while He was still with them in the flesh, supporting them by supernatural indications of His protection, when they returned unto Him, telling Him of "what things they had done." But, on a subsequent occasion, He is still with them indeed in the ship, but He is asleep, and the storms arise; He is with them, but apparently powerless and helpless. And here, indeed, it is a strong trial to them; they are in jeopardy indeed, and, to all human appearances, in danger of sink-

[5] Matt. iv. 18.   Mark i. 16.   [6] John xv. 16.
[7] Ch. v. 11.

ing, both themselves, and their vessel. Then He arises, and stills the storm, and reproves them for being wanting in this trial; not as devoid of faith, but for being of little faith: not for expecting death, for there were all appearances of it, but for fearing death, or any thing that portended it, while they were with Him. One can scarcely fail to recognize in this circumstance a preparation and training of them against the time of His death[s], when He should be asleep, and the storm should arise, and beat vehemently, so that their little boat was nearly covered by the waters. We hear at once, in these His words to them, the very words and voice of Him who, after the Resurrection, "appeared to the eleven as they sat at meat, and reproved them for their unbelief and hardness of heart." Beautiful, indeed, and interesting is this lesson, conveyed by miracle. Fear, on the appearance of shipwreck, was natural. They knew not enough of God's ways to know they were not to perish in that storm, as circumstances seemed to indicate that they were likely to do. But what they needed was, in spite of appearances, in spite of their hopeless and helpless condition, to trust in Him. This was what they needed at the Crucifixion: He arose, "and there was a great calm."

But they have another and still higher lesson to learn, and the next appearance of our Lord with His disciples on the Lake is again, like the preceding, accompanied with the miraculous display of His power. It is midnight upon the Lake: they are alone, and are sent forth apart from Him. As our Lord had been before asleep, and thus taught them, so does He now proceed to teach them a higher lesson, by His absence, and by His being with them when they know it not; but still they hardly

[s] See Passion, pp. 335—338.

venture to believe it, and St. Peter goes out upon the waters before the rest. The whole occurrence appears full of some miraculous and significative teaching, both of prophecy and of doctrine, and especially that mysterious action of St. Peter in walking on the waves, and supported by the hand of his Lord. What may be signified respecting the future condition of the Church, and as it may be especially respecting the Church of St. Peter, is beyond the thought of man to divine; a more immediate reference to the self-confidence and fall of St. Peter is more evident, from the coincidences and correspondences in the two events. It occurs, it may be observed, after the sending forth of the Apostles, and that mysterious multiplication of the loaves; and the close of all is remarkable, that when our Lord entered the boat "*immediately*[9]" it was at its destination. So shall it be we know at the end;—when the storms of persecution shall be at their height, He shall appear, and when our cries are addressed to Him, He shall be talking with us, and saying, " It is I, be not afraid;" and when He shall appear to His Church, and with them, it shall be at the end.

Once more is our Blessed Lord with His disciples at the Lake; but it is now morning—the twilight of the eternal morning; and He is seen, not with them, who are toiling on the deep, but on the shore. That all this occurrence has a mysterious reference to the final consummation of all things, has been shown by St. Augustine in so striking a manner, as to carry conviction and wonder to every reader[1]. And Origen had before enlarged on the preceding incident, as containing within it a mystical import, full of spiritual meaning and prophecy, re-

[9] John vi. 21.   [1] Comm. in Johan. ad loc.

specting the probation of our souls, in passing the waves of this troublesome world to our heavenly country[2].

Thus these incidents on the Lake, taken successively, appear like emblematic pictures, representing the successive scenes of the ministry of those who, from being humble fishermen, became fishers of men. Our Lord first invites them to Him, when they are apart from Him. In the next place He gets into the same boat with them to teach and to work miracles; He gives them commission but keeps them with Him. Then again He is still with them, but asleep. Then He sends them alone, but comes to join them in their journey. Then He is seen by them on the shore, and invites them to that mystical repast which indicates the gathering in of the Elect.

On the first miraculous draught of fishes, in St. Luke, the multitude of fishes is vast and *unnumbered*, the net breaks, and the ship begins to sink: and thus now the net of Church discipline is broken, and the ship is sinking, from the multitudes that flock into it of all kinds, caught by Apostolic ministries. But not so in this last miracle in St. John, at the close of all things; for the final Elect, that are to be with God, are numbered, "the twelve thousand" of each tribe[3]; it is "full of great fishes, an hundred and fifty and three; and for all there were so many, yet was not the net broken."

---

[2] Com. in Matt. ad loc.   [3] Rev. vii. 5—8.

SECTION IV

DIFFERENCES OF CHARACTER IN THE TWELVE

AND now, as our Blessed Lord thus dealt with the
Apostles, revealing Himself to them, and schooling them,
and proving them, for their destined office in His Church,
so also among the Twelve themselves we find distinctions
and differences, while our Lord appears to have acted
towards them according to the dispositions and circumstances of each. Thus, as we have seen that He revealed
Himself to His disciples, with a freedom and intimacy
which He did not observe towards the rest of the world,
so even among the disciples themselves, He admitted some
to a nearer approach and converse with Him than other
disciples.

One instance of this kind of distinction is on the very
surface of the narrative, that of the Three, on some
occasions, being drawn by our Lord to Himself, in preference to the rest of the Twelve : and this may serve as
an indication, and afford us a clue to differences of the
same kind being made by our Lord, among them all
respectively, and perhaps furnish us with reasons for such
distinctions. First of all, the name of "the beloved
disciple" proves that there was one who stood pre-eminent
above all the others, in the degree of intimacy to which
he was admitted, although nothing is recorded of the
circumstances of that intimacy. We have no indication
of two being thus separated, and set apart from the others,
by a particular degree of the Divine favour ; for although
we have two, as St. Peter and St. John, often thrown
together, yet it is not by our Lord Himself in admitting

them more intimately to His divine Person. But with
regard to the three we find it very distinctly, as on the
raising of the daughter of Jairus to life, on the Transfiguration, and in the Agony in the garden, when St. Peter,
St. James, and St. John, are thus distinguished from the
others, in so marked a manner as to render it probable
that it was often the case. After this distinction it
appears, on two occasions, that another, St. Andrew,
is added to their number, so that four are present; for
such was apparently the case in the healing of St. Peter's
mother-in-law[a], and at the discourse on the Day of judgment[b]. After this we find that other individuals among
the Twelve are, on one or two occasions, singled out for
express mention, as St. Philip on the miracle of the
loaves. From all these circumstances an interesting
inquiry might be made, viz. whether any thing could be
ascertained respecting the character of each, and our
Lord's conduct towards them severally. The subject
is altogether the more interesting from the consideration
that our Lord does probably act towards us all, and deal
with us now, in the same manner as He did with them :
—that we are admitted to' Him, or put far from Him,
according to certain indications of disposition in ourselves.
And indeed that His conduct to the Apostles, and His
revelation of Himself to them, and choice of them, was
not any thing peculiar, but precisely according to the same
laws, with which He will deal with all men to the end of
the world, may, I think, be considered to be intimated in
His own words. This He appears, on more than one
occasion, to have declared to them, when there was any
contest between them, calculating on their relation to
Himself and the priority of their call, as affording them

[a] Mark i. 29.   [b] Mark xiii. 3.

some degree of preference also in the ultimate Divine favour and acceptance. Thus on the suit made by their mother for Zebedee's children, they were told that their final place in God's kingdom would not depend on any favour, or arbitrary respect of persons, but would be given to those for whom it was prepared of the Father; and on St. Peter asking with respect to the Twelve, what they should have who had left all to follow Him, our Lord said in answer, that there were last who should be first, and first who should be last.

These distinctions I have spoken of are with respect to intimacy with our Lord Himself, and apparent gradations in the knowledge of Him ; but perhaps there were other distinctions observed by our Lord, and certain favours conferred by Him of a different kind, according to the peculiar character of each, so that each may, in some point of view or other, have had some mark of pre-eminence. Thus, as St. John was the first in the love of his Lord, and St. Peter perhaps in spiritual authority among his brethren ; so even Judas Iscariot in one way had, as it were, the first place of pre-eminence, namely, in the care of their worldly property entrusted to him. A consideration of no account indeed among them, but of no little moment with the world ; and indeed, power of this kind, and possession of worldly wealth, is now considered among ourselves as the highest and most enviable distinction among the successors of the Apostles, and that which chiefly marks the most desired pre-eminence. In like manner others also among them may, in some particular point of view, have had a priority and privilege assigned them, as limbs composing that spiritual Body, which have each their own respective endowments and offices to fulfil.

That our Lord did thus differently deal with different persons is, indeed, to be observed throughout : it is so even with whole classes of men : there is a marked difference between His mode of speaking to the Pharisees and that of His replying to the Sadducees ; again, He deals, generally speaking, differently with Jews and with Gentiles ; and it has been shown with what a marked distinction of intimacy He received the Apostles, apart from the people at large.

. The point therefore to be considered will be, what the respective characters of the Apostles were ; what were the circumstances in which they were severally placed ; and what were the various degrees of intimacy and favour to which our Lord admitted them. But satisfactorily to trace out these points would require more facts than we are furnished with ; and to enter at all fully into the characters of the Apostles, even from those circumstances with which we are acquainted, would exceed the limits and intention of the present undertaking.

SECTION V

THE GRACE OF GOD SEEN IN NATURAL WEAKNESS

THE object of this little volume has been rather to throw out hints and suggestions, such as have occurred in various points, and such as may be followed up hereafter, rather than to establish all that might be done by a lengthened induction, and by tracing out all the facts and incidents on which such an induction might be founded. And on this subject there are one or two points, of such general inquiry, which might be mentioned. The first of these is, whether it is not the case, in considering the characters and dispositions of persons in Holy Scripture, that where Scripture has pronounced, or shown any intimation of the Divine judgment on the Saints of God, it is often rather different, if not quite the contrary, to that which we should have been otherwise inclined to form concerning them:— different from that which the facts of the case seem *at first sight* to warrant? If it be so, this will afford us, of course, some little difficulty in deciding on their characters ; but a difficulty which is found in many similar cases will often supply some clue to the solution of itself, by affording us a case of analogy, and thus suggesting a principle on which such analogy is founded. Such difficulties which appear on the surface of Holy Scripture, will almost always, in the explication of them, furnish us with some valuable truth, important for our well-being. Now the phenomenon here mentioned, respecting the characters of Holy Scripture, may, I think, be observed so often, that it seems to lead us to this remarkable inference, that in the Saints of God the character, acquired by the gift of the Holy Spirit, is often that which is most opposed to the natural tendencies and dispositions. And this may be connected with some great mystery in our probation ; it may be that the victory of faith consists in overcoming natural infirmities ; so that in this, as in so many other matters, the strength of God is perfected in human weakness ; in like manner, as in the Old Testament, the miraculous victories of God usually take place not only without human means, but under the greatest apparent weakness and difficulty, as far as the strength of man is concerned.

The fact alluded to may be more clearly seen by refer- ring to the Saints of the Old Testament. Thus Abraham is known to all as "the father of the faithful," and stands forth pre-eminent beyond all mankind, for that faith which is the transcendental crown and perfection of all graces and virtues, so much so as to have been called "the friend of God." But if there is any thing which *appears* like a weakness recorded of him in Holy Scripture, any thing which in the narrative of his life might *seem* to human eyes as a blemish, it was on the two occasions when, first to Pharaoh and afterwards to Abimelech, he did not venture to declare Sarah to be his wife. Now in both of these instances, if the holy Patriarch fell short of his high character, we should attribute it rather to want of full confidence in God and His protection, than to his failing in any other grace. The one infirmity of his nature would appear to us to have been a deficiency in that faith, for which he was on the whole so singularly distinguished.

And as Abraham was distinguished for his faith, so was Moses for his meekness ; for Scripture has declared that he was "very meek, above all the men which were on the face of the earth[*]." Yet, judging from facts recorded of him, we should be inclined to suppose that he was by nature remarkable for sensitiveness and hastiness of temper, —that this was his one besetting infirmity. Such appears to have been evinced when he slew the Egyptian ; when he twice smote the rock in the wilderness : and on that occasion when he was "punished," as the Psalmist says, "because they provoked his spirit, so that he spake unadvisedly with his lips ;" and when he broke the two Tables of stone. Something of the same kind appears to have been the case with our own Hooker, whose biographer attributes to him such singular meekness, while his private writings indicate a temper keenly alive and sensitive to the sense of wrong.

[*] Numb. xii. 3.

Again, the patriarch Jacob has been pronounced by Holy
Scripture to have been a plain or simple-hearted man,—
"a plain man dwelling in tents':" and, indeed, our Lord
Himself seems to allude to this his simplicity of character;
for as those whose faith was remarkable were designated
in Scripture the true children of Abraham, so that man
seems to have been called by our Lord "an Israelite indeed," i. e. a true son of Israel, "in whom is no guile⁸."
And yet, if in this case we look to the natural man, and
judge according to human judgment, we should probably
have thought otherwise. For does there not appear in
many actions, which have been left on record of this holy
Patriarch, something like deceit, so much so, as to have led
some to suppose that subtilty, approaching to guile, was
the marked tendency of his natural character? Such were
those acts of Jacob in deceiving his aged father, in increasing the number of his flock, in beguiling his father-in-law
by his flight, in discreetly arranging his flock to meet his
incensed brother Esau. All these important events of his
life might seem to intimate artfulness of character, rather
than guilelessness, as some men might have thought.

Again, if we may venture to say it, may there not be
supposed something of this kind in Job, whose patience
has so signally received the praise of God; are not his
expostulations and complaints,—sublime, holy, and touching as they are,—yet are they not apparently marked with
somewhat a little like a tone and expression of impatience
occasionally,—till God's holy discipline had perfected His
strength in that his natural weakness?

In like manner, to whom should we attribute the
epithet of holiness and loyalty of heart, more than to
him who has pre-eminently attained the title of the

7 Gen. xxv. 27.   8 John i. 47.

" holy " David, " the man after God's own heart "? And
yet, the sin by which he was so signally tempted and
overcome, is one of those which are said especially to
" take away the heart ;" so much so, that the great crime
of which he was guilty, was that which has given the
name by a figure to those who are alienated from God,
and disloyal in heart to Him ; for they are called by the
Prophets and by our Lord Himself "adulterous :" whereby it is implied, that no word intimates more strongly
unholiness of heart than adultery. We may well ask
how this can be in such a character, that things so opposite should have been found, and doubtless, it is a part
of " the mystery of iniquity ;" and yet if we might venture
to add, it contains in it something of "the mystery of
godliness " also : so does "deep call unto deep." For,
surely, nothing can be more opposed to that purity of heart,
which has the privilege of seeing God, than this crime.
And it was accompanied with murder also, than which nothing is more opposed to God, Who is love and life. Yet,
contrary to all this, no one had more strongly an abiding
sense of God's presence ; and a principle of holiness is no
where seen more deeply, than in that penitential Psalm in
which he laments his crime. It is all as if he who arose
by Grace so immeasurably high, would have been by nature
tempted to the lowest depths.

Now, if we take the instances which most prominently
occur in the New Testament, they will appear to be
examples of this principle. It was indeed no other
than the disciple of divine love, who would have called
down fire from heaven to destroy ; until the zeal of
the "son of thunder" was so perfected in that love that
"casteth out fear," that he could at last give utterance to
no words but those of, " Little children, love one another."

Of the sacred character of St. Peter, we have indeed no very distinct evidence : but the name of the Rock would lead us to attribute to him all firmness and stability of purpose.   For, I think, we cannot but suppose that, in giving him that name, our Blessed Lord had some reference to his character : to that character which by the Grace of God he was about to obtain, and which was so necessary for him who was to be one of the chief foundations of the Church ; one who, when he was himself converted, was to be the strength of others—the strengthener of Apostles[9].   But now, if we were to judge according to human judgment, from the facts that come before us, would not that failing which we should attribute to St. Peter, rather consist in a want of firmness? All the faults and failings recorded of him indicate a want, —not of love, not of zeal, not of self-denying earnestness, not of faith,—but of firmness ; of firmness to render consistent and stable a mind pre-eminently gifted in all other respects ; a character of singular zeal, ardour, and faithfulness, but naturally deficient in firmness to support endowments so great.   Thus, when he attempted to walk upon the sea, it was at first an act of pre-eminent faith, but it was firmness that he needed to support it ; when he made confession of our Lord's Divinity, he was raised as it were to the third Heaven of all blessedness, by our Lord's gracious words of acceptance, but so wanting in firmness, to keep him to this height, that soon after our Lord said unto him, "Get thee behind Me, Satan, thou art an offence unto Me ; for thou savourest not the things that be of God, but those that be of men[1]."   And above all, in the Hall of judgment, his denials, so strongly contrasted with his former earnest and sincere professions,

[9] Luke xxii. 32.   [1] Matt. xvi. 23.

were owing especially to a want of firmness. Courage and faith took him into that place of danger, when others fled, but that courage and faith needed stability to support him there. Even afterwards, if we may consider it a failing in this great Apostle, when he was rebuked by St. Paul, for not abiding to what he had before taught, " fearing them of the circumcision [2]," it was in a want of firmness that he failed. This is evidently implied in what St. Paul says of the circumstance.

And may we not see something of the same kind of contrariety in the history of St. James the Great, one of the most favoured three? The circumstance remarkable respecting him is, that we know so little of one so highly favoured and distinguished; for what we have recorded of him is next to nothing at all. What we do know of him is, that he, with his brother, wished to call down " fire from heaven [3]," but was afterwards of another spirit, being willing to sustain suffering rather than to inflict it. He at one time aspired to be great [4], but our Lord gave him His promise that he should indeed be great, but it should be from pre-eminence in sufferings ; and his greatness consists in his being hid with God from the eyes of all mankind. No Gospel, no Epistle, left to be a memorial of him ; no word spoken by him, no act performed in the kingdom of Christ ; whatever he did, he did previously to the establishing of the kingdom,—then was he indeed most great in the greatness of his humiliation and littleness, in being most of all hid from human greatness—being hid with Christ in God. He asks for the first place in the future kingdom, and nothing is again heard of him but his death.

[2] Gal. ii. 12.　　　[3] Luke ix. 54.　　　[4] Mark x. 35.

And indeed something of the same kind might be said of all the Apostles generally; our attention is particularly arrested, and our wonder excited, by something that appears like ambition, before our Lord's death: they are seeking for pre-eminence: they come before us as not having attained that virtue of humility for which they were to stand first, but as being like other men, seeking for the first place; and we may well suppose that they did indeed attain unto the first place in Christ's kingdom for their surpassing humility; for they afterwards came to know, and themselves beyond all to exemplify the doctrine, that they, who were the lowest in the estimation of themselves, would be the highest in God's kingdom. The history evinces them to have been by nature opposed to that which they were by Grace to be, and afterwards by Grace so signally became.

To take again the character of St. Matthew; as in other cases, we have very slight indications indeed from which we can form any judgment of his character, or of the circumstances in which he was placed. But, from what we know of him, one would naturally conclude that of all the disciples he was, beforehand, most in danger of wealth, and most inclined to covetousness; for his office was that of a publican, not only a gainful office, but one which implied for the love of gain a sacrifice of sacred caste and privilege. Such therefore may have been his tendency by nature; for what but the desire of money could have ever tempted one of the seed of Abraham to become an outcast? And the large and promiscuous feast given at his house to Pharisees, and publicans, and disciples of our Lord, and those of the Baptist, seems to indicate something of wealth. Now, though we know little indeed of his character, as formed by Grace in

Christ's kingdom, yet that little would mark him as especially "poor in spirit;" so as to be peculiarly suited to be the first to unfold to us the kingdom of Christ, of which the first requisite is poverty of spirit. This St. Matthew puts at the door as the first beatitude. For all that we know of him is, that he "immediately gave up all;" and this was relinquishing a gainful occupation and livelihood. Two circumstances are noted of him, both of which indicate a poverty of spirit; they are on occasions of speaking of himself; that he alone of the Evangelists places himself behind Thomas, and he alone designates himself, not with the more honourable appellation of Levi, but with the despised name of Matthew, and to this adds also, "the publican." The very style of his Gospel is marked by this simplicity throughout, and an absence of any thing like ostentation or vanity; and style in composition is the result of character. Here therefore, again, the strength of God is perfected in weakness; from the rich seat of the usurious publican is brought poverty of spirit. And moreover, from the despised Publican, not worthy of the name of a Hebrew, and cut off from the children of Abraham, comes forth that Evangelist, who is the especial Evangelist of the Hebrews; for throughout all his Gospel, it is the Gospel of the Hebrews. In the new kingdom, which he is the first to reveal to us, the Publican becomes the Hebrew of the Hebrews, the true son of Abraham.

And this is all quite in character with that Gospel dispensation, which "hath chosen the weak things of the world to confound the strong;" which out of death brings life; out of suffering highest blessing; out of sickness greatest health of soul; out of humility highest greatness; that Gospel, which, it may be observed, is not only itself like a contradiction, but does especially deal with contradictions, declares things contrary to what man's judgment would suppose. As it is the case in the Beatitudes, that the blessing conferred is the opposite to that which would have been inferred by the world; for poverty of spirit is most opposed to a kingdom, and meekness to the possession of earthly inheritance, and persecution to the ecstasies of joyful delight which are promised: so also it is but consistent with all this, if it be the fact, as is here suggested, that the virtue bestowed in Christ's kingdom is that which was most wanting; the most opposite to the natural character and tendencies. And surely they are "more than conquerors," who obtain by Grace that temper most pre-eminently, which by nature they pre-eminently needed.

SECTION VI

NATURAL WEAKNESS AND EXTERNAL TRIALS

The other point to be observed in the probation of God's Saints is this,—that the providential dispensations of God respecting them, the external trials with which they were exercised, seem to have consisted, mostly, in occasions wherein their natural weakness was most tried, and in mastering which their spiritual strength was attained. The characters brought before us in Holy Writ, seem to have their probation in one particular line, or sphere; and the circumstances of life in which they are placed, are especially adapted with a view to this one particular object. Thus it is that the internal tendencies and external temp-

tations, combined together, make up the course of probation; which in each case takes the particular shape here
described; and thus the character stamped upon them, when
approved by Scripture, is the result. It is therefore from
this cause that it becomes eventually the very opposite to
their natural bias and temper; and this circumstance occasions at first sight this doubt respecting the true character
of God's saints, as it was shown in the former Section.

Thus, as Abraham stands pre-eminent in God's book for
his faith, so all the trials of his life seem especially calculated to be trials,—not of temper,—not of courage,—not
of charity throughout, so much as—of faith. His first
call,—his sojourn in a foreign land,—his long waiting for
the promises,—his sacrifice of his only son,—his being in
the hands of powerful men and strangers; all these things
seem especially trials of faith, as distinguished from every
other virtue. This faith was indeed productive of every
other virtue in a singular degree, but faith was the ruling
principle of his life, and that quality which marked his
character: and only by consequence proved productive of
every other grace, for such necessarily arise out of the inherent strength of that genial soil of faith. Hence it follows
that the two points in which he may have been supposed
to fall short in the probation, were especially marked by a
want of faith, inasmuch as his trials were of this kind, and
through many victories, and a few failures, he obtained that
crown which had been held out to him.

To take again the life and trials of Moses, whose characteristic excellence was meekness, as far as any virtue can
be considered independent of others, for they are all necessarily connected: and his constitutional bias, it has been
observed, was marked with an apparent sensitiveness, not
to say irritability. His residence in the Egyptian court,

and his position afterwards, as a Governor and Lawgiver, would have been calculated to promote this natural tendency, as may be seen in the usual effect it had on Eastern Kings, in rendering them incapable of brooking contradiction, and having their wills thwarted. The conduct and fickleness of Pharaoh; and the ingratitude, the stubbornness, and waywardness of those whom he came to deliver; and almost every step in the wilderness with that people; their murmurings, their rebellions, their idolatries, their turning back to Egypt; the harassing situation of a leader; hope delayed, and the weariness of protracted journeyings; the conduct of his wife, of his sister, and of his brother; and the final disappointment of all his hopes; these things were all, in an especial manner, trials of temper. And his own natural character, if such as it has been supposed above, coincided to render them so. In these things, therefore, once and twice he fell, and in these he was by God Himself made to stand; whose declaration concerning him in His Book on earth already precedes His final judgment, and the declaration of His Book in Heaven. For through these things he was so perfected, as to be in character a type of Him who said, " Learn of Me, for I am meek."

In like manner, the trial of Job consisted in something very different from that of Abraham, or of Moses. Satan had sought to have him and to sift him as wheat, and doubtless tried him in that point in which he was most vulnerable; even unto that which is the sorest trial of patience, viz. when the body is touched. In Job, not the domestic affections, not his temper, not his faith, not his courage, not his love, but his patience throughout is put to the proof; for " tribulation worketh patience." But in all these things " Job sinned not with his lips,"—" nor charged God foolishly ;" and he came forth as "gold that hath been tried seven times in the fire :" he overcame, and is made a pillar in God's house, and is held out by Holy Scripture as an example to all ages ; to all of which it may be said, "Ye have heard of the patience of Job!" As victory implies a struggle, and a struggle implies liability to be overcome, we may well suppose that Satan should try and assail in the very place of weakness, "Behold," says our Blessed Lord, "the devil shall cast some of you into prison, that ye may be tried : and ye shall have tribulation ten days : be thou faithful unto death, and I will give thee a crown of life⁵."

Again, there are others of whose characters we may form a judgment, although it may not have been pronounced of them by Holy Writ itself ; and in these also something of the same kind is observable. In Joseph all the events of his life seem not to affect his irritability, as in Moses ; not his impatience, as in Job ; did not put to test his courage, as in Joshua, nor his faith, as in Abraham ; but in all things seem to try his forgiving disposition and gentleness of heart. His being the favourite of his father, the unkindness of his nearest relatives, the undeserved persecution of his master, and the perfidiousness of his master's wife, the forgetfulness of the chief butler, and the power of retaliation afterwards afforded him as a Ruler ;—if any circumstances would have called forth ill-will, and revengeful feelings, and the darker passions of the soul, they were those with which Joseph was tried. Now although the character of Joseph does not seem to be stamped by any express declaration of Holy Scripture, yet it appears to have been remarkable for a singular sweetness of disposition, and absence of all malice ; this is evident from many circumstances,

⁵ Rev. ii. 10.

and we have an instance of it in the last words recorded of him: "And Joseph said unto them, Fear not, for am I in the place of God? But as for you, ye thought evil against me ; but God meant it unto good, to bring it to pass, as it is this day, to save much people alive. Now therefore fear ye not: I will nourish you, and your little ones ; and he comforted them, and spake kindly unto them⁶." Now whatever the natural temper of Joseph might have been, his trials were all such, that his generous character could not have been produced but by the especial aid of Him, Who by His Grace "worketh great marvels." Men are apt to mention any of the circumstances with which he was tried as a natural reason why the disposition of any person should have been soured, and rendered bitter or malevolent.

It may not be irrelevant to notice even slighter cases than this. The virtue required of Joshua was courage, and in wars he was tried. "Be strong, and of good courage," is the command repeatedly addressed to him. Samuel was tried with wicked men, and with men against whom the Divine displeasure was denounced ; but his disposition among the Saints is marked with a love for others, and a desire of obtaining God's love towards them. His character is one of intercession, and a commiseration for sinners. He is in the temple from a child ; in Saul's transgression, it is said, it "grieved Samuel, and he cried unto the Lord all that night ;" and afterwards, emphatically, "Samuel mourned for Saul⁷:" and to the people, he says, "God forbid that I should sin against the Lord in ceasing to pray for you⁸." But this man of compassion chiefly comes before us as carrying God's judgments

⁶ Gen. l. 20, 21.   ⁷ 1 Sam. xv. 11, and 35.
⁸ Chap. xii. 23.

to others;—to Eli, to Saul, to Israel. Thus was his
charity severely tried, but such instances called out and
exercised his spirit of intercession, which became not
stifled and impaired, as by nature it would have been, but
the more kindled, from the wickedness of those with
whom he had to deal.

In like manner it may be seen, in all the trials of St.
Peter, that it is his firmness especially which is put to the
test, in those points in which he failed, or seemed to
human eyes to fail—it was in firmness and faithful con-
stancy alone that he was tried. As in zeal, and energy,
in devotion to his Lord, and self-sacrifice, he was pre-
eminent, as became the chief of Apostles, these qualities
do not seem to have undergone the test; as if he needed
only this firmness to give stability to those graces. His
conduct throughout, notwithstanding those occasional
failures, and all his language, as seen in his Epistles,
indicate great strength and manly energy of character;
and might it not have been that these great and martyrlike points of his character were thus by trials, and
through a sense of imperfection occasioned by failings,
at length developed and perfected: and indeed the expressions of our Lord to him, and that question thrice
repeated at last, might be to point out the way to this
confirmation,—it may have been that by feeding the
"lambs" of Christ's flock, he should obtain the stability
and at length arrive at the power of feeding the "sheep"
also.

Thus all the Saints of God had to bear their own
peculiar cross, which was found in their natural infirmity
and temptations, until that cross became their crown, and
their very trials and weaknesses became the subject of
their rejoicing and glory. From hence it is that St. Paul,

after enumerating the Saints of God who overcame through faith, adds his appeal to us, to lay aside " the sin which doth so easily beset us," indicating that it was mainly by overcoming that besetting sin, that we should be joined unto that " cloud of witnesses," the company of Saints and Martyrs. And in his own case, that sore trial which he calls "the thorn in the flesh" became to him the source of joy and thanksgiving, and "the power of Christ resting" upon him ; for this secret was revealed to him ; " My grace is sufficient for thee, for My strength is made perfect in weakness. Most gladly, therefore, will I rather glory in my infirmities,"—"for when I am weak then am I strong."

Temptations are indeed as necessary to form the good character as they are conducive to the bad, and the more frequent and strong they are, the more do they draw out, strengthen, and establish this part of the character which needs confirmation. And, indeed, one can see some obvious reasons, why temptations should assail a person in that point in which he is most tender, and feels them the most. Each person has perhaps some affection, passion, or inclination, which most of all hinders him from the love of God ; even in good men, there exists some natural tendency, or some object to which the heart turns, which most obstructs its free rise to things heavenly. And since God chastens those whom He loves, and sends them afflictions in order to wean them from the world, and draw them to Himself ; such arrows of the Almighty will necessarily find them out in those weak points in which they will feel them the most ; will attack them in those places in which the world has the strongest hold upon them. It is their constitutional bias which makes men gravitate to the earth,—whether it be parental fondness, or covetousness, or ambition, which most reigns in their weakness; in these points they will be thwarted, and tried, and weaned to Almighty God. And thus, of course, those two points which have here been noticed, will have a mutual reference to one another: for natural weakness is only shown under temptation; for otherwise it is dormant and latent; and such external temptation could not exist without that internal weakness, which is liable to feel it. When therefore the infirmity is greatest, and the temptations are most frequent, then is that cross most severe; and the more severe the cross is, the brighter is that crown, when internal weakness and external temptation are both overcome. Thus are they formed who compose the army of Saints and Martyrs; formed by that "faith which *overcometh* the world."

Nor is it only in the probation of the good; but in those also who seem to fail and fall short in their course of probation, is the same thing apparent. The probation also, in this case, takes one line and course, and such as affords the greatest scope to that one infirmity in which they most fail. This may be seen in the one instance of the kind, with which the history of the Apostles furnishes us. Judas had one besetting sin, and had it not been for that, he might have believed, and continued steadfast; but the circumstances in which he was placed, drew out especially that one ensnaring temper, of covetousness; he "had the bag, and bare what was put therein." Thus when any evil temper of any kind is gaining the mastery in any character, it naturally puts itself into all those conditions of life which afford the greatest indulgence to its inclinations; and thus men are prone by the mere force of their evil nature when unrestrained, to place themselves in that very position in which their weak point is tried and most beset; as the covetous seek places of wealth, the ambitious of authority, increasing thereby both the occasions of sin and the tendencies of it. By Grace, on the contrary, men seek to avoid those places and snares of their weakness. Zaccheus sacrifices his wealth; St. Matthew his profitable calling; St. John his domestic ties. Thus do men, as they advance in Grace, not only grow out of the infirmities of their former nature, but also become freed from those occasions which combined with those infimities to draw them away from God. And it may be that the devil ceases to tempt them at length in those points, which become to them only the occasions of greater vigilance and prayer, and consequently of increasing strength[9]. For that which is to him who lives by nature the occasion of sin, is to him who lives by grace only an opportunity of victory. Of this latter case therefore it is said, "Blessed is the man who endureth

---

[9] Thus it is given as a rule of piety:—"Cum pugnas cum hoste, non satis tibi, si ictum illius declines aut etiam repellas, nisi fortiter arreptum telum in ipsum auctorem retorseris, suomet illum gladio jugulans. Id ita fiet, si ad malum solicitatus, non solum non pecces, sed hinc tibi arripias occasionem virtutis. Et quemadmodum eleganter fingunt poetæ, Herculem objectis ab iratâ Junone periculis animo crevisse atque induruisse, itidem tu quoque da operam, ut hostis instigatiouibus non solum pejor non fias, sed etiam evadas melior. Solicitaris ad libidinem? imbecillitatem tuam agnosce, ac plusculum etiam tibi de licitis voluptatibus interdicito, ad castas et pias occupationes apponito nonnihil auctarii. Instigaris ad cupiditatem, ad tenacitatem? auge eleemosynas. Incitaris ad inanem gloriam? tanto magis demitte te in omnibus. Ita fiet ut unaquæque tentatio sit tibi renovatio quædam sancti propositi tui, et pietatis incrementum. Neque enim prorsus alia ratio tam efficax conficiendi profligandique hostem nostrum; verebitur enim te denuo provocare, ne, qui impietatis auctor esse gaudet, pietatis ministret occasionem."—Erasm. Enchiridion Milit. Christiani, Canon xii.

temptation, for when he is tried he shall receive a crown of life[1];" but of the other, to whom temptation becomes but an occasion of falling, it is said, "Let no man say when he is tempted, I am tempted of God,"—"but every man is tempted when he is drawn away of his own lust, and enticed[2]."

One can hardly pass from this subject without noticing the character of the Holy Baptist, for whatever his natural disposition may have been, he certainly does come forth at last as rendered by the Grace of God the very opposite to what one would have expected. He had been sanctified by God in the womb, born of Priestly and holy parents; living apart from men from childhood: as a stranger and sojourner before God he looked on earth for no continuing city, but as the Patriarchs of old, sought for one that had foundations whose Builder and Maker is God: showing this belief not as the Patriarchs, by living in tents, amidst flocks and herds and domestic comforts; but houseless, homeless, solitary, he looked for a place in the house of God, "and a name better than of sons and of daughters;" while reared up as the child of the desert amidst fastings and watchings, he listened like Elijah of old for the still small voice of God in solitude. What, therefore, should we have expected from such a Preacher as this, when he came down among the cities of men, and found himself surrounded by promiscuous multitudes given up to sins of which he knew nothing? One might have expected that he would have said something of the desert, of his own more excellent way, of retiring from so wicked a world, nay even of the virginal life, and perfection, and contemplation, nursed by austerities and solitude. But not a word of all this: he was as gentle and considerate to

[1] James i. 12. [2] Ibid. i. 13, 14.

others, as unsparing and severe to himself; they confessed
their sins; he entered into all their temptations, and instead
of requiring difficult and great things, he led them on—
each to overcome his own besetting sin or the peculiar
temptation of his calling, even the Publican, the soldier,
the Pharisee. He called them not to the camel's hair and
the locusts of the desert, but merely to relinquish super-
fluities. Not a word of his own mode of life; unlike the
Pharisees, he bore himself heavy burdens, but required not
of others to touch them with one of their fingers. So
gentle indeed was he, that he could speak so as to be
listened to and heard with gladness by the adulterous
King, though he preached to him repentance. He descended from the desert into kings' houses, and he who
lived on the food of the wilderness and was so hardly
clothed, could be listened to by them who wore soft
clothing and lived delicately in Royal courts. Full of
gentleness and compassion, the preacher of repentance had
a joy of his own, which " the stranger intermeddleth not
with," while in all lowliness and gladness his heart beat
even as an attendant at a wedding festival. "He that
hath the Bride is the Bridegroom, but the friend of the
Bridegroom, which standeth and heareth Him, rejoiceth
greatly because of the Bridegroom's voice; this my joy
therefore is fulfilled. He must increase, but I must
decrease."

Surely this is a very remarkable instance of one coming
forth by the grace of God, perfected in a manner so
different to the children of this world under the like circumstances. It may also serve as an instance in point, of
one "out of weakness made strong;" in whom the bitter-
nesses of life had turned to sweetness; of one coming
forth from the austerities of the desert, whose tongue

dropped manna and honey as from the stony rock; for while his life was in the wilderness, his heart had been in heaven.

But to return from this digression. Considering the characters of Sacred History, and the dealings of Christ with men, these two points especially have occurred to the writer, as affording us rules, and it may be important guides, that we may not mistake occasional failures for the disapprobation or desertion of God, nor natural tendencies for the ultimate and true characters of God's Saints. It seems not improbable that the whole of our probation may be according to some general laws; and the numerous circumstances which there are of this kind, may indicate something of what those laws may be; and with regard to ourselves, these two considerations which have been pointed out, are of the very highest interest and importance, as they prove, that which is of all things the most difficult to persuade others and ourselves, viz. that the temptations to which men are most subject, and their strong natural bias and propensities, are no excuse for sin, but rather opportunities of growing in Grace. Thus nicely and beautifully adjusted is our probation in the hands of our great Disposer, weighing us day by day in the scale; while He, Who is the Great Witness, is present to watch the struggle, and to lead us, as our Lord did of old His associates in the flesh, to the fuller knowledge of Himself.

SECTION VII

FURTHER MARKS OF CHARACTER IN THE TWELVE

It is as an assistance to us in this study, that these things are remarked; for as no study can be so valuable, so nothing can be more important than any observation which may assist us in this study, or furnish us with any hints that may lead us to the knowledge of those qualities in His disciples which recommended them to our Lord, and drew them on to the more unreserved revelation of Himself.

A few more observations of this kind may be added. Even in the very highest characters there is a difference. There is indeed a love which rises above what is earthly, and seems to have its conversation in things heavenly; and there is also a Divine love, which makes earthly things themselves the steps by which it arrives at this wisdom: not as yet buoyed up by that instinctive contemplation and knowledge of things unseen, but which eagerly embraces all means of ascending to it. Thus of St. John perhaps it might be said, in St. Paul's words, "Though we have known Christ after the flesh, yet now henceforth know we Him no more[3];" and therefore, as was the case with our own Bishop Ken, the very style of his composition partakes of this; he deals not much in human things, human incidents and affections, but in contemplation of those things which are in Heaven, and therefore speaks more in abstract terms and general expressions, as "the world," "the Truth," "the true Light." Whereas St. Peter may be described perhaps in the words of the same

[3] 2 Cor. v. 16.

inspired Apostle, "I count not myself to have apprehended; but this one thing I do, forgetting those things
which are behind, and reaching forth unto those things
which are before, I press toward the mark"—"that I may
apprehend that for which also I am apprehended of Christ
Jesus[4];" for so indeed had he been apprehended, and
caught, and sustained, at one time by his Master's hand,
and at one time by His look, and at another by His kind
reproving voice. And all his Epistles express that which
he had himself so much by experience learned, the
necessity of gradual growth in Christ.

But on these two characters of St. John and St. Peter,
so much has been said by the writer in other places [5], as to
preclude the propriety of dwelling more at length on them
in this place, much as it bears on the present subject.
And, indeed, these characters are so holy, that they are
"hid with Christ in God," and our earthly eyes are unable
to follow them. It is curious and interesting to observe
others of the Twelve, who came not within the hallowed
precincts of these three ; such as were admitted indeed into
the garden of Gethsemane, but were left afar off at the
entrance of the garden. How eagerly does their Blessed
Lord seem to watch them, and to watch over them, with
no less care, indeed, than over those three, to bring them
into that sacred choir nearer unto Himself! One or two
instances of this kind may be mentioned.

Such appears to have been the case with St. Andrew
and St. Philip, from the few casual circumstances in which
the mention of them occurs, sufficient to afford some clue
to their characters, and indication of our Lord's conduct

---

[4] Phil. iii. 12, 13.

[5] Tracts for the Times, No. 80, Part i. p. 31. Plain Sermons,
Sermon cxiv. also Part i. Sect. vii. of this Vol.

towards them. Philip would seem to be a person of singular simplicity and goodness of heart,—open and easy of access, and marked by strong indications of Christ's preference and regard. But there appears to have been in him a want of the deeper habits of meditation, of watchful observation and self dependence. His character seems marked with that cheerful love of mankind, which is apt to look to and to lean upon others, rather than that which looks to and leans on the laws of God only : this latter therefore was that which he had to learn more perfectly ; and such a disposition, by discipline and care, will come to realize the other also, and to convert earthly into heavenly love. Thus our Lord at a very early period calls him to follow Him, and we hear nothing more than that he finds and brings unto Him Nathanael,—that simple-hearted and guileless person, with whom, under the name of Bartholomew, he seems ever after associated. We afterwards find, on the miracle of the loaves, that he is the person whom our Lord addresses in order to prove him : "When Jesus then lifted up His eyes, and saw a great company come unto Him, He saith unto Philip, Whence shall we buy bread, that these may eat? And this He said to prove him[6]." This preference to Philip in the address of our Lord on this occasion may, indeed, have been owing to the fact of his knowing Bethsaida,—of which he was a native, —which made him the fittest person to be addressed on such a matter ; for it was in the neighbourhood of Bethsaida that this miracle was wrought[7]. But this could scarcely have been the sole reason, although it rendered the question to Philip not an unsuitable one ; and indeed our Lord's purpose is stated : it was in order "to prove him." Nor does St. Philip seem to apprehend any intention of the miracle.

[6] John vi. 5, 6. [7] Luke ix. 10.

But here again He probably turns to St. Andrew; for it is St. Andrew that makes the reply, and a reply that implies a watchful suspicion of something great and marvellous; and perhaps on this as on every other occasion, our Lord's question was to elicit that faith without which He wrought no miracles. But again, this kind and friendly dependence on others, which marks St. Philip, makes a character to whom others naturally look. And the next mention we find of him, is when the Greeks come to him desiring to see Jesus : selecting him for this purpose of all the twelve. On this occasion, too, it may be that Gentiles would naturally look to one of Bethsaida, a city in the border of the Gentiles, which rendered him more acquainted with their customs and dialect : for in this place St. John, in mentioning the circumstance, repeats that he was of Bethsaida. But it seems likely that he was one of those whose natural kindness made him accessible to others, as he looked to them. And here, likewise, we find him, as on the two former occasions, going to St. Andrew, and with St. Andrew to our Lord : "Philip cometh and telleth Andrew, and again Andrew and Philip tell Jesus *." Now all this in St. Philip would indicate one to whom our Lord would look with watchful care and encouragement, but not one whom He would admit to witness His glory, and to be with the three chosen ; but, on the contrary, it all falls in with the character of one, of whom, after all, our Lord had to complain at last : "Have I been so long time with you, and yet hast thou not known Me, Philip?" The expression has a particular force when we consider how early, and afterwards how signally, and perhaps how frequently, our Lord had invited him,—to draw him forth, as it were, after Him. For our Lord's words seem to indicate some degree

* John xii. 22.

of complaint at his not having made that progress which he might have done by a corresponding readiness to perceive those truths which his gracious Master had so often brought before him.

St. Andrew, on the contrary, being a step in advance, improves the hints afforded on all occasions, and seems to have in his character that which was wanting in St. Philip, and therefore made meet to approach nearer; for on two occasions he seems to be combined with the three first Disciples. He appears not to have been of that lively and clear belief, to be worthy to have been in the room where the Ruler's child was raised from death to life, or to witness the Transfiguration, and the Passion in the garden of Gethsemane; but from that more slow, but ever watchful and observant faith, still hoping against hope, and catching at intimations of that Divine power and goodness which were emanating from the sacred Person of his Lord. Thus on each occasion when he is mentioned, by watchful observation, he approaches very high towards that faith which needed no manifestation; his act in bringing the loaves was the foundation of that great miracle,—was, as it were, "the oblation" of the Bread; and the observation on the stones of the Temple, which our Lord had just declared should be left desolate, appears not unlikely to have been St. Andrew's: for St. Mark mentions the observation as being made by "one of the Disciples," and St. Andrew is connected with the other three immediately after, in asking, "When shall these things be?" which led to that most awful and important discourse as they sat on the Mount of Olives, looking down on the Temple, during that solemn evening of His last departure from it. In observant and watchful piety, there appears something similar in the two brothers; but perhaps there was some natural slowness in

St. Andrew, which rendered a longer time necessary for his character to be developed in the higher acts of faith, or in the understanding of mysteries : so that as his younger brother, St. Peter, from ardent zeal of temper, was formed by nature for the first place, St. Andrew,—although first called, and continuing to be with those three, the former associates of his calling, and strongly united as they all were together, partly in blood and partly in friendship, as St. Peter with St. John, and all in union of heart and purpose :—yet St. Andrew, from some deficiency in natural or moral disposition, was sometimes not admitted with the other three. And thus, by the ancient Masters, he is represented in picture with a slowness which contrasts with the ardour of his brother. Why his name should occur with St. Philip, more than once, is not evident ; perhaps from his being more advanced in age, and more thoughtful in character, St. Philip would naturally turn to him as his fellow-countryman, being both of Bethsaida. It is moreover interesting to observe how, in these instances, as is often the case in His moral Providence, the ties of friendship are made by Christ the means of drawing men unto Himself : for even earthly friendships seem sanctified as being in some sense like parts of that love, which leads men to that ineffable union and oneness which is with God.

With regard to three being apparently selected, and on one occasion four, perhaps in these things, as in the number of Twelve being that of the Apostles, there was some hidden fitness and appropriateness in the numbers, according to their mystical and sacred import : for as Three is the holy number, three are taken apart to be with Christ and God ; but as four is a going out of and beyond that sacred number into the world,—as the Gospel when it is revealed to the world goes forth by four

Evangelists, and as the river of Eden when it passed from Paradise into the world was divided into four heads,—so when Christ looks on guilty Jerusalem, and the subject is of judgment and the guilty world, it is no longer to three, but to four Disciples[9].

The Apostle St. Thomas likewise comes before us three times, by express mention, in St. John, and something of the same character is indicated on each of these three occasions. Unlike St. Philip, for he did not lean and depend on others, but speaks out for himself, and even to advise or contradict his brother Apostles; unlike St. Andrew, for he did not, by probable evidence and observant induction, come at once to high conclusions of mysterious Divinity: and he is associated in our minds with slowness of faith. And yet of him and of others, men in these days judge more harshly than we should do of God's Saints. It is with him, as with St. Philip, that our Lord's endearing use of his name[1], in His condescending kindness to relieve him of his difficulties, doubtless evince a singular and tender love towards him: although such an expression, as when addressed to St. Peter and St. Philip, is not unmixed with gentle reproof. There appears no reason to doubt his perfect fidelity and sincerity, and, indeed, it appears of the highest kind; but he seems to have been constitutionally deficient in what is often considered poetry, or imagination, of character: slow to take upon trust and to realize things unseen;— from a timid distrust, indeed, but that nearly allied to honesty and truth of character. In some respect he appears to be contrasted with St. John, who "had not

[9] See Nativity, p. 406.
[1] See Christian Year, St. Thomas's Day.

seen, and yet had believed;" but St. Thomas seems to represent a class of persons, whose faith is genuine indeed, but too much blended with what would be esteemed worldly prudence. And yet this fidelity, as far as earthly things go, is of the highest kind. It may be remembered, that the great poet of antiquity has represented the most exalted instance of human fidelity as thus distrustful, in the character of Penelope, upon the recognition of Ulysses. Thus on the first occasion when he is mentioned, when our Lord is going to raise Lazarus from death, St. Thomas says, "Let us also go, that we may die with Him," indicating a despondency arising from a want of that faith which "hopeth all things;" but yet he had fidelity and courage to die with his Master. And thus, when at the Last Supper St. Thomas says, "Lord, we know not whither Thou goest, and how can we know the way?" he seems to have no apprehension of the awful mysteriousness of our Lord's words, while we must suppose, from our Lord's declaration, that the other Disciples must have had some faint sense of it. Yet, on the three occasions on which he speaks, he seems to have no hesitation in judging for himself, and in expressing that judgment to take the lead, as it were, of the Twelve, either to advise or to oppose them. Thus, as on one occasion, he says to his fellow-disciples, "Let us go, that we may die with Him;" and on another, he declares that he cannot believe their statement, and must have stronger evidence than that with which they were disposed to acquiesce,—"Except I see and feel, I will not believe."

Such a character as St. Thomas has often a decision of purpose which more refined minds, and those of quicker susceptibilities, have not; and from that very decision and self-confidence are disposed to take the lead, to claim for themselves a certain degree of deference and authority,—a deference which may well be afforded to them in practical matters of daily life ; but when they expect the same in the life of faith, which is superhuman and spiritual, then it is of something better and more heavenly, even than this good character, that it is said, " Blessed are they who have not seen and yet have believed." But it must be remembered that St. Thomas's faith at last is no less emphatic than his former doubt,—his confession is full and perfect. And it may be observed that the doubts and inquiries of persons of this character, do at all times give rise to palpable confirmations of the faith, and practical sensible evidences, useful to weak believers ; while our Lord's words of blessing support and defend those whom the world despises, because they need not such evidence.

In all these things we must remember that Holy Scripture speaks of men with a holy sternness and simplicity, in a manner unlike that of human writers, when they speak of their friends. And, by the way, in speaking of this stern simplicity, and absence of any thing like an appeal to human favour, which characterizes God's Word, it may be asked, do not the companions and relatives of our Lord speak with less sanguine hopefulness of mankind than others :—with less enthusiasm, and therefore with more apparent severity? Contrast, in this point of view, the words of St. James's Epistle, and of St. Jude, with those of St. Paul ; the character of St. Matthew's Gospel with that of St. Luke ; and even St. Peter's Epistles with St. Paul. No one has spoken so fully of Judas as St. John : no one so incessantly dwells on the necessity of keeping the commandments as the Disciple of Divine Love, as if partaking throughout of our

Lord's apprehension, that in this men would be found wanting.

But I have already, perhaps, ventured too far even in these suggestions; for when we speak of the friends and associates of our Lord in the flesh, we approach so nearly to His own sacred Person, which cannot be done without some danger of irreverence to our Blessed Lord Himself; and one trembles to think, that one may have appeared to be judging those, in whose presence we shall ourselves be judged: those who, " in the Regeneration, when the Son of Man shall sit on the throne of His glory, shall also sit upon twelve thrones, judging the twelve tribes of Israel."

CONCLUSION

Now all these subjects of inquiry in this volume have been thought important, as bearing on a Commentary on the Gospels, and as explaining some of the rules thought necessary for such investigations; or rather, perhaps, as containing some leading points which have occupied the writer's mind, and have given a character to his views in many cases; which renders it necessary to explain the principles on which they are founded.

The first Part, which forms the opening of the Book, has been an attempt, not only to explain the characteristic differences between those four Gospels, and therefore as a preliminary matter very necessary to be considered, but also places the whole subject in that point of view in which it can alone be safely approached. For Inspired Writers, being more immediately instruments in the hand of God, cannot be ever safely considered, as they too freely have been, according to the laws of human composition; for such a mode of inquiry commences the investigation itself, by supposing them uninspired: and so goes throughout on a false supposition, in order to bring them down to the level of human criticism.

The next topic of consideration is of a still higher nature, and has respect to the Author of Inspiration, and the Subject of the Gospels Himself, and has for its purpose to indicate the necessity of devout humility on our part, and sincerity of life, in order to approach and comprehend matters so high and Divine ; and to be admitted to be with Him, Who reveals all His ways and Himself also in the Holy Gospels, according to faith and holiness of life, whether to those who saw Him of old, or read of Him now. There is nothing more necessary for every Christian student, than seriously to consider this method of the Divine dealings, in blinding some, and leading others to the knowledge of His truth, according to that seriousness of mind with which they draw near to Him. There can be no stronger warning against making such a study a mere intellectual pursuit.

Immediately connected with the foregoing inquiry is that of our Lord's own interpretation of Holy Scripture, for hereby we are at once furnished with a rule, at the Fountain-head of all wisdom. And certainly it is a point of all others the most needful in commenting on the Gospels, to show that we have such a sanction for the mode in which we interpret Holy Scripture, which may appear new to some because it is old. For if, in the expounding of sacred passages, the appeal is to the opinion of the Fathers, it will be found that their mode of interpretation, which is called by some mystical and fanciful, is in fact according to those laws of faith, and not of human reason, which our Lord has Himself set before us : and this is founded on a principle which falls not far short of this, that His Spirit Who speaks in His Church Catholic, is no other than Ho Who spake to us in the flesh. So that although certain expositions are but human and peculiar, yet the whole tone and method of such, generally, may be Catholic and Divine.

And this necessarily leads to the next topic of investigation—that of analogy. For faith itself, which has been shown to be the interpreter of Scripture, is itself built up on analogy. And it is requisite to say something in defence of explanations of our Lord's words and works, which attribute to them different and distinct meanings, but without derogation from the authority of other senses, which may be equally true. For it seems not improbable, nay, indeed, highly reasonable, to suppose, that our Lord's ways were according to vast incomprehensible laws;—that there were around Him what might seem a waste and profusion of miraculous powers, of which glimpses only and indications have been seen, and yet even of these but a few have been recorded to man[2]. And indeed such things which appear miraculous to us, are only so because we know not the laws on which they are founded. The things, moreover, which we behold, and things we behold not, things natural, and things revealed, seem to be under the same analogous systems, so as often to allow an appeal to things sensible, concerning the invisible laws of God[3]. Hence numerous expressions are used by the Prophets of the Old Testament, which seem to point out the Hand of God in the phenomena of events passing in the world, or seen in nature, which are again taken up and made use of, or alluded to, in the Book of the Revelation;—clearly indicating thereby that such things have their higher fulfilment in matters Divine and spiritual, in the Christian kingdom upon earth, or in the final Judgment. So that in all Christian matters we may apprehend some great and

---

[2] John xxi. 25.

[3] Δεῖ γὰρ ὑπὲρ τῶν ἀφανῶν τοῖς φανεροῖς μαρτυρίοις χρῆσθαι. Arist. Ethic. bk. ii. ch. 2.

hidden analogy to exist, and may reverently point out such intimations of it as appear.

The next subject, on the introduction of spiritual Beings in so remarkable a manner in the Gospels, may not at first sight appear so necessary as a preliminary dissertation: but it affords us so lively a representation of the dignity of the new dispensation into which we are introduced by the Gospels, that perhaps no other subject is calculated to set before us more strongly the truth and force of ancient Catholic teaching, in distinction from that low manner of treating the inspired writings, which has so much prevailed for the last century and a half. And one subject such as this will serve more to set before the mind this principle, than many general statements.

The other two subjects which have been introduced are of a different nature; but in another point of view have been considered not unimportant towards that mode of illustrating and explaining the Gospels which it is purposed to pursue. For although it is most necessary for us to bear in mind, that our Lord was "perfect Man" as well as God, yet it has always appeared to the writer that, as such, His actions have been too much considered as capable of being explained according to views of human policy and expediency; whereas they were doubtless controlled by some principle far greater and more mysterious, than such as human wisdom, and human expediency in teaching, would suggest to us;—some great and deep law of self-sacrifice, some doctrine of the Cross which was set forth in His life, as well as in His death, in overcoming the world. For let it be considered how unlike any thing that worldly greatness or the economy of human wisdom would have suggested, is the whole narrative of our Blessed Lord's life in the flesh. If it is according to infinite

E e

wisdom, yet it is not such as appears so to the natural man. But as St. Paul when he speaks of knowing nothing but "Christ crucified," mentions, as an instance and proof of this, that he "came not with excellency of wisdom," but was with them "in weakness, and in fear, and in much trembling," that their "faith might not stand in the wisdom of man, but in the power of God." "Howbeit," he says, "we speak wisdom among them that are perfect, yet not the wisdom of this world," . . "but we speak the wisdom of God in a mystery, even the hidden wisdom⁴." And thus no doubt the places of our Lord's abode, and the circumstances of His ministry, were regulated by some great laws of Christian humiliation and submission. For "wisdom"—the wisdom by which He dealt with mankind—"is justified," not of the men of the world, but "of her children." They alone who have the Spirit of God, see His ways, and justify His wisdom therein. To others it is foolishness.

The seventh and last discussion of all, is one which tends to bring home the whole subject of our Lord's life and teaching to ourselves, as drawing attention to His mode of dealing with all mankind, and more especially with those more immediately around Him, according to the diversity of their moral character, and progress in Grace: for so doubtless does He now deal with us, according to the same laws as He did with them. This brings all the historic narrative of Inspiration down to ourselves, or rather raises us up to it, sets before us Jesus Christ, as "the same yesterday, and to-day, and for ever"—the Alpha and Omega, the First and the Last, the Beginning and the End, and our beginning and our end as being in Him. And here in conclusion, perhaps, it will not be

⁴ 1 Cor. ii. 1—7.

unsuitable to say something on the very high subject on which we are engaged, to which it seems desirable to be ever recalling our attention, that these inquiries may not degenerate into a mere critical or scholastic dissertation.

The study of the holy Gospels is in this respect different from any other that can occupy the mind of man, that it is so very intimately of our very selves that we read. For when we consider the omnipresence of Jesus Christ Who is therein revealed, we become ourselves in such relation towards Him that spoke those words, and did those deeds there recorded, as if we were ourselves of that crowd that attended on Him. And in reading these sacred words, it is not only that we are admitted to be with the people which thronged, and saw, and heard Him—to see with their eyes and to hear with their ears,—but to see and hear with the eyes and ears of Apostles themselves. Nay, indeed, yet further, though it may seem bold to say it, we are thereby trained and taught, if we be willing to learn, to see and to hear all things in this world with the eyes and ears of Jesus Christ Himself; to judge of things with that judgment which He expressed. To study the Gospels, therefore, is to study the mind of Christ,—"the mind of the Spirit," and of God. It is Immanuel or God with us. It is with Jesus Christ Himself that we are admitted to be.

The mind of Christ is the very opposite to the mind of the world, of that which we see and hear around ; and the more we withdraw ourselves from this outer state of things in order to understand His sayings and observe His doings, the more do we come to that mind which is the Truth itself. But the world will be ever busy, not only to instil into us another lesson, but to persuade away even the lesson of Christ itself, to suggest something of its own instead of the meaning of the Spirit; the world comprehends not its spiritual depth and power; the instrument with which it would fathom unsearchable deeps is human reason, not faith; human expediency is the court which it would establish in order to explain Divine laws; it will tell us that the commands of the Gospel interfere not with modern practices, because they suit them not, but speak of ancient times and custom. But O! blind man, whoever thou art that art travelling to that unknown country, from which none hath returned, with no one but He that holdeth this divine light to guide thee, let not such worldly wisdom entice thee: for if thou wouldest be wise with the wisdom of Christ, thou wilt appear a fool to the many around thee: yea, what if thou even appear as Christ Himself to His own brethren, as one "beside thyself." Listen not to them who say, the narrow way and the strait gate was for them of old, and spoke of persecutions—but the wider path is for thee. Let not the difference of nation, nor of age, nor of custom deter thee from entering into the fulness of that knowledge, to which Christ inviteth thee in the Gospels. Say not this was needful for them, but less is required of me. For this is to put away from thee the mind of Christ, and to take the world to thee again, to be thy counsellor in things Divine. If thou needest an interpreter, for thou art thyself by nature blind, take no other interpreter but the Spirit, let Christ Himself be thine interpreter, Who dwelleth ever in the union of His Church. Thither go thou as to the pool of Siloam, and there wash away the earthly clay—the affections of the carnal mind—from thine eyes, that thou mayest see. Say not Christ spake thus to them of old, but not so now to us; know rather, that as the Scriptures of old set forth the Gospel in type and shadow, so doth the Gospel itself set forth in living type and emblem that which is now. For as of old in the flesh, so is Christ now in His Church, as seen by that faith which would realize things unseen amid things that are beheld. How does He still go about in mourning, " a Man of sorrows and acquainted with grief," as among the disciples of old, wandering from place to place, with nowhere to lay His head, for He can find no place of rest, but in the pure and undivided heart. He in whom Christ dwells must still be as his Master, " without form or comeliness," and " rejected of men." Without indeed, in that aspect which the world presents, it is all activity, " the temple of the Lord, the temple of the Lord," and " Lo, here is Christ, and Lo, He is there." But where is that pastor who would wish to have no thought but to win souls unto Christ? how is he daily among a few solitary worshippers ! and even they, when he would lead them on to that which is mysterious and Divine, seem to go back, and of them in the solitude of the heart he seems to say, " Will ye also go away⁵?" In His own Temple Christ preacheth now as of old, and is there in His own pastor as one that mourneth ; but when perchance He sitteth in the vestibule, and among the costlier offerings of the rich He may find the spirit of that poor widow with two mites ; and to soothe the aching heart a gleam of worth among Christ's little ones. He is still to be seen in His poor, for where suffering humanity is, there is He, as He has promised : and He is to be seen in His servants to whom he has given charge : for where His spiritual authority is, there is He, as He has promised. Yea, indeed, are there now on earth some that bear the keys of Christ's kingdom, and sit on spiritual thrones with authority which

⁵ John vi. 67.

is of God. In them also is Christ seen and present. It may be, indeed, that they are not of His spirit, for doubt. less they who seek the chief rooms, even though it be in His kingdom on earth, and in order, as it seemeth to them, to be called Benefactors, yet such are not of His spirit; for proud Pharisees sat in the seat of the meek Moses, yet their pride was not thereby converted into meekness; and to those who seek for the first place, He hath not promised to give wisdom nor aught of His spirit, nay, He hath promised to take His spirit from them, and to give the same to them who seek the lowest place :—yet though they be not wise by His Spirit, and though such may be the first here and the last hereafter, yet nevertheless is He seen and present in His kingdom below in their authority.

Wonderful are the changes of Providence, while under various and manifold circumstances, it is still eliciting and setting forth to view the same form of evil and of good : and faith and unbelief still wait on Christ in His kingdom in essence the same, though continually assuming a new form and aspect. Such as were under the Law come forth again under the Gospel. And disclosed in a new shape, the old enemies of Christ are still with us. The stubborn Jew that strove with Moses in the wilderness, and the impenitent idolater that mocked at Jeremiah, were again seen in the garb of the over-righteous Pharisee : and Korah, Dathan, and Abiram had put on the robe of Caiaphas, and said, We will not have This Man to reign over us. In altered semblance it was still that enemy of old, and that same also is now seen in pride of place, despising Christ in His little ones, and hating Christ in him who calleth to mourn and to leave the world. And there is Judas also now, though he carrieth not the bag nor walketh barefoot, yea, haply may be clad in state, while he heapeth up riches to himself, and it may be even from the revenues of Christ's Church and poor entrusted to him. And Martha, too, is engaged about much serving, and would show forth glad welcome and much abundance, but complaineth of Mary that sitteth idle, because she is at Christ's feet, to hear His words, knowing nothing, and desiring to know nothing but of that good part which she hath chosen. Yea, even now the proud Pharisee entertaineth Thee, but with cold welcome ; for he loveth little because he hath been forgiven little, and he hath been forgiven little, because he thinketh that he hath but little that needeth forgiveness[#].

But where, save in Thy blessed Gospels themselves, shall we find the love and the faith of Thy holy Apostles ? in these we must live, into these portals must we enter, and in these we must ever be, that we may be with them. There do I behold Thine own beloved disciple, on whose outward form the painter labours to bestow youth and beauty :—as if that within his soul, which rendered him lovely in Thine eyes, must needs render him lovely in the eyes of all mankind ; but Thou hadst Thyself no form nor comeliness, and when we behold Thee there is no beauty that we should desire Thee : but I see him full of contemplation of things Divine and Heavenly ; and love, as a stream of light from Thee, around all his actions and his words, and seeing in all Thy words what others understood not, and what even Peter did not comprehend. And holy Peter, too, is there, as one in a struggle between Divine fear and human energy, the one drawing him back into the shade, and bidding him stand afar off, the other urging him on to be the chief of Apostles, until both Divine fear and human energy were lost and

---

[#] Luke vii. 47.

overwhelmed in the love of his Master, for Whom he was
willing to endure the loss of all things.

But oh! let me turn from all—from proud Pharisees
that stand aloof in scorn, and from the company that
throng Thee, and from Thine own Apostles, to hear Thine
own gracious words.   Make that unpleasing unto me
which doth not savour of Thy poverty, that I may have
sympathy with Thy poor, and in them with Thee : let
" the zeal of Thine house eat me up," that I may appear
vile and " base in mine own sight [7]," if transported with
righteous indignation against the pollutions of Thy
sanctuary, and by mine own abasement hallow and
glorify Thy name.   And so at length from the evil of the
world and the strife of tongues may I long to be hid with
Thee, thinking over Thy words, and living in Thy Gospel :
of these may my meditation be day and night ; may this
contemplation be my daily food and the light of mine
eyes.   That whatever else I read, it may all come to this,
and whatever else I see, it may all come to this ; that this
may be to me the treasure hid in a field, in secret meditation ; that it may be to me in the world the net that
gathereth of every kind ; that I may become wise unto
Thy kingdom, and of Thy treasures bring forth things
new and old, in order the better to understand Thine
Evangelical Word.   Open unto me the great deep of Thy
wonderful counsels, that I may ever be trading therein, as
the merchant seeking goodly pearls, till I find that pearl
beyond all price, the knowledge of Christ crucified.

By comparing together day by day the hues that come
on the clouds, and the ways and motions of water and of
wind, men come to see through the order and harmony of
nature, and to discern the face of the earth and the sky.

[7] 2 Sam. vi. 22.

By comparing together, man comes to know the order of the stars, the movements and the appearings of the heavenly bodies. By comparing together, man comes to know in the Gospels the signs of what is to be to himself, and the order of things here below, and also the mysterious ways of things heavenly.

But let me not read and know without realizing also those things of which I read, considering them not as good only, but also as real and true : and not as real and true only, but also as concerning and important unto me. To know of Christ, and to believe of Christ, and of heaven, and of hell, of the fire that goeth not out, and the worm that cannot die ;—in these things all men among us are much alike ; though the learned have arguments more fair in show, and are able to set forth with more bright and convincing proof what they know, yet in the mere fact of knowing these things are all much alike. The hoary and impenitent sinner, who hath grown old in wickedness, will confess on the bed of death that he hath known these things full well at all times—of Jesus Christ and His miracles, the impenitent have heard and known as well as others. But in considering these things as real, and substantial, and true, in this there are all differences, in extent as wide apart as heaven and hell. In this one man differeth from another ; there is no other distinction among mankind but this ; rich and poor, learned and ignorant, noble and mean, between them all there is no real diversity, but in this alone;—in the evidence which the soul hath attained of things eternal, the substantial reality which it hath learnt by proof of things hoped for.

This, therefore, I crave mercy that I may attain unto, this I would seek to know, that I may look on those things of which I speak as Divinely true, and concerning

unto me, more than those things which I behold around;
that I may apprehend and lay hold of Thee Who art the
Truth and the Light; and that I may apprehend Thee I
must pray : and I cannot pray unless Thou first apprehend
and draw me after Thee, by the sweet fragrance of Thy
love constraining me.   Helpless by the road side, and
blind, I lay, and begging help of all that pass; and Thou
art passing by, going Thy way to the heavenly Jerusalem,
and art almost already gone by and passed; but still the
loud and importunate cry will reach Thee, that Thou wilt
turn back unto me, and bid me to be brought unto Thee,
and by Thy Word wilt open mine eyes if I have faith in
Thee.   Anoint Thou mine eyes with eye-salve that I may
see; that I may see the wonderful things of Thy law;
that I may behold Thy kingdom which, wonderful to
speak, is spread abroad in the world, and open unto all,
and yet is a hidden treasure, only discerned by a few;
that I may receive Thy kingdom within me, the light of
Thy presence and the knowledge of thy mysteries.   For
what are Thy miracles, but manifestations of Thyself and
of Thy presence, on the way that leadeth to the Heavenly
City? and what are those Evangelical commandments,
but the stones that pave the road, and to miss of which
is to fail of the way? nay, rather, what are they but
those precious stones and jewels, that pave the streets of
the true Jerusalem, which has come down to be with
men? Open Thou mine eyes that I may behold the
beauty thereof, and that Thy words may be to me more
precious than gold and silver, being weighed in the scales
of Thy sanctuary.

O the wonderful mystery, and greatest of Evangelical
miracles! The Divine Light is burning in the kingdom
of darkness, and yet unpolluted by that which surrounds

it; the Kingdom of God is set up in the midst of Satan's kingdom; the world hath received into her bosom that which condemns herself and prophesies her destruction; the very seat and tribunal of the Judge, and His living Word that shall judge it, are already upon the earth by His Gospels. Man, unbelieving and yet believing, bears about, and extends throughout the world, that great Witness that reproveth himself. Ignorance and poverty of Apostles hath made its way through the wisdom of the world, which boweth down before them, and listeneth to their voice; the pride of man beareth about in his hand the law of meekness; the impure offspring of Adam spreadeth abroad the tidings that the pure in heart alone shall see God; worldly riches are spent to teach the blessedness of poverty; and have thereby their greatest use and privilege. The four Living Creatures go about the world in marvellous ways,—in all directions at one time,— and the Spirit of God is within them, and rules them, as if they were of earth, yet not of earth, and where they are is the Heavenly Kingdom; and the four-and-twenty Elders fall down and worship wherever they are: for in the midst of them is the Lamb that hath been slain, "having seven horns and seven eyes, which are the seven spirits of God sent forth into all the earth[a]." For with them are all the Churches of God, worshipping with them, and where they enter there is the Lamb that was slain, and the all-searching Spirit of God. And through all things they pass with wonderful access; through palaces of kings, and poor cottages, and through armies and courts, and through the opposing passions of men: and wherever they are, there is the Eye and the Spirit of God,—hum-

[a] Rev. v. 6.

bling every heart to glorify His Name, wherever His Word entereth by the Gospel.

For therein is His Eye that searcheth the heart,—that searcheth by His Word into those things which the secret spirit knoweth,—those things which man dares not disclose to the wife of his bosom, lest she should loathe him ; nor confess unto his Priest, who standeth in Christ's stead to receive his confessions, lest the key of gold should become iron unto him.   Even all these things His Eye in the Gospels searcheth out.   And if according to the fear which He hath implanted in man, so is His displeasure,—yet, according to His knowledge, so is His mercy also ; and therefore, on account of that mercy, is He the more to be feared.   He knoweth whereof we are made, and therefore He hath pity on us.

The Holy Gospels are no less than the life of God upon earth, and written by His Spirit !   Oh, who can fathom the depth of His words !   What mortal shall measure the height, and breadth, and length of this Temple, in which the living God dwelleth !   For even as a living Temple is this His Gospel, wherein the Almighty is Himself present : wherein His Death and Cross is as the Altar, and His Birth the Fountain that goeth forth to all the world. O ! marvellous mirror of infinite Love, who will not hope for pardon when he gazeth on Thee !   O ! marvellous mirror of infinite Holiness, who will not tremble lest he fall short when he beholdeth himself in Thee !   To study the Gospels is to gaze on Almighty God, and to behold oneself in the brightness of His presence.   Oh, who will not wish to hide himself when seen in that Presence, in which the Heavens are not clean, and the Angels hide their faces in fear !   For God is Himself in some sense in His Gospels, and therefore they are in some sense the

Kingdom of Heaven; and to be in them, in contemplation and in prayer, is in some sense to be in heaven: for
that is Heaven where He is revealed. For Heaven is not
so much a local habitation, as that place wherein God is
discovered. But as Heaven would be no Heaven to those
who have not the temper of those blissful inhabitants, but
rather a place of banishment from their own pleasures of
sense; so this Gospel is no Gospel, this Heaven is no
Heaven, to those who are not of the temper and disposition required therein. It is love and obedience that
maketh Heaven to be Heaven, and perfect union with
God in those His creatures who have no will but His will:
who have no delight but in submission to His pleasure;
no love for created things independent of God, but love
and rejoice over those penitents and humble ones over
whom Christ rejoices, and whom He loves. To those,
therefore, who have this love of God, the Gospel itself
will be a Kingdom of Heaven, where Christ is heard, and
Christ is seen, and His power is manifested, and His will
is declared, and His creatures are before him. This is as
a Heaven upon earth, within whose hallowed precincts the
vanities of this world enter not: from which we may look
forth and behold the things of earth as Angels behold
them,—nay, see them in the light in which they behold
them who are now with Christ, those whom they can influence and charm no more. Here in these living oracles
of God we know who are truly blessed, and on whom woe
abideth; here we learn by what means to approach Him,
and what tempers He draws near unto Himself: here we
are taught to realize the things unseen around us, and to
behold Angels ministering.

But it is not study that it needeth to enter into this
Kingdom of the World,—it is not study, but worship, and

adoration; and adoration is not barren wonder kindling
into delight at the greatness of the verities, and the mysteries there disclosed : but is an earnest feeling after God,
from a life devoted to Him, and ways of life and desires
conformed to that Gospel. For what sympathy with
Lazarus can he have who liveth like Dives? and how can
he understand the narrow way who is looking about how
he may rise in the world?

The Kingdom of God is within thee ; for there is the
throne of Him Who trieth thine inmost reins, and bidding thee pluck out from thence the mote or the beam
that is in thine eye, that thou mayest see His Kingdom,
which is love to God and man. It is not human knowledge and intellect which is the key unto those "treasures
of darkness ;" but that repentance which groweth in
humility, and cleanseth the eye of the soul. If thou art
poor, lose not the blessings of thy poverty, and poverty
in spirit shall lead thee to a Kingdom. If thou hast
wealth, sell what thou hast and give alms, that thou
mayest follow Christ ; let thy loins be girded about, and
thy light burning ; let thy treasures be poured into His
treasure-house, that thy heart may be there also : and if
thy heart be there, thou wilt thyself be there, and wilt
know His Kingdom ;—for where thy heart is, there wilt
thou thyself be.

If thou art upon earth as a stranger and sojourner
before God, nor tied by human home and affections, then
take heed that thou lose not nor sully this thy crown, by
impurity of heart, or curiosity too bold into the unseen
things of God. For the human soul, restrained at the
door of sense, will ofttimes run out too curiously into the
mysteries of the Spirit. Go thou on, and prosper, and
"let no man take thy crown ;" yea, God " will send His

Angel with thee and prosper thy way[9]." Go on, seeking no rest below, unto the place of thy rest,—unattached and solitary, as thy Lord, and therefore the more free to follow Him. And blessed art thou if thou knowest this thy blessedness; for unto thee "shall be given the special gift of faith, and an inheritance in the temple of the Lord more acceptable to" thy "mind;" thou shalt know the things of God, and teach mankind His parables: thou shalt have more abundantly the knowledge of mysteries revealed unto thee, as Daniel, the "man greatly beloved," and beloved John: and so as thine eye of sense is dim, thou shalt have thy spiritual eye open to things of Heaven,—yea, thine heart, thine eye, and thine ear shall be in Heaven. Thou shalt have "manifold more in this present time," and the company of Christ and holy Apostles more abundantly vouchsafed unto thee in more than earthly nearness, and what thou losest in things of the sense, thou shalt find in joys of the spirit; for the pure in heart shall behold God in His Gospel.

But if earthly bonds hold thee, and domestic ties, and the affections of thy choice,—these things shalt thou find in the Gospels hallowed to a more excellent mystery. And if thou hast lost thereby the higher and better part[1], and canst not from henceforth be ever of the number of those who have given up all to follow Christ, then let this thought humble thee, and it will more profit thee in Divine treasure, and advance thee more in the knowledge of Christ, than if thou hadst given up all and wert proud of the same: and the prize thou hast lost may be thy gain. Thou shalt "have trouble in the flesh," for so hath the Apostle promised; but if that trouble subdue thee, and becometh not that sorrow of the world that worketh

[9] Gen. xxiv. 40. [1] 1 Cor. vii. 38.

death, but be converted into a Divine sorrow, then may it render thee more fit for those consolations which are with the mourner.

Let earthly joy and sorrow depart, that I may learn the joy and the sorrow of Christ; for even He also had joy on earth, because God hath made known His Kingdom to the humble in heart. Far away be the disputers of this world, that I may hear Christ speaking unto me !—far away be the stir of controversy, and the novelties of the latter and evil days, that I may enter into that ancient Temple, where the echo of Christ's voice is still heard amidst His silent and reverend worshippers of old; nay, where His voice itself is still new and fresh in His Gospels. "The Lord is in His holy Temple, let all the earth keep silence before Him." Well may we say, let all things else be silent, that we may hear Christ speaking to us. Hushed be the sounds of earth, the noise of things passing by that are fleeting on to decay and ruin, that we may listen to that "Word of God" that "abideth for ever." Hushed be the sounds, not of strife only,—the wranglings of the market and exchange, and the councils of nations,—but hushed be the sound of human affections, of human thought, and of all things fleeting, and of all things that cannot pass the barrier which divides us from things unseen: that we may be able to hear His words who hath said, "Heaven and earth shall pass away, but My words shall not pass away." "Let all the earth keep silence before Him." Hushed be the steps of hurrying waters that speak of fleetness; and silent the sea, whose sound is of restlessness, and of change, and of motion; and silent the winds, that speak of mutability and change;—hushed be the earth and the heavens, that are passing away; and the voice of hurrying days and of years, that we may hear God speaking unto us,—speaking unto us as man unto man, as brother unto brother, in His Gospels. "The time is short; it remaineth, that they that weep be as though they wept not, and they that rejoice as though they rejoiced not." The sun of life is going down,—and the year is on the wane,—and the busy sounds of day are declining: and even now the silent stars begin to appear, like the lights of immortality. Let Prophets and Apostles speak no more : no more the obscure sign and the dead ordinance,—the oracle on the breast,—and the smoking sacrifice ! Christ Himself in these His living oracles is speaking unto us. Let His creatures be set aside, that we may hear our Creator,— may hear His voice, and see His face ! The Maker of the world, He that " layeth the foundation of the earth, and formeth the spirit of man within him[2]." He that knoweth every movement of the heart is flesh and blood ; nay, wonderful and unspeakable the mystery, He is of my flesh and blood, even " bone of my bone, and flesh of my flesh[3]:" for my life hath been taken from His side. His body is one with my body, which hath partaken of Him ; yea, therefore, His Resurrection is my Resurrection, and the Transfiguration of His flesh is the Transfiguration of mine also ; for He shall change our vile body, that it may be like unto His glorious Body ; and even now, with these eyes of the flesh, is it given us to gaze on Him in the flesh, and even to be converted into the same image.

" Of such a one will I glory," for he is the new creature in Christ ; " but of myself I will not glory :" for oh, what abasement is sufficient for these things ! How can he feel sufficiently his own vileness and nothingness who has thus

[2] Zech. xii. 1.   [3] Gen. ii. 23.

F f

to stand before God,—to stand before Him in filthy gar-
ments, with Satan at his right hand [4] ?   If the holy
Prophet exclaimed, "Woe is me ! for I am undone, because
I am a man of unclean lips : for mine eyes have seen the
King, the Lord of Hosts [5] ;" what therefore should we say,
who are admitted into that Temple wherein we hear, not
Seraphims crying unto each other, but the Lord of Hosts
Himself speaking unto us, and behold His eye fixed upon
us in His Gospel !

   [4] Zech. iii. 1.   [5] Isa. vi. 5.

"Thou Who, on man's transgressing Thy command,
and falling,
didst not pass him by, nor leave him, GOD of goodness;
but didst visit in ways manifold,
as a tender Father,
supplying him with Thy great and precious promise,
concerning the Life-giving Seed,
opening to him the door of faith,
and of repentance unto life,
and in fulness of the times,
sending Thy CHRIST Himself,
to take on Him the seed of Abraham ;
and, in the oblation of His life,
to fulfil the Law's obedience ;
and, in the Sacrifice of His death,
to take off the Law's curse ;
and, in His death,
to redeem the world ;
and, in His resurrection,
to quicken it :—

O Thou, Who doest all things,
whereby to bring again our race to Thee,
that it may be partaker
of Thy divine nature and eternal glory;
Who hast borne witness
to the truth of Thy gospel
by many and various wonders,
in the ever-memorable converse of Thy saints,
in their supernatural endurance of torments,
in the overwhelming conversion of all lands
to the obedience of faith,
without might, or persuasion, or compulsion :—
Blessed be Thy Name,
and praised, and celebrated,
and magnified, and high exalted,
and glorified, and hallowed;
its record, and its memory,
and every memorial of it,
both now and for evermore."

Bishop Andrewes's Devotions.

INDEX OF TEXTS

ST. JOHN.

THE END.

www.ingramcontent.com/pod-product-compliance
Lightning Source LLC
Chambersburg PA
CBHW022017110726
47901CB00006B/1565